PRAISE FOR *ANGELS IN THE SKY*

"Robert Gandt understands pilots and he understands flying, which are not always the same thing. *Angels in the Sky* is . . . an enjoyable, balanced description of the origin of one of the world's leading air forces. Strap in tight, turn up the oxygen, and set the gunsight for 'pegged range' because it's a wild ride."

—BARRETT TILLMAN, AUTHOR OF *WHIRLWIND: THE AIR WAR AGAINST JAPAN, 1942–1945*

"*Angels in the Sky* is the best of Robert Gandt. He details the extreme measures that were required to get aircraft out of the United States, Britain, and other countries and into Israel in 1948. But more importantly, he gives life to the aircraft buyers, mechanics, and pilots that were to make up what would become one of the most formidable air forces in the world. Gandt shows us the joy, sorrow, comradeship, and trust that was shared by the foreign and Jewish members of the group. A terrific read for anyone."

—DAVID NORTH, FORMER EDITOR-IN-CHIEF, *AVIATION WEEK & SPACE TECHNOLOGY*

"A well-told aviation history unlike any other. Beech Bonanza bombers, B-movie Beaufighters, ersatz Messerschmitts, a bogus airline, and battle-tested veterans from every corner of the world—all to save a new nation in terrible peril. A truly amazing yarn."

—WILLIAM GARVEY, EDITOR-IN-CHIEF, *BUSINESS & COMMERCIAL AVIATION*

"It takes a serious pilot to adequately describe serious aerial adventures, and Robert Gandt does that better than anyone. *Angels in the Sky* digs into one of the most exciting chapters in aviation history: the three-dimensional battle for the birth of a nation—Israel. He brings the ragtag pilots and their ragtag air force to life in a way that gives new dimension to the meaning and value of independence."

—BUDD DAVISSON, EDITOR-IN-CHIEF, *FLIGHT JOURNAL*

ANGELS
IN THE SKY

ALSO BY ROBERT GANDT

Mastery (2015)

The President's Pilot (2014)

The Twilight Warriors (2010)

Intrepid (2008)

Black Star Rising (2007)

The Killing Sky (2005)

Shadows of War (2004)

Black Star (2003)

Acts of Vengeance (2002)

With Hostile Intent (2001)

Fly Low Fly Fast (1999)

Bogeys and Bandits (1997)

Skygods (1995)

China Clipper (1991)

Season of Storms (1982)

Roy Cisnell

ANGELS
IN THE SKY

How a Band of Volunteer Airmen
Saved the New State of Israel

ROBERT GANDT

W. W. NORTON & COMPANY

Independent Publishers Since 1923

New York   London

For information about permission to reproduce selections from this
book, write to Permissions, W. W. Norton & Company, Inc.,
500 Fifth Avenue, New York, NY 10110

For information about special discounts for bulk purchases, please
contact W. W. Norton Special Sales at specialsales@wwnorton.com
or 800-233-4830

Manufacturing by QUAD Graphics, Fairfield
Book design by Ellen Cipriano
Production manager: Beth Steidle

Library of Congress Cataloging-in-Publication Data

Names: Gandt, Robert L., author.
Title: Angels in the sky : how a band of volunteer airmen saved
the new state of Israel / Robert Gandt.
Description: First edition. | New York : W.W. Norton & Company,
[2017] | Includes bibliographical references and index.
Identifiers: LCCN 2017028807 | ISBN 9780393254778 (hardcover)
Subjects: LCSH: Israel-Arab War, 1948–1949—Aerial operations |
Fighter pilots—Biography. | Israel. Ḥel ha-aṿir—History. | Airplanes,
Military—Israel—History.
Classification: LCC DS126.96.A3 G36 2017 |
DDC 956.04/248095694–dc23
LC record available at https://lccn.loc.gov/2017028807

W. W. Norton & Company, Inc.
500 Fifth Avenue, New York, N.Y. 10110
www.wwnorton.com

W. W. Norton & Company Ltd.
15 Carlisle Street, London W1D 3BS

1 2 3 4 5 6 7 8 9 0

To Mitchell Flint,
Commander, United States Navy Reserve,
Major (Rav Seren), Israeli Air Force,
who lived this story.

With thanks and profound admiration.

Contents

PART TWO: BESIEGED

PART THREE: FORTUNES OF WAR

Prologue

One after the other the Messerschmitt fighters rumbled down the runway. The deep bellow of each V-12 engine echoed like thunder between the tin-roofed hangars.

Their target was only 10 miles away. In the cockpit of the lead fighter, Lou Lenart squinted in the fading light. He was trying to pick out Ishdud from the string of villages on the coastline. Each village looked alike.

Then he spotted it. Lenart was stunned by what he saw.

A column of Arab military vehicles stretched for over a mile along the coastal road. The center of Ishdud was filled with trucks, tanks, thousands of troops. An armored brigade was jammed up at the downed bridge over the Lachish River. The enemy was busy erecting a temporary new bridge.

At that moment the Egyptians spotted *them*. The sky over Ishdud erupted in oily black puffs of antiaircraft fire. Lenart felt the *whump* of flak bursts exploding around his fighter.

Lenart swung his head to look behind his wing. The other three Messerschmitts in his flight were strung out in a combat formation. Lenart reached to the panel at his knee and armed the fighter's cannons, machine guns, and the release switch for the two 70-kg bombs.

The flak bursts came closer. It seemed as if every gun in the mile-

long armored brigade was firing at the fighters. Lenart rolled the fighter
up on its wing. A Hebrew phrase came to his mind: *ein brera*. It meant
"no alternative."

The volunteer fighter pilots had no alternative. The fate of Israel
would be decided in the next few minutes.

Lenart pointed the Messerschmitt's nose down toward the target.

———

It was the first combat mission for the volunteer aviators in Israel. Lenart
worried that it might be the last. Four junk fighters—Czech-built ex-Nazi
Messerschmitts—versus an entire Arab army. David against Goliath.

The armies of five Arab nations were converging on the heart of
Israel. The fast-moving Egyptian armored division had advanced to
within 22 miles of Tel Aviv. If the Egyptians were not stopped, they'd
be in the city by morning. Israel's two-week-old war of independence
would be over.

The four Messerschmitts—and the pilots—had arrived in Israel only
a few days earlier. Their existence was still a secret to both Arabs and
Israelis. Lenart and his squadronmates had barely begun learning to fly
the Messerschmitt in Czechoslovakia when the Arabs invaded Israel on
May 15.

It was the end of training. Ready or not, the pilots and the disassembled fighters were bundled into C-46 and C-54 transports and flown
to Israel where they would learn to fly Messerschmitts the hard way.
In combat.

What Lenart had already learned was that he hated the Messerschmitt. "The worst piece of crap I have ever flown," he said. It wasn't
even a real Messerschmitt, the classic German fighter of WWII, but a
bastardized model produced in Czechoslovakia.

Despite its flaws, the clunky Messerschmitt carried significant
firepower—two 13.1-mm nose-mounted machine guns and two 20-
mm cannon on the wings. Each fighter had two 70-kg bombs suspended
beneath the wings.

Lou Lenart was a wiry WWII veteran with curly black hair and dark, piercing eyes. The twenty-seven-year-old was born in Hungary and grew up in Pennsylvania. At the age of seventeen he joined the Marines because he heard they were the first to fight. "I wanted to kill as many Nazis as I could, as fast as I could." Nobody told him that the Marines would be fighting in the Pacific. Lenart wangled his way into flight training and wound up on Okinawa, where he finished the war as a decorated Corsair fighter pilot.

The first target of Israel's new fighter squadron was supposed to be the Egyptian air base at El Arish, in the Sinai just below the border of Egypt and Israel. The Messerschmitts would take off at dawn and bomb the rows of parked Egyptian Spitfire fighters at El Arish.

The evening before, everything changed. The four pilots were huddled in their squadron shack at Ekron Air Base when a new report came in. The Egyptian Army had reached Ishdud, just to the south of Tel Aviv. Israeli sappers had blown the last bridge on the main road to the north, temporarily halting the Egyptians. The Egyptians would have the bridge repaired in a few hours and resume their advance. The two-and-a-half rifle companies of the Israeli brigade, exhausted, would be overrun.

The surprise El Arish strike was canceled. From Tel Aviv came the volunteers' new orders: Take off and attack the Egyptian brigade at Ishdud. *Now.*

━━━━━

The target was swelling in Lenart's gun sight. The airframe of the Messerschmitt was humming as the fighter accelerated in its dive. The front of the Egyptian armored column was framed in the narrow panel of Lenart's windshield.

He waited . . . watching the target expand . . . jammed the release button. There was a jolt as the two 70-kg bombs dropped from the belly of the Messerschmitt.

Lenart pulled up over Ishdud, setting up for a strafing pass. He couldn't see whether his bombs landed on target. From the side of the canopy he glimpsed the brownish shapes of other Messerschmitts diving through the curtain of flak.

Lenart dove back down on the target, aiming for the concentration of troops. He could see them scattering like ants toward the fields outside Ishdud. Lenart squeezed the trigger on the control stick. He felt the hard rattle of the wing-mounted cannons.

And then nothing.

Damn. After only a few rounds, Lenart's cannons had stopped firing. It was the first time the cannons had been tested. And they had failed.

Lenart could see the other fighters darting like hawks through the bursts of flak. Were *their* cannons working? *Was anyone hit?* Lenart didn't know. The radio in his Messerschmitt didn't work.

With flak bursts nipping at his tail, Lenart pulled off the target and headed for Ekron. He plunked the fighter down on the concrete runway, then did the delicate rudder dance he'd learned in Czechoslovakia to keep the fighter rolling straight. When he reached the hangar he saw that one of the Messerschmitts was already there.

A few minutes later they saw the silhouette of a third Messerschmitt landing. The fighter rolled straight for a hundred yards, then abruptly veered to the right. Dragging its left wingtip, the Messerschmitt swirled off the runway, kicking up a geyser of dirt.

The Messerschmitt was wrecked.

The pilots stood in the deepening shadows and peered to the west. Three of them had made it back to Ekron. The number four pilot was still out there somewhere.

Darkness fell. There was no sign of the missing airman.

An hour passed. Then came a report. Israeli troops had seen an airplane engulfed in flames go down 7 miles southwest of Ekron. Egyptian troops had already seized the area. Judging by the impact, the Israelis were certain the pilot was dead.

A pall of gloom settled over the little band of airmen in the Ekron operations shack. The mission had been a disaster. They'd inflicted no significant damage on the enemy. In the space of forty minutes they had lost half their airplanes and a quarter of their airmen.

The pilots were dejected. What had they accomplished? They'd come to help save a new nation. And they'd failed.

Not until later that night when the intelligence reports came in would they learn the truth.

They hadn't failed. They had accomplished a miracle.

They helped every man his neighbour;
And every one said to his brother: "Be of good courage."

—Isaiah 41:6

The bravest are surely those who have the clearest vision
of what is before them, glory and danger alike, and yet
notwithstanding, go out to meet it.

—Thucydides, *Greek historian c. 460–c. 400* B.C.E.

Part One

A WAR WAITING TO HAPPEN

You may not be interested in war,
but war is interested in you.
—LEON TROTSKY

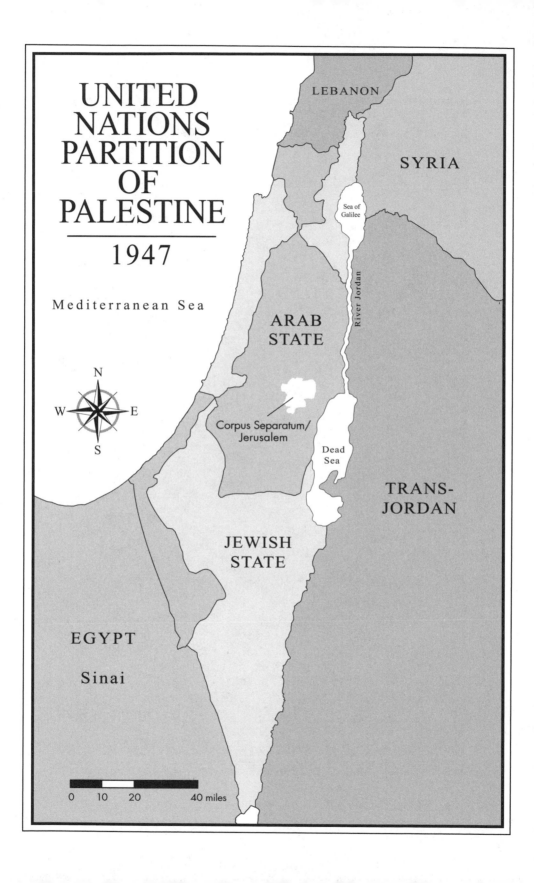

UNITED
NATIONS
PARTITION
OF
PALESTINE

1947

Mediterranean Sea

LEBANON

SYRIA

Sea of
Galilee

River Jordan

N
W   E
S

ARAB
STATE

Corpus Separatum/
Jerusalem

Dead
Sea

TRANS-
JORDAN

JEWISH
STATE

EGYPT

Sinai

0   10   20   40 miles

— 1 —

Yakum Purkan

JERUSALEM
NOVEMBER 29, 1947

It was nearly midnight, but no one in the city was sleeping. The streets of Tel Aviv and Jerusalem were filled with singing, dancing, deliriously happy people. Every café and bar throbbed with excitement. On street corners people built bonfires, clasped hands, swirled in spontaneous *hora* dances.

Watching the celebration from a balcony was a stocky little man with untidy shocks of white hair sprouting from either side of his head. More than anyone of his generation, David Ben-Gurion was responsible for this historic moment.

For most of his adult life the sixty-one-year-old Zionist had labored to create a Jewish state. He was president of the Jewish Agency Executive and the de facto head of the Jewish community in Palestine. Tonight should have been his moment of triumph.

Instead, Ben-Gurion was watching the jubilation with a heavy heart.

The cause for the revelry was an event 6,000 miles to the west. In a massive gray building that had once been an ice skating rink in Flushing Meadow, New York, a long debate had come to an end. The delegates of each nation, one after another, declared their vote. When the final tally was done the result was flashed across the ocean and transmitted over the Palestine Broadcast Network.

In a thousand homes, cafés, and meeting halls, breathless listeners heard the crackling radio announcement: "The General Assembly of the United Nations, by a vote of thirty-three in favor, thirteen against and ten abstentions, has voted to partition Palestine."

Partition. The UN resolution meant that Palestine would be divided into two states—Arab and Jewish. To the joyful dancers in Tel Aviv and Jerusalem and every Jewish settlement and kibbutz in Palestine, it was an ancient prophecy come true. *A Jewish nation.* After two thousand years of exile, war, pogroms, brandings, expulsions, and genocide, the children of Abraham would have their own nation on an arid sliver of land between the Mediterranean and the Jordan River.

The resolution also meant the end of the British Mandate, the onerous thirty-year rule of Palestine by Great Britain. In May 1948, the one-hundred-thousand-man British occupying force would leave and the Jewish settlers of Palestine would determine their own fate.

David Ben-Gurion didn't join the rejoicing in the streets. "I could not dance," he wrote. "I could not sing that night. I looked at them so happy dancing and I could only think that they were all going to war."

And so they were.

At 8:30 the next morning a man in a business suit was standing beside the main road from Netanya to Jerusalem. As the scheduled bus rolled toward him, he flagged down the vehicle. When the bus slowed almost to a stop, half a dozen Arab men standing along the road pulled out their concealed submachine guns. In a burst of fire they killed five Jewish passengers and wounded several more.

Half an hour later they struck again. Two more Jewish bus passengers died in a machine-gun ambush.

The same day snipers began firing from the Arab city of Jaffa into adjoining Tel Aviv. Massive Arab riots erupted throughout Palestine. The troops of Great Britain, the official peacekeepers of Palestine, stood by while rioters sacked and burned Jewish shops in the commercial district of Jerusalem.

Within hours a full-scale Arab–Jewish civil war was raging in Palestine. It was just the beginning.

━━━━━

In his Jerusalem office, Ben-Gurion was shaking his head in sadness. It was happening just as he feared. Like it or not, they were going to war with the Arabs. But the Palestinian Arabs, Ben-Gurion was certain, were not the greatest danger.

"The Land of Israel is surrounded by independent Arab states that have the right to purchase and produce arms, to set up armies and train them," he told the Zionist Congress. "Attack by the Palestinian Arabs does not endanger the Yishuv (the body of Jewish residents in Palestine), but there is a danger that the neighboring Arab states will send their armies to attack and destroy the Yishuv."

Ben-Gurion knew that when the British withdrew in May, the armies of five surrounding Arab countries—Egypt, Syria, Iraq, Lebanon, Transjordan—would roll like a seismic wave across Israel. With a sixty-to-one numerical advantage, the Arab armies would invade with tanks, armored gun carriers, field artillery, antitank and antiaircraft guns.

The Egyptian Army totaled fifty-five thousand troops, with an air force of forty Spitfire fighters and a fleet of C-47 Dakotas configured as bombers. The eight-thousand-man Syrian Army was French trained and well equipped with modern armor and artillery. The Syrian Air Force consisted of Harvard AT-6 trainers equipped as dive bombers. Iraq boasted a twenty-eight-thousand-man British-trained army also equipped with tanks, heavy guns, and British-supplied fighter aircraft. The four-thousand-man French-trained Lebanese Army was the smallest of the invading forces.

Geography was on the side of the Arabs. The UN-designated Jewish state was a long, thin strip of territory, squeezed in the middle, vulnerable on all sides. Jewish settlements were scattered in isolated pockets throughout the territory. Each would have to defend itself against the onslaught of entire armies.

Israel's only defense force was an underground militia called the

Haganah. Haganah had weapons for less than a third of its soldiers. They had enough ammunition for three days' fighting. Haganah had no heavy guns, no warplanes, no warships, no machine guns.

Nor could they import them from the United States or Britain.

There was no shortage of surplus armaments in the world during the years after WWII. Vast inventories of it—ships, vehicles, planes—were in the United States, and most were available for sale through the War Assets Administration.

But not to the Haganah.

Although President Truman had supported the UN resolution allowing a Jewish state, less than a week later, on December 5, 1947, the United States ordered an embargo on the export of *all* arms to the Middle East. It was an example of the schism within the Truman administration—the president voicing support for Jewish statehood while his anti-Israel State Department, led by America's eminent statesman, George Marshall, was doing everything possible to thwart it.

The Arab nations surrounding Israel were not affected by the embargo. While the British Royal Navy maintained its blockade of immigrants and war materials to Jewish Palestine, the British government continued its tight relationship with its Middle East clients: Egypt, Transjordan, Iraq, Syria. All were being provisioned with modern British warplanes, tanks, heavy artillery.

The few armaments in the Haganah's arsenal entered the country by sea or were clandestinely manufactured in cowsheds and tin shacks. Smuggling *anything*—weapons, ammunition, or the thousands of desolate European refugees—past the British naval blockade of Palestine was nearly impossible.

Ben-Gurion realized that Israel's only chance of survival must come from the sky.

———

Putt-putt-putt-putt.

Night after night the kibbutz dwellers and isolated settlers in Jerusalem peered up in the darkness at the clattering sound. They could barely make out the ghostly silhouettes in the night sky. The sixty-five-horsepower engines sounded like farm machines.

They were hearing the rattle of the little airplanes of the Haganah's air service. It had a proper name—Sherut Avir—but the settlers gave it an oxymoronic label: the "underground air force." The little air force amounted to two dozen flivver sport planes—Piper Cubs, Taylorcrafts, British Auster observation planes, a couple of de Havilland Tiger Moth biplanes—all flown by amateur pilots of an organization called the Palestine Flying Club.

The *putt-putt* of the little airplanes boosted the morale of besieged settlers. Beneath the noses of the British occupiers, the air service made daring night supply runs to isolated kibbutzim (-*im* is a suffix indicating plural in Hebrew). They landed on carved-out strips illuminated by trucks' headlights. They made regular flights into Jerusalem, where the Haganah had smoothed a 2,000-foot stretch in a wadi beside the Monastery of the Cross.

In the midst of pitched battles between besieged villagers and Arab irregulars, a Piper Cub would appear overhead, a machine gunner firing out the open door at the enemy below.

The kibbutz dwellers and the Jerusalemites gave the airplanes a name—Primus. On their spindly landing gear the little planes resembled the three-legged stoves called primuses that villagers used for cooking.

Ben-Gurion watched the Primuses in action. He shook the hands and clapped the shoulders of the brave airmen. But Ben-Gurion knew the truth. When the Arab armies swarmed into Israel, the Primuses would be swatted from the sky like mosquitoes.

The white-haired little statesman knew that if Israel were to survive, it *had* to have an air force. A *real* air force to combat the Egyptians' squadrons of British-supplied Spitfire fighters, the two squadrons of C-47 Dakotas configured as bombers, the Iraqi and Syrian Air Forces equipped with state-of-the-art warplanes.

While the streets of Tel Aviv and Jerusalem were still throbbing with celebration, Ben-Gurion dispatched a team of undercover operatives to

Europe, South Africa, the United States, and Canada on an urgent mission: Acquire weapons and warplanes. Recruit pilots to fly them. And find a way to bring them to Israel.

The operation took a name: *Yakum Purkan*. It came from a line in an ancient Aramaic prayer: "*Yakum purkan min shemaya* . . ." It meant "Salvation will come from heaven." Or, in this case, from the skies.

One of their early recruits was a Jewish American with an inconvenient first name: Adolph.

The chilly days of late autumn had arrived as Adolph "Al" Schwimmer made his way down the busy Manhattan street. Still, Schwimmer was perspiring. This was his third visit to Hotel Fourteen, a residential hotel at 14 East 60th Street. Nicknamed Kibbutz Fourteen, the hotel was the unofficial headquarters of the Jewish Agency in the United States.

Each time, he had come to offer his services. What the Palestinian Jews needed, Schwimmer kept telling them, was airplanes. Airplanes to haul people and armaments. Airplanes with guns and bombs to defend the country. Airplanes were the key to their survival. Schwimmer wanted to help make it happen.

Each time, he had been rebuffed.

Al Schwimmer was a thirty-year-old veteran of WWII and a flight engineer with TWA. He was a bland-faced young man with a stocky, athletic build. Like many engineers, Schwimmer had a quiet, unflamboyant demeanor, preferring to listen before speaking.

Schwimmer loved every aspect of aviation—the flying, the maintenance, and especially the organization. During the war years he had been fascinated by the Flying Tigers, the band of American volunteer pilots who flew with the Chinese air force in 1941. Such a cadre of volunteers was exactly what the Palestinian Jews needed, Schwimmer believed. And he was just the guy to organize it.

So Schwimmer kept coming back to Hotel Fourteen. By now he was acquainted with the head of the agency, a taciturn Palestinian and ex–British army major named Shlomo Rabinovich. Rabinovich was a suspicious man. He clearly didn't trust this newcomer off the streets.

Rabinovich shook his head. Having airplanes would be nice, he said. Then he listed the reasons why it was impossible. How would they buy airplanes? Where would they get the money? Where would they get the crews and mechanics to make them fly? What would they do for facilities?

Schwimmer was unfazed. It could all be worked out, he told Rabinovich. He knew ways to make such things happen. Everything was possible.

A thin smile crossed Rabinovich's face. He dismissed the young man. "Come in again sometime."

Schwimmer came in again. He kept receiving the same answer, but he knew that the agency had checked him out, making sure he wasn't a phony or an infiltrator. They would have learned that Al Schwimmer was a New Englander who, like many kids of his generation, grew up being crazy about airplanes. In his home town of Bridgeport, Connecticut, he'd hung around the airport, tinkered with planes, earned his pilot's license as well as a mechanic's and flight engineer's ticket, then went to work at the Sikorsky plant in nearby Stratford. From there he'd gone to the Martin aircraft factory in Baltimore, then out to California to work at Lockheed.

Schwimmer joined TWA in 1942 and spent the war years in a USAAF uniform, flying throughout Asia and the Middle East. At war's end Schwimmer continued as a flight engineer for the airline, based in California.

On one of his airline trips to Europe he visited a WWII German concentration camp. It was a life-changing moment for Al Schwimmer. On the list of victims he found the names of his mother's parents and most of her relatives who had been brought to the camp from Hungary.

The revelations of the Holocaust were the beginning of a journey for Schwimmer. Soon after his experience in Germany, he learned about an organization called the Haganah that was smuggling Holocaust survivors to Palestine.

Schwimmer knew he had found a mission.

Gradually Rabinovich loosened up with Schwimmer. He asked a few questions, solicited Schwimmer's opinion—but nothing more. And then in November 1947, with the UN decision on partition looming and a subsequent war ever more likely, Schwimmer was introduced to a new arrival. He was an energetic man with gray, swept-back hair and a vaguely sinister look. His name was Yehuda Arazi. Schwimmer would learn later that Arazi was the Haganah's star spy and smuggler.

Unlike the cautious Rabinovich, Arazi was immediately excited by Schwimmer's ideas. He bombarded Schwimmer with questions.

What were the best airplanes for hauling cargo? How much did they cost? What about warplanes? Which were the best suited for Palestine? How quickly could they get them?

Schwimmer had an answer for each of Arazi's questions. The Haganah agent was impressed. At their next meeting he handed Schwimmer a fistful of dollars.

Schwimmer asked what the money was for.

"Expenses," Arazi explained with a wave of his hand. Schwimmer was leaving immediately for California. He was going to buy airplanes for the Haganah.

2

A Righteous Cause

Fighter pilot. Of all the labels applied to Mitchell "Mike" Flint, that was the one he liked best. It had just the right macho ring to it, describing the action heroes he had worshiped in comic books and Saturday matinees. And it described the job Flint had performed with distinction until three years ago.

It was a mild winter evening in Berkeley. Mike Flint was sitting alone in his room with his eyes closed. With perfect clarity he was seeing an old image: a tiny winged silhouette. The silhouette was as sharp in his memory as when he spotted it that summer afternoon in 1945. Flint recognized the greenish drab color, the long narrow fuselage, the distinctive red ball painted on each wing.

A Nakajima C6N "Myrt." It was the fastest carrier-based Japanese warplane in service, and it was coming directly toward him.

Flint shoved the throttle full open and yanked the Corsair fighter into a high, arcing 180-degree turn. After a nerve-wracking hound-and-hare pursuit, he sliced inside the Myrt's turn.

The tracers from Flint's six .50-caliber machine guns arced ahead of the enemy plane, drifted back, then converged on the nose of the hard-turning Myrt. There was a flash and then . . . *Kabloom.* A ball of fire appeared where the Japanese warplane had been. Instinctively Flint yanked back on the stick, barely missing the roiling mass of debris.

As he returned to his carrier, USS *Wasp*, Flint thought about what had happened. Had he not shot the kamikaze down, the Japanese warplane might have killed hundreds of Americans and possibly sunk a ship.

Flint had the feeling that he'd served a righteous cause. Sometimes he wondered if he'd ever have that feeling again.

━━━━━

By almost every measure, Mike Flint had the world by the tail. He was a slender, good-looking young man with flaming red hair, twenty-five years old, a decorated navy fighter pilot from the Pacific war.

Flint knew that fortune had smiled on him. For the past two years he'd been surrounded by attentive female students at the University of California at Berkeley. He'd not only survived the greatest of wars, but he would also soon graduate from a prestigious school and embark on a glittering career.

Since his acceptance at Berkeley, Flint had taken classes straight through the summers and was graduating early. He was also active socially, especially in a fraternity called Hillel, a Jewish campus organization. The hottest discussion topic among Hillel members was the plight of Holocaust survivors and their quest to settle in Palestine.

Many of the students, like Mike Flint, were veterans. They argued among themselves about what should be done. They had military skills. What could they do to help? What *special* qualifications did they have?

Flint knew.

It was late, after midnight. Mike Flint peered out at the darkened Berkeley hills. He was thinking about the images that had emerged from the Holocaust. He knew that if his grandparents hadn't emigrated from Austria-Hungary, they would have been in the death camps. Seared into Flint's memory were the faces of the survivors, refugees without home or country, desperate to settle in Palestine. In those faces he saw his relatives.

He saw himself.

On the table beside him Flint had a yellow legal pad. He was a logical young man, not given to impulsive decisions. On the pad Flint had drawn two columns. One was a Go list, the other a No-Go list. The No-Go list was the longer column. It included items like girlfriends at Berkeley, post-grad school, the London Olympics that he'd promised himself he'd attend as a graduation present, and most important, his widowed mother. He felt responsible for her, especially since she'd already endured three years of worrying about him in the Pacific war.

The Go list was shorter. And more abstract. Flint was like many of his generation, kids who grew up in the Great Depression and then were thrust into the cauldron of WWII. They were a generation who viewed the world in terms of heroes and villains. Good and evil. Right and wrong. Righteous causes. Their war had been the epitome of righteous causes. There had been no question about whether they should join the fight.

Now this. Was Israel's war a righteous cause? Should he volunteer to go fight? Was it worth risking everything—life, citizenship, future career, his status as a naval reserve officer?

Flint continued jotting on his legal pad and staring out at the night. Gradually the darkness paled. The yellow pad filled with his notes.

It was almost dawn when Flint realized he had his answer. He had only one remaining problem.

What was he going to tell his mother?

———

Lou Lenart squirmed in his seat in the crowded Los Angeles temple. Lenart was following the speaker's words, but his thoughts were on his grandmother.

The speaker was a former British officer, Major Wellesley Aron. The dapper military man was talking about the fighting in Palestine and the war that lay ahead. Aron spoke about the shiploads of refugees from Europe, most of them Holocaust survivors. They were being turned back from Palestine by the British naval blockade.

Lenart closed his eyes for a moment. He saw his grandmother's face. She had chosen to remain in Hungary when the family immigrated to

America. His grandmother and thirteen other family members were murdered in the Holocaust.

Lou Lenart had been born Layos Lenovitz. At the age of nine, he immigrated with his parents to Wilkes-Barre, Pennsylvania. Lenart grew up feeling not only the sting of anti-Semitism but also bullying because of his Eastern European accent. When he was fifteen, he took a Charles Atlas bodybuilding course, after which, he liked to say years later, "Nobody bullied me anymore."

It was a juncture in his life. In 1940 he changed his name to Lou Lenart and joined the Marine Corps. After a year and a half as an infantryman and with war breaking out, Lenart talked his way into flight training. He won his wings and by war's end was a veteran combat aviator with the rank of captain in the Marine Corps.

When Lenart returned to civilian life he tried to put his Eastern European good looks and swashbuckling style to good use. He married a movie starlet and began trying to carve out a career in Los Angeles. Nothing seemed to work for him. His life was adrift, and he had only a vague sense of what he wanted to do.

Listening to the speaker in the temple, something clicked in Lenart's mind. At last, something was making sense. After the lecture Lenart drove directly home and pulled out his WWII military résumé. He delivered it to the speaker at his hotel that night.

Nothing more happened for several weeks. One day he received a telephone call. Without introducing himself, a man said, "I understand you're interested in flying."

"No," said Lenart.

The man persisted. He said he understood that Lenart had expressed an interest in a certain kind of flying assignment. And then Lenart remembered. He agreed to meet the agent the next day in downtown Los Angeles. Two weeks later, Lenart was accepted.

Another recruit named Sam Lewis, an ex-TWA captain, contacted Lenart and gave him an envelope with $5,000 in hundred-dollar bills. As a veteran, Lenart was entitled to buy a war-surplus airplane. He was instructed to go to the Federal Building with the money and purchase an ex-military C-46 Curtiss Commando cargo plane. When he was asked what he was going to do with the airplane, he would declare that he and some colleagues were starting a new airline.

Which was close to the truth. The C-46 Lenart purchased was one of ten acquired by a new company called Schwimmer Aviation. They were the beginning of the Haganah's air force.

Lenart was sent to New York to help recruit more pilots. After a couple of weeks, he was on a plane headed for Europe.

===

In a Newark, New Jersey, synagogue, a young man named Gideon Lichtman was listening to a talk by a former crewman from the SS *Exodus*. The crewman was telling his audience how the British Royal Navy had forcibly boarded the *Exodus*. The ship was en route from France to Palestine with 4,515 immigrants, most of them Holocaust survivors. After a pitched battle in which two immigrants and a crew member were killed and thirty others injured, the immigrants were deported back to Europe, to detention camps in Germany.

As he listened to the story of the *Exodus*, Lichtman was filled with a growing anger. Like his father, he was a Zionist, a supporter of the reestablishment of a Jewish homeland in Palestine. And like almost every Jew in the United States, Lichtman had seen the images of the Holocaust, knew families of those who perished in the death camps, sensed the deep yearning that compelled the survivors to board ships like the *Exodus*.

Gideon Lichtman had been out of the military for nearly two years. He'd been a P-51 Mustang fighter pilot with the 3rd Air Commando Group. He'd seen action in New Guinea, Okinawa, and over Japan escorting B-29 bombing missions.

As much as Lichtman liked the Army Air Force, he didn't like it enough to stay in. By the spring of 1946, he was on his way home. He rejoined his family, enrolled at New York University on the GI Bill, and started a new life. Gideon Lichtman was finished with war.

Or so he thought.

Lichtman waited until the lecture was finished. As the crowd began to disperse, Lichtman walked up to the *Exodus* crewman and asked how he could volunteer to fight for Israeli independence. The crewman told him to write to an organization called Land and Labor for Palestine, at 14 East 60th Street in New York.

What happened next played out like a low-budget spy movie. After he'd written to Land and Labor, Lichtman received a questionnaire inquiring about his experience and qualifications. He filled it out and returned the questionnaire. Then came a telegram directing him to call a number. He was told by phone that he should meet a guy on 57th Street. He'd be wearing a red rose in his lapel.

Lichtman found his man, and they talked. "No names were exchanged," remembered Lichtman. "It was all secret. He said that Israel was setting up an air force and there was a need for fighter pilots."

Lichtman was told to come back to 57th Street the next day to meet a different man.

Again they talked. This time Lichtman was introduced to a young man named Steve Schwartz. Schwartz was the newly appointed vice president of an outfit called Service Airways—and a busy recruiter for the Haganah.

"What will I be flying?" Lichtman asked.

"I don't know," said Schwartz. "Could be fighters, bombers, or transports."

"I'm a fighter pilot," Lichtman snapped. He had no interest in flying a clunky C-46 or any other multimotored flying truck. "What kind of *fighters* will the Israeli Air Force have?"

Again, Schwartz was vague. "P-51s, maybe. Maybe P-47s. Maybe something else."

Bullshit, thought Lichtman. He walked away.

A few days later, Lichtman's parents told him someone had called the house asking for him. Lichtman returned the call, and later that week came a certified letter.

Inside was an airline ticket to Rome.

3

Schwimmer and Company

BURBANK, CALIFORNIA
JANUARY 10, 1948

For a long while Al Schwimmer stood gazing at the gray shapes parked on the ramp. It was a chilly day in California. Schwimmer was wearing his usual business attire—leather sports jacket, slacks, no tie.

Behind Schwimmer lay the sprawl of the Lockheed plant in Burbank where new Constellation airliners were rolling off the assembly line and entering service with international airlines like TWA and Pan Am.

But the objects of Schwimmer's attention at this corner of the field weren't factory-fresh airliners. These were war-surplus transports. Thirteen of them were stuffed on this obscure ramp where they wouldn't detract from their glittering new sister ships. They were the military transports Schwimmer had flown around the world with TWA during the war.

That was behind him now. Following his handshake deal with Yehuda Arazi, Schwimmer had burned his bridges and resigned from TWA. Now he was buying airplanes for the Haganah.

Among aircraft aficionados, transport aircraft never won beauty contests. The winners were sexy fighters like the P-51 Mustang and the P-38 Lightning, with their slick lines and built-for-speed looks. Fighters and race planes were the sports cars of aviation. Thick-bodied transports like the DC-3 and C-46 were the trucks.

That was before the Connie.

When the Lockheed Constellation made her debut in 1943, she changed everyone's thinking about clunky transports. She had a long, curvaceous fuselage and a sleek, three-finned tail. Her wing design was almost identical to that of the P-38 fighter, differing only in size. The Connie was as fast as many WWII fighters, with a maximum speed of 375 miles per hour. She could carry eighty passengers in a pressurized cabin at altitudes over 25,000 feet and over distances of 3,500 miles.

The Constellation had been the dream child of aviator tycoon Howard Hughes, a man with an eye for all things sexy, including airplanes. Hughes had visualized a graceful four-motored, long-range airliner as the flagship of his international airline, TWA. Because of Lockheed's wartime commitments, only thirteen Connies were built during the war. All had been inducted into military service. They'd seen hard duty hauling troops and war materiel throughout Europe and the Far East.

Schwimmer leaned against the fence and kept staring at the beat-up Connies. Their military paint job was peeling. Their tires were deflated. Puddles of oil lay beneath the engines. Al Schwimmer didn't care. The most important thing about them was that they were for sale.

Schwimmer had already done his homework. He knew three of the Constellations could be bought from the War Assets Administration for $15,000 each. Besides the Connies, Schwimmer had located a fleet of surplus C-46 Curtiss Commandos.

The C-46 was a brute of an airplane, in its time the largest two-engine transport in the world. During the war the C-46 had hauled millions of tons of cargo over the Hump in the China-Burma-India theatre, the dangerous eastern Himalayan range that separated India from China. Schwimmer intended to purchase ten C-46s for $5,000 each.

There were problems, of course. The biggest was the fact that each of the tired old birds required thousands of hours of reconditioning and many more thousands of dollars in expensive replacement parts. Another niggling problem was the requirement by the government that such aircraft must be registered for use in the United States.

To Schwimmer, these were all solvable problems. He had a plan.

He turned away from the fence and walked purposefully back to his car in the parking lot. Schwimmer was on his way back to New York.

He had to sell his plan to his Haganah boss.

———

A look of shock passed over Nahum Bernstein's face. Schwimmer had already told him the price tag of the three Constellations plus ten C-46s. But that wasn't what caused Bernstein's reaction. Schwimmer was explaining that to meet the Civil Aeronautics Commission's requirement for civil registration, the aircraft would have to be retrofitted with some expensive alterations.

How expensive? Bernstein wanted to know.

Schwimmer kept his voice impassive. The bill would come to $200,000 each to have the three Constellations modified at the Lockheed plant. The C-46s were another matter. Each would have to go through an overhaul, and that could be expensive also.

Bernstein listened. Behind his narrow-frame glasses, his eyes bulged.

Until now, Schwimmer had known Nahum Bernstein only by reputation. Bernstein was a prominent Manhattan lawyer. He was a slightly built man with a shock of brownish hair atop a narrow, bespectacled face.

He was also, Schwimmer learned, the man through whom money flowed in the murky Haganah arms purchasing operation. Yehuda Arazi might be the idea man, the concocter of outrageous capers, but Bernstein was the dispenser of funds. In any case, Arazi was not present in New York. He was off to Europe on another underground mission.

Nahum Bernstein had been an early inductee into the Haganah network. As a young lawyer-investigator before WWII, Bernstein had distinguished himself exposing insurance claims rackets. During the war he had been an Office of Strategic Services agent, and it was this qualification—expertise in intelligence work—that made him a prize catch for the Haganah's underground operations.

Now Schwimmer and Bernstein were conferring behind closed doors at the agency's suite in Hotel Fourteen. And Bernstein was still shaking his head. The numbers Schwimmer was proposing simply wouldn't work. The network couldn't spend $600,000 on three airplanes, let alone the ten C-46s Schwimmer was asking for.

Schwimmer nodded, maintaining his trademark bland expression. Bernstein's response was exactly what he expected. Schwimmer had already thought all this through, and there was another way. If he could persuade Lockheed to provide the technical expertise and some temporary space at the plant in Burbank, he could hire enough skilled mechanics and do the work themselves. The bill, Schwimmer believed, would amount to far less than the $600,000 that had been quoted.

They continued talking through the evening and past midnight. Bernstein listened to Schwimmer's ideas. He raised objections. Then he listened some more.

Little by little, Bernstein came around. There was something about this fellow Schwimmer, that calm, unruffled manner, the sheer confidence in his voice, that made Bernstein believe, yes, perhaps it *was* possible.

What Bernstein was seeing—and hearing—was the beginning of the Al Schwimmer legend. As Bernstein and everyone in the Haganah network would come to learn, Al Schwimmer was not intimidated by obstacles. Once Schwimmer had seized on an idea, he clung to it with a bulldog tenaciousness.

When Schwimmer left New York the next day, he carried with him a check from Bernstein for $45,000. His next stop was Washington, D.C., and the office of the War Assets Administration. He was going to buy three surplus Lockheed Constellations.

———

The Haganah's secret headquarters in Tel Aviv was an obscure pink building on the beach called the Red House. On a glimmering winter afternoon, David Ben-Gurion was gazing thoughtfully out the window of his office in the old structure.

He turned back to the old friend sitting across the table from him. Dr. Otto Felix was a Czech-born lawyer, and he had come to

Ben-Gurion's office bearing news of great interest. Felix's native Czechoslovakia had been a major arms producer for the Axis in WWII.

Felix had just picked up a snippet of precious information. Czechoslovakia still had large inventories of munitions—rifles, machine guns, tanks, heavy armor, even warplanes. Even though the cash-starved country was already in the process of being absorbed into the Soviet bloc, the Czechs were interested in selling surplus arms.

It was exactly the news Ben-Gurion had been hoping to hear. A large smile creased Ben-Gurion's weathered face. He rose and clapped his old friend on the shoulder—and handed him a job.

Felix was to return immediately to Prague on an arms-buying expedition.

The rotund little lawyer carried out his orders with precision. Within two weeks Felix made his first big score: a stash of weapons, including 4,300 rifles, which still bore the markings of the German Wehrmacht. There was more where that came from, Felix reported.

And then, a couple of weeks later, Felix surprised Ben-Gurion with another item of information. The Avia company in Czechoslovakia had been a wartime manufacturer of the German Luftwaffe's premier fighter, the Messerschmitt Bf 109. In the postwar years, the company had continued to build the fighter for the Czech Air Force.

According to Felix's contacts, they were interested in selling twenty-five of the Czech versions of the Messerschmitt, called the Avia S-199.

Messerschmitts? Ben-Gurion didn't like the idea. Much as they needed combat airplanes, Ben-Gurion was leery of becoming too entangled with Czechoslovakia. Such a relationship, with its Cold War implications, would only worsen their already tenuous relations with the United States and Britain.

Beyond that, Ben-Gurion and the Haganah were still hoping to acquire a more modern fighter than the Messerschmitt, which was a design from the 1930s.

Yehuda Arazi had been in negotiations with a shadowy arms dealer in Mexico who went by the name of "Mr. Brown" for the purchase of P-51 Mustang fighters, a far better warplane than the Messerschmitt.

And Al Schwimmer was working on another deal for P-47 fighters, also from Mexico.

In any case, Ben-Gurion and the Haganah commanders had found a source of arms. But there was one major problem that was still unsolved. There was no way to ship the contraband weapons from landlocked Czechoslovakia to Palestine.

None except Ben-Gurion's proposed Yakum Purkan airlift. In January 1948, it still existed only in the dreams of a young man in California.

Al Schwimmer paused at the entrance and allowed himself a big grin. It was his boyhood dream come true. The door of the office he had just leased in the Lockheed Air Terminal at Burbank now bore a black-lettered sign: "Schwimmer Aviation Services."

Exactly *what* services Schwimmer's company would be offering was still undetermined. For the time being its only mission was the refurbishing of the three Constellations and the ten C-46s that were coming.

For the next several days Schwimmer and his old wartime buddy, Rey Selk, culled lists of available aircraft mechanics. With the postwar glut of trained mechanics who wanted to keep working in the aviation industry, they could choose the best. Schwimmer was paying well—$1.95 an hour, top wages for aircraft mechanics in 1948.

Most of the mechanics Schwimmer hired in Burbank were non-Jews. They were told that the big Connies and the C-46s that were coming were part of a start-up international airline flying out of Rome.

International airline? It sounded good to most of them. Schwimmer's mechanics, almost all WWII veterans, were calling themselves the Cobbers, a slang label picked up in wartime Australia when they maintained army and navy war birds. The Cobbers were all anxious to get back in the aviation game.

Schwimmer had already put down the money for five C-46 Commandos at $5,000 each and placed an order for five more. All were parked at a war-surplus boneyard at CalAero Airport in Ontario, California.

The C-46s were in even rougher shape than the Connies. The big twin-engine transports had seen hard wartime service followed by years of neglect. The airframes would have to be treated for corrosion, and the Pratt & Whitney R-2800 engines would require reconditioning. Schwimmer sent a team headed by mechanic Robert Frieburg to CalAero to get the big transports airworthy.

Schwimmer's fleet of transport aircraft was coming together. But who was going to fly them?

=== 4 ===

Dark Suits and Fedoras

LOS ANGELES, CALIFORNIA
JANUARY 18, 1948

"Here comes Smilin' Jack," Sam Lewis's buddies always said. Lewis had heard it enough times. He just flashed his trademark grin and went about his business. Captain Sam Lewis was a dead ringer for the aviator hero in the Zack Mosley comic strip *The Adventures of Smilin' Jack*.

Lewis was a muscular man with a thin, dark mustache and a yen for adventure. He was also one of those pilots, other pilots said, who could fly anything.

Lewis had been one of the few Jewish airmen at TWA to become a captain. Even before being approached by Schwimmer, Lewis and another wartime pilot and flight instructor named Leo Gardner had been kicking around the idea of starting an airline to fly refugees and cargo from Europe to Palestine.

On a gray winter evening in Los Angeles, Lewis and Gardner were sitting across a table from Al Schwimmer at Lewis's home. It was a classic Schwimmer pitch. Schwimmer was explaining in detail not only the problems his new airline faced but convincing the men that he *knew* how to overcome them.

And then Schwimmer played the card he knew would win them over. Lewis and Gardner would not only be realizing their individual dreams of helping build a new airline, but they would also be serving a higher purpose.

They would be saving their fellow Jews.

Lewis and Gardner looked at each other. Schwimmer's pitch was right on target. Leo Gardner missed flying and was already looking for something besides the family loan and jewelry business. He had grown bored.

Sam Lewis had another motivation. He loved the Constellation airliner. This guy Schwimmer just happened to have *three* of them.

Before the evening was over, both men signed on. Not only would Lewis and Gardner become Schwimmer's first pilots, but they would also be his chief recruiters. They would spread the word through aviation circles that an outfit called Schwimmer Aviation was hiring.

Within a couple of weeks, the roster of employees swelled. And as the company grew, there was gossip. And whispered questions.

Where does someone like Schwimmer get the money to buy these airplanes?

What does he really plan to do with them?

What's the big rush getting them airworthy?

Where are they really going to fly?

And the questions were coming not just from the employees.

———

They were easy to spot, the guys in dark suits and fedoras. Schwimmer saw them lurking around the hangar, parked outside in black sedans, pretending to be doing something other than snooping. They wore different outfits, but they all had the same unmistakable look about them.

One day in January 1948, Schwimmer was walking out of the Lockheed terminal. One of the fedora-topped men got out of his car and come across the ramp toward him. He had sandy hair and a purposeful stride, and he was peering at Schwimmer as though he recognized him.

The man said he had some questions for Schwimmer. He flipped open his credential case. His name was Bernarr Ptacek. He was a special agent of the FBI.

Schwimmer, being Schwimmer, showed no change of expression. He'd been expecting this. Acquiring thirteen large military transport aircraft for an undisclosed mission was a sure way to draw the attention of the Feds.

What Special Agent Ptacek wanted to talk about was a $20,000 check that had been paid to Schwimmer Aviation Services by an entity called Foundry Associates. The same Foundry Associates had just been implicated in an arms smuggling operation uncovered on the East Coast.

Schwimmer was ready. Yes, he told the agent, it was true that he was receiving help from various sources in starting an airline for the purpose of flying into Palestine. They intended to commence flights as soon as the British Mandate came to an end and there were no restrictions against such an operation. None of his purchases had been warplanes. The agent was welcome to look around the facility and see for himself that the aircraft were all intended for civilian use.

The agent was unimpressed. He reminded Schwimmer that the shipment of any kind of armaments to Palestine was unlawful. There were severe penalties for violating the US Neutrality Act, which had been in force since 1939, and specifically prohibited unlicensed arms trades to foreign entities.

Schwimmer put on his most sincere face. Ship armaments? Violate the US Neutrality Act? They were loyal Americans. They certainly had no intention of doing such a thing.

The agent gave him a dubious look. He had no further questions for now, but he'd be back.

Schwimmer watched the agent walk to his car. He was sure the visit was a fishing expedition, but it signaled danger. To fly his airplanes out of the country, Schwimmer needed the cover of a legitimate airline. The problem was, Schwimmer Aviation Services was a maintenance facility, not a commercial airline certified by the CAA—Civil Aeronautics Administration.

A few days later, as if on cue, appeared a tall, curly-haired young man from Florida. His name was Irwin R. "Swifty" Schindler. He said he owned an airline.

At least on paper.

On their first meeting, Schwimmer learned instantly where Swifty Schindler got his nickname. Schindler did everything in a hurry. He bustled from one appointment to another. He ate fast. He drank fast. Most of all, he talked fast.

Schindler had dark hair, deep-set piercing eyes, and a long, angular face. As with many who'd flown for the ATC—Air Transport Command—during the war, flying was in Swifty Schindler's blood. And like Lewis and Gardner and Schwimmer, his burning ambition was to someday operate his own airline.

Back in 1944, while he was still in uniform, Schindler and his wife, Edyth, who was also a pilot, had incorporated Service Airways, Inc. After the war they bought a four-passenger Beechcraft. Together they operated charter flights out of tiny Aeroflex Airport in Andover, New Jersey.

And promptly went broke.

Schindler went to work as a copilot for an international non-sched (charter) airline. He hated it. He hated it mostly because he knew he was locked forever in the copilot's seat. His boss had made it clear: he'd be goddamned if he'd have a Jew as a captain.

One evening during a layover in London, Schindler was telling the navigator on his crew, a cigar-smoking ex-ATC airman named Steve Schwartz, about his dissatisfaction with the airline. Schindler happened to mention he still had the operating certificate for his defunct airline, Service Airways, Inc.

What happened next was mostly a mystery to Schindler. There were phone calls from "a friend of Steve's" asking about his airline-on-paper. Then came meetings in New York, and finally a conference in New York with a lawyer named Nahum Bernstein.

Sitting across the table from Bernstein, Swifty Schindler could barely believe what he was hearing. The Haganah agent was offering him the presidency of an . . . *airline?* It would be a newly activated Service

Airways, Inc., freshly equipped with three Constellation airliners and a fleet of C-46 cargo haulers.

To make it work Schindler would have to drum up some business flying legitimate cargo, probably to Latin America and Europe. Then when it became feasible, they'd be transporting immigrants and, perhaps, cargo to Palestine.

Special cargo.

A huge grin spread across Swifty Schindler's face. It meant that his old dream might finally be coming true. Not only would he be running a *real* airline, but he'd also be living an historic adventure. He'd be saving Jews in Palestine.

The next day he did what he'd been dreaming about for a year. Schindler told his boss at the non-sched airline that he was finished. Take his copilot job and stuff it.

A few days later, Schindler was ensconced in his new office on West 57th Street. His navigator friend, Steve Schwartz, resigned from the same non-sched airline and was now a vice president. Rey Selk, Al Schwimmer's mechanic buddy and cofounder of Schwimmer Aviation Services, was another vice president.

Service Airways, Inc., was in business. Swifty Schindler had airplanes, pilots, mechanics, and money in the bank.

Only one item was still missing. To fly their transports to Europe, Service Airways needed a legitimate cover business. Schindler's airline needed a franchise somewhere beyond the scrutiny of US treasury agents.

But where?

A few days later, over drinks in Manhattan, Schindler heard the answer.

━━━━

Panama, explained Martin Bellefond. Panama happened to be where Martin Bellefond owned a franchise for a flag-carrying airline.

Schindler swirled the ice in his drink. The possibilities raced through his brain. He and Martin Bellefond were old friends from the non-sched business.

Bellefond was a large, blond-haired pilot with movie-star good looks. He had been an air force major during WWII and in the postwar years a swashbuckling aviation entrepreneur, founding a non-sched airline called World Airways.

Because of CAA regulatory pressure on his operation—flying between Puerto Rico and New York—Bellefond was looking for a new area of operations, a place free of the stringent US bureaucracy.

Bellefond found what he needed in Panama. The officials of the Panamanian government were eager to exploit their country's unique position as a bridge between two continents and two oceans. Panama had just made a multimillion dollar investment on the Pacific side of the isthmus, Tocumen International Airport. The airport was being ignored by the international airlines. It was an opportunity waiting to be exploited by someone like Martin Bellefond.

After considerable legal machinations, Bellefond obtained a franchise for an airline to be called Lineas Aereas de Panama, Sociedad Anonima. LAPSA for short, it would be Panama's flag carrier.

But then, a problem. The majority stockholders of Bellefond's creation, World Airways, became exasperated with his free-wheeling management style and booted him out of the company he had founded. Suddenly jobless, Martin Bellefond owned his sought-after Latin American franchise, but it was only a third of what was required. Bellefond had neither airplanes nor an airline to go with his Panamanian franchise.

Listening to this, Swifty Schindler knew he had found what he was looking for. He clinked glasses with Martin Bellefond. The long-awaited airlift to Palestine was about to begin.

5

"How Much Would We Have to Pay You?"

MONTREAL
JANUARY 25, 1948

Montreal was in the grip of a bitter winter. The icy streets and gray skies only added to the boredom of Canada's greatest flying hero.

Twenty-six-year-old George "Buzz" Beurling had been the RCAF's top scoring ace in WWII, with thirty-one confirmed kills and a shared credit for another. The one-on-one, kill-or-be-killed pandemonium of combat had been Buzz Beurling's reason for living.

Now he was a man without a mission.

Beurling learned to fly in Canada as a teenager. An indifferent student, Beurling dropped out of the ninth grade to be a bush pilot. With the outbreak of WWII, he tried to join the RCAF but was rejected because of his lack of academic credentials.

Determined to get into the war as a pilot, Beurling sailed across the Atlantic on a convoy to Scotland, where he attempted to join the RAF. He was turned down because he'd neglected to bring his birth certificate. After a return trip across the ocean, his ship taking a German torpedo en route, he presented his birth certificate to the RAF and was accepted for pilot training.

Flying the Supermarine Spitfire, Sergeant Pilot Beurling was assigned to bomber escort missions and fighter sweeps across the English Channel. After gunning down two German FW190s over France and being reprimanded for attacking a target without permission, Beurling requested transfer to an overseas post. He was shipped to the Mediterranean island of Malta, which in 1942 was the most-bombed patch of ground on earth. German and Italian warplanes were making daily raids on the British-held island.

Beurling's squadron commanding officer remembered Beurling as "untidy, with a shock of tousled hair, penetrating blue eyes, smiled a lot, was highly strung, brash and outspoken . . . something of a rebel."

Some of Beurling's success could be attributed to those eyes. Beurling became famous for his ability to spot the tiny specks of incoming warplanes long before anyone else in his flight.

The skies over Malta were Beurling's aerial combat laboratory. Between missions he jotted copious notes in a black book about angles, speeds, bullet drop, shots that had scored, shots that missed. He developed a set of equations for calculating precise deflection angles.

Deflection shooting—aiming his guns a correct distance ahead of a hard-turning target—became Beurling's passion. He built models of Spitfires and Messerschmitts. He mounted them on sticks and used them to simulate air combat tactics.

Beurling was a cool killer. *Too* cool, in the opinion of some of his critics. Fellow pilots would be repulsed—sometimes nauseated—by Beurling's matter-of-fact descriptions of his kills. He could recite in gory detail how he'd come within a hundred yards of an Italian fighter. He had aimed precisely at the enemy pilot's cockpit. Then he watched his cannon shells sever the man's head from his body. Beurling described how the blood from the headless pilot streamed like crimson paint over the tail of the Macchi fighter.

This was too much even for combat-toughened pilots at Malta. Most walked away in disgust.

Not even Beurling's worst critics could deny his marksmanship, though. After one mission he claimed downing a German fighter while firing only five rounds. No one believed him until they found the wreckage of the enemy plane with the pilot inside. Five neat holes were punched through the side of the cockpit.

In fourteen days of swirling dogfights over Malta, Beurling broke all the records: twenty-seven Axis aircraft shot down, eight more damaged, three more scored as probable kills. Twice Beurling was shot down. The first time he belly-landed his Spitfire in an open field. The second time he was wounded in a dogfight and had to bail out at low altitude.

On his way to a recuperation facility aboard a B-24 Liberator, his airplane crashed off Gibraltar. Of the twenty-four passengers and crew aboard the Liberator, only Beurling and two others survived.

A bona fide war hero, Beurling was sent back to Canada to participate in a war bond drive. It was a public relations disaster. Beurling hated the appearances, the autographs, the speeches, and he didn't mind saying so. After a dismal tour of selling war bonds, Beurling was sent back to England to an RCAF Spitfire squadron.

He was still a rebel, even more so. Never a team player, Beurling exasperated his new commanders for the same old reasons: disobeying orders, leaving his formation to engage enemy aircraft on his own. He was never discreet about criticizing flight and squadron leaders, or pointing out what he considered sloppy airmanship.

After multiple chewings-out and threats of court-martial, the RCAF had finally had enough of Beurling. He was sent back to Canada and discharged from the air force in 1944.

It was the worst possible punishment for a man like Beurling. The war was still on, and Beurling was out. He tried to rejoin the RAF, where his military career had begun. He was rejected. He applied to join the US Army Air Force, even offering to change his citizenship. He was turned down by the Americans.

"I would give ten years of my life to live over again those six months I had in Malta in 1942," he said. "Combat, it's the only thing I can do well; it's the only thing I ever did that I really liked."

Beurling was never the same. World War II ended, and Beurling moved through a succession of desultory jobs—bush flying, air show pilot, life insurance salesman. Nothing worked for him. His brief marriage to a young woman he'd met during his bond tour foundered.

What Buzz Beurling needed more than anything was another war.

Beurling politely refused the drink being offered him. He was a teeto-taler, and in any case he had come here to talk about Palestine.

Beurling's host was a man named Syd Shulemson. Shulemson headed the Montreal recruiting branch for the Haganah, and he knew Beurling by reputation. What worried him was that Beurling was not a Jew. That made him a mercenary or, worse, possibly a British or Arab agent. The battle for Israel, Shulemson believed, should be fought by Jews.

Beurling had sought out Shulemson in early 1948. He'd heard the rumors that a Jewish underground was recruiting pilots for an air force in Palestine. After his first feelers were ignored, Beurling arranged a meeting with Shulemson.

For all his brashness, Beurling could demonstrate genuine passion. He insisted to Shulemson that he cared deeply about the plight of the Jews in Palestine. He knew about the Holocaust, was troubled by the refugees interned in British camps on Cyprus, understood the Jewish yearning for a homeland. He wasn't interested in the money. He would volunteer for nothing more than expense money.

The inner circle of Haganah recruiters in Montreal and Toronto finally decided that Beurling was too valuable an asset to pass up. Any fighter pilot who could shoot down twenty-seven Axis airplanes in four-teen days would be the scourge of the Arab air forces.

A week later, Buzz Beurling was on his way to Rome.

Aaron Finkel was asleep in his 9th Avenue apartment in New York when he realized he wasn't alone. A stranger was sitting on his bed.

"Are you Aaron Finkel?" said the stranger. He spoke with an accent.

Finkel stared at the stranger. Did his roommate let this guy in?

"Yeah," said Finkel.

"You are Jewish?"

Finkel nodded. Before he could ask the guy what the hell he was doing in the apartment, the stranger told him in broken English.

"I would like you to go to Palestine to be a fighter pilot."

Finkel was wide awake now. Later he would learn that someone had supplied the Haganah operatives in New York with a list of ex–air force pilots with Jewish-sounding names. Finkel's name—and his war record—jumped out at them.

Aaron Finkel went by "Red" even though his hair was rapidly vanishing in front. He was a muscular, wisecracking Brooklynite, twenty-nine years old, who had flown P-47 Thunderbolt fighter-bombers in the China-Burma-India theatre in WWII. In the three years since the war Finkel had been making his living as a salesman of radio components.

Finkel knew about the fighting in Palestine. He liked the idea that the Jews were fighting for their cause. "For once the Jews were *not* turning the other cheek," he recalled.

But *him?* Go to Palestine as a fighter pilot?

Finkel needed only a few minutes to think about it. Hell, why not? Such an idealistic adventure was exactly what Red Finkel had been looking for.

"How much would we have to pay you?" the stranger asked.

Finkel considered for a moment. "How about a bottle of whiskey, cigarettes, and thirty dollars a month?"

The Haganah man's expression didn't change. In his strange accent he gave Finkel instructions to go to a downtown address, which turned out to be the offices of an outfit called Service Airways. Three days later Red Finkel was boarding a TWA Constellation.

He was headed for Rome.

6

Service Airways

The icy blast of air hit Schwimmer as he stepped down the boarding ladder of the Constellation. Schwimmer was wearing his customary light leather jacket and cotton slacks. The temperature was two degrees below freezing. A frigid wind swept in from nearby Delaware Bay.

Seven hours ago Schwimmer and Sam Lewis and Leo Gardner had left the balmy climate of southern California. Now they were stepping off the Constellation in the frozen flatlands of New Jersey.

It had been a peculiar flight for Sam Lewis, the Smilin' Jack look-alike. As the captain, he was in command of the aircraft. The other crew members were all subordinate to him. But Schwimmer, the flight engineer, also happened to be Lewis's boss.

Schwimmer had chosen the Millville airport because of its proximity to Manhattan—a two-hour drive but far enough to escape unwanted attention. Millville lay in the southern part of New Jersey, a sleepy tomato-farming district. The field had been a wartime air force training base and had everything Service Airways needed: hangar and shop space for the incoming fleet of transports, and a 5,000-foot runway, long enough to accommodate Schwimmer's growing fleet.

A few days after the Constellation arrived, a new sound rumbled over the flat New Jersey terrain. It was the throbbing noise of the big R-2800 engines of the first three C-46s arriving from California.

A dozen men climbed down from the transports, shivering and flapping their arms against the cold breeze. They were the Cobbers—the ex-WWII mechanics who had served in Australia—whom Schwimmer had hired in Burbank. They were joined the next day by another fifteen newly recruited air crewmen, moving to Millville from their temporary New York quarters.

The little Millville base was coming to life.

In his New York office on West 57th Street, newly minted Service Airways vice president Steve Schwartz was studying the printed list on his desk. A wartime buddy of Schwartz had placed in his hands an item of immense value: a roster of New York Air National Guard airmen.

With Schwartz in his office were four of his newly recruited airmen. Schwartz had given them a job. They were going over the roster, picking out Jewish-sounding names, and phoning the prospects.

They'd say they were calling to see if the prospect was interested in a flying job. When the pilot asked *what* kind of flying job, Schwartz would keep it deliberately vague. A start-up overseas airline. You know, cargo and charter flying.

Nothing was ever mentioned about Palestine, hauling contraband, or the possibility of being castrated and killed by irate Arabs. If the candidate was interested, he should come down to the Manhattan office of Service Airways.

Several came. The word got around to other colleagues. Gradually the pilot roster of Service Airways grew.

One of Schwartz's early recruits was an ex-B-17 pilot and New York City fireman named Norman Moonitz, who was accustomed to being told he looked like actor William Bendix. Moonitz was soon joined by another New York fireman and former cop, a large and boisterous man named Ray Kurtz, who had also flown B-17s over Europe in WWII.

Kurtz and Moonitz became a team of playful bears, clowning and playing jokes on the others, inserting their brand of New York humor into the volunteer band.

At the Bakersfield airport in California, Hal Auerbach climbed out of his private airplane and walked across the ramp. Auerbach was a good-looking bachelor and a ladies' man, and he was following up on a tip. A buddy told him that if he landed sometime in Bakersfield, he should look up an attractive woman named Elynor Rudnick. She had her own airport and ran a flying school.

The thirty-one-year-old Auerbach had been a PBY Catalina patrol plane pilot in the Pacific during the war. After the war he wanted to keep flying, so he had gone to work as an examiner with the Civil Aeronautics Administration in California.

On the sunshine-filled airport at Bakersfield, Auerbach met Miss Rudnick. And everything Auerbach had heard about Miss Rudnick was true. She *was* attractive. She was well-to-do, and she *did* own a school and an airport.

But no romance came of the meeting—at least between Auerbach and Rudnick. Instead Auerbach was tantalized by an item of information the lady passed to him. She had heard about some kind of start-up airline in Burbank. They had acquired three Constellations, and it was rumored that they were planning on flying them to Palestine.

Constellations. A new airline. Palestine. It was enough to send Auerbach's hopes soaring. Auerbach was familiar with the discrimination in the airline hiring process. Getting an airline job was tough. It was tougher for Jews.

Auerbach climbed back in his airplane and flew directly to the Lockheed terminal at Burbank to meet the president of Schwimmer Aviation Services.

The two men developed an instant rapport. Auerbach was more mature and experienced than most of the young airmen Schwimmer had been recruiting. He was just the kind of guy Schwimmer had been looking for.

In a few days Auerbach had moved to Millville, New Jersey to take up his new role: Director of Operations of Service Airways.

—————

It was early evening. The airmen were clustered around a table in the bar of the Henry Hudson Hotel in Manhattan. The Hudson had become their hangout of choice, mainly because the drinks were reasonable and the place filled with single women this time of evening.

Millville, New Jersey, they had already determined, had two serious deficiencies. There were few bars and almost no available women. When they weren't involved in training flights, the airmen jammed into their cars and headed for New York.

The Service Airways airmen had begun to bond as a group. They were developing the sort of camaraderie peculiar to elite military units, the sense that they were involved in something larger than themselves.

Radio operator Harold Livingston remembered that "We first began envisioning ourselves as true life, bigger-than-life, honest-to-God Yankee adventurers. A latter-day Flying Tigers volunteer group, risking life and limb this time for a noble, glorious Jewish cause."

It was a good feeling. It helped them overlook the awkward facts that they were working for a phony airline, flying beat-up airplanes not suited for a long flight across the Atlantic, and running a serious risk of being indicted as traitors.

But what the hell, they were in it together.

With them was a thirty-five-year-old ex–air force major named Bill Gerson. With his slight build and fatherly manner, the balding Gerson was immediately tagged as the Old Man. Gerson was a passionate believer in the cause of the Jews in Palestine, so much so that he left behind his successful Los Angeles flying school and his wife and two young daughters to join the band of volunteers at Millville. Because of his even-tempered, confidence-inspiring manner, the Old Man had been put in charge of training the new pilots at Millville.

Not all the new airmen were Jewish. Trygve "Tryg" Maseng was a twenty-six-year-old blond-haired Norwegian American. Maseng was a former air force captain who had flown the demanding B-26 Martin Marauder in combat over Europe. Instead of working for an airline or non-sched after the war like many of his fellow volunteers, he had become a student at Columbia, studying creative writing.

Which made Maseng an oddball, at least to his fellow pilots. *Creative writing?* What drew a guy like him to *this* job, especially a non-Jew? Maseng wasn't the kind to talk about himself or rationalize his motives. When pressed, he'd say that since he'd been too young to volunteer for the Spanish Civil War, this was the next best thing.

The truth was that Tryg Maseng was one of those rare birds—a pure idealist. In the plight of the Palestinian Jews, Maseng had found his own righteous cause.

———

When will your airplanes be ready?

Schwimmer was expecting the question. He'd driven his old LaSalle coupe from Millville to New York to meet with Arazi and Bernstein.

Arazi was more intense than ever. The dapper spy had recently returned from Palestine and a meeting with Ben-Gurion. The civil war between the Haganah and Arab paramilitary forces in Palestine had taken a bloodier turn. The British naval blockade was still firmly in place, making it nearly impossible to import the munitions they were gathering in Europe.

Arazi wanted to know: When will the airlift begin?

Soon, Schwimmer said, sounding more certain than he felt. He told them about Martin Bellefond, who was in Panama City finalizing the details of the LAPSA—Lineas Aereas de Panama, Sociedad Anonima—franchise. Bellefond had rented office space and living quarters for the air crews. LAPSA was in business—at least on paper. The only missing pieces of the new airline were a few essentials—airplanes, pilots, mechanics.

But Schwimmer was working on that. He said goodbye to Arazi. The next day he was on a commercial airline flight back to California.

By now Schwimmer had nearly two hundred mechanics working on the airplanes in the Burbank hangar. They were stripping all the military accoutrements from the Constellations—bucket seats, toilets, primer-coated metal paneling—and installing five-abreast upholstered passenger seats, separate men's and women's lavatories, and carpeted aisles, making them appear to be airliners.

The C-46s were receiving the same treatment. All the vestiges of wartime service were being yanked out not only to make the aircraft lighter but also to maintain the image of a commercial freight hauler.

Schwimmer recognized a familiar figure standing outside the Burbank hangar. He was there almost every day. Keeping a discreet distance but making no effort to be unnoticed was the tall, fedora-topped silhouette of FBI Special Agent Ptacek.

But now he was doing more than watching. Ptacek was having conversations with some of Schwimmer's employees.

Which gave Schwimmer something else to worry about. Were some of the mechanics he'd hired government spies? Were the Feds also watching the Millville base?

———

It was mid-afternoon when Swifty Schindler spotted them on the road outside his Millville base. The same ones Schwimmer had told him about.

Unsmiling guys in their black sedan. They were doing their best to appear nonchalant while they observed the comings and goings of the air crews.

But these weren't FBI agents. They were T-men—Treasury Department agents—and Schindler had already been told that they suspected Service Airways was planning to haul contraband materials.

The agents rotated shifts, one black sedan relieving the other every evening. Each time one of the cars passed a group of the airmen, the pilots gave them great exaggerated salutes.

What worried Schindler was that the T-men would make their suspicions a reality by planting *real* contraband onto one of the airplanes. He posted watchers to keep an eye on the T-men. The watchers took shifts sitting in Schindler's new canary yellow Packard convertible or

Schwimmer's LaSalle, parked across the ramp from the black sedans. Neither side spoke with the other.

———

The Constellation's engines bellowed. The airliner gathered speed. Sam Lewis eased the nose up and the heavy transport lifted from the runway and turned south.

All the way to Panama. It was March 13, 1948, and Panama's official airline, LAPSA, now had a flagship—Constellation RX 121.

It had been pure luck—and government bungling—that Lewis slipped away without being snagged. Presidential Proclamation 2717 of February 14, 1947, required State Department permission for the export of any aircraft weighing over 35,000 pounds, a category that included the Constellation.

Now the Feds were keeping a tight watch on the other two Connies, one at Millville, one still in Burbank. The C-46s fell beneath the weight requirement and were good to go—at least in theory. But then on March 26, the Truman administration threw down yet another obstruction. Proclamation 2776 superseded the previous order and expanded the list of nonexportable arms, ammunition, and "implements of war" to include *all* commercial aircraft regardless of weight.

The order was clearly aimed at exports to Palestine. The new proclamation would go into effect April 15, 1948.

An export ban! The news set off another frenzy in Hotel Fourteen and the Service Airways shops at Millville. Even the unflappable Schwimmer felt the pressure of time running out. Five of the big freighters were still in Burbank, and four on the East Coast. Not one was ready to fly overseas.

Nor were the crews. Most of the volunteers had come to Service Airways with zero experience in C-46s. The new pilots were still grinding around the traffic pattern at Millville with Gerson or Maseng instructing them. Few were ready to make the long overwater flights to Panama and onward to the Middle East.

Schwimmer made yet another hurried trip to confer with Bernstein in New York. Then he met with Schindler and Auerbach at Millville. Schwimmer could tell from their worried expressions they didn't like the idea. Not a bit.

But the airplanes *could* be flown, the men reluctantly agreed. Not safely or professionally even, but they were airworthy. More or less.

They didn't have enough pilots to fly all nine C-46s at once. They'd ferry the Millville airplanes to Panama, then send crews back up to Burbank to retrieve the last five C-46s. The most experienced pilots would have to manage without a qualified copilot. A radio operator or navigator would be in the right seat.

By any measure it was a dangerous operation. Unqualified crewmen, overloaded airplanes, inexperienced pilots. There was no alternative.

=== 7 ===

Black Sedans

MILLVILLE, NEW JERSEY
APRIL 10, 1948

Swifty Schindler saw them coming. It was almost departure time. The black sedan drove right up to where Schindler was standing. Out climbed four grim-looking T-men in fedoras and overcoats, the same ones who had been lurking outside the Millville base the past few weeks.

Today was different. They parked the sedan on the apron directly in front of the C-46s that were about to take off for Panama.

Each C-46 had a newly-assigned Panamanian registration number. They would be flown by the four most experienced captains: navy veteran Hal Auerbach, ex-fireman Norm Moonitz, Bill Gerson, still called the Old Man by his pupils, and Larry Raab, a baby-faced ex-army bomber pilot whose speech and teenage countenance always got him ID-checked at the Henry Hudson bar.

The crews had spent the previous day scrambling to collect the gear they needed: survival vests, sidearms, cigarettes, canned food, maps. They made phone calls to girlfriends and wives and parents, being vague about where they were headed or when they might return.

Gone for the moment were the raunchy banter and sophomoric jokes. The reality of the situation—*Hey, we're on our way to a war*—had a sobering effect on all of them.

The C-46s were heavy—*too* damned heavy, in several pilots' opinions. The airplanes' loads included two disassembled Vultee BT-13 trainer aircraft, spare R-2800 engines, tires, and assorted parts for both the C-46s and the Connies. There had been no time to train the pilots in heavy-weight takeoffs. No one had bothered with such niceties as fuel burn predictions or precise weight and balance calculations. It would be a learn-as-you-go operation.

The plan was to fly southward along the Atlantic coast, over Cuba, landing in the morning at Kingston, Jamaica. After refueling they'd fly the shorter leg to Panama.

One of men from the black sedan walked up to Schindler and presented his card. His name was Fisher, and he was a US Customs agent. He told Schindler that these airplanes—he waved at the C-46s—would not be permitted to depart.

Schindler stared at the agent. *Not be permitted?* They already had State Department clearance to depart, Schindler said. On what basis were they preventing their departure?

On suspicion of carrying contraband, the agent declared. He was empowered by federal law to detain any aircraft suspected of hauling contraband cargo.

Schindler invited him to inspect all of the cargo. He'd see that there was no contraband. In any case, he reminded the agent, these aircraft weren't US-registered airplanes and therefore weren't subject to the statutes the agent was talking about.

The agent pointed to the closest C-46. "They have US numbers," he said.

Schindler said they hadn't had time to change them. They'd do it in Panama.

The agent was unmoved. The airplanes were US registered, he said. That meant they wouldn't be permitted to leave.

Schindler was getting the picture. The agents *had* to find a reason to hold up the departure of the airplanes.

"I'll be back in a second," Schindler said and headed for the hangar. When he reappeared, he had two mechanics with him. One carried a bucket of blue paint and the other had a ladder. Wordlessly, they leaned the ladder against the aft fuselage of the first C-46. One of the mechanics climbed the ladder with the bucket in his hand. On the windowless area between the cabin and the tail of the aircraft, he painted first a big "R," then an "X," then the airplane's Panamanian registration number, "135."

They moved to the next C-46 and painted its assigned number. Within minutes, all four C-46s were labeled with the messy new numbers. With the small amount of blue paint left, the painter went back and added a final flourish—the letters "LAPSA" on the fuselages.

The paint job wasn't pretty. Already the blue paint was starting to run in little rivulets down the fuselage.

Agent Fisher wasn't impressed. To show how unimpressed he was, he ordered the black sedan positioned directly in front of the lead C-46.

Schindler stormed inside the hangar to telephone Hotel Fourteen and have someone, maybe Bernstein, obtain an injunction. Schindler was told it would take a while. An injunction would have to come from a federal judge, maybe even from someplace higher up the chain. Fisher, in the meantime, was talking by phone with his own district office.

The standoff continued. The agents watched from the black sedan while the sun dipped closer to the western boundary of the airport. With each passing minute Schindler was growing more frustrated. If they delayed much longer, it wouldn't be possible to make the flight south, refuel, and make it to Panama before sunset tomorrow.

Schindler stomped over to the black sedan. These airplanes were taking off immediately, he declared. He didn't wait for the agent's reply. Schindler yelled at his crews to start their engines.

The Customs agent was out of his car, shouting that the crews were prohibited from leaving the United States. The airmen ignored him. They were all trotting toward their airplanes.

"If you want to stop them," Schindler yelled to Fisher, "you'll have to shoot them down."

The agent seemed to be considering this suggestion when he was startled by a whining, coughing noise a few feet from his head. It was the left engine of Auerbach's C-46. The big four-bladed propeller was turning. The R-2800 engine belched smoke and rumbled to life.

Seconds later the right propeller was turning. The engines of the other three C-46s across the apron were starting up, growling like omnivorous beasts.

The black sedan hadn't moved. Auerbach gunned the right engine of the C-46, swinging the tail around. With a blast of power, he passed a wingtip over the agents' heads, scattering their fedoras with the prop blast.

Schindler watched from his cockpit. *Will they really use guns? Will they block the runway?*

Minutes later he had the answer. With its lights twinkling, Hal Auerbach's C-46 was roaring down the 5,000-foot strip of concrete. Each of the overloaded transports followed.

The black sedan hadn't moved. The agents watched the twinkling lights vanish in the south.

═══════

They all made it.

One after the other in the midday hours of Sunday, April 11, the four C-46s swept in over the gulf coast of Panama. The last to land was Larry Raab and his crew with a hairy tale of having to land in Cuba with only drops of fuel remaining. Norm Moonitz, experiencing the same fuel overconsumption problems, had dropped into Nassau to refuel.

Only Swifty Schindler, whose copilot, Bill Gerson—the Old Man—knew the C-46 better than any of them, made it all the way to the scheduled fuel stop at Kingston, Jamaica.

The exhausted crews were shuttled to nearby Ancón, where Bellefond had arranged plush quarters for them in the Tivoli Hotel. In the lounge of the hotel they slammed down drinks, clapped each other on the back, and toasted their successful flights to Panama.

Tired as he was, Auerbach joined the celebration. But Auerbach knew they'd been lucky. Before they attempted the dangerous transocean flights from Central America to Italy, the crews—including himself—needed a lot more training. They'd have to sharpen their skills in everything: navigation, instrument flying, and, especially, fuel management. Auerbach gave them a day off. Then the classes would begin.

They were still celebrating when Auerbach gave them something else: a new nickname. As soon as they heard it, they raised their glasses and roared their approval.

The Bagel Lancers.

They loved it. It struck just the right note for the cocky young aviators—a mix of schmaltz, chutzpah, and self-deprecating humor.

Armed with their new name and a few extra drinks, the Bagel Lancers, most in their twenties and in robust fine health, were already embracing the classic illusions of young warriors. They were invincible. Indestructible. Hell, maybe even immortal.

The illusion would last exactly eleven more days.

———

Schwimmer called from Burbank. Looming over them was the April 15 deadline, and the five remaining C-46s were still stuck in Burbank. Also stuck, probably permanently, were the other two Constellations, their applications for export denied by the State Department. Bernstein had filed yet another application, this one proposing to export them to South Africa under the ownership of Transcaribbean Air Cargo Lines, Inc.

To no one's surprise, it was denied.

Schwimmer thought if they acted immediately, the five C-46s could be flown out of Burbank before the West Coast government agencies connected them with the near shoot-out in Millville.

The problem was, he was short of crews. Auerbach and Gerson would have to leave Panama immediately and come to Burbank.

———

"Where's the weight and balance sheet?" was Auerbach's first question.

A weight and balance sheet was a computation showing how much every item of cargo weighed and its position relative to the aircraft's center of gravity.

There wasn't one, the chief loader told him. There hadn't been time.

Auerbach just nodded. He was still creaky from the long flight to Panama and then the commercial trip to California. When he and Gerson arrived at the Burbank hangar on April 13, Auerbach was surprised at what he found. The C-46s were already loaded, gassed, ready for departure.

It was a replay of the Millville departure. Each airplane was crammed with tools, machinery, engines, wheels—all the paraphernalia that belonged to Schwimmer Aviation Services.

Auerbach knew they were overloaded. Even if he'd insisted on unloading and weighing the cargo, it was too late. They had one day left before the April 15 deadline. In his navy days and CAA examiner days, Auerbach would never have accepted shortcuts like this. But this was different. There was no alternative.

Anyway, reasoned Auerbach, hadn't they just made it out of Millville with their airplanes a good 5,000 pounds over maximum? This flight should be no different.

= 8 =

Incident in Mexico

LOS ANGELES
APRIL 14, 1948

It was still early morning when Sam Lewis led the gaggle of C-46s to Mines Field in Los Angeles to clear US Customs. Because Lewis had the most experience in heavy transports, Schwimmer put him in charge of the five-plane flight. The others would follow like geese.

As the transports trundled across the field, Lewis's eyes scanned the ramp. He saw no black sedans. No agents in fedoras. Lewis breathed a sigh of relief.

In a matter of minutes, all five planes had cleared Customs. As they hoped, the slow-moving US Customs Service hadn't yet connected *these* C-46s to Swifty Schindler's group at Millville.

The first leg was short, across the border to Tijuana, where they cleared Mexican Customs for the next two legs through Mexico. From Tijuana they flew down the Gulf of California, stopping to refuel at the coastal airport of Mazatlan.

The pilots realized just how overloaded the C-46s were when each barely made it off the short 3,300-foot sea-level runway. By the time they landed in Mexico City, they knew all about the wallowing, heavy-weight characteristics of their airplanes.

They were hosted in Mexico City by the Haganah's representative, an affable attorney named Herbert Rothman. Rothman seemed to have an unlimited expense account. The aviators were fed at lavish restaurants, entertained at the most posh nightclubs. They loved it. If they were on their way to war, this was the way to go.

Still in a euphoric mood, their spirit of adventure renewed, the aviators took the long ride back out to the Mexico City airport for the last leg, the scenic journey over the mountains, down to Tocumen Airport in Panama.

———

Mexico City had a long runway, over 8,000 feet. But the airport, like Mexico City itself, nestled atop a plateau 7,382 feet above sea level. At such altitude, the airplanes required a far greater takeoff roll to reach flying speed.

It was the afternoon of April 21, 1948. Positioned at the end of the runway, the pilots ran up the engines. Each checked his magnetos, making sure they could squeeze maximum power from the R-2800 engines.

Lewis took the lead. Behind him came Marty Ribakoff, a classic flyer of fortune. A short, beak-nosed man, Ribakoff had been a volunteer in the Spanish Civil War, a wartime C-46 pilot in Asia, and then become one of the thousands of ex-military pilots in the non-scheds and knockabout flying outfits before landing at Service Airways. Ribakoff was also the best friend of Bill Gerson, the Old Man, in the number three slot behind him. The last C-46 was flown by a recent recruit, a veteran pilot named Si Sorge.

Lewis revved his engines to full power and rolled. And kept rolling. The other airmen held their breath, watching Lewis's airplane gobble up runway. On its main gear, tail in the air, the C-46 was nearly at the end of the runway.

When there was almost no remaining concrete beneath it, the big transport labored into the air. But the C-46 didn't climb right away. The heavy aircraft skimmed the cactus and sagebrush for a mile beyond the end of the runway.

From the ground, the other four pilots watched with intense interest. A sobering truth struck each of them: *This is dangerous.*

Next went Ribakoff. It was a repeat of Lewis's takeoff. Ribakoff's C-46 consumed nearly the full length of Mexico City's runway before it grudgingly staggered into the air.

It was Bill Gerson's turn. Like the first two, Gerson's C-46 rolled and rolled. And kept rolling. All the way to the end.

And beyond. A plume of dust appeared behind each main wheel. The C-46 rumbled briefly through the dirt off the end of the runway, and then the plumes stopped. Clinging to the thin cushion of air, the C-46 wallowed to an altitude of a hundred feet.

And then something happened. The left wing dropped. The C-46's nose angled toward the ground.

———

Marty Ribakoff saw it from the air. He had taken off a minute ahead of Gerson, and his airplane was in a climbing left bank. Ribakoff craned his neck to peer back at the airport when a surge of alarm shot through him. The silver, distinctive shape of Gerson's C-46 was in a steep bank close to the ground.

Ribakoff knew exactly what would happen next.

Gerson's C-46 struck the ground left wing first. The rest of the airplane disintegrated around it like a collapsed building. A geyser of dirt and smoke erupted from the dry river bed.

Through his cockpit window Ribakoff stared at the rising column of smoke. *Damn!* Gerson was his colleague in what was supposed to be a grand adventure.

Watching from the opposite end of the field, Hal Auerbach gunned the engines of his C-46 and taxied at high speed down the mile-and-a-half length of the runway. He could see the wreckage of Gerson's airplane in the distance.

Auerbach shut down his engines and clambered down from the cockpit. He and his copilot, panting in the thin air, ran for nearly a mile through the sagebrush and dirt mounds to the crash site. They arrived at the same time the airport crash truck pulled up with its red lights flashing.

It looked like a scene from hell. Debris was scattered over a fifty-square-yard area. Small fires were burning in several locations. They saw the right engine half buried in the dirt. The fuselage was broken apart at the front, and both crewmen had been thrown from the aircraft. Glen "Bud" King, the mechanic who was serving as Gerson's copilot, was dead, killed on impact.

They found Gerson still alive. He was crumpled and moaning. Gerson had been crushed by the left engine and was badly burned. Auerbach and the crash crew transported Gerson on a canvas to the ambulance.

Auerbach rode along on the traffic-clogged, siren-wailing drive through Mexico City streets to the hospital. Gerson drifted in and out of consciousness while Auerbach kept giving him words of encouragement. By the time they reached the hospital, he had fallen into a coma.

At seven o'clock that evening Bill Gerson, the Old Man, was dead.

———

So they weren't immortal after all. Not invincible, not indestructible, not even crash proof. The deaths of Gerson and King hit the Bagel Lancers like a seismic shock. Gone was the euphoria, the sense of derring-do, the grand adventure. Their war hadn't even begun, and already they were losing people. Worse, they were losing them for senseless reasons.

Or so it appeared.

They would never determine exactly what caused the crash. Gerson was a pilot's pilot and a role model for the younger airmen, but it seemed that he made a fatal decision during the long takeoff roll.

Concerned that they might not get off the ground, Gerson had lowered the C-46's flaps. The flaps momentarily produced enough lift to pop the overloaded transport off the runway. But with the extra drag in the high, thin air, a temperature of 100 degrees, the overloaded transport was flying on the edge of a stall.

Most of the airmen believed that at this critical moment, Gerson's left engine failed. The evidence was the sudden left wing drop that Auerbach and Ribakoff had witnessed. In the mini-seconds available to him, Gerson didn't have time to feather the propeller or raise the flaps.

Bill Gerson had used up all his luck. So had Glen King, a non-Jew who had the distinction of being the first volunteer airman to die for the new Jewish state.

But to the bitter young aviators dissecting the circumstances of the crash, the *real* culprit was obvious. *The damned airplane was overloaded.*

Gerson had been carrying most of the communications equipment for Service Airways, putting the airplane at least 4,000 pounds over the maximum allowed gross weight. Why, the pilots were demanding to know, were they carrying loads like that out of a high-altitude field like Mexico City?

There was more. In Mexico and Panama, the aviators, whose compensation was supposed to be a secret but ranged from almost nil to a few hundred dollars a month, had seen the lush life being led by their Haganah bosses. Expensive restaurants, nightclubs, women—money seemed to be no object.

The worst rumor, however, was that the $10,000 life insurance policy that was supposed to be in force for each of them had been canceled. If this were true, Bill Gerson's and Glen King's bereaved families would get nothing.

It was in this spirit, the mood growing uglier among the crews in Panama, that Al Schwimmer flew down to confront his angry aviators.

Schwimmer's eyes roamed the room, looking at each airman. They were all crowded into a conference room at the Packard House where Bellefond had established LAPSA's offices. The sullen pilots smoked cigarettes and sprawled on couches and chairs and glowered at Schwimmer.

One of the most sullen was Swifty Schindler, the president and boss of Service Airways. In a heated clash before the meeting, Schwimmer told Schindler that he was fired as president of Service Airways. Fine, snapped Schindler. In fact he was quitting from the whole damned operation.

Few of the pilots knew much about Schwimmer, only that he was the brains and guiding spirit behind the airlift. They saw him as a mild-mannered, soft-spoken man who got things done in an undemonstrative way. Only a handful of insiders like Sam Lewis and Leo Gardner had seen the strong-willed, decisive side of Al Schwimmer.

It was this side they were seeing now. In a firm voice Schwimmer said, "I'm told you guys are blaming me for Gerson's death."

There were coughs, the sound of feet scraping, the metallic snap of Zippo lighters igniting cigarettes. No one spoke. This was not the easygoing Al Schwimmer they knew.

Yes, he told them, Gerson's airplane was overloaded. *All* the airplanes were overloaded. If overloading caused Gerson's death, said Schwimmer, then it was he who murdered him. *He* was a murderer.

More silence.

Schwimmer told them that Gerson had been satisfied that his airplane was okay. In fact, Gerson was carrying the lightest load of all. And while they might never know what caused the accident, it seemed likely that the combination of an engine failure and Gerson's lowering of the flaps had been a deadly combination.

A few heads nodded in agreement. Some of the hostility was melting.

Schwimmer went on. He promised that never again would he ask them to fly with such loads in those conditions. And about the $10,000 life insurance policy—they had his word that it was in force and was being paid to Gerson's and King's widows.

It was a command performance. The airmen exchanged glances, lit more cigarettes, and began to relax on the couches and chairs. Schwimmer was restoring some—but not all—of their shattered confidence.

But Schwimmer wasn't finished. He'd brought with him two other Haganah operatives. One was a tall, rugged-looking ex-infantry major named Hank Greenspun, who had served on General George Patton's staff in WWII. Recruited by Schwimmer, the thirty-nine-year-old Greenspun had given up his Las Vegas public relations business to run the Haganah's arms smuggling operation in Mexico.

Most of the volunteers had heard the Greenspun stories. A month earlier, when Greenspun was transporting machine guns to a waiting freighter in Mexico, the yacht captain he had hired to haul the contraband cargo balked. He refused to move his vessel. Greenspun solved the impasse by jamming the muzzle of his Mauser automatic pistol against the captain's temple. The captain could deliver the cargo as agreed or he could have his brains splattered across his yacht's cockpit.

Suddenly possessed of a clearer understanding, the captain nodded his agreement. Greenspun's machine guns were delivered.

The other man with Schwimmer had a less imposing countenance. He was a wiry, American-born Palestinian in his late twenties who had been a B-25 navigator in WWII. He introduced himself as Hy Marcus, though his real name was Hyman Sheckman. Soon he would take a Hebrew name—Haman Shamir—when he became Deputy Chief of Staff for the Israeli Air Force.

Sheckman began by telling them he had come here on behalf of the Jews fighting for their lives in Palestine. The war had already begun in Palestine, and Jews were dying every day. Arab militias were attacking cities, kibbutzim, medical convoys. They had laid siege to the Old City of Jerusalem. They were ambushing supply convoys, massacring everyone in them. Without *you*, Sheckman told the airmen, the Jews of Palestine had no chance. They needed everything—arms, reinforcements, tools, ammunition, airplanes. Every single item would have to be flown in— at this Sheckman paused for effect and gazed at his audience—*by you.*

When Sheckman finished, the room fell silent. The appeals from Schwimmer and Sheckman had struck a nerve. The transformation— just as Schwimmer had hoped—was happening.

The rebellion was over. None of the airmen had quit, not even Swifty Schindler. In a quiet moment after the meeting, he pulled Schwimmer aside and said that if it was all the same with Schwimmer, he'd keep on flying as a line pilot.

Schwimmer gave him the old bland-faced Schwimmer smile. The two men shook hands.

Schwimmer said goodbye to his airmen and headed back to the air- port. He was on his way to Europe with good news.

The Great Flyaway

PRAGUE, CZECHOSLOVAKIA
APRIL 23, 1948

A soft afternoon rain was falling when Dr. Otto Felix, carrying an umbrella and wearing his three-piece suit and a homburg, walked into the office of the Avia factory manager. He had come, he said, to place an order for ten Messerschmitt fighters.

The Czech manager scoffed. *Ten fighters?* That was nothing. You'll soon have to replace them. If the Jews want to purchase fighters, they should buy the entire lot of twenty-five the Czechs had for sale.

Felix left the office to make a hurried query to Tel Aviv. Ben-Gurion, who was still trying to convince the Haganah command that there would be an invasion and that warplanes were critical, told Felix to stick with the lot of ten fighters. It was all they could afford.

Felix returned to the manager's office and placed the order for the ten Messerschmitts. Then, on his own, he executed a private option with the manager for the additional fifteen fighters.

Each Messerschmitt would cost $44,600. Auxiliary equipment for each machine would run an extra $6,890 plus $120,229 for ammunition and weaponry—a total of nearly $1.8 million. Included in the price was the training of Israeli pilots by Czech Air Force instructors.

As warplane acquisitions went, it was not a good deal. In the United States a surplus P-51D fighter—the premier propeller-driven fighter in the world—was selling for $4,000, but only to approved buyers. Even the crafty Al Schwimmer had been unable to purchase fighters from the US War Assets Administration.

But Schwimmer's efforts in North America had not all been in vain. His search had taken him south of the US border, and there he had struck gold.

Slumped in the padded hotel room chair, Schwimmer closed his eyes and massaged his temples. It was what he did whenever time zone changes and lack of sleep and stress converged on him like a swirling vortex.

Schwimmer had just made the journey from Mexico to the United States to Europe, all the way to Rome. Now he was in Arazi's hotel suite. They were conferring with Shaul Avigor, the Haganah's new point man in Europe for purchasing armaments.

As usual Arazi was nattily clad in suit and tie, long graying hair combed back in continental style. Avigor was a balding, dark-eyed man in his late forties. He was a founder of the Haganah's intelligence service and had directed the post-WWII illegal immigration of European Jews. On Ben-Gurion's orders, Avigor had come to Rome to head up the Haganah's European arms procurement operation.

Despite his fatigue, Schwimmer was excited. He had brought with him important news. He had just concluded an agreement with the Mexican government for surplus fighter planes. Although the hoped-for P-51s were not available, the Mexicans were ready to release twenty-four P-47s.

It was perfect timing, Schwimmer told Avigor. His fleet of C-46s and the Constellation in Panama were positioned to begin ferrying the fighters to Israel. The P-47 was the ideal fighter for—

Avigor cut him off. It was too late. They had just made a deal with Czechoslovakia. The Haganah was buying ten of their Avia S-199s—the Czech version of the Me-109 Messerschmitt. They had an option for fifteen more.

For a moment Schwimmer lost some of his legendary coolness. *Messerschmitts?* He told Avigor that they were crappy, obsolete warplanes.

The Czech-built Messerschmitts would be a nightmare for American-trained mechanics and pilots. The P-47 was a far superior fighter. It had range, could carry a big load of bombs, and was a better air-to-air platform. Many of the American pilots they'd recruited already had combat experience in the P-47.

Avigor let Schwimmer finish his rant. Then he shook his head. Sorry, it was a done deal. In any case there was no money left for arms purchases in Mexico. For better or worse, Israel's air force was going to war in Messerschmitts.

Schwimmer tried to contain his disappointment. After all the close calls, the cat-and-mouse games with the Feds, he'd gotten most of their precious transports out of the United States and positioned in Panama under the cover of the pseudo-airline LAPSA. For what? They wouldn't be hauling fighters or heavy weapons from the Americas to Israel. Their only mission now was to pull up stakes and fly to Europe.

The sooner, the better.

———

At his Red House office in Tel Aviv, Ben-Gurion had to shake his head in sorrow when he heard the latest count. It was the beginning of May, and the number of Jewish dead in the civil war had passed 1,200. The toll was increasing daily.

Haj Amin al Husseini, the Grand Mufti of Jerusalem, a devotee of Hitler during WWII, had delcared a *jihad* for the liberation of Palestine. His force of two thousand paramilitary troops had laid siege to Jewish settlements in and around Jerusalem.

Supply convoys to Jerusalem were taking heavy losses. In March 1948, sixty-four Jews were killed attempting to reach Jerusalem in trucks. Another forty-six died in an ambush on their way to reinforce a besieged village in the Galilee.

On April 4, forces of the Syrian-backed Arab Army of Liberation attacked Jewish settlements around Haifa in an effort to sever the port from Tel Aviv and from the northern territories.

But by the end of April, Haganah fighters had gained the offensive.

The Arab paramilitary units had been driven out of most of the settlements and outposts they had captured.

To Ben-Gurion, it was the silver lining in the past five months of violence. It meant the Haganah's ragtag fighting units were—*maybe*—beginning to operate like a real army. It also meant that they needed more than ever the vital armaments that could only come into the country by air.

And the airplanes that could bring them were still in Panama.

———

Umm . . . just when do you think LAPSA will be commencing its scheduled airline flights?

It was a question the Panamanian government sponsors of LAPSA were asking with greater regularity. Almost daily someone would drop by LAPSA's office to inquire about progress. All these airplanes and crews here in Panama, and nothing seemed to be happening. When would the airline begin service?

Martin Bellefond gave them the same answer he always gave. Soon. Very soon. Just a few more route survey flights, a little tweaking, and the new airline would be in business.

While the LAPSA crews prepared for the flyaway to Europe, Bellefond was doing his best to maintain the charade. He had contracted for a few cargo flights of beef and dairy around the country. The frequent C-46 training flights he described to the officials as "charters." Just rehearsals, you know, for the *real* airline operation.

More airmen were joining the group already in Panama. Schwimmer had rounded up enough captains for all the airplanes, but the copilot for most of the flights would be a radio operator, mechanic, or navigator. Each aircraft was fitted with a 400-gallon auxiliary fuel tank for the upcoming transatlantic flight.

When the day came for the flyaway, Bellefond saw to it that the airplanes received a festive send-off at the new Tocumen airfield. To an audience of government officials and a battery of reporters, Bellefond proudly announced that the five aircraft were embarking on a "route survey." The purpose of the survey was to establish LAPSA's new routes through South America and across the Atlantic. The flag of Panama would be flying the international airways.

The crowd waved and wished them well. The C-46s fired up their engines. They taxied to the long runway and roared into the air. For good measure Hal Auerbach, in the lead aircraft, turned back and made a pass over the crowd.

The crowd was still waving as the C-46s flew away from Panama. Never to return.

———

They made a refueling stop in Paramaribo, Dutch Guiana, and then another at Natal on the coastal salient of Brazil. As usual, there were problems with the beat-up transports: hydraulic leaks, runaway propellers, failed oil pumps. The crews checked in to the El Grande Hotel, the swankiest in Natal. There they met a congenial group of British pilots eager to drink and talk with fellow airmen. When the Brits figured out that the Americans were *not* innocent airline crews but, quite likely, arms smugglers to Palestine, the relationship turned frosty.

A message from Schwimmer reached them in Natal. Their European destination had been changed. Their original base at the Ambrosini airport in Castiglione del Lago in the interior of Italy was not suitable for heavy transports. The Haganah's Rome agent, Danny Agronsky, had come up with a better facility: Catania, on the island of Sicily.

After two days in Natal, three of the C-46s set off at night to cross the South Atlantic. Auerbach had to return almost immediately with a failed propeller governor. The other two, Ribakoff and Raab, made the eleven-and-a-half-hour journey safely, landing in Dakar on the morning of May 14. After a brief rest they wearily climbed back in their C-46s and flew to Casablanca.

The crews were having lunch in the airport coffee shop at the Casablanca airport when Larry Raab looked up from his plate. He realized there was a buzz of excitement in the shop.

Raab asked the English-speaking waiter what was going on.

The Jews have announced their statehood in Palestine, the excited waiter told him. And the Arab countries surrounding them have declared war.

Raab had to force himself not to cheer. Then he glanced around. Everyone in the vicinity—waiters, guests in the coffee shop, guards, drivers, airport officials—was Moroccan Arab. They seemed to be peering with greater than normal curiosity at the two C-46s parked outside.

Raab was getting a bad feeling. What would happen when they learned that these airplanes were bound for Israel? That they were carrying war supplies?

That the crews were Jewish?

Raab didn't want to find out. They had to get the hell out of Morocco. They were taking off again for their next stop, Catania, on the Italian island of Sicily. A place where they would be welcome.

=== 10 ===

When in Rome

ROME
MAY 8, 1948

Wearing his sky-blue zoot suit, Gideon Lichtman stepped off the train in the middle of the city. As he headed down the avenue toward the Hotel Mediterranee, he realized people were staring. It was the suit. "Everyone spotted me for an American right away."

Lichtman had plenty of company in Rome. Nearly fifty volunteer airmen were there—fighter pilots, transport crews, utility plane pilots—scattered in small hotels around the city. They still didn't know where they were going or what they'd be flying. With nothing else to do, they did what rambunctious airmen always did. They raised hell.

The Haganah's point man in Rome was a tall, round-faced young man named Danny Agronsky. Agronsky was the American-born son of a Palestinian newspaper publisher. He'd been involved with Yehuda Arazi in the Haganah's arms procurement schemes in Europe.

Now it was Agronsky's job to keep the airmen occupied, answer their endless questions and, with increasing frequency, get them out of trouble with the *polizia*.

The problem was, the Haganah still had no airplanes. No *real* airplanes except a small collection of Canadian-built Noorduyn C-64 Norseman single-engine bush planes that were based at the small Urbe airport outside of Rome. Schwimmer's fleet of C-46 and Constellation transports was still trying to escape a tightening web of red tape in the United States.

And they still had no fighters. The unruly pilots in Rome badgered Agronsky every day with the same questions.

How long are we going to be here?

What kind of fighters are we going to fly?

Where are the damned fighters?

Agronsky fed them information, but only a little. Umm, yes, the Haganah *was* buying fighters. They might be P-51s. Or P-47s. Or something else. Agronsky claimed he didn't know.

But he had heard rumors.

———

Laughter and the sound of clinking glasses filled the bar. The place was called La Biblioteca, and it was the favorite watering hole of the volunteers in Rome. Lichtman was there. So was another recent arrival, a thin, intense-looking young man named Buzz Beurling.

Like all the pilots, Lichtman knew Beurling by reputation. Beurling was one of the highest-scoring aces of the war. No one liked Beurling, he had heard. Beurling was a loner.

But here in Rome, Beurling was being one of them. Even though the Canadian was a nondrinker, he was laughing as loud as any, telling war stories, ogling the dark-eyed Roman beauties.

The next day Lichtman joined up again with Beurling. He was curious. Lichtman wanted to hear more about Beurling's war experience in Malta, his techniques, his reason for being here.

The two became buddies. Lichtman, the frustrated P-51 pilot who joined the war in the Pacific too late to engage in the great swirling dogfights off Japan, was intrigued with Beurling's fanatical zeal to be the deadliest fighter pilot in the world. Beurling's voice would grow animated when he went into descriptions of combat over Malta, talking about deflection angles, kill shots at close range. His ice-blue eyes would shine with a new intensity.

One night Beurling offered to show Lichtman how he trained with his wooden fighter models. In his room at the Mediterranee Hotel, Beurling pulled down the window shade. With the light behind him, he projected onto the shade the shadows of two dowel-mounted model airplanes—one a Spitfire, the other a Messerschmitt. He maneuvered the shadows of the two warplanes, demonstrating how he'd shot down thirty German airplanes.

Lichtman was impressed. He'd known hotshot fighter pilots before. None was like this guy. Air combat for most fighter pilots was a visceral, gut-driven pursuit. For Beurling it was a religion.

———

Lichtman spotted the strange woman in the lounge at the Mediterranee Hotel. She was sitting at the far end of the bar, and she was exchanging gazes with him. She was a brunette, and there was no mistaking that look, the knowing smile, the way she propped one hand on her hip.

Lichtman had seen the woman before—and been warned about her. The Shoo-Shoo boys—the Haganah intelligence agents—had already tagged her as a possible Arab agent.

One of the Haganah's main worries in Rome was spies. The presence of the rowdy young airmen was attracting unwanted attention from foreign agents. Agronsky warned his pilots: Keep your mouths shut. Avoid intimate discussions with strangers. Especially strange women.

Agronsky was wasting his breath.

Lichtman kept looking at the woman, then made a snap decision. To hell with the Shoo-Shoo boys. He was a fighter pilot, damn it. He knew how to handle himself with women. Even women spies.

Soon Lichtman and the woman were engaged in a lively conversation. She was cute, inquisitive, more than friendly. After a drink together, she suggested they go up to her room. Lichtman gave one more fleeting thought to the warnings. This was too good to pass up.

They reached her room. She opened the door and motioned for Lichtman to enter. He was almost through the threshold when he stopped. Something wasn't right. He glanced inside the room and glimpsed the fleeting shadow of a man disappearing from view.

Lichtman's survival instinct kicked in. It was a set-up. He reversed course in the doorway and, glancing over his shoulder, beat it down the hall.

Back at the bar Lichtman slammed down a drink and thought about what happened. Yeah, he had probably dodged a bullet. The Shoo-Shoo boys were right. Perhaps he had learned a lesson.

And perhaps not. After another drink, Lichtman was remembering the brunette's smile, the look in her eyes. What the hell, he thought. This was Rome. The place was full of gorgeous brunettes. Another would come along soon enough.

The volunteers continued to raise hell, mostly in public places. Even Beurling the teetotaler was caught up in the activities, causing yet more headaches for Agronsky, whose job it was to keep the presence of so many unruly airmen a secret from the Italian press. And then one night, despite Agronsky's efforts, the secret was blown.

It happened at La Biblioteca. The hour grew late, and the babble of pilot talk and the clink of glasses grew louder. Incoherent arguments arose between English speakers and Italians. Someone—it was never reported *who*—started the brawl. Chairs flew and punches were thrown. Into the bar stormed the *polizia*, and most of the occupants were hauled off to jail.

One of them was Buzz Beurling.

By next morning, the Rome newspapers had the story. A famous Canadian pilot was in Rome. So were a number of other ex-military airmen. The foreigners were here for the purpose of flying arms and warplanes to—where else?—Palestine.

It meant Agronsky's headaches were only going to get worse. The unruly pilots needed a mission. Agronsky had something in mind.

Fly a Norseman?

Buzz Beurling didn't have to think twice about it. He'd fly anything, even the big lumbering single-engine transport.

At the Urbe airport outside Rome, the Haganah had accumulated a small fleet of Canadian-built Noorduyn C-64 Norseman single-engine transport airplanes. The Haganah's energetic arms procurer in Europe, an ex-RAF bomber pilot named Freddy Fredkens, had managed to purchase twenty of the cargo haulers from the US military inventory in Germany, using several layers of cover companies and brokers.

The Norsemans were desperately needed in Palestine to supply the Arab-besieged outposts. Of the five Norsemans so far delivered, two had already made the perilous nonstop flight to Palestine, flown by volunteers Lou Lenart and Milt Rubenfeld. Three more were at Urbe, being stripped and readied for the fourteen-hour flight.

The fighter pilots were not thrilled about flying the Norseman. The big utility plane had none of the sleek beauty of a Spitfire or a Mustang fighter. It was a high-winged, strut-braced truck with a fixed landing gear and round, blunt nose, designed for the rough fields and tundra of northern Canada. The Norseman was a single-engine iteration of unlovely transports like the C-46 and C-47, built for gritty, hard-knuckled wartime duty.

Which was fine with Beurling. He had been flying bush planes in Canada since he was a teenager. If the Norseman was the only airplane available, he'd fly it. He'd fly it all the way to Israel.

But first, he had to put in a training flight. That evening he asked Gideon Lichtman if he would come along as copilot. Lichtman, having nothing better to do, agreed.

Later that evening Lichtman had something better to do. She was tall, Italian, and available. Lichtman had met her at the hotel bar. They'd had dinner, partied most of the evening, then wound up in his room.

"We spent the night getting it on," Lichtman recalled. Knowing he'd be in no shape to fly in the morning, he called Beurling and begged off.

By now Beurling knew Lichtman. He laughed and said he understood. He'd get someone else to fly with him.

═════════

A high ceiling of puffy cumulus clouds covered the Urbe airfield. It was 08:30 in the morning, and Beurling was making another touch-and go landing. Before him the runway at Urbe stretched out like a green carpet.

Despite its ponderous size the Norseman was an easy airplane to fly, at least for a pilot like Beurling. In the right seat was Leonard Cohen, an ex-RAF pilot from Liverpool. Because Cohen was the most familiar of the pilots with the landscape of Israel, he had been placed in overall charge of the upcoming ferry mission.

Len Cohen was nearly as famous a wartime pilot as Beurling. He had earned the title "King of Lampedusa" during the siege of Malta. His plane had been hit by ground fire, and he was forced to land on the Italian-occupied island of Lampedusa. Waving his revolver, Cohen stormed out of his crashed airplane and convinced the Italian commander on the island that he was the advance man of a coming invasion. The entire Italian garrison surrendered to Cohen.

Beurling and Cohen were on their fourth touch-and-go landing at Urbe. They were sweeping over the field boundary when there was a muffled explosion. To spectators on the ground, it sounded like a distant thunderclap.

The Norseman was still 50 feet in the air when a sheet of flame enveloped the front section of the airplane.

———

Bill Malpine saw it first. Malpine was an Italian-American from Providence, Rhode Island, and a former Air Transport Command pilot during WWII. Designated as one of the ferry pilots, Malpine had already completed his own touch-and-go practice in the Norseman. Now he was standing beside the runway watching Beurling and Cohen go around the pattern.

Malpine stared in disbelief. Something had gone badly wrong. Flames were belching from the cowling of the Norseman. It looked as if the engine exploded. The airplane was wobbling, plunging toward the runway, dropping a wing.

It took one more second. The Norseman caught a wingtip and cartwheeled across the field, shedding parts and sliding to a stop. The crumpled airplane erupted in a towering blaze.

Malpine sprinted toward the crash. No fire truck, no ambulance, no vehicles had arrived. By the time Malpine reached the burning airplane, the flames were so intense he couldn't open the cabin door.

Through the fire and smoke he could see the two men inside, slumped and unconscious. Clenching his fists, Malpine watched helplessly while the raging fire consumed the Norseman and its occupants.

It was over in minutes. The column of black smoke rose several hundred feet into the morning sky.

Soon after the arrival of the emergency vehicles came a cadre of men with cameras and notebooks. They were reporters who somehow had learned almost instantly about the crash at the Urbe airfield. From the Italian airport authorities they determined the identities of the dead pilots.

The next day's newspapers were filled with the story of the volunteer pilots. And why they were in Rome.

═══════

A cloud of cigarette smoke hovered over the bar in the Mediterranee. The pilots were gazing thoughtfully into their drinks. A single question was bouncing back and forth between them. *What caused the crash?*

None of them believed that Beurling and Cohen, both masterful aviators, had been killed by a botched landing. Or by a failed engine.

Gideon Lichtman had already made up his mind. "They wanted to get Beurling," he said flatly, "and they did."

Sabotage. Few of the volunteers doubted it.

But who were "they?" Rome was full of agents from all camps—Arab, British, American, Jewish. After Beurling had been tossed in jail a few days ago, his presence in Rome was no longer a secret. As the killer of thirty-one enemy warplanes in WWII, he represented a genuine threat to the Arab air forces. Eliminating Beurling before he reached Israel would have been a master stroke.

Later, experts would theorize that the explosion was caused by a problem in the Norseman's six-hundred-horsepower Pratt & Whitney engine. According to the theory, the flames ignited a fuel source and the airplane became an inferno.

It was an improbable scenario. The R-1340 engine had seen service in thousands of military aircraft and had a reputation for great reliability.

There were other circumstances too peculiar to ignore. The arrival of the reporters on the field only minutes after the crash suggested a prior knowledge of something about to happen. Crewmen had often complained about the lack of security at Urbe. The Norsemans spent every night unattended, leaving plenty of opportunity for sabotage.

There was an unconfirmed report from a Haganah operative that a British agent—a former British army sergeant named Levingham—had been assigned to do "whatever he could do to prevent planes and volunteers from reaching Israel." Following the crash, according to the operative, the British agent had been kidnapped and summarily executed.

No hard evidence was ever uncovered. The Italians wanted to wash their hands of the whole messy affair. The cursory investigation concluded that the fire was "due to a backfire caused by the engulfment of the carburetor."

There would be little opportunity to make a detailed analysis of the crash. Israel's war for independence was beginning. The death of the famous fighter ace Buzz Beurling was now international news, and the Haganah's Rome operation was under heavy scrutiny.

By now Lichtman and the other pilots in Rome knew that the rumors about the Haganah buying Messerschmitts in Czechoslovakia were true. What they didn't know was that some of their fellow volunteers were already there.

=== 11 ===

Meeting the Mule

ČESKÉ BUDĚJOVICE, CZECHOSLOVAKIA
MAY 11, 1948

Across the grassy apron of the Czech airfield the volunteers could see the row of long-snouted, narrow-geared fighters. They looked like menacing predators.

Messerschmitts.

The newly arrived airmen were getting their first look at the warplanes they were going to fly. It was then that the strangeness of their situation struck them. They were Jews. They had come to a Communist country to fly, of all things, *ex-Nazi fighters*.

Americans Lou Lenart and Milt Rubenfeld and South African Eddie Cohen were part of the Machal, the Hebrew acronym for *Mitnadvei Hutz La'aretz* (overseas volunteers). Less than two weeks ago, the three volunteers had flown the first pair of Norsemans on the long overwater ferry flight from Italy to Palestine.

The other seven pilots in the group were sabras—native-born Palestinian Jews. They had been pilots in the Haganah's secret air service, Sherut Avir, flying light planes on support missions for the beleaguered settlements. Of the sabras only Ezer Weizman and Modi Alon, both ex-RAF fighter pilots, had military flying experience.

From Israel the ten airmen had flown to Cyprus, Rome, and finally Geneva. Haganah agents hustled them onto a train for Zurich where other agents hauled them to the airport to board a flight to Prague.

When they arrived behind the Iron Curtain they were confronted at the airport by armed Czech border police. The pilots did exactly what they had been instructed to do.

They asked for Dr. Otto Felix.

It worked. Within minutes the bespectacled, officious lawyer was on the scene. Reams of Communist bureaucratic red tape dissolved. Felix deposited the pilots in the old Flora Hotel, which would soon be the new Israeli embassy in downtown Prague. After two days they were whisked aboard a Czech military Ju-52 and flown to a small airfield south of Prague with a tongue-twister of a name.

—————

You say it like this, Felix told them, pursing his lips: *Cheska-booda-jo-veechay.*

However they pronounced it, the pilots thought České Budějovice was a depressing place. The small town was perched in the rolling countryside south of Prague, halfway to Vienna. České Budějovice was just as gray and melancholy as the rest of Czechoslovakia.

They were kept isolated from all the Czech personnel on the base except for the handful of instructors working with them in the airplanes. The Communists had recently taken control of the government and a cloud of suspicion and paranoia enveloped Czechoslovakia.

Their quarters were in a drafty old former wartime barracks. Trying on their new outfits—ex-Luftwaffe flight jackets, coveralls, boots, and parachutes—the pilots cracked up at the irony. Jews wearing Nazi costumes so they could fly German fighters.

Their instructors were Czech pilots who had flown in the British RAF during the war. All spoke excellent English and seemed genuinely interested in helping the airmen become combat ready. Over drinks at night, most expressed the belief that the Communists were just as bad for Czechoslovakia as the Nazis had been. But they were pragmatists. This was their homeland. Flying fighters was what they did. The Czech pilots were making the best of it.

But not all. One Saturday morning, when no one was flying and the volunteers were in the barracks swapping stories, they heard the roar of a multiengine airplane low over the building. They rushed outside in time to see a transport skimming the rooftops. It stayed at low altitude, headed south at full throttle.

The base officials tried to suppress the story. The pilots soon learned what happened. A senior flight instructor and half a dozen other officers had stolen the airplane and defected with it to Austria. The affair only added to the aura of suspicion and paranoia that pervaded České Budějovice.

The commanding officer at the base was a red-faced, heavy-set colonel named Hlodek. Colonel Hlodek was another pragmatist. He had flown both for the RAF and later for the Soviets and had little sympathy for the Communists.

The colonel laughed a lot and drank voluminous quantities of vodka. Like his instructors, he supported the cause of the Jews in Palestine. Hlodek liked to host the students in his quarters, where he'd tell his wartime stories and offer toasts to the defeat of their Arab enemies.

Before flying the single-seat Messerschmitt, the students were given dual instruction in two-seat Arado trainers. The Arado wasn't a fighter, but it was close enough to give the students the feel of flying a high-performance airplane. It soon became obvious that the sabra light plane pilots lacked the experience to move up to fighters. One by one all were dropped from training.

After a few flights in the Arado, the remaining five were ready for the real thing.

Lou Lenart was the first. Even for a man with Lenart's wiry build, the Messerschmitt cockpit felt cramped and claustrophobic. His shoulders were jammed against each side of the narrow compartment. His legs were squeezed into the narrow tunnel beneath the instrument panel.

Lenart's Czech instructor stood on the wing outside the cockpit pointing at gauges and knobs and giving last-minute instructions. Lenart understood only a fraction of what the instructor was saying.

The instructor hopped down. A coveralled mechanic inserted the crank for the starter in the nose section and began winding up the flywheel. Instead of a heavy electric starter, the Messerschmitt had a weight-saving inertia starter. When the inertia starter had whined up to full speed, the mechanic yanked out the crank and gave Lenart the signal that he could start the engine.

Lenart gulped once, turned on the magneto switches, advanced the throttle, and tugged the starter actuator handle. The big paddle-bladed propeller spun around. After a couple of revolutions the twelve-cylinder engine barked, coughed a cloud of smoke from the exhaust stacks, and settled into a deep-throated staccato rumble.

Lenart lowered the clamshell canopy over his head. It only deepened his feeling of claustrophobia. He could see nothing over the long, uptilted nose. His only view was out either side. He taxied in a zigzag route across the field, making his way to the takeoff position. After he'd run-up the engine, Lenart tightened his straps and looked around him. He could see his fellow volunteers standing back at the apron watching him.

There was no main runway at České Budějovice, just the sprawling open field. Lenart shoved the power up on the Messerschmitt. The engine noise deepened to a throaty roar. There were no visual references outside the cockpit, only the gray-green blur accelerating beneath him. Lenart tried to keep the fighter going straight ahead using his peripheral vision.

The numbers on the airspeed indicator were in kilometers, not miles per hour or knots. When it read 150 kilometers per hour, he nudged the control stick forward to raise the tail.

For the first time Lenart could see ahead. What he saw horrified him.

Ahead of him were two large hangars. The Messerschmitt was headed directly between them, toward a tall chain link fence.

Lenart hauled back on the stick. The Messerschmitt hadn't yet reached flying speed. The fighter lifted off the grass. It barely cleared the fence, then settled back down on the far side.

Careening over the field, Lenart fought to keep the fighter from rolling into a fireball. He coaxed the airplane back into the air, gathering speed in the thin blanket of air between the wings and the ground.

The rest of the flight—it was supposed to be a familiarization session—was uneventful. Lenart flew around for a while in the narrow airspace between České Budějovice and the Austrian border, gathering up his nerve to come back and land. When he touched back down on the airfield, he managed to keep the fighter reasonably straight.

Lenart shut down the engine and opened the canopy. Then he saw them. His fellow volunteers were standing there, mouths agape. They had witnessed the whole show—the detour between the hangars, the rabbit-hop over the fence, the rooster tail of dirt as he sashayed across the pasture.

They were amazed that Lenart was alive.

To a man the volunteers reached a conclusion about the Messer-schmitt: *This goddamn thing is dangerous.*

———

The Czech Air Force had their own name for the Messerschmitt: *mezek*. It meant "mule." Every volunteer who flew the mean-spirited Czech Mule thought it was an appropriate name.

Part of the Mule's meanness was due to the power plant. Soon after the war the Czechs had lost their supply of the powerful Daimler-Benz DB 605 engines, the standard power plant in the German-built Messer-schmitt Me-109. For the Avia S-199—the Czech-built Messerschmitt—they substituted the heavier and less powerful Jumo 211F engine, a power plant intended for the multiengine Heinkel He 111H bomber. Worse, they matched it with the oversized paddle-bladed propeller from the bomber.

The ungainly propeller created a powerful leftward torque, causing the fighter to take violent swerves on takeoff. To compound the problem, the fighter had no rudder trim, a tab that could be adjusted by the pilot to counter the leftward yawing tendency. As Lenart learned, the Avia S-199 pilot had to literally be on his toes to keep the fighter going straight.

Lenart, Weizman, Alon, Cohen, and Rubenfeld flew the Messer-schmitt daily. Each flight was a hair-raising experience. No one changed his feelings about the Czech Mule.

In the evenings they listened to the radio. The news from Palestine was worrisome.

The pilots of the Haganah's little observation planes had no trouble spotting the enemy. The dust clouds were visible from miles away as the armored vehicles rolled into position. The armies of five Arab nations were gathering on the borders of Jewish Palestine, waiting for the clock to run out on the British Mandate.

Already operating inside Palestine were two paramilitary units, the Arab Liberation Army and Arab Home Guard, each waiting for support from the invading armies.

Despite their superiority in numbers, the Arab nations were handicapped by their conflicting objectives. Between King Abdullah of Transjordan and King Farouk of Egypt simmered a long rivalry. Neither wanted the other to emerge from the coming war as the champion of the Arab cause. Abdullah viewed the war as an opportunity to annex to his kingdom all the territory allotted to the Arabs in the UN partition plan, which included the area west of the Jordan River called the West Bank. Farouk, for his part, wanted to seize all of southern Palestine for Egypt.

The leaders of the other three coalition members—Syria, Iraq, Lebanon—had their own plans for annexing portions of northern Palestine.

Transjordan wasn't waiting for the official war to begin. On May 12, forces of the Arab Legion, Transjordan's British-led and British-supplied army, attacked the Etzion Bloc, a cluster of Jewish settlements 9 miles southwest of Jerusalem. British troops were still nominally in charge in Palestine. They stood by and did nothing.

On May 13, one of the settlements in the besieged bloc, Kfar Etzion, surrendered after a two-day battle. The defenders, soldiers and civilians alike, were massacred by Arab villagers. The next morning, May 14, as the British were beginning their withdrawal from Palestine, the Etzion Bloc and all its settlements fell. The entire southern approach to Jerusalem lay in Arab control.

That evening in České Budějovice, the volunteers were again huddled around their radio. Crackling over the speaker came the news they had been expecting.

=== 12 ===

"Will They Bomb Tel Aviv Tonight?"

TEL AVIV
MAY 14, 1948

The black limousine pulled up to the Dizengoff House on Rothschild Boulevard. Out of the vehicle stepped the five-foot-tall, sixty-one-year-old dynamo whose entire adult life had been directed toward this day.

With his head erect, David Ben-Gurion strode past the honor guard of white-belted Haganah cadets and entered the building. The spacious hall was already jammed with expectant observers, Jewish Agency leaders, Haganah officers, and dozens of reporters.

At precisely four o'clock Ben-Gurion rapped his gavel on the lectern before him. Reading from the scroll of white parchment in his hand, Ben-Gurion spoke of "the self-evident right of the Jewish people to be a nation, as all other nations, in their own sovereign state."

Then he came to the words they'd been waiting for: ". . . by virtue of the natural and historic right of the Jewish people and of the Resolution of the General Assembly of the United Nations, we hereby proclaim the establishment of the Jewish state in Palestine, to be called Israel."

In unison the audience rose to its feet. They cheered and clapped. Someone began singing "Hatikva" (The Hope), their new national anthem, and the entire joyful crowd joined in. One by one the Jewish leaders affixed their signatures to the scroll.

The entire ceremony had taken thirty-two minutes. Eleven minutes later in the United States, President Harry Truman surprised his anti-Israel State Department with his announcement of the United States' de facto recognition of the new nation.

The streets outside the Dizengoff House filled with the sounds of rejoicing. Celebrants were dancing and singing and toasting their new-born country. It was a repeat of the jubilation on November 29 when the UN announced its partition plan.

As before, Ben-Gurion didn't join the celebrations. The new prime minister was already on his way to the Red House, the Haganah head-quarters on the beach.

He was preparing for the inevitable.

That evening Ben-Gurion sat alone his office. After thinking about the historic events of the day, he pulled out his diary. "I am like a mourner among the merrymakers," he wrote. "Will they bomb Tel Aviv tonight?"

They struck just before dawn.

Ben-Gurion had risen early to make an international radio broad-cast. He was sitting at the microphone when he heard the low drone outside the studio.

Ben-Gurion kept speaking as the drone swelled in volume. He knew instinctively what was about to happen.

The first bomb exploded. Then another. More bombs crashed nearby, punctuating Ben-Gurion's broadcast.

Spitfires of the Royal Egyptian Air Force were bombing downtown Tel Aviv. Through Ben-Gurion's microphone, it was a sound heard around the world.

The armored columns of the Arab armies rolled into Israel. The Syrians attacked from the northeast, intending to capture all of the Galilee. Lebanese forces were charging down from the north along the coastal plain toward Haifa. Iraqi troops and armored columns were headed due west across central Palestine. The Iraqis would need only a short 20-mile advance before they reached the sea and severed Israel in half.

Transjordan's Arab Legion intended to secure the territory and outposts around Jerusalem. From the south came the Egyptian Army, the largest of the invading forces. One brigade was charging straight up the coast with the objective of seizing Tel Aviv. Another was heading across the Negev Desert to capture Beersheba and link up with Transjordanian forces to take Jerusalem.

On every border, the new state of Israel was under siege.

———

In their damp Czech military barracks, the volunteers were huddled around their radio. Lenart, Rubenfeld, Cohen, Weizman, and Alon heard the crackly voice of David Ben-Gurion describing the air attack on Tel Aviv that morning.

The pilots were seething. The war had begun—*without them*. It was terrible not being there. They no longer had the patience to study. Israel was hanging on by a thread, and they were far away from it all.

Three days later the radio brought even more stunning news. Egyptian bombers had struck Tel Aviv's central bus depot. Forty-two civilians were killed. The air raid had been virtually unopposed.

That did it. The pilots came to a unanimous decision. No more training. They wouldn't sit there in Czechoslovakia while the war ran its course without them. They announced that they were leaving.

Their Czech instructors thought they were kidding. "Not yet, you still have lots to learn. Wait," they said.

The instructors were right, of course. In any *real* air force, training on a new fighter required fifty or more hours. Each of the volunteers had flown the Messerschmitt no more than a few hours. They'd had no training in air-to-air combat, strafing, bombing, or any kind of offensive tactics.

It didn't matter. There was a war on. They had to be there. The advanced tactics they would learn on the fly when they got back to Israel.

That night the five men sat down for a vodka with Colonel Hlodek, the affable base commander. They told him they were going to leave.

"What?" said the Czech. His cheeks puffed out. "You haven't even fired yet. You have to learn to shoot."

The pilots assured the colonel they would have lots of opportunity to learn to shoot. The Arabs would provide them unlimited shooting practice.

Hlodek tried to talk them out of it, but he saw that it wasn't working. Fortified by more vodka, the colonel said he knew how they felt. If he didn't have a family to worry about, he'd be going with them.

And then the colonel gave them some advice about tactics: "Fuck them on the ground," he said. "Fuck them on the ground before they have a chance to take off."

The pilots looked at each other. Then they poured more vodka. The colonel's advice was making sense. After a few more vodkas it made even more sense. Yeah, that was the way to beat the Arabs. *Fuck them on the ground.*

———

The next day they made a phone call to Ehud Avriel, Israel's new ambassador to Czechoslovakia. Avriel didn't try to dissuade the airmen from leaving, but he told them there was a problem transporting the Messerschmitts to Israel. Ferrying the short-ranged fighters was out of the question. Sending them by surface ship was risky and would take too long.

The only possibility was by air. Don't worry about it, Avriel said. He was working on it.

The ambassador was true to his word. Within hours he had rounded up the fly-for-hire C-54 crew that had smuggled the first load of Czech guns to Israel on March 31. From Tel Aviv came the okay to use Schwimmer's C-46s, which were still scattered across the Mediterranean from Catania to Žatec to Israel. Each C-46 could haul half of a disassembled Messerschmitt fighter.

On May 19, the five partially trained fighter pilots said goodbye to their instructors at České Budějovice. When they arrived at the Žatec air base, nestled in the Sudetenland northwest of Prague, they were astonished. After the bleak and secretive atmosphere of tiny České Budějovice, Žatec looked like a thriving air terminal.

Which, in effect, it was. The chartered C-54 was already there. So was a Messerschmitt fighter, ferried up from the Avia factory near Prague by one of the Czech Air Force pilots.

Ezer Weizman ambled over to the Czech pilot and introduced himself. The Czech was friendly. He also confirmed what the volunteers already suspected about the Czech Mule. "They're tricky airplanes," the Czech said. "We're glad to be rid of them."

The cargo loaders were having a problem with the disassembled Messerschmitt. They couldn't stuff the fuselage through the narrow cargo door of the C-54. Over two hours passed while they jiggled and maneuvered the delicate-skinned fuselage, trying to slip it nose first through the door. It wouldn't fit.

Finally one of the C-54 crewmen came up with an idea. Try inserting the fuselage *tail first*. They did and—*caramba!*—the fuselage slipped neatly inside the cabin.

Crammed in with the Messerschmitt fuselage were the fighter's wings, propeller, crates of munitions, several Czech mechanics—and fighter pilots.

Not far behind the C-54 came the C-46s. Each hauled half a Messerschmitt—either a fuselage or a pair of wings—plus crates of parts and weapons.

The volunteer fighter pilots were on their way to war. Ready or not.

=13=

The Sound of Spitfires

The war came to Tel Aviv at 05:25 in the morning. In his room at the Yarden Hotel, Boris Senior was awakened by the unmistakable sound of twelve-cylinder Rolls Royce Merlin engines, a sound that he knew came from Spitfire fighters.

Arab Spitfire fighters.

The twenty-six-year-old commander of the Sde Dov airfield climbed into his jeep and roared off toward the field. He knew what he'd find. He had seen the black smoke billowing from the hangar complex. The Spitfires were already withdrawing from the dawn raid.

Senior was livid. It was precisely what he had warned the senior officers would happen if they left all the airplanes parked at Sde Dov. They would be picked off like targets in a shooting range.

And so it had happened. The Sde Dov airfield was demolished. So was most of the Sherut Avir—Israel's little fleet of utility airplanes. The Bonanza passenger plane that Senior had personally flown all the way from South Africa only ten days ago was a wreck.

Two C-47 Dakotas, one a transient aircraft belonging to Air France and the other a Pan Africa freighter hired by the Haganah, had taken heavy damage. There was a gaping hole in the wall of the only hangar. A munitions shed was burning fiercely.

Five Sherut Avir crewmen had been killed and nine injured in the attack. Caught by surprise, the antiaircraft gunners at the field had put up hardly any fire before the Spitfires were finished with their raid.

This was not Boris Senior's first war. He was a swashbuckling South African who had flown fighters in WWII. He had survived being shot down in his P-40 in March 1945, during an attack on the Italian port of Mestre. After bailing out and nearly dying in the freezing Adriatic, Senior was rescued by a courageous American PBY Catalina crew, who plucked him from the water while under heavy fire from German shore batteries.

After the war Senior was studying in London when he made a life-long friend, Ezer Weizman. The two were founding members of Haganah's secret little air force. Senior would claim the distinction of being the first Machalnik—overseas volunteer—in the Israeli Air Force.

Standing amid the wreckage at the Sde Dov airfield, Senior was exasperated. Only the day before he had flown a reconnaissance flight over the borders of the new country. Senior had been shocked at what he saw. Massed along Israel's borders were thousands of Arab troops, armored vehicles, troop carriers. Many of the Arab units were already inside the proposed new border even though the British occupying force had not yet pulled out.

Senior landed back at Sde Dov and rushed to general headquarters to report what he had seen.

"Yes, we know," replied chief of staff Yigael Yadin with a shrug. Senior requested that his squadron of utility and spotting airplanes be dispersed to outer airfields. He was denied permission. Yadin told him the aircraft might be needed there at Sde Dov.

Senior was still fuming about his destroyed airplanes when he heard it again. The sound of Merlin engines. The Spitfires were back.

Senior dived for shelter behind a pile of concrete blocks. From there he watched the second pair of Egyptian fighters shoot up the airfield.

The sound of the Merlin engines was still fading when Senior saw a black sedan trundle across the wooden bridge at the edge of the airfield. The sedan rolled up to the apron. Out climbed a stocky, white-haired man carrying a pair of binoculars.

Ben-Gurion. Senior couldn't restrain himself. In a minute-long tirade he sputtered his feelings about the stupidity of leaving airplanes out here to be shot up by the goddamned Arabs. "I warned them and now look at this. What idiocy!"

And then Senior caught himself. Hurling abuse at the prime minister was bad form, even in wartime.

Ben-Gurion didn't rebuke him. The prime minister remained silent. He gazed thoughtfully at the still-smoking wreckage. Then he climbed back in his sedan and left.

Minutes later, as if on cue, the Spitfires came again. In an impotent rage, Senior drew his pistol and blazed away at the fast-moving fighters. It was ridiculous, but—*damn it*—at least he was doing something.

Again the Spitfires withdrew. And then came back—for an unbelievable *fourth* time.

During each attack the Spitfires had received little opposition from Israeli guns. But now the gunners on the three 20-mm antiaircraft batteries at Sde Dov had had practice. And they were angry.

One of them scored a hit.

Senior spotted the telltale sign: a long white stream of fluid streaming from one of the Spitfires. It was the coolant fluid that kept engines like the Merlin running. One of the antiaircraft gunners had put a round through the Spitfire's coolant system.

Senior knew exactly what would happen because it was the same kind of lucky shot by a German gunner that punctured his P-40's coolant system and dumped him in the Adriatic in 1945.

This Spitfire wouldn't make it back to Egypt.

Senior watched the enemy fighter pull up and fly northward. It was the opposite direction from Egypt. Senior guessed that he was trying to make it to the still-occupied British base at Haifa.

Senior leaped from behind the block shelter and raced to the hangar. He found the squadron's second Bonanza—one that *hadn't* been shot up in the raids—and fired it up. Minutes later Senior was roaring hell-bent for where he'd last seen the Spitfire.

The Spitfire had made it only 10 miles north. Just as Senior expected, the Merlin engine, without its coolant, had seized. The pilot put the fighter down on its belly on a stretch of open beach near Herzliya.

Flying in a tight circle around the downed fighter, Senior saw that one wing was damaged, but otherwise the Spitfire was intact. The cockpit was open. There was no sign of the pilot.

Senior put the Bonanza down on a nearby grass strip. He yanked out his revolver—the same one he'd fired at the passing Spitfires—and went hunting for the Egyptian pilot.

He didn't have to hunt for long. The twenty-three-year-old Egyptian pilot, Flight Lieutenant Mahmoud Barakat, was in a nearby brick factory building where he was being held by the Israeli troops who captured him.

Senior had the prisoner blindfolded and, with an armed escort, loaded into the Bonanza. He flew the Egyptian back to Tel Aviv where, in the general headquarters building, he was interrogated by Senior and the senior air force officers, Aharon Remez and Dan Tolkowsky.

From the talkative young pilot they learned one especially interesting item of intelligence. The Egyptian Air Force had staged an entire squadron of Spitfires as well as Dakota bombers at El Arish Air Base just beneath the Sinai border.

Less than a hundred miles from Tel Aviv.

Mahmoud Barakat's Spitfire wasn't the only Egyptian fighter shot down that week. Early on the morning of May 22, a pair of Egyptian Spitfires swooped down on Ramat David Air Base. Either through egregiously bad intelligence or target misidentification by the pilots—it was never officially determined—the Egyptians didn't realize the base they were bombing and strafing was still occupied by the British.

The Egyptian fighter pilots managed to destroy two RAF Spitfires on the ground and badly damage eight others. Infuriated, the RAF sent up a combat air patrol, just in case the Egyptians were brazen enough to do it again.

They were. More Egyptian Spitfires showed up, *still* mistaking the British-held field for an Israeli air base. This time they shot up two Dakota transports that had just arrived, killing several British airmen. The patrolling RAF fighters caught two of them as they were departing Ramat David. Both were shot down in flames. A third was downed by the combined fire of several British Bren gunners on the ground.

Incredibly, the Egyptians came back a third time. Again they were met by RAF fighters. Again, Egyptian warplanes were shot down. By the end of the morning the Egyptian Air Force had lost five valuable fighters and pilots, including their squadron commander.

It was a stunning loss for the Arabs—and an unexpected gift for the Israelis. One of the Spitfires belly-landed a few miles south of the Israeli Kibbutz Dalia where the pilot was captured by Israeli soldiers.

Again, Boris Senior went to fetch the pilot and hauled him blind-folded back to Tel Aviv for questioning. The prisoner was Flying Officer Abd al Rahman Inan, a thickset, wooly-chested man who turned out to be less talkative than Mahmoud Barakat, captured on May 15.

Little useful information came from the prisoner, but Senior was thinking about the crashed Spitfire. Some of the remains of the downed Egyptian fighters were salvageable. They already had a cache of parts and power plants scavenged from British scrap heaps.

From those jigsaw puzzle pieces, could they build a *real* Spitfire?

———

On the afternoon of May 16, Larry Raab and Marty Ribakoff landed their C-46s in Catania, Sicily, after a nine-hour flight from Casablanca. Catania, the tired pilots quickly discovered, was no more welcoming than Casablanca. The airport manager was a red-faced Sicilian. He was not pleased to see the two tramp freighter planes rolling up to the ramp at his airport.

The Italian airfield was a leftover Axis base from WWII—a few shacks, Quonset huts, a makeshift control tower. The hangars were still ruined from bomb damage.

Waiting for the C-46s was the Haganah agent, Danny Agronsky, and Haman Shamir, whom they'd last seen during the crew rebellion back in Panama. When Agronsky negotiated LAPSA's landing rights at Catania, he had promised the airport manager that *airliners* would be flying scheduled trips out of Catania. The obscure airport on Sicily would become an international terminal.

Now the manager was pointing at the C-46s, ranting that these clunky freighters were obviously *not* airliners. These people were up to something illegal. With a snort the manager stalked away. He said he was reporting this to his superiors in Rome.

Agronsky loaded up the crews and hauled them into town. That evening he told them what they'd already figured out. The Catania base wasn't going to work. The US government had informed the Italians that LAPSA was a cover for an arms smuggling operation to Palestine. The airport manager was threatening to impound the airplanes and have the crews arrested.

Raab and Ribakoff would have to leave in the morning. Their next landing would be in a war zone.

Twenty-four hours later, an exhausted Larry Raab was peering down at a thin strip of beach. It was his first glimpse of Israel. Darkness was settling over the land.

The darker the better, Raab thought. He'd been warned that Egyptian fighters were on the prowl at dawn and dusk. They shot up everything that moved. The two lumbering C-46 Commandos—Marty Ribakoff was flying a few hundred yards behind Raab—would make juicy targets.

Standing behind Raab in the red-lighted cockpit was Haman Shamir, who had joined them in Catania. Shamir had helped organize the Yakum Purkan airlift. Now he was arriving with its first load. In the cabin of the C-46 was a tied-down and disassembled BT-13 military trainer.

The radios were silent. No one at their destination, Ekron Air Base, was answering on the discrete frequency. Shamir was worried that the field might have been captured by the Arabs. To be safe, Shamir told Raab, they should land instead at the Sde Dov airfield at Tel Aviv.

It was a near-disastrous decision. As they neared Tel Aviv at an altitude of only a thousand feet, the night sky erupted in antiaircraft fire. Tracers arced toward the pair of C-46s. What they didn't know was that Egyptian warplanes had earlier bombed the city. Israeli gunners had been newly equipped with 20-mm Hispano-Suiza antiaircraft guns. Now they were looking for payback.

With the lights out and full power on the C-46's laboring engines, Raab yanked the airplane to the west and over the Mediterranean. Again using the prearranged code signals he tried making radio contact with Ekron.

He received a response. None of it matched the prearranged code.

Then the runway lights at Ekron illuminated.

The airmen argued in the darkened cockpit. If the Arabs had captured Ekron, they'd try to lure the incoming airplane with the lights. What was the better choice? Return to Tel Aviv and be shot down by Israelis? Ditch in the sea? Land at Ekron and be captured by Arabs?

Raab made the call. They would land at Ekron. Descending toward the flickering lights of the runway, every pair of eyes in the cockpit peered into the darkness. The same question was on every man's mind: *Who's waiting down there for us?*

Raab kept his hand poised on the throttles. He plunked the wheels of the C-46 down on the edge of Ekron's runway, then rolled to the mat at the end. Ribakoff landed close behind and followed him to the runway end.

Raab kept both engines running. He swiveled the tail around, ready for an emergency getaway. Figures were coming toward them out of the darkness. A truck emerged from the gloom. Its lights were out.

Raab sent Shamir to the cabin door, armed with a .45 automatic. "Talk to them in Hebrew and see what answer you get."

Shamir opened the door. He offered a greeting in Hebrew to the first man he saw approaching the door.

The man answered—in Hebrew. Shamir burst into a grin. He had just met his boss, Aharon Remez, who was about to become the new commander of the Israeli Air Force.

It took the men on the ground forty-five minutes to unload the cargo and the disassembled BT-13. Fatigued from the ten-hour flight and the tension of the arrival at Ekron, Larry Raab fell sound asleep in his cockpit seat.

Raab was still dozing when he felt a tap on his shoulder. It was Shamir. Sorry, he said, but the plans had changed. The planes couldn't stay in Israel. The Egyptians had bombed the field just before dark. They'd surely be back in the morning.

Raab and Ribakoff would have to fly back where they came from. Before dawn.

Nothing had changed at Catania. Nothing except the airport manager's attitude. It was even more hostile than before.

"You are either smugglers or thieves," the manager said in the way of greeting. To make his point, he had the crews arrested.

The airmen didn't resist. After the round trip to the Middle East, they were too tired to give a damn.

The arrest, as it turned out, was a formality. The exhausted airmen were allowed to check into their hotel. Within hours the hard-working Danny Agronsky was back in Catania to dispense money and smooth relations, at least temporarily, with the Sicilians.

The Catania base was still inhospitable. For the moment, it was all they had.

One by one, the LAPSA C-46s completed their passage across the South Atlantic. Despite mechanical delays and holdups in Dakar and Casablanca, each made it to Catania except for Swifty Schindler, who diverted to Rome because of weather.

The hospitality in Catania wasn't improving. The red-faced airport manager was making louder noises about impounding airplanes and detaining crews. While Agronsky worked hard to dissuade the Italian government from revoking LAPSA's landing rights, Haganah operatives were searching for a safe haven in Europe.

The original plan—to base the aircraft in Israel—was no longer an option. There was no way to protect the big transports from the daily Arab air raids.

In the lounge of their hotel in Catania, the crewmen had gathered for drinks when they saw Agronsky came in. He was smiling.

Agronsky had news for them. The Bagel Lancers would soon be flying to the Haganah's new secret base. It was a place where the C-46s could stage round trip supply flights to Israel.

The airmen lowered their drinks and focused on Agronsky. The Haganah operative paused for dramatic effect. He leaned in close, away from eavesdroppers, and whispered the location of the secret base. Then he told them its code name: *Zebra*.

=== 14 ===

Zebra Base

From a mile away the town looked like a gingerbread village. Swifty Schindler could see the twisting cobblestone streets, ancient buildings with beam-and-stucco façades, the horse-drawn wagons meandering down narrow lanes.

But when he brought the C-46 low over the town, Schindler noticed something else. The entire front façade of a main building was festooned with a huge red star. On the adjacent building hung a giant banner emblazoned with a hammer and sickle.

Schindler and his copilot, who wasn't a pilot but the wisecracking radio operator, Harold Livingston, peered at the banner. The reality of where they were struck them.

The town was called Žatec. It was in Czechoslovakia.

Behind the Iron Curtain.

Since the end of WWII the United States and the Soviet Union had been engaged in the ideological dispute known as the Cold War. The Soviets had cordoned off their new satellites—Czechoslovakia included—behind this invisible barrier. And now US citizen Swifty Schindler and his all-American crew were about to take up residence there.

The Zebra base was 5 miles from Žatec. The single long ribbon of concrete, about 5,000 feet long, was clearly visible against a green patchwork of hay and hops fields. During the war it had been a Luftwaffe fighter strip, and now it was a Czech Air Force base.

Schindler made a low pass over the base. At one end of the field he could see what appeared to be military facilities. At the opposite end were a few obscure hangars and—*aha!*—a familiar shape. Another C-46 was parked on the ramp, LAPSA markings clearly visible on the fuselage. Coveralled workers waved at the low-flying transport. They were loading what looked like the fuselage of a fighter plane into the C-46.

To Schindler it was a lovely sight. The Bagel Lancers finally had a home.

———

"Zebra" was just one of the codenames used for staging bases. The Haganah, the volunteers were learning, loved ciphers, cryptology, codes. In message traffic the United States was "Detroit." Everything south of Panama was "Latin Detroit." Italy was "Illinois."

From the Zebra base the crews would fly to Ajaccio, Corsica, codenamed "Jockstrap," before making the ten-hour journey to "Oklahoma," the name for Israel. The Czechoslovakia-Israel airlift was called "Operation Balak." It came from the biblical name for the son of Zippor, one of Moses's wives. Zippor in Hebrew meant "bird."

Airplanes took codenames too. The big four-engine Constellations became "Cadillacs." The clunkier C-46 Commandos were "Dodges." The name chosen for the Czech-produced Messerschmitt caused some knowing head-nods. The codename was *Messer*, the Yiddish word for knife.

———

Jhaa-tets, said Dr. Otto Felix. It was the way the airmen were supposed to pronounce Žatec, the Czechoslovakian city that would be their new home.

The portly little Czech lawyer was waiting at the Zebra base to meet each new crew. He showed them where some of Schwimmer's mechanics—the Cobbers—had set up shop. Among them was Ernie Stehlik, the brilliant TWA mechanic Schwimmer had recruited early in the operation at Burbank.

Stehlik possessed another vital skill at the Zebra base. He spoke Czech.

Also at the base was a balding thirty-eight-year-old man named Sam Pomerance. Pomerance had been one of Swifty Schindler's early recruits for Service Airways. Pomerance had impressive credentials: he was an aeronautical engineer, brilliant mechanic, and a competent pilot. Pomerance was now supervisor of all maintenance operations at the Zebra base.

At the far end of the field they could see the Czech Air Force experimenting with their own airplanes. One was a new Soviet-built jet fighter. Felix warned the pilots not to get curious.

"Stay away from the Czechs," he warned them, "especially the military. And assume that spies are everywhere—Czech, Russian, Arab, British"—he shrugged—"even American."

Fussing over his newly arrived airmen like a schoolmaster tending twelve-year-olds, Dr. Otto Felix bundled each crew into a taxi and escorted them into Žatec.

They drove into the main square where the Kremlin-shaped town hall—the building Schindler spotted from the air—bore the huge hammer-and-sickle banner. Directly opposite the town hall was their hotel with its freshly painted new name over the entrance: Hotel Stalingrad.

The Bagel Lancers had a new home. The Stalingrad was where they exchanged news, picked up mail ferried in by arriving crews, and did what young off-duty aviators historically did: They drank, played cards, smoked, and prowled the local bars in search of women.

The meager monthly salary most of them received was immediately exchanged on the black market for Czech kroner, multiplying its value by about ten times. But there wasn't much in Žatec to spend it on. Booze was already cheap. American cigarettes—Camels, Luckies, Pall Malls—were hauled in for them. Most of the local girls kept a wary distance from the strange-talking, khaki-clad Americans.

Swifty Schindler flew his first trip to Israel and back to Zebra. When he returned to Hotel Stalingrad, he was handed a sealed envelope.

Secret orders? He opened the envelope. Reading the message, he was instantly awake.

Schindler was leaving for the United States immediately. Schwimmer had a special mission for him.

———

Who are those guys?

Raab and Livingston and half a dozen others were drinking and kibitzing in the big, high-ceilinged bar in the Hotel Stalingrad. Another crew showed up, guys they didn't recognize. The crew stayed to themselves, but the volunteers quickly figured out that they belonged to the C-54 parked on the tarmac at Zebra.

They were a contract crew. Mercenaries. *Not* idealists like themselves, meaning they weren't in the same pay bracket as the Bagel Lancers, some earning the grand sum of a hundred bucks a month.

For the next hour the two groups maintained a wary distance. Gradually curiosity, an abundant flow of booze, and the common bond between aviators melted some of the frostiness. The airmen began talking.

The C-54 belonged to an American charter outfit, Atlantic Northern Airlines, Ltd., based at le Bourget airport in Paris. The boss was an ex-USAAF major named Gerald Rowland. Only one of the crew, navigator Seymour Lerner, was Jewish.

None showed any special interest in Palestine or the new state of Israel. For them it was a job.

Rowland told them that their first supply flight to Palestine had been back in March, when they made a dangerous nighttime flight to a deserted airfield in Arab-occupied territory to deliver guns and ammunition to the Haganah. It had been that load of weapons that enabled Haganah fighters to open the crucial Tel Aviv-to-Jerusalem road.

The C-54 crew had returned to Czechoslovakia last week. Already they'd made two round trips to Israel. The big four-engine C-54 Skymaster could carry a greater load than the C-46 and could fly from Zebra to Oklahoma nonstop.

A silence fell over the volunteers as they absorbed this information.

Finally Larry Raab, emboldened with cheap Czech booze, asked the question that was on all their minds. Umm, just how much might they be getting paid for these flights?

Rowland just smiled. Enough, he told them. Enough to make it worth their while.

One hundred fifteen miles to the south, at the Czech air base in České Budějovice, Gideon Lichtman was getting his first close-up look at a Messerschmitt. "What the hell is that?" he blurted. Lichtman knew it couldn't be a *real* Messerschmitt. Not with that grotesque propeller that looked better suited for churning butter.

It was the last week of May, and Lichtman had just arrived from Rome, via Geneva and Prague. Agronsky's people had told him that he wouldn't need a visa for Czechoslovakia. On arrival Lichtman was supposed to ask for Dr. Felix, Israel's mysterious point man in Czechoslovakia. Lichtman had been instructed to buy several cans of Nescafé in Geneva as a special treat for Dr. Felix.

When Lichtman landed in the Prague airport, the Czech immigration officers demanded to see his visa. He had none. The Czechs promptly placed him under house arrest in a nearby boarding house.

Lichtman called the emergency number he'd been given for Dr. Felix. "Get me out of this place *now*," he said, "or I'm going home."

Eventually the rotund lawyer showed up and Lichtman was released. Felix's first words were, "Where's my Nescafé?"

Lichtman, in the best of times, had a short fuse. He felt like clobbering this fat lawyer with the cans of Nescafé. But he didn't. Fuming, he kept his mouth shut and followed Felix out of the airport. The next day he was on his way to České Budějovice to meet the Messerschmitt.

Peering at the fighter parked on the grass apron, Lichtman had a sinking feeling. He was a fighter pilot, and flying machines like the P-51 Mustang and the P-40 Warhawk had been a sensual experience for him. There was nothing sensual about this paddle-bladed beast.

The feeling didn't go away. After a brief training session in the two-seat Arado, Lichtman received his first—and only, as it turned out—training flight in the Messerschmitt.

"There was no cockpit check," he recalled. "One of the mechanics stood on the wing and wound up the inertia starter. The instructor leaned in the cockpit and pointed to the start lever. That was it. I started the thing, and I was on my own."

Lichtman stayed over the airfield, did a few stalls, steep turns, a couple of aileron rolls. Then he landed back on the open grass field at České Budějovice.

And that was it. The next day, with thirty-five minutes of total flight time in the Messerschmitt, Lichtman was climbing into the cabin of a C-46. He shared space with a disassembled Messerschmitt and another volunteer fighter pilot, a Brit named Maury Mann.

They were headed for Israel.

═══ 15 ═══

Or Die Trying

ROME
MAY 22, 1948

The Haganah's cover in Rome was blown. Buzz Beurling's death had sent the city's journalists on a fact-finding frenzy. Now the newspapers were reporting that Beurling was a member of a band of aviators in Rome who planned to smuggle contraband warplanes to Israel.

Worse, the US embassy in Rome was ordering all the Americans connected with the Haganah operation to present themselves at the US embassy.

No one intended to comply with the order. They all knew what it meant. Their passports would be revoked and they would be shipped back to the United States.

To Danny Agronsky, the Haganah's point man in Italy, it meant the Rome base was finished. The volunteer airmen had to leave town, and so did the airplanes. Already the US State Department was pressuring the Italians to seize any aircraft they suspected was bound for Israel.

The two remaining Norsemans had to be flown to Israel immediately. Agronsky's problem was, no one wanted to fly them.

═══

In their usual corner at the Mediterranee Hotel lounge, the pilots sipped at their drinks and talked about the proposed ferry flight. *Something* caused Beurling's plane to crash. The big radial engine blew up because of lousy maintenance or it had been sabotaged. If someone had tampered with Beurling's plane, they could have done it to all of them. The Norseman had just killed two pilots.

Now they wanted someone to fly the damned things for fourteen hours over the water.

It was a gut-check moment. After all the idealistic talk about saving Israel, it came down to a lonely overwater journey in a clattering single-engine airplane they didn't trust. They could die by drowning at sea. Or they could be captured by Arabs who would execute them. For what? A penny-ante war in which few of them had a personal stake?

That day the airman who had been scheduled to lead the flight, a veteran military transport pilot they all respected, had quit. To hell with it, he was going home.

Bill Malpine had been scheduled to be his copilot. Malpine had been an eyewitness to Beurling's crash and was convinced the airplane had been sabotaged. Malpine was still wrestling with his decision about whether to go when another pilot named Bob Fine, a seasoned wartime airman and one of the early recruits to Service Airways, volunteered to take the place of the man who quit.

Fine wanted Malpine to come with him.

Malpine had been on the verge of quitting. After some serious thought, he finally agreed. Okay, he would fly with Fine.

The impasse was broken. In quick succession a British navigator, Hugh Curtiss, piped up and said he'd fly with them. Two more airmen, a Dutchman named Vic Wijnberg and Al Trop, a pilot from Cleveland, said they'd fly too.

And that was it. Two crews for the two Norsemans. If any of them was having second thoughts, it was too late. They were going to fly across the Mediterranean, all the way to Israel. Or die trying.

It wouldn't be the first such flight. On May 2, two Norsemans had made the long overwater journey to Palestine. It was in the pre-independence era, and the British Mandate was still in effect. Both airplanes and crews were greeted by joyous Haganah fighters, and the planes were immediately pressed into service supplying outposts in the besieged Etzion Bloc.

But that had been three weeks ago. The crews' greatest worry after the long flight was being met on landing by Arab irregulars, an unlikely scenario, or by British occupying troops, who would simply impound the airplanes.

Now it was different. There were no British occupying troops. Instead, there were entire Arab armies.

━━━━━

It was the night of May 24. Through the windscreen of the Norseman, Bob Fine saw only blackness. He didn't need reminding what would happen if his 600-horsepower engine failed. Ditching at night in *any* airplane was a catastrophe. Ditching a big bush plane was worse. The huge extended landing gear would grab the water like a sea anchor and flip the airplane onto its back.

Even if he and Malpine and their radio operator survived the crash, they'd be stranded in the middle of the Mediterranean with no chance of rescue. They'd filed no flight plan. No one would ever know what happened to them.

The two Norsemans had been stripped of every ounce of excess weight. A rubber bladder tank holding 1,200 gallons of gasoline had been stuffed into each cabin. With another 1,200 gallons in the main fuel tanks, the Norsemans were far over their maximum takeoff weight. They were flying bombs.

They'd made an unwanted stop at Heraklion on Crete. The fuel transfer valves in both airplanes were inoperative. It meant that half their fuel was unusable.

Bob Fine already had experience with stopovers in Greece. None of it was good. Greece had been notoriously unsympathetic to the cause of the Jews in Palestine. In April Fine had been flying one of four Avro Anson twin-engine light bombers bound for Palestine. When they stopped for fuel on Rhodes, the Greeks seized the airplanes and jailed the crews.

To Fine's great relief, the Greek officials at Heraklion were friendly. They even offered to help repair the airplanes. Still remembering his experience at Rhodes, Fine decided not to push his luck. By two o'clock the next afternoon the two Norsemans, fuel valves repaired, were airborne and headed eastward.

That was six hours ago. Now Fine was peering into the darkness. They were near the coast of what he hoped was Israel. He saw nothing he recognized. No city lights, no airfield. The war had begun ten days ago, and the country was blacked out against air attacks.

The radio operator, Hugh Curtiss, was crouched behind Fine and Malpine in the cramped cockpit. Curtiss was trying to obtain bearings with his radio direction finder. Nothing was working. No one on the ground was responding to their prearranged radio calls.

Their fuel was running low. Fine had to gamble. Guessing they were near Haifa in the north of Israel, he turned the flight to the south, in the direction of Ekron Air Base.

Another half hour passed. Fine still saw nothing. Thinking they must be near the Egyptian border, he turned north again.

The fuel situation was critical. Fine told Curtis to send a distress signal on an open radio frequency. To hell with codes.

In response to Curtis's distress call, a flare shot into the night from somewhere in the interior. Then another. Fine turned toward the flares. Al Trop, flying the second Norseman, followed him.

More flares arced into the sky. Fine flew directly toward them. He spotted what looked like a landing field. Its edges were illuminated by the lights of trucks. It definitely wasn't Ekron—or any other field Fine recognized.

It didn't matter. In the next moment Fine's engine stopped from fuel starvation.

With an ominous silence coming from the big radial engine, Fine glided the Norseman down through the darkness to the landing strip.

Except it wasn't a landing strip. The Norseman's wheels dropped into a ditch and the airplane went up on its nose. Trop and Wijnberg were luckier. They landed on another part of the field, missing the ditch and staying upright.

Fine, Malpine, and Curtis scrambled out of the upended Norseman. They saw in the darkness what looked like orange groves. Were they in Israel? Was this a kibbutz? They walked toward the still-illuminated headlights.

Fine yelled out what little Hebrew he knew: "Shalom!"

He received an immediate reply. *Rat-tat-tat-tat.* A burst of machine-gun fire. Then another. Someone shouted something in Arabic.

"They're fucking Arabs!" yelled Malpine.

The sickening reality struck them like a hammer blow. After all their preparations, a forced landing in Greece, a dangerous fourteen-hour overwater flight, a pitch-black landfall, they'd landed in enemy territory.

All three men sprinted for the nearby orchard. Machine bullets kicked up the dirt around them. They made it to the orchard and climbed into citrus trees.

After what seemed hours but was in fact only several minutes, they heard an English-speaking voice over a loudspeaker.

"This is the Egyptian Army," said the speaker. "We will give you ten minutes to surrender." In perfect English the speaker assured them they would be treated according to the rules of the Geneva Convention.

Fine and Curtiss made a gut-wrenching decision. They would surrender. The two walked toward the sound of the loudspeaker where they were met by an Egyptian lieutenant colonel. They learned that Trop and Wijnberg had been captured as soon as they exited their airplane.

That left Bill Malpine. He had heard the stories about what the Arabs did to prisoners. Malpine had no intention of becoming a prisoner. He slid down from his tree and ran. Malpine could hear machine-gun fire raking the trees where he'd been. He slipped through a barbed wire enclosure, crawled to another citrus grove, and climbed into a tree.

Malpine remained hidden for three nights without food or water and almost no sleep. Nearing the end of his endurance, he set out toward what sounded like a gun battle. If he was lucky, he'd come up on a friendly side of the skirmish.

Malpine wasn't lucky. He stumbled onto a machine-gun nest manned by Arab irregulars. One of the Arabs walloped the pilot with a rifle butt. The others beat him repeatedly while he was down. At the last minute before he was about to be killed, an Egyptian officer arrived. Malpine was hauled away, blindfolded, interrogated, and eventually transported to Abbassiye prison in Cairo.

After two weeks of solitary confinement Malpine was finally reunited with Fine, Curtiss, Trop, and Wijnberg.

The five men had earned an unwanted distinction. They were the first volunteer airmen to become prisoners of war in Israel's war for independence.

They were the fortunate ones. Downed airmen in the future would not live to be prisoners.

= 16 =

Where Is Moonitz?

EKRON AIR BASE, ISRAEL
MAY 24, 1948

It was nearly midnight. Beneath him, Norm Moonitz saw only a dark blanket of fog. A low-hanging moon was shining on the top of the fog layer. The entire coastal plain south of Tel Aviv was obscured. Somewhere beneath the fog was their destination, Ekron Air Base.

Norm Moonitz and Hal Auerbach were flying a pair of C-46s into Israel. In the cabin of Moonitz's C-46 was a tied-down Messerschmitt fuselage. Auerbach's airplane was carrying the fighter's wings. Stashed in every remaining nook and space in both airplane cabins were crates of weapons and ammunition.

"Find out where Auerbach is," Moonitz told the radio operator, Ed Styrak.

"I heard them give the clear-to-land signal," said Styrak. He was huddled just behind Moonitz in the darkened cockpit.

Moonitz nodded. Auerbach's C-46 had arrived over the coast just a few minutes behind them. If Auerbach had enough visibility below the fog layer to make it into Ekron, then Moonitz could, too.

It was their first flight into Israel. The night before, Larry Raab and Marty Ribakoff had made their first flights. They had to come and go in darkness to avoid Egyptian fighters.

Norm Moonitz, the William Bendix look-alike, was one of two New York City firemen and ex-WWII bomber pilots recruited for Service

Airways. The other was the oversized Ray Kurtz, who worked as hard as Moonitz at being colorful.

During their down time in Natal, Moonitz and Kurtz had each acquired a pet monkey. To go with his pet, Moonitz acquired a bush jacket, khaki shorts, and a swagger stick. During the evenings in Natal he liked to walk the streets in his new garb, smoking a cigarette in an ivory holder, the monkey perched on his shoulder. Moonitz liked to tell everyone that he was teaching the monkey to fly so it could replace his copilot.

Moonitz's real copilot was a young ex-bomber pilot named Sheldon Eichel. Moonitz and Eichel had a brotherly love-hate relationship. They got into raucous quarrels in the cockpit, ignored each other for hours at a time, then patched it up over drinks on the ground. Tonight, so far, there had been no fights.

Standing beside Styrak in the eerie, red-lighted cockpit was Moe Rosenbaum, the navigator. Rosenbaum, a recent addition to the volunteer crews, was a pleasant young man in his mid-twenties. He'd been a WWII air force captain and, until just a few weeks ago, an engineering student at Cornell University. As the most experienced navigator in the group, Rosenbaum had been put to work training the others back in Panama.

Rosenbaum's job tonight was finished. He'd plotted their course all the way from the refueling base at Ajaccio, Corsica, precisely hitting their landfall on the Israeli coast. The rest was up to Moonitz and Eichel.

Ekron had no precision approach, no localizer or glide path, just a primitive low-frequency radio beacon. Already Moonitz had made two passes at the field. He'd flown out to sea, past the coastline where the fog bank began, and tried coming in just above the water, hoping to fly beneath the cloud layer. Each time he'd flown into solid fog and had to pull up.

And then, circling over where they thought the field ought to be, Eichel glimpsed a break in the clouds. Through the break they saw it— *runway lights*!

Ekron was in sight.

Moonitz shoved the nose down toward the opening. Just as he entered the hole in the overcast, it closed. Visibility back to zero.

Again Moonitz pushed the throttles forward and pulled the C-46 back into the clear sky above the cloud deck.

Moonitz kept trying. Four more passes, four more pull-ups. He asked Eichel how much fuel they had left.

Eichel checked the gauges. "Maybe thirty minutes."

Moonitz decided to try again. He would time the approach, descending at 500 feet per minute, hoping he would see the runway threshold when they broke out of the cloud deck. *If* they broke out.

Into the fog bank they went again. He called for Eichel to lower the landing gear. Then the flaps. Eichel was calling out altitudes: Eight hundred . . . seven hundred . . .

Then, a hole in the clouds. Eichel yelled that he saw the flashing beacon on the field.

And then he didn't. The hole closed again. Back on his instruments, Moonitz continued the descent. Eichel called out their altitude. "Four hundred . . . three hundred . . ."

In the fog-shrouded darkness they didn't see the 200-foot-high hill rushing toward them. The C-46 slammed into the hillside.

Inside the cargo space the Messerschmitt fuselage ripped loose from its fastenings and shot forward like a missile, smashing into the navigator's station in the front of the cabin.

The C-46 caromed along the hillside, shedding parts and bursting into flame.

———

Where is Moonitz?

Haman Shamir peered into the moonlit sky around Ekron Air Base. Moonitz's airplane was nowhere in sight. Twenty minutes had passed since Shamir first heard the C-46's engines droning over the field. Now there was only silence.

Shamir, formerly known as Hyman Sheckman, had just been appointed second in command of the Israeli Air Force. He'd come to

Ekron to meet the incoming C-46s. Standing beside Shamir was Hal Auerbach, who had landed nearly half an hour ago.

Auerbach was worried about Moonitz. He insisted that they refuel his airplane so he could take off again and look for the missing C-46. Shamir refused. He wasn't going to risk another airplane searching for one that may already be lost. In any case, they were still unloading Auerbach's cargo, which included half a Messerschmitt. The other half was in Moonitz's airplane.

The two men were still discussing the whereabouts of Moonitz and his crew when they abruptly stopped. An apparition was emerging from the darkness at the end of the runway.

It was Norm Moonitz. He was staggering under the 200-pound weight of his radio operator, Ed Styrak, whom Moonitz was hauling on his back. Stumbling along with them was Sheldon Eichel. The three figures looked like phantoms, illuminated by the eerie glow of the runway lights.

The fourth crewman, Moe Rosenbaum, wasn't with them.

They were in bad shape. Moonitz and Eichel had burns from the fire that had enveloped their cockpit. Styrak's leg had been broken in the crash, and he hadn't been able to free himself from the burning wreckage. Moonitz and Eichel had managed to shove the six-foot-two radio operator through a cockpit side window, then drag him away from the burning airplane.

Moe Rosenbaum was dead. He'd been at his navigator's station in the cabin. He was killed instantly when the Messerschmitt fuselage broke free from its tie-downs and hurtled forward.

Moonitz, Eichel, and Styrak were rushed to a hospital in Tel Aviv. Moonitz and Eichel would return to flying duty in a couple of weeks. Styrak's leg would take longer to mend, but within a month he had rejoined the Bagel Lancers.

———

On Shamir's orders, the C-46 that Auerbach had brought in was unloaded and refueled. The previous evening Egyptian warplanes had bombed and strafed Ekron Airfield, and they were expected to return at first light. Before sunrise the C-46 was on its way back to Europe with a fresh crew.

Then, more bad luck. An hour into the flight, the C-46's right engine stuttered, belched smoke, and wheezed to a stop. With the propeller feathered, the crew was forced to make an emergency landing in Greece.

The precious C-46 was impounded by the Greek military.

It was an ominous beginning for Operation Balak—the codename given to the Czechoslovakia airlift. In less than twenty-four hours they'd lost two of the four C-46s from the Zebra base, plus half a Messerschmitt. Three crewmen were hospitalized in Tel Aviv. Another lay dead.

Moe Rosenbaum had become the third Bagel Lancer to lose his life in the war.

At the bar in the Stalingrad Hotel the airmen stayed to themselves. They spoke in somber voices, smoking cigarettes and sipping cheap vodka while they wondered: *How many more are we going to lose?*

═ 17 ═

Ad Halom

EKRON AIRFIELD, ISRAEL
MAY 25, 1948

It became a nightly ritual. Out of the blackness over the Mediterranean would come a low drone. The noise of the two synchronized engines would swell in volume as the invisible shape flew nearer Ekron.

At the last minute, runway lights flashed on. The ghostly silhouette of a large transport plane would sweep over the end of the runway. *Chirp, chirp*—wheels stroked the concrete. Seconds later the runway lights extinguished again.

Even before the C-46's engines had shut down, cargo unloaders were swarming over the airplane, jabbering in half a dozen exotic languages, gently extricating the precious Messerschmitt components.

As each fighter was unloaded at Ekron, it was quickly hustled inside a hangar and out of sight. The existence of Israel's new warplanes had to be kept secret.

By day, as marauding Egyptian Spitfires swept over Israel, Ekron looked like a deserted former British field. No sign of activity, no indication that a lethal new weapon had arrived. By night the base was a bustling terminal.

For the Messerschmitt pilots—Lenart, Weizman, Alon, Cohen, Rubenfeld—these were days of frustration. They still had no fighters to fly. Reassembling the Messerschmitts was proving to be a more difficult process than disassembling them had been. The Czech technicians who came with the first Messerschmitts worked day and night alongside Israeli mechanics in the Ekron hangars.

On May 28, 1948, by an ordinance signed by Ben-Gurion, the Haganah and the other splinter fighting groups were unified into the Israeli Defense Forces. At the same time the Sherut Avir—the Haganah's air service—became, officially, the Israeli Air Force.

That evening in their concrete-walled operations shack at Ekron, the five fighter pilots reached a unanimous decision. Now that they were part of a real air force, their little unit should be a real squadron. With a real designation.

It was the kind of democratic process that would be peculiar to the Israeli Air Force, the pilots being allowed to choose their own designation. That night they announced that henceforth they were the . . . *101 Fighter Squadron.*

Everyone loved it, even the headquarters staff and Ben-Gurion himself. The designation had just the right boldness to it. It implied that Israel had *many* fighter squadrons instead of one secret little five-plane, five-pilot unit that had not yet flown a single mission.

It was the end of May, and the two-week-old war wasn't going well. The sporadic thunder of artillery boomed down from the Golan Heights and through the Jordan valley. Anxious kibbutz dwellers near the coast watched the light show in the hills to the east of them. Each night the rumble of the big guns sounded nearer to them than the night before.

In the north, armored columns of the Syrian Army were driving southward from the Golan Heights, overrunning kibbutzim and settlements in the Jordan valley. Iraqi brigades were invading from the West Bank and were within a few miles of the Mediterranean coast. Jerusalem was under siege by two brigades of the Arab Legion.

But the greatest danger was in the south. The Egyptian Army, the largest of the five invading forces, had launched a two-pronged invasion of the Negev. One brigade was headed toward the Judean Hills to link up with Transjordanian Arab Legion forces already there, while the fast-moving Egyptian 2nd Armored Brigade was driving up the coast, aimed like an arrow for Tel Aviv.

There was nothing to stop them. The fighters of the new 101 Squadron were still not ready.

For the newly trained fighter pilots, it was a maddening time. "We couldn't sit around doing nothing," recalled Ezer Weizman. So he didn't. On the late afternoon of May 25, Weizman climbed into the air service's little Beechcraft Bonanza at the Tel Aviv Sde Dov airfield. The Bonanza was an American-built family airplane, not a warplane. It didn't matter. With his bomb-chucker passenger aboard, Weizman took off and flew south. When they were 4,000 feet over Gaza they opened the door and flung out incendiary bombs.

It was a purely symbolic gesture. The Egyptians didn't even bother shooting at them. Weizman didn't care. At least he was doing *something*. In any case, the next time he went calling on the Egyptians, they'd pay attention.

He'd be in a *real* fighter.

The debut mission of Israel's secret new fighters was supposed to be spectacular. For nearly two weeks the Haganah chief of staff, Yigael Yadin, and the acting air force chief, Aharon Remez, had been planning a surprise air strike.

Reconnaissance flights confirmed what they'd learned from the Egyptian pilot captured the first day of the war. The Egyptian Air Force had moved an entire Spitfire squadron to the El Arish air base in the western Sinai just below Gaza. At least twenty-five Egyptian fighters were parked in a neat long row on the El Arish ramp. Parked near them were several C-47 Dakotas.

The same Dakotas they'd been using to kill civilians in Tel Aviv.

Ripe targets. The pilots of 101 Squadron would be following the vodka-inspired advice they'd gotten from Colonel Hlodek in Czechoslovakia: *Fuck them on the ground*.

The five-fighter raid was planned for the morning of May 28. As dawn drew near, the Czech and Israeli mechanics had managed to get only three Messerschmitts ready to fly. Not enough for the debut surprise attack. They needed at least four.

The strike was postponed. They'd go the next morning.

Then another delay. Though four Messerschmitts were ready to fly the next morning, the ordnance loaders couldn't get the bombs armed.

The strike was postponed again. They'd go that evening.

The hours of the long, anxious day ticked past. In their operations shack, the pilots fidgeted, peered at their maps, tried to remember what little they knew about flying the Messerschmitt.

And then in the late afternoon a jeep came racing onto the airfield. It was carrying Shimon Avidan, commander of the outnumbered little Givati Brigade that was holding off the Egyptian Army south of Tel Aviv.

"We need your planes now," Avidan said. The Egyptian Army had stopped at the Lachish River in the town of Ishdud where Avidan's troops had blown the bridge. In a few hours the Egyptians would have the bridge repaired. Avidan's little unit couldn't stop them.

The Egyptians could be in Tel Aviv by morning.

Orders and countermanding orders flashed between Ekron and Tel Aviv. Ahoran Remez argued that using the fighters at Ishdud would ruin any chance they had of a surprise attack on El Arish. Avidan said it didn't matter if the war was already ended before the fighters went into action.

Finally the Haganah chief of staff, Yigael Yadin, settled the matter with a direct order: The fighters would attack the Egyptians at Ishdud now.

Ein brera. No alternative.

———

Lou Lenart threw a leg over the edge of the Messerschmitt cockpit and slid inside. It was the first time he'd been in the fighter since they'd terminated their training in Czechoslovakia nearly two weeks ago. The cockpit was just as cramped and claustrophobic as he remembered it. Lenart settled himself onto the hard seat and cinched up the seat belt and shoulder harness.

The fighters were still hidden inside the hangar. Ekron Air Base had been strafed by Egyptian Spitfires that afternoon. Though none of the Messerschmitts was seriously damaged, it was too dangerous to expose them to another enemy air raid on the tarmac at Ekron. They would warm the engines, then make a quick departure from inside the hangar.

Through the open door of the hangar Lenart could see dusk settling over the Israeli countryside. Their target—the coastal village of Ishdud—was only 10 miles away.

Lenart had been tapped to lead the mission because he had the most combat experience. His wingman would be Modi Alon, a handsome young sabra and ex-RAF Spitfire and Mustang pilot.

Leading the second two-plane section was Ezer Weizman, also an RAF-trained pilot. On his wing was Eddie Cohen, a veteran of the South African Air Force who had flown Spitfires in combat in North Africa. In 1947 Cohen had moved from South Africa to a kibbutz in Palestine and soon after joined the Sherut Avir along with Alon and Weizman.

With four fighters and five pilots, the odd man out was Milt Rubenfeld, an American who had flown Spitfires with the RAF in the early days of WWII, and then transferred to the Air Transport Command with the USAAF. Rubenfeld would fly the next mission.

If there were more missions after tonight.

In their briefing, no one talked about the fact that none of the newly assembled fighters had been test flown. The guns had never been fired. None of the bomb racks had been tried. The radios in most of the fighters didn't work.

What they least of all felt like talking about was that none of them had flown the Messerschmitt in combat. Or even on a gunnery range. Another snippet from their conversation with Colonel Hlodek was coming back to them: *You haven't even fired yet. You have to learn to shoot.*

None of it mattered now. Sitting in his cockpit, Lenart felt himself filled with a sense of urgency. It was the same urgency he'd seen in the faces of the other three as they huddled over their maps.

"There is no making light of this moment," Lenart would say later. "Behind us is Israel, the Jewish people hanging by a thread. Ahead of us is the enemy, advancing to destroy everything we love."

On Lenart's signal the Messerschmitts' engines chuffed to life. The hangar filled with a steady popping rattle and clouds of sweet-smelling high-octane exhaust. The first three pilots waited anxiously while Cohen's propeller ticked over. The balky Jumo engine refused to start. Finally, on the third try, Cohen's engine sputtered, belched smoke, and joined the rumbling chorus in the hangar.

They took off an hour before nightfall. Lenart kept the flight low, making a wide turn back to the west and heading out over the water, climbing to 7,000 feet. Ishdud lay near the coast. Lenart's plan was to coming sweeping down from out of the sun, hoping for complete surprise.

It wasn't much of a plan. As he turned the flight back to the east, Lenart peered at the string of villages along the Israeli coast. He'd been in the country less than two weeks. *Where the hell is Ishdud?* Every village had the same cluster of red-roofed buildings, same minaret, same north–south road passing through the village.

Lenart's radio didn't work. He twisted in the cramped cockpit and signaled to his wingman, Modi Alon, who had grown up in Palestine. Lenart pointed straight ahead and then gave a palm up questioning gesture. Alon slid up wingtip to wingtip with Lenart's fighter and pointed toward a village off to the right.

In the next few seconds the location of Ishdud became stunningly clear. Lenart saw the column of vehicles backed up to the south for over a mile. Hundreds of trucks, tanks, troops were swarming in the Arab village. A mile and a half north of the village was the downed bridge over the Lachish River.

If Lenart needed further evidence he'd found the target, it came in the next few seconds. Egyptian gunners were putting up a roiling black canopy of antiaircraft fire.

Lenart armed his guns and bomb release. Approaching the north side of the village, he rolled the Messerschmitt up on its right wing and went into his dive. On either side of him blossomed black puffs of 40-mm ground fire. The air noise around the Messerschmitt's cockpit rose to a howl as the fighter gathered speed in its dive.

Keeping the target fixed in his gun sight, Lenart stabbed the release button. *Whump.* The 70-kg bombs released.

The untested bomb racks worked. Next, the guns.

As Lenart pulled out from his dive, he could see the largest vehicle concentration at a curve in the road about 300 yards south of the village. He yanked the fighter around in a climbing left hand turn and then pointed his nose down toward the clustered vehicles.

Lenart lined up on a row of vehicles, held them in his sights, squeezed the trigger. The wing-mounted cannons rattled for a couple seconds—then stopped. Both 20-mm cannons had jammed.

Lenart pulled up again, this time to the right, flying a cloverleaf gunnery pattern just as he'd learned back when he was a Marine Corsair pilot in the Pacific.

He fixed another cluster of vehicles in his gun sight. He fired again. The cannons didn't work, but the pair of nose-mounted 13-mm guns fired. They kept firing for several more seconds. Then they ran out of ammunition.

Lenart got a glimpse of the other Messerschmitts. One fighter—he thought it was Weizman—was diving from the south. Not far behind was another Messerschmitt, probably Cohen. Below and to his side he saw Modi Alon, who was following Lenart's cloverleaf pattern. Flak was bursting all around them.

They had no plan to rejoin after the attack. With antiaircraft fire exploding around him, Lenart pointed the Messerschmitt to the northeast. He could see the long runway at Ekron only 10 miles away.

The Messerschmitt's wheels bonked down on the concrete. Lenart worked the rudder pedals, remembering the Czech Mule's tendency to resist going straight ahead. He rolled up to the hangar he'd left forty minutes ago.

Another Messerschmitt—it was Weizman—was already there. The mechanics were hauling the fighters into the hangar when Lenart and Weizman saw the dark silhouette of a third Messerschmitt approaching the runway. The fighter's wheels chirped on the concrete, rolled straight ahead for a hundred yards, then abruptly veered hard to the right.

Lenart heard a *pop*—the sound of a tire blowing—then a metallic screech as the left wingtip scraped the concrete. The fighter careened off the runway and slid to a stop in a geyser of dirt. The Messerschmitt's canopy flew open, and out climbed the pilot.

When Lenart and Weizman arrived, Modi Alon was standing beside the fighter glowering as if he wanted to shoot it. Alon's Messerschmitt had performed a classic ground loop, swiveling out of control and swapping ends. It was a maneuver the Czech Mule would repeat with regularity in the months to come.

Three Messerschmitts had made it back from Ishdud. The fourth—flown by Eddie Cohen—hadn't returned. Weizman thought he'd seen Cohen's airplane burning from an antiaircraft hit. But then the controller in the Ekron tower reported that earlier they'd received a radio call from Cohen that he was inbound.

The pilots stood on the tarmac at Ekron listening for the distant growl of a Messerschmitt's engine. They heard nothing.

An inky darkness was falling over the countryside. There was no chance that the Messerschmitt was coming back to Ekron. *Where was Cohen?*

An hour later they knew. Eddie Cohen was dead. His burning fighter had crashed a mile and a half from the Beit Daras airfield, 7 miles from Ekron.

Had his Messerschmitt been hit by enemy fire over Ishdud? Or had Cohen mistakenly tried to land at the wrong airfield? No one knew. The wreckage was in Arab-held territory.

A grim mood fell over the pilots at Ekron. During their time in Czechoslovakia and then in their newly formed fighter squadron, the five men had bonded. Now they'd lost a brother.

It was especially hard for Weizman, who had known Cohen from the Primus air force days flying Piper Cubs on raids against Arab militias. He remembered the jubilation he and Cohen felt when they were selected to fly the new fighters.

Eddie Cohen had been a reluctant warrior. He was a quiet and scholarly young man, fond of classical music, not given to the swaggerings of many fighter pilots. He had volunteered to fight for Israel for no reason except that he thought it was the right thing to do. Eddie Cohen had just become the first pilot in the war to be killed in action.

The commander of the outgunned little Givati Brigade, Shimon Avidan, was standing beside his jeep on the ramp. Lenart was still sweat-soaked from the forty-minute mission. He took a deep breath and walked over to Avidan.

Lenart gave the soldier the grim news. He was very sorry. What little damage the Messerschmitts did to the Egyptians would have no effect on their advance. In the morning, Avidan's depleted rifle companies would face the full might of the Egyptian Army.

Avidan nodded. He climbed back in his jeep and motored off to rejoin his troops.

Lenart was discouraged. He had been the leader of a desperate, disorganized, botched strike. Once they'd found the target, each pilot had been on his own, diving and firing without any coordination with the others. They'd lost half the squadron's valuable fighters and one of its precious pilots. As far as Lenart could tell, the strike at Ishdud was a failure.

Lenart was wrong. Israeli monitors had intercepted a radio message from the Egyptian commander, Major General Ahmed Ali al-Mwawi, to his superiors in Cairo:

We have come under attack by enemy aircraft, we are dispersing.

The Egyptian general was stunned by the appearance of fighters with the Star of David emblazoned on their sides. Neither he nor his intelligence officers had any idea that Israel possessed such warplanes.

That night Shimon Avidan's Givati Brigade dragged out their few *Napoleonchik* 65-mm mountain guns and began a bombardment of the enemy troops across the river. For the rest of the night and throughout the next several days, the outnumbered Israeli brigade kept up a series of commando raids on the bivouacked Egyptians. The demoralized Arab troops hunkered down and dug in for a long stay.

The Egyptian brigade would not cross the bridge at Ishdud. They would march no deeper into Israel.

Tel Aviv was saved. And so, for the moment, was Israel.

Part Two

BESIEGED

I declare a holy war, my Moslem brothers.
Murder the Jews. Murder them all.
—HAJ AMIN AL HUSSEINI,
MUFTI OF JERUSALEM, 1948

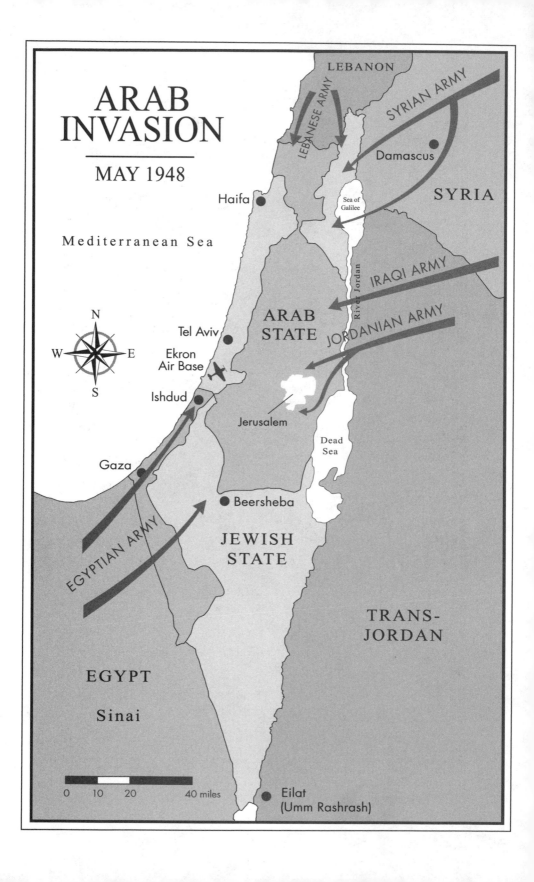

ARAB INVASION

MAY 1948

Mediterranean Sea

LEBANON

LEBANESE ARMY

SYRIAN ARMY

Damascus

SYRIA

Sea of Galilee

Haifa

River Jordan

IRAQI ARMY

ARAB STATE

JORDANIAN ARMY

Tel Aviv

N
W E
S

Ekron
Air Base

Ishdud

Jerusalem

Dead Sea

Gaza

EGYPTIAN ARMY

Beersheba

JEWISH STATE

TRANS-
JORDAN

EGYPT

Sinai

0 10 20   40 miles

Eilat
(Umm Rashrash)

=== 18 ===

Gefilte Fish

Only twelve hours had elapsed since the 101 Squadron's first mission, the strike at Ishdud. The Egyptians had been stopped in the south, but another threat was advancing in the north. A massive Transjordanian–Iraqi armored column was 10 miles from the coastal city of Netanya. If they cut the critical north–south highway connecting Tel Aviv to Haifa in the north, the Arabs would divide Israel and surround Tel Aviv.

At dawn the Arabs' 30-mm cannons had begun shelling the Jewish settlement of Kfar Yona, their only obstacle on their march to the sea. Opposing them was a single Israeli unit, the Alexandroni Brigade. The little unit was just as beat up and depleted as the Givati Brigade at Ishdud.

Only two flyable Messerschmitts were left after the raid at Ishdud. Early on the morning of May 30, air force chief Remez sent the order: The fighters would attack the enemy column in the north. Ezer Weizman and Milt Rubenfeld, the only pilot not yet to fly, would execute the mission.

Milt Rubenfeld was a swarthy, athletic twenty-nine-year-old from Peekskill, New York. He'd learned to fly as a kid and was earning a living teaching aerobatics when WWII began in Europe. He volunteered to fly with the RAF, fought in the Battle of Britain, and ended the war in the USAAF Air Transport Command ferrying almost every military aircraft in the inventory.

Rubenfeld was a classic fighter pilot. When he was recruited by the Haganah in 1948, his interviewer jotted in his notes that Rubenfeld was "so cocky he seemed to swagger even while sitting down."

Rubenfeld was sent to Rome, where he hung out with the other idle fighter pilots until he and Lou Lenart made the first long Norseman ferry flight from Italy to Palestine. Three days later Rubenfeld was in the first group on their way to České Budějovice to learn to fly the Messerschmitt.

Today was Milt Rubenfeld's first combat mission since 1941. In the thin light, he was having trouble finding his target. It was a few minutes past dawn. The landscape of northern Israel was covered in long shadows.

Then Rubenfeld saw the target. Not one target but *hundreds*—tanks, trucks, armored carriers—stretching for miles along the east–west road from Tulkarm to Netanya. The Iraqi forces at Tulkarm possessed more armored vehicles than the entire Israeli Army.

As Rubenfeld peered down at the enemy column, explosions erupted around him. The Arabs had spotted the incoming fighters. A curtain of flak was going up over Tulkarm.

Weizman led them in a wide left turn, then he lined up in a slanting approach from east to west. Diving down through the antiaircraft bursts, the pilots planted their bombs in the Tulkarm railway station where the Arab vehicles appeared to be staging.

Rubenfeld could feel the thud of the nearby explosions. Five minutes into his first mission he was dropping bombs, strafing, dodging flak—all the special skills they hadn't had time to learn in České Budějovice.

Rubenfeld knew about the jammed guns during yesterday's mission at Ishdud. The Israeli armorers had promised him his guns would fire today.

And they did. He squeezed the trigger, and 13-mm bullets and 20-mm cannon shells poured into the convoy in front of him. He released the trigger and pulled up for another pass.

The flak was getting thicker. And closer. Then, a hard *thump*, as if something had slammed into the nose of the fighter. Seconds later black smoke gushed from the cowling of the Messerschmitt. The deep baritone of the V-12 Jumo engine changed to a death rattle.

Every fighter pilot knew the dictum that dated back to the First World War: *It is never a good idea to bail out over a place you have just bombed.*

Rubenfeld had just bombed Tulkarm. He definitely did not want to bail out there.

A string of commands rushed through Rubenfeld's adrenaline-charged brain: *Climb. Head for the water.* He could see farms below. Ahead was the beach. He didn't know whether the Arabs had gotten to the coast yet.

It no longer mattered. The Messerschmitt's engine was dying. Rubenfeld was a little over a thousand feet above the terrain. He yanked the canopy release and the cockpit filled with the roar of air noise.

Rubenfeld unfastened his straps. He stood in the wind stream and hurled himself out of the Messerschmitt's cockpit.

———

Ezer Weizman was rolling in for his next firing pass. He looked around for his wingman. *What happened to Rubenfeld?*

Then he saw the smoke—a long black ribbon, heading west. At the head of the smoke trail was the unmistakable shape of a Messerschmitt. While Weizman watched, a tiny object separated from the smoking Messerschmitt. A few seconds later, Weizman saw the round canopy of a parachute blossom, descending to the countryside below.

Weizman was stunned. *How can this happen?* He'd flown two combat missions in the Messerschmitt. Each time he'd lost a wingman.

Weizman had no more time to think about it. He heard a *whap*, followed by shards of glass and a hurricane blast of wind in his face.

The front windshield of the Messerschmitt was smashed. Weizman tilted his head to the side, trying to avoid the blast of wind. He yanked the Messerschmitt up and away.

When he was far enough from the flak around Tulkarm, he slowed the fighter down. He peered back over his shoulder. Rubenfeld's Messerschmitt was gone. So was the parachute.

———————

Rubenfeld watched the water rush toward him. He'd made it all the way to the beach before he bailed out. Seconds after his parachute opened, Rubenfeld was splashing down in the Mediterranean.

Everything hurt. His side and his groin ached, and he was bleeding from several wounds. He didn't know whether it was from the flak bursts or hitting the tail on the way out of the fighter.

He was several hundred yards offshore. After trying to swim for what seemed like hours, Rubenfeld realized that the water was so shallow he could walk.

Dripping wet, aching all over, he limped through the shallow surf toward the beach. Rubenfeld's optimism was returning. He'd just survived a shoot down and a bail out. He was still a free man.

Blam. A gunshot rang out. A plume of water erupted beside him. *Blam, blam.* More gunshots, more plumes. Then he saw them. They were clustered on the beach, a group of men with weapons. The bastards were shooting at him.

Arabs or Israelis? It didn't matter who they were if they killed him. Rubenfeld raised his hands in surrender. He limped toward the dry shore. No one had shot him yet. They were lousy shots or else they were waiting to kill him at close range.

Some of the men on the beach held rifles. A few had pistols. Others were waving pitchforks and spades. They were farmers, Rubenfeld guessed, probably from the nearby Kfar Vitkin *moshav*—a collective farm. And he could see that they were *furious*. They were brandishing the weapons as if they wanted to make mincemeat of the pilot.

Then it dawned on Rubenfeld. They thought he was an *Arab* pilot. The existence of an Israeli fighter squadron was still a secret. Worse, Rubenfeld *looked* like an Arab. His naturally dark complexion had been burned darker by the Mideast sun.

Rubenfeld spoke no Hebrew. His mind was racing to come up with something—*anything*—that these wild-eyed dirt farmers would understand. He threw his arms in the air and yelled the only Yiddish words he could think of.

"*Gefilte fish! Gefilte fish! Shabbes! Shabbes!*"

The farmers stared at him as if he'd just landed from outer space. *Gefilte fish?* They kept their pitchforks and rifles at the ready as Rubenfeld hobbled onto the beach.

One of them snatched Rubenfeld's pistol. Another frisked him and came up with the identification folder from the pocket of his flight suit. The farmer examined the folder, then held it for all of them to see. It was a black-and-white photo of Milton Rubenfeld with his name and rank as a pilot in the Israeli Air Force. In Hebrew.

The pitchforks lowered. The exuberant Israelis took turns embracing the American volunteer in the air force they didn't know they had. It was time for a celebration.

───

Ezer Weizman had stopped thinking about Rubenfeld. He had problems of his own. His windshield was shattered and he was trying to get the Messerschmitt back on the hard, unforgiving concrete at Ekron. With his goggles down, wind blasting his face, Weizman landed the Messerschmitt and managed to keep the fighter on the runway.

When he shut the engine down back at the hangar, he was met by Yehuda Pilpel, the squadron's tough senior mechanic. Weizman gave him the bad news. They'd lost another Messerschmitt.

Then he showed him his own combat damage. "I seem to have been hit," said Weizman, with a touch of drama in his voice.

Pilpel could see the smashed windshield. He crawled into the cockpit. Seconds later he emerged wearing a wry smile. He showed Weizman the remains of the bird that had smashed the windshield.

Weizman would have laughed, except he couldn't. He'd just lost another wingman. The past twelve hours had been a violent mixture of

high drama and comedy. He'd taken battle damage to his own fighter—
he looked again at the bloody bundle of guts and feathers—from a *bird*.
It was a hell of a war.

With his shoulders slumping, a depressed Weizman trudged over to
the squadron operations shack.

Seconds later, his spirits were surging again. The report had just
come in from the north. Rubenfeld was alive. He'd been rescued by villagers from the Kfar Vitkin kibbutz. Rubenfeld had some injuries, but
as soon as he was patched up at the Hadassah hospital he'd be joining
them at their quarters in the Yarden Hotel in Tel Aviv.

A broad smile spread over Ezer Weizman's face. It was the first good
news he'd received since going into combat with the Messerschmitts. If
there was ever a reason to throw a blow-out party, this was it.

The Sparrow and the Condor

TEL AVIV
MAY 30, 1948

t was the first in a series of legendary 101 Squadron bashes. This one they convened in the posh bar at the Yarden Hotel on Tel Aviv's Ben Yehuda Street. Present for the party were the remaining four pilots from the first Messerschmitt class—Lenart, Weizman, Alon, Rubenfeld—plus an assortment of ground staff and a few transient airmen from the Operation Balak airlift.

The lanky, twenty-four-year-old Weizman was already known as a hard-drinking, woman-chasing carouser. Tonight he did his best to live up to his reputation.

His fellow sabra, Modi Alon, had just been appointed commander of the new fighter squadron, and Alon was taking his role seriously. Alon was drinking little, wearing an indulgent smile while he watched his pilots getting shitfaced.

Milt Rubenfeld was a mess. He was wearing a broad grin and an assortment of bandages and patches. Rubenfeld was still in obvious pain, but the booze was already taking effect.

The pilots had good reason to celebrate. Not only had they gotten Rubenfeld back from the dead, but the little two-plane attack on the Arab column had also produced the same effect as the previous evening's raid on Ishdud. The actual damage inflicted was minimal, but the appearance of Israeli fighters intimidated the Arab commanders.

The Iraqi–Transjordanian march to the sea was halted. The beat-up Israeli Alexandroni Brigade had time to retrench and fortify their defensive positions. The city of Netanya was safe, and so was the road to Tel Aviv.

Even Rubenfeld's Messerschmitt was not a total loss. The farmers of Kfar Vitkin—the ones who nearly pitchforked Rubenfeld—salvaged the machine guns from the shattered fighter. They had already mounted them at their *moshav* for their own defense.

Beneath the noisy chatter and the singing and raunchy jokes lay a worrisome reality. The little 101 Fighter Squadron, such as it was, was down to one flyable airplane and three pilots.

Milt Rubenfeld wouldn't be coming back. His injuries were serious enough that by the end of the month he would return to the United States for more advanced treatment. Rubenfeld's five minutes over Tulkarm were his first—and last—combat mission in the war.

––––––––––

Later, few of them would remember how long the party lasted. Sometime after midnight they wobbled off to their quarters, mumbling that they'd regroup in the morning. After all, there was a war going on.

Modi Alon, in keeping with his job and his personal nature, was awake and clearheaded early the next morning. Alon headed off to Ekron in the squadron's jeep, knowing that the other pilots might require more recovery time.

Later in the morning Ezer Weizman came down looking for a ride to Ekron. He saw that Alon had thoughtfully left his motorcycle. With his head throbbing and his throat dry, Weizman threw one long leg over the bike, kick-started the motor to life, and set off for Ekron.

He made it nearly halfway. The four-way intersection of main highways called the Beit Dagon crossroads had recently been blown up by Arab irregulars and the holes weren't fully repaired. As Weizman sped through the intersection, the front wheel of the motorcycle dropped into a pothole. Weizman sailed over the handlebars, smacked the asphalt road, and rolled like a bowling pin across the road.

At the Hadassah hospital they confirmed what Weizman already guessed. He'd broken a bone in his left wrist. Weizman's arm would be encased in plaster for the next month.

Now the 101 Squadron was down to *two* pilots.

———

That same morning, May 31, hard-pressed Israeli brigades across the country were screaming for close air support. Air force boss Remez ordered the single flyable Messerschmitt into action against Transjordanian gun positions blocking the construction of a supply route—the Israelis were calling it the Burma Road—to besieged Jerusalem.

Alon and Lenart were the only two pilots available. Alon drew the mission by the flip of a coin. Less than an hour later he was making low-altitude strafing passes on the Transjordanian positions. On each pass, Alon heard the *ping* of small arms fire hitting the Messerschmitt. It was as if he were flying through a shooting gallery.

When Alon landed back at his base, his mechanic's eyes bulged. "The Messerschmitt was so full of holes," he reported, "we didn't know how he kept it flying."

Remez was there too. Gazing at Alon's bullet-holed Messerschmitt, he shook his head. Remez was already taking heat from the general staff. Israeli morale was plummeting because Egyptian bombers were making almost daily raids over Tel Aviv.

Remez reached a decision. Performing both missions—supporting the ground troops and patrolling the skies—was not feasible. Henceforth, he ordered, the single fighter would be used *only* for air defense.

Alon and Lenart rotated the patrols. For two days the pilots patrolled the skies around Tel Aviv. They encountered no enemy warplanes.

And then on June 1, just before dusk, everything changed.

———

Lenart and Alon were in the Ekron operations shack when they heard the sound, swelling like the growl of an incoming storm. It was the deep crackle of Merlin engines.

Spitfire engines.

The pilots glanced at each other, then sprinted for the trenches outside the hangar. The first bombs were exploding as the men dove into the shelter.

From their trenches they watched the Egyptian Spitfires swoop over Ekron, dropping bombs, blazing away at the hangars with machine guns.

The raid had come without warning. The squadron's only operational fighter was hidden in a hangar, awaiting its next patrol. Caught by surprise, the Israeli antiaircraft gunners were peppering the sky, hitting nothing. Untouched by flak, the Egyptian Spitfires finished their work and peeled away back to the south.

The airmen climbed up from their trenches and peered around. Smoke was streaming from one of the hangars that had been strafed. When they checked, they found that two of the Messerschmitts awaiting reassembly had taken some damage.

They could be fixed. The other hangar where the remaining fighters were housed was unscathed. Only luck—and the Egyptian pilots' lousy aim—had spared the squadron from being decimated.

It meant the secret was out. The Arabs knew that Israel had fighters. And they knew exactly where they were hidden.

That same evening a decision was made at air force headquarters. The fighter squadron had to move. Ekron was too easy a target. The field was not only too close to the Egyptian guns at Ishdud, but one lucky Spitfire pilot could also wipe out *all* their fighters.

They had to find a field farther north, not so identifiable as a fighter base, and beyond the range of Arab guns. The job of locating a new base went to Modi Alon and Ezer Weizman, both of whom had grown up in Palestine.

The choices were limited. The Hatzor airfield was farther to the south and an even easier target for Arab gunners. So was the Lydda airport, not far from Ekron. The former RAF base at Ramat David was suitable, but it was too far north for the short-range Messerschmitts to reach targets in the south.

And then in a patch of sand dunes and orange groves 8 miles north of Tel Aviv they found what they were looking for. Herzliya was a sleepy farm community a mile from the beach. An east–west runway could be bulldozed in the verdant orange and banana groves. The orchards provided good concealment for parked fighters. Alon liked the idea of a dirt runway after his landing calamity on the hard concrete at Ekron.

Earth-moving equipment rolled into Herzliya. Within days they had smoothed out a mile and a half of surfaced dirt. Bulldozers carved out square revetments in the orange groves large enough to accommodate a fighter covered with camouflage netting. Builders erected a 20-foot concrete water tower which, equipped with a radio, wind sock, and field telephone, would be the base's control tower.

It would be mid-June before the 101 Squadron's secret new base was ready. One after the other the Messerschmitts would be flown to Herzliya and hidden in their camouflaged revetments. The pilots would take up residence in a small pension called the Falk House, nestled off the end of the runway in the village of Kfar Shmaryahu. The best thing about the Falk House, the pilots determined, was that it would be an easy walk from the local beer garden.

———

The order came a few minutes before noon on June 3: *Scramble the Messerschmitt.* The headquarters of the IDF—Israel Defense Forces—at Ramat Gan, to the east of Tel Aviv, was under attack by Egyptian Spitfires.

It was Modi Alon's turn to fly the squadron's single operational fighter. By the time he reached the area, the Spitfires were finishing their raid and heading south. Alon managed to slide in behind the trailing Spitfire, bring his sights on the enemy's tail—and open fire.

He saw some of his tracers hitting the fighter. But only for a second. The startled Egyptian pilot managed to dive away and speed out of range. Unable to catch the faster Spitfire, Alon gave up the chase and landed back at his base.

Mordecai "Modi" Alon possessed a cool, studied demeanor that seemed more mature than his twenty-seven years. Square-jawed with thick, sandy hair and piercing blue eyes, he looked typecast for the role of fighter pilot. Alon reinforced the image with his aviator sunglasses, which he wore indoors and out. Alon had recently married an attractive Israeli nurse named Mina, with whom he spent every minute when he wasn't with his squadron.

A WWII British-trained fighter pilot, Alon had finished his RAF career in his native Palestine flying P-51 Mustangs at the Ramat David RAF base. After leaving the service in 1946, Alon became an architecture student at the Technion, Israel's principal technical university. Then the fighting erupted following the UN partition plan in November 1947.

Until he went to Czechoslovakia to fly the Messerschmitt, Alon had been commander of the Tel Aviv squadron of the Sherut Avir. Alon and his pilots had flown their collection of rickety light airplanes on dangerous supply missions and bombing raids in support of besieged Jewish settlements.

After failing to shoot down any of the Egyptian Spitfires, a frustrated Modi Alon stomped into the squadron operations shack to write his after-action report. He knew *someone* was going to be the first to shoot down an enemy warplane. Alon had missed his chance to make history.

That evening at seven o'clock, the Egyptians gave him another chance.

———

The evening sun still blazed over the rim of the Mediterranean. Alon was flying in a high orbit around the capital when he spotted them: four silhouettes, down low, flying up the coast. Two were large aircraft, the other two smaller. They were coming up from the south, headed for Tel Aviv.

There was no question whether they were friend or foe. Alon knew he was the *only* friendly warplane in the sky.

Alon swung out over the water, putting the sun behind him. As he drew nearer, he was able to identify the silhouettes. The two multiengine aircraft were C-47 Dakota transports configured as bombers. The Egyptians had used them for fifteen separate air attacks on the civilian population of Israel.

The smaller, elliptical-winged escorts were their escorts. *Spitfire fighters.*

Alon was outmatched in numbers and firepower. He was counting on the factor of surprise. So far the Gyppos—the word they'd adopted for referring to the Egyptians—had shown a remarkable lack of real tactical skill.

Alon swept down from out of the sun. As he had hoped, they didn't see him. He locked on to the tail of one of the bombers. The Spitfires continued straight ahead, still oblivious to the danger.

Alon opened fire. The Messerschmitt rattled and vibrated from the combined chatter of the cannons and machine guns. To his surprise, the Dakota was making no evasive maneuvers. It continued toward Tel Aviv as if it were touring the city.

With his greater speed Alon overtook the bomber. He swung around for another close-range firing pass. The Spitfires still hadn't joined the fight, the pilots muddling along straight ahead.

Alon opened fire again on the Dakota. This time the bomber shuddered, dropped off sharply on one wing, and turned away from Tel Aviv.

And then exploded. Pieces of the shattered Dakota were tumbling like confetti on the nearly deserted port city of Jaffa.

The Egyptian Spitfire pilots came to life. One made an ineffective attempt to latch onto Alon's tail. Alon could tell that the Egyptian pilot was a novice. He yanked the Messerschmitt's nose up and inside the Spitfire's turning radius.

The Spitfires, he decided, were no threat. Alon went looking for the other bomber.

There. The second Dakota was headed for the coastline. The Egyptian pilot was no longer interested in bombing. He was at full throttle trying to escape.

It was too late. Alon swung in behind the bomber and opened fire again. A bright orange blaze spewed from beneath one of the wings, swelling until it enveloped the entire wing. The doomed bomber crashed into the sand dunes a few miles south of Tel Aviv.

Finished with the bombers, Alon looked around for the Spitfires.

They were gone. With nothing left to escort, the Egyptian fighters had disappeared in the south.

━━━━━

Everyone in downtown Tel Aviv saw it. With faces uptilted, thousands of astonished Israelis watched the show—Egyptian bombers pursued by a tiny growling fighter, the bursts of gunfire, the bombers going down in flames.

Someone captured the scene in a photograph that appeared in the next day's newspaper. It looked like a sparrow chasing a condor.

A wave of joy swept over Israel. *We have fighters!* After all the bombings, the killing of civilians by the hated Egyptian warplanes, the grim news from the battlefields, an unidentified Israeli pilot had just blown two Egyptian warplanes out of the sky.

It didn't take long to identify the pilot. Modi Alon's room at the Yarden Hotel was swamped with flowers, cakes, cognac, bottles of champagne from adoring citizens. The handsome young fighter pilot had just become Israel's new national hero.

= 20 =

Bogeys

EKRON AIR BASE, ISRAEL
JUNE 3, 1948

It was warm, even this late in the evening. Stepping down from the C-46, Gideon Lichtman could smell the dry, sweet smell of the countryside. He could see the outlines of the hills to the north and east.

A feeling swept over Lichtman like a pleasant breeze. *I'm in Israel.* After the weeks of secretive contacts and mysterious agents and trips across the world and a fourteen-hour plane trip, he was in the ancient land of his people.

For all Gideon Lichtman's swaggering and tough talk, he was, at heart, an idealist. He was one of the few who had volunteered to fight in Israel for *zero* pay. Lichtman was here for the sole purpose of helping to save the new nation.

The feeling deepened during the jeep ride into town. At roadblocks along the route they were halted by uniformed IDF soldiers. "It thrilled me," Lichtman recalled. "I saw Jews protecting their own country."

Tel Aviv was blacked out. The jeep pulled up to a darkened building along the beach. In the darkness Lichtman could barely make out the sign: *Park Hotel*. Hefting their duffel bags, Lichtman and his fellow fighter pilot, Maury Mann, trudged up to the main door.

The place looked deserted. Then they opened the door.

The light almost blinded them. Raucous noise spilled out the door.

Music blared from a phonograph. Inside the big open room couples were dancing. Someone was singing. A buzz of conversation permeated the air. The lounge was packed with partiers, men in uniform, dozens of cute women, some also in uniform.

At the bar he met his fellow fighter pilots in the 101 Squadron. One was a tall, skinny guy who introduced himself as Ezer Weizman. His left arm was in a plaster cast, he explained, due to a stupid motorcycle cock-up a few days ago.

Lichtman was introduced to Milt Rubenfeld, still banged up and bandaged from being shot down on his first mission only a week ago. He met Lou Lenart, the Hungarian American ex-Marine who had led the first Messerschmitt mission against the Egyptians.

Tiredly, Lichtman tossed down his drink. He needed sleep. He wondered how long he would have to wait before they sent him into combat.

═══════

Lichtman was asleep when he felt someone tapping his shoulder. "Giddy, wake up. Wake up."

It was Modi Alon. He was wearing a flight suit, and he had a serious look on his face. It was the morning of June 8. They were in the bunkroom at Ekron Air Base. Lichtman had moved out to Ekron so he'd be closer to the Messerschmitts when it was time to fly.

It was time.

"Get your parachute and flight gear, Giddy. We've got a call. Four Spitfires are heading north toward Tel Aviv."

Lichtman was instantly awake. He pulled on his flight suit, trying to listen while Alon rambled through a mission briefing. ". . . no radios, so I'll give you a circling motion with my hand, then point to the bogeys . . ."

Lichtman just nodded. "Bogeys" was a term coined in WWII. It meant aircraft suspected of being hostile. If the bogeys were Spitfires, they were automatically hostile.

With their parachutes flopping against their butts, the two men trotted across the ramp to where the Messerschmitts stood waiting. The *only* two in the air force that happened to be flyable.

Alon was still talking. ". . . and stay on my wing when I make the intercept so we can cover each other . . ."

Lichtman kept muttering, *"B'seder, b'seder."* *B'seder* meant "okay." It was one of the few Hebrew words he knew.

Things were happening too fast. They reached the parked fighters, and it was the end of Alon's briefing. He was already climbing into his Messerschmitt.

A mechanic helped Lichtman into his cramped cockpit. He fumbled with the straps and then set up the switches for engine start. It came rushing back to him how short his training at Budějovice had been.

The mechanic was winding up the inertia starter. It sounded like a cat being tortured—a low howl rising in pitch. The mechanic yanked the crank handle out and gave Lichtman the signal to start.

Lichtman peered around the cockpit. *Where the hell is the start handle?* The mechanic pointed to the handle by Lichtman's left knee. *Oh, yeah.*

Lichtman pulled the handle and the paddle-bladed propeller whirled in a jerky rotation. The Jumo engine rumbled to life.

Lichtman was still trying to set the flaps and the engine mixture and the trim for takeoff when he looked up. Alon's Messerschmitt was already rolling. Lichtman powered up his own fighter and hurried to catch up. At the end of the runway he stopped alongside Alon's fighter, slammed down the clamshell canopy of his fighter, and gave his engine a quick run-up. Lichtman was trying to make sense of his gauges when he glanced up.

Alon's fighter was gone. It was halfway down the strip, tail raised, accelerating like a runaway Doberman. Lichtman shoved his throttle forward and pointed his own Messerschmitt down the runway.

As they headed out toward the coast, Lichtman was fuming. He was at full throttle and he still wasn't catching up with Alon. Worse, at this high power setting the Messerschmitts were burning nearly *twice* the normal amount of fuel. At this rate, they'd be out of gas before they ever engaged the enemy.

Lichtman couldn't transmit on the radio. These goddamned airplanes didn't *have* radios. The low-hanging sun was blazing into Lichtman's face. Tears gushed from his eyes as he tried to stay in formation.

He saw Alon making a circling movement with his left hand and then he pointed down and left. Lichtman blinked away his tears and gazed down.

He spotted the elliptical-winged shapes. *Spitfires.* Four of them, cruising along in a loose formation.

The pair of Messerschmitts swept down on the Spitfires from behind. Lichtman was still groping in the cockpit. *Where is the arming switch for the guns?* He couldn't find it.

He kept flipping switches. None of them worked.

Closing the range, Alon opened fire. As his tracers spewed through the formation, the Spitfires scattered like a covey of quail.

Lichtman hadn't fired a shot. He watched the four Spitfires duck into a layer of cloud. He kept his eye on the cloud, waiting for a Spitfire to emerge, while he fumbled with his switches.

Aha! He found one that worked. He gave the trigger on his stick a short squeeze and heard a satisfying *Brrrrappp.*

Then he realized he was running out of fuel. At full throttle chasing Alon, he had consumed most of the Messerschmitt's minuscule fuel load. Now they were far from their base. He was still thinking about his fuel when he saw it.

A Spitfire. Coming of the cloud bank.

Lichtman whipped the Messerschmitt into a pursuit curve behind the Spitfire. At two hundred yards, he opened fire. It was the first time he'd actually fired the guns or cannons on a Messerschmitt. He saw the two streams of cannon tracers arcing toward the Spitfire.

And missing. The tracers were spewing past the Spitfire on either side. Even in his hyper-excited state, Lichtman knew what was happening. The guns hadn't been sighted in to *converge* at the optimum range.

The Spitfire pilot abruptly reversed his turn and put the fighter into a dive. Lichtman stayed on his tail. He fired again, kicking the rudder pedals to spray the cannon fire across the Spitfire's airframe. This time he saw hunks of metal spewing off the Spitfire. The enemy fighter was coming apart, heading for the floor of the desert.

Lichtman pulled up and away. *Is the Spitfire down?* It no longer mattered. Lichtman's attention was riveted on the fuel gauge in his Messerschmitt. The needle was ominously close to the bottom mark.

He throttled back to an economy power setting. As he flew back to his base, it occurred to him that running out of gas would be a hell of way to complete his first mission.

He made it. When he rolled up to the hangar opening and shut down the Jumo engine, Modi Alon and Ezer Weizman were waiting for him. Weizman was bubbling with excitement. "We just got a confirmation. A Spitfire was shot down. That was you who shot him down, wasn't it?"

For the first time that morning, Lichtman allowed himself to relax. Frozen in his memory was the sight of his tracers pouring into the enemy fighter. He still saw the pieces flying off the Spitfire as it headed for the desert.

It was what he had come to Israel for.

"Yeah," he said, "that was me."

———

Such an event, of course, called for another party. The squadron convened that evening at the Park Hotel bar, where they were joined by a few of the transient Operation Balak airmen from the Zebra base.

As usual, toasts were proposed. Songs were sung, tales told, and Lichtman's achievement was properly celebrated. Though Modi Alon had made the squadron's first air-to-air kills when he shot down the Egyptian Dakotas, Lichtman had just scored the first kill of an enemy *fighter*.

On his first mission.

As usual, Weizman was in the center of the party, cracking jokes, egging everyone on. Also as usual, squadron commander Alon presided over the rowdy pilots like an indulgent father watching teenagers.

Someone got around to asking Lichtman what it felt like to shoot down the Egyptian fighter. By now Lichtman was in his tough-talking fighter pilot mode. "It was wonderful," he said. "Better than getting laid."

At that, the pilots all laughed. But no one believed him.

=== 21 ===

Message to Amman

*B*omb Amman?

In his command shack at the Sde Dov airfield, Boris Senior read the order that had just been handed to him by Ezra Omer, the adjutant to the commanding general. Amman was the capital of Transjordan, which straddled the Jordan River to the east of Israel and, until its independence in 1946, had been a British protectorate. The country was heavily defended by Transjordanian Air Force fighters and antiaircraft guns. Amman also happened to be the site of a major military air base of the British, who maintained a watchful presence in the country.

Senior shook his head. How were they going to bomb a city? His little squadron at Sde Dov consisted of a handful of utility planes—Piper Cubs, Austers, Fairchilds, a Dragon Rapide biplane, and a Beechcraft Bonanza. He had no bombers or fighters. Fewer than two dozen airmen were assigned to the unit. None except Senior was military-trained.

Ezra Omer was a tall, taciturn soldier who didn't mince words. He hadn't come here to be told all the reasons why something couldn't be done. There was a good reason to bomb Amman. IDF headquarters had received intelligence reports that the top officials of the Arab League were meeting that night in Amman to discuss progress in the war against Israel. This was a perfect moment to send them a message.

Senior just nodded. It was a crazy idea, but no less crazy than most of the ideas headquarters had come up with. So far in this short war the IDF general staff had displayed a notable lack of understanding of the limits of their tiny air force.

Senior's little band of pilots had already become amateur bombers. They chucked explosives from the open doors of all their light planes—Austers, Norsemans, Dragon Rapide transports, even Boris Senior's V-tailed Bonanza.

Bomb Amman? Sure, said Senior. They'd do it.

It would have to be at night, if the attack were to have any chance of success. Even then there was no guarantee that Transjordanian Spitfires wouldn't swat them down like moths.

Senior assigned himself to lead the mission in the Bonanza. He would be first over the city and drop incendiaries to mark the target, just as the Pathfinder aircraft had done during heavy bomber raids over Germany. The heavy bombers, in this case, amounted to a Fairchild F-24 Argus light plane and a twin-engine Rapide biplane.

That evening the crews were standing in the darkness at Sde Dov, about to depart on the mission. One of the pilots was having second thoughts. His name was Asher Breier, and he was a member of the old Palestine Flying Club. Already that day Breier had flown two missions over the embattled town of Sdom by the Dead Sea.

Breier declared he wasn't going on this one. Even if they found the target in the darkness, they'd be shot out of the sky by the fighters that would surely come up after them.

A silence fell over the little group. Ezra Omer, the army major from headquarters, broke the impasse. He pulled out his pistol and shoved the muzzle against the pilot's head.

"If you do not fly, you get a bullet in the head."

Asher Breier's eyes widened. So did the eyes of the others. They all knew Omer. No one doubted that the battle-hardened officer would do exactly as he said.

Without a further word, the pilot turned and climbed into the cockpit of the Rapide. Minutes later the three little planes were on their way to bomb Amman.

Senior couldn't see a light anywhere on the ground. There was only a sliver of moon, a glitter of stars, the glow of the Bonanza's instrument lights. Flying with Senior was his bomb-chucker, a tough, thirty-year-old volunteer named Dov Judah. Judah was a Johannesburg lawyer and a former navigator in B-26 Marauders in the South African Air Force during WWII.

The three slow-flying aircraft droned eastward, crossing the Jordan River into Transjordan. They could see the moonlight reflecting from the Dead Sea. They'd been flying less than an hour when Senior spotted the lights of Amman ahead. There was still no gunfire, no sign that the country was at war.

Senior headed the Bonanza across the city toward the target. The incendiary bombs were long sticks of shiny metal with handles attached so the bomb-chucker could hurl them out the Bonanza's baggage door. Like much of the Israeli Air Force's weaponry, the bombs were homemade.

Senior tried to guess the drift and arc of the bombs. Over the target he yelled to Judah to chuck out the incendiaries.

In a left bank, Senior could see the trail of exploding incendiaries in the city. City lights were extinguishing. Behind Senior, the Fairchild and the Dragon Rapide made their own runs, aiming at the incendiaries that were twinkling like fireflies down below.

Seconds later came the expected response. Flashes appeared in the sky around them, followed by the thud of explosions. Tracer rounds, some green and some red, arced into the sky.

The three light aircraft zoomed toward the unlighted terrain in the west. At regular intervals Senior turned the Bonanza to look behind. No fighters were chasing them down.

After half an hour of droning in the darkness, Senior spotted a flashing light on the ground ahead. As he flew closer he saw that it was the airfield at Lydda, only about 15 miles from Tel Aviv. The field was still in Transjordanian hands, and the beacon on the tower was in full operation.

Senior and Judah broke out in laughter. After the tension of the dangerous bombing raid, it was comic relief. The Jordanians had thoughtfully left the lights of Amman on so that the bombers could locate the target. Now they were providing a homing beacon for the trip home.

As expected, the bombing raid caused little actual damage, but the *real* mission had been accomplished. An unmistakable message had been delivered to the Arab League officers gathered in Amman. The war they had promised would be ended in two weeks was just beginning. By attacking Israel, they had exposed *their* homeland to attack.

The Amman raid produced an unintended consequence. Three of Senior's incendiaries had fallen on the RAF air base at Amman. So had three bombs from the other two aircraft. One scored a direct hit on the base's main hangar. There were no casualties, but the bomb damaged two Anson aircraft and wrecked numerous military offices and storage facilities of Great Britain's Royal Air Force.

There was a howl of protest. The British Consul-General at Haifa warned the new government in Tel Aviv that if any RAF aircraft or installations in Amman were bombed again, "We would be bound to defend ourselves and attack Jewish aircraft on the ground or in the air." To back up the threat, all British units in Transjordan were placed on alert.

No one in Tel Aviv, least of all David Ben-Gurion, felt like apologizing. Jabbing a thumb in Jordan's eye had given Israel a badly needed morale boost. But drawing the British into the war was a worrisome prospect. Ben-Gurion gave the order that there would be no more air raids on Amman.

A clash with the British Royal Air Force had been averted. For now.

Baron Wiseberg was strapping into the Messerschmitt on the tarmac at Ekron Air Base. The 101 Squadron hadn't yet moved its fighters to the new Herzliya base. A burly mechanic was winding up the fighter's inertia starter. Wiseberg yanked the starter handle and the Jumo engine barked to life. A few minutes later he was roaring down the runway.

Wiseberg was a slender, dark-haired Englishman. He had been tapped for the mission because he was a former British Fleet Air Arm pilot and the only ex-navy pilot who had experience bombing ships.

After Modi Alon's downing of the two Dakota bombers, the Egyptians had given up attacking Tel Aviv from the air. Now they were coming from the sea. On the afternoon of June 4, an Egyptian flotilla was spotted heading for the Tel Aviv coast. An urgent order went to the 101 Squadron: *Send fighters to attack the enemy ships.*

Attack ships with Messerschmitts? It was yet another ill-suited mission for the fighters. In any case, only one Messerschmitt was flyable.

Baron Wiseberg was still new to the quirky Messerschmitt. As Wiseberg went hurtling down the runway, his old navy habits kicked in. Instead of raising the tail of the bomb-loaded Messerschmitt, he took off in a three-point, nose-high attitude.

The Messerschmitt rose no higher than 10 feet above the runway. Then it stalled. The fighter settled back to the runway. Shedding pieces and propeller blades, the Messerschmitt careened along on its belly to a stop.

The stunned Wiseberg opened the canopy. He sat there for a moment thinking about what happened. Then he lit a cigarette.

Wiseberg was still sitting in the cockpit smoking when the crash truck came roaring up.

"Get that bloody thing out, you fool!" yelled a fireman. "You've got petrol and bombs."

Wiseberg looked at the fireman. The man had a point. Wiseberg did as he was told. It was the shortest combat mission he had ever flown.

Wiseberg had crashed the last available fighter. The Egyptian flotilla was still bearing down on Tel Aviv. The tiny Israeli Navy had nothing that could engage the Egyptian ships.

Another urgent order went out, this one to Boris Senior's little band of amateur bombers at Sde Dov. Minutes later the same trio of flivvers that bombed Amman—the Bonanza, Fairchild Argus, and the Rapide biplane—were headed out to engage the Egyptian Navy.

It seemed a parody of a World War I scene—desperate airmen tossing bombs from the cockpits of wood-and-fabric airplanes. They'd gotten away with it because until now all their missions had been in darkness over land targets. This was mid-afternoon in a clear Mediterranean sky. The Egyptian warships were armed with antiaircraft guns firing 3-lb shells.

They didn't have far to fly. The Egyptian ships were less than 4 miles from the beach. They were steaming directly toward Tel Aviv.

Senior was the first in the Bonanza. Dodging antiaircraft fire, he managed to put one 50-kg bomb in the water close to the big flagship. With his second bomb he scored a direct hit on its deck.

Behind him came the bi-wing Rapide, putting down a stick of bombs from fore to aft. Last was the plodding Fairchild, a high-wing cabin monoplane. Each plane made multiple round trips, rearming at Sde Dov and returning to harass the Egyptian ships.

By late afternoon, the Egyptians had had enough. The flotilla headed back to the south.

But one of the bombers hadn't returned. Missing was the Fairchild flown by David Shprinzak and his bomb-chucker, Mattie Sukenik. With darkness coming, Senior took off again in the Bonanza. He searched the sea where the action had taken place. He found no trace of the lost aircraft.

He searched again in the morning. Still no trace. Senior had to conclude that the Fairchild had been downed by the ships' gunfire and disappeared in the sea.

Later they learned the truth. The Egyptian Air Force had acquired a new fighter—a Hawker Sea Fury. A charismatic Egyptian squadron leader named Abu Zaid, the Egyptian Air Force's most successful fighter pilot, had flown the Sea Fury on its first combat mission that day. On his return to his base at El Arish, Zaid reported shooting down an Israeli aircraft.

Nothing was ever found of the Fairchild or the lost airmen.

===

There's gotta be something better than the goddamned Messerschmitt.

It was a common refrain among the fighter pilots, especially after a few rounds at the bar. To a man they loathed the Czech Mule. There *were* better fighters out there. Lots of them. The Mule was still the only fighter available to the Israeli Air Force.

Or was it? The Israelis were short on everything but ingenuity. They had already cobbled together an inventory of weapons from scraps and leftovers—tanks, heavy guns, warships. Why not a fighter?

When the British departed Palestine, they left behind at Ekron Air Base a scrap heap containing the remains of a number of Spitfires. There were also salvageable parts from the Egyptian Spitfires shot down on May 22 during their ill-informed attack on the RAF base at Ramat David. But the real prize was the nearly intact Egyptian Spitfire ditched on the beach near Herzliya on the first day of war.

The myriad Spitfire pieces and scraps were collected and delivered to the air force's maintenance center at Sharona in the lower Galilee. In charge of the team to build the fighter was a brilliant former RAF mechanic named Jack Freedman. In February 1948, Freedman had defected from the RAF and joined the Haganah. Like many immigrants, Freedman took a new name: Yakov "Freddy" Ish-Shalom.

The collection of scraps looked like a giant jigsaw puzzle. The pieces weren't even from similar models. The scraps left by the RAF were from advanced versions, and pieces from the Egyptian airplanes were older models. The mechanics had no manuals, no technical documents.

Another problem was the Spitfire's Merlin engine. Though the British had left several scrapped Merlins behind, they'd made them unserviceable. From the scrap piles at the various British bases, Ish-Shalom's crew came up with enough matching parts to construct a few workable engines.

By the end of June 1948, they had stitched together an airplane. The wings were from a photo-reconnaissance Spitfire. The fuselage came from a different model.

Shrouded in canvas, the Spitfire was hauled down to the Herzliya airfield for testing. It already had a name: the Frankenstein fighter.

——————

Boris Senior settled himself into the Spitfire's cockpit. Lined up by the runway were mechanics, pilots, squadron officers, all watching like vultures. No one else had wanted the job of test-flying the new fighter. None had confidence in the ragtag team of mechanics who had assembled the disparate pieces of the fighter.

Now Senior was having second thoughts. Though he had experience in the Spitfire, it had been in WWII. He hadn't yet flown the Messerschmitt, nor had he flown *any* WWII fighter in over three years.

Senior started the engine. He remembered that sound. There was no other aircraft noise in the world like the Rolls Royce V-12 Merlin engine.

The plan was to make a couple circuits around Herzliya, then fly to the nearby strip at Ma'abarot where Ish-Shalom's crew would install the operational equipment—guns, radio, gun sight, and oxygen system. The antiaircraft units along the route had been alerted not to shoot at the Spitfire, which now bore Israeli markings.

When Senior landed, Ish-Shalom and his crew of gritty mechanics were cheering, pumping the air with their fists.

Israel had a new secret weapon. And this one was just the first.

22

Bombers

MIAMI, FLORIDA
JUNE 12, 1948

They called it Cockroach Corner. It was the section of the Miami airport where derelict aircraft, fly-for-hire freighters, and tramp charter planes were stashed so they'd be out of view from the main terminal 2 miles away.

Even among the other beat-up aircraft moldering in Cockroach Corner—old C-46s, C-47s, a dented C-54—Al Schwimmer's airplanes were hard to miss. They were B-17 Flying Fortresses. They were the once-mighty warplanes that had reduced the cities and factories of Nazi Germany to rubble.

The evening had cooled, but Schwimmer was perspiring. In the pale light, he could see the three olive drab–painted bombers. In just a few minutes the bombers would be cranking up. They'd leave the country—if the guys in fedoras and black sedans didn't show up to stop them. So far the coast was clear.

Schwimmer was proud of his new acquisitions. Acquiring *any* warplanes, even trainers and transports, from the War Assets Administration had become increasingly difficult. But *strategic bombers?*

Schwimmer had found a loophole. The WAA had already released a number of WWII bombers. They were demilitarized with gun turrets and bomb racks removed for civilian use as freighters and personal airliners.

Schwimmer tracked down four of them. Under the cover of a dummy corporation, he bought two from an operator in Tulsa, Oklahoma. One had been delivered to Miami while the other was still undergoing maintenance in Tulsa.

The other two were already in Miami. A businessman named Charlie Winters had purchased the surplus warplanes to use on a fruit-hauling business between Miami and Puerto Rico. One day Schwimmer approached Winters about selling the airplanes. And, while he was at it, would he consider "guiding them to somewhere in Europe?"

Charles Thompson Winters, age thirty-six, was not Jewish. He was a stocky, round-faced Irish Protestant from Boston. Later, when asked by federal prosecutors why he agreed to help Jewish agents smuggle warplanes to Israel, Winters shrugged and offered the explanation used by most volunteers: It was the right thing to do.

Gazing at his bombers, Schwimmer felt a wave of excitement surge through him. The big three-bladed propellers of the R-1820 engines were rotating. Within minutes the air was filled with the rumble of twelve big radial engines.

The shabby-looking bombers, one behind the other, trundled past where Schwimmer stood and headed for the active runway. Schwimmer again glanced over his shoulder. Still no black sedans. He knew that rumors were swirling around Miami about the B-17s, that they were involved in some kind of clandestine operation. Perhaps the war in Palestine.

Schwimmer didn't move from his spot on the tarmac until the last of the bombers had taken off and disappeared to the south.

Charlie Winters was true to his word. Waiting in San Juan were ten contract airmen who would fill out the crews to ferry the B-17s across the Atlantic. None had been told their true destination, just "someplace in Europe." They'd be given the details after they'd arrived in Santa Maria, in the Azores.

The next day the three fully fueled bombers lumbered into the sky from San Juan. Because Puerto Rico was still within US jurisdiction, Winters had declared to US Customs that the aircraft were only leaving US airspace for a short while, making an aerial survey of the Azores.

The Customs officers in San Juan were familiar with the comings and goings of Winters's fruit-hauling airplanes. None raised an objection. Later, a State Department official would write, "Due diligence on the part of customs officials at San Juan was lacking."

The flight didn't go smoothly for all the bombers. Each airplane carried twenty-four hours of fuel for the twenty-one-hour flight, which required precise navigation to find the Azores island group. Most of the B-17s' navigation systems had been removed. Each had a single low-frequency direction finder radio with a range of only about 200 miles. The navigators' Plexiglas turrets had been removed and covered with plywood. To take celestial sightings, the navigator had to remove the plywood hatch and then stand up in the 140-mile-per-hour wind with his octant while crew members hung on to his legs.

In the left seat of the third B-17 was a former B-24 pilot named David Goldberg. Goldberg had been assigned as the copilot, but the command pilot, an ex-USAAF colonel, showed up at departure time roaring drunk. Goldberg and navigator Eli Cohen poured the colonel into the back.

They had been flying for ten hours when the colonel returned to the cockpit, more or less sober. Exhausted, Goldberg turned the airplane over to the colonel. He went back to take a nap, and so did Eli Cohen.

In the mid-cabin, Goldberg was five minutes into his nap when he was awakened by screams. The screams were loud enough to be heard above the din of the engines. Startled, Goldberg ran toward the nose of the bomber.

He saw the source of the screams. Eli Cohen had stepped on a plywood panel in the bottom of the compartment.

And fallen through. Cohen's lower half was flopping in the 140-mile-per-hour wind stream 9,000 feet above the Atlantic. Cohen was clutching the interior of the compartment with outstretched arms, hands, fingernails. Inch by inch, Cohen was being sucked out of the airplane.

Goldberg yelled for help. He was joined by three other crewmen. Someone called to the cockpit for the colonel to slow the damned airplane down. With all of them yanking Cohen's arms, his head, his clothing, they finally dragged him back inside the cabin.

While Cohen lay on the deck, gasping and incoherent, Goldberg considered their situation. The colonel, still fog-brained from his bender in San Juan, was back in the captain's seat. They were somewhere over the Atlantic, eleven hours from the Azores. Eli Cohen, the navigator, was useless.

"By a stroke of luck we were able to pick up the airway radio beacon from Santa Maria," recalled Goldberg.

But the weather had gone bad. The ceiling was low. Peering out the windshield, the colonel declared that the island was mountainous and an instrument approach would be too risky. He was going to ditch the plane off the coast.

Goldberg was aghast. *Ditch the plane?* Forget it, *he'd* make the approach.

The colonel refused. He wasn't getting out of his seat.

Goldberg grabbed a fire extinguisher. He held it over the colonel's head. "I'm going to crush your skull if you don't get out of the fucking seat."

The colonel's eyes widened. He saw that Goldberg meant it. Reluctantly, he climbed out the seat. Minutes later Goldberg was landing the B-17 on the runway in Santa Maria.

Charlie Winters was waiting for them.

Winters was exhausted, and he knew all the other B-17 crewmen were just as tired. But they couldn't stay in the Azores. The arrival of three heavy American bombers would not go unnoticed by the press—or the US State Department.

Winters pulled out the sealed envelope Al Schwimmer had given him before the departure from Miami. Winters had always figured that the B-17s were headed for Palestine, but when he opened the envelope and read Schwimmer's instructions, his eyes narrowed.

They were going to a place called . . . Žatec. Where the hell was that?

For twelve more hours the bombers droned eastward over Spain, France, Germany. They had filed a flight plan for Ajaccio, Corsica. They communicated with no one, relayed no position reports to air traffic control. Passing the invisible border of the Iron Curtain, the bombers descended over the Alps to the airfield at Žatec, Czechoslovakia.

Zebra base.

On their arrival, an Israeli agent relayed the information to Ajaccio, Corsica, where another operative reported to air traffic control that the three B-17s had arrived safely in Corsica. According to flight plan.

Charlie Winters climbed creakily down from the B-17. He was astonished at what he saw. All around him were C-46s in various stages of loading, unloading, or maintenance. Messerschmitt fighters were lined up in a row, some disassembled, some being stuffed into transports. At one end of the field stood a Constellation airliner. Next to it was a C-54.

Just as astonished were the crews of Operation Balak. Pilots, mechanics, loaders all gaped at the apparitions that had just rolled up. *B-17s!*

A few of the pilots—ex-firemen Ray Kurtz and Norm Moonitz, as well as Bill Katz and Al Raisin—were gazing at the B-17s as if they were long-lost girlfriends. Kurtz's WWII bomber had flown him to Germany and back over a dozen times.

Charlie Winters just wanted to go home. He'd done what Schwimmer asked. But Winters hadn't heard the last of the B-17 story. Someone had already found out what he'd done.

By June 16, newspapers in the United States had sniffed out the story about the vanished B-17s, first reporting that two of the bombers had landed in Ajaccio, then departed for Palestine. Another paper reported that the third B-17 had gone missing and was presumed crashed in the ocean. When French officials in Corsica denied that the bombers had ever arrived in Ajaccio in the first place, the speculation ratcheted upwards.

Where were the missing B-17s? Palestine? Or somewhere else?

The US State Department already knew. Back in May the BBC in London had reported the existence of a mysterious airlift operation in Žatec, Czechoslovakia. The American embassy in Prague was being regularly tipped off by observers at Žatec about the number and identities of aircraft on the base.

The whereabouts of the missing B-17s was not a secret.

It was the beginning of the end for Al Schwimmer's warplane smuggling operation. With the FBI closing in, Schwimmer began laying preparations for one last audacious flyaway.

They were closing in on Charlie Winters, too.

On a sultry day in Miami, Winters stood in his doorway while unsmiling men in fedoras asked him questions about the missing B-17s.

When he sold them, was he aware that they were leaving the country?

Did he, by any chance, leave with them?

Did he know the penalty for violating the US Neutrality Act?

Winters knew. And he knew he was going to need a lawyer.

═══ 23 ═══

A Truce of Sorts

Red Finkel looked up from his poker hand. He didn't like what he was hearing. The C-46's right engine was making a stuttering, laboring sound like a sick cow.

Finkel exchanged glances with his traveling partner, Sid Antin, with whom he had been playing cards. They were stuck in the back of the C-46 along with a cargo of machine guns and ammunition. One of the machine-gun crates was serving as their poker table.

Aaron "Red" Finkel and Sid Antin had been P-47 Thunderbolt pilots in WWII. The two had gone to Czechoslovakia together to train in the Messerschmitt. They had just completed the course at České Budějovice, and now they were being hauled to Israel, via the interim refueling base at Ajaccio, along with a planeload of munitions. En route they had been sucked into a poker game with the radio operator, Sol Fingerman.

The stuttering noise from the right engine grew more persistent. Finkel put his cards down on the machine-gun crate. He had the helpless feeling fighter pilots always had when they were passengers in a clattering freight hauler. He was trapped.

Two hours ago they had left Zebra base in Czechoslovakia. The C-46 climbed into the thin air at 14,000 feet to cross the Alps. It was then that the right engine began its sick-cow stutter.

"Carburetor ice," yelled the captain over his shoulder. He was a thirty-five-year-old ex-airline pilot named Dan Kosteff.

The engine coughing and stuttering persisted. Kosteff announced that they were going to land at the Italian military field in Treviso. Though the Italians had given the Panamanian-registered transports a hard time at other airports, the base commander at Treviso had been extraordinarily friendly to Hal Auerbach and his crew when they made an unscheduled stop there for maintenance a few weeks earlier. The Italian commandant had taken Auerbach's word that the plane carried no contraband cargo. They were hauling civilian material to Central America.

When the C-46 rolled up to the main hangar at Treviso, it was met by the same commandant. Colonel Arturo Bracci looked like a character from a Puccini opera. He was a heavy-set man with a mane of gray hair and a huge black mustache. Bracci spoke excellent English, which, he explained, he had learned while he was a POW in the United States during WWII.

As he had done with Auerbach, the commandant was willing to take Kosteff's word that the C-46 contained no contraband cargo. He didn't bother looking inside.

But then the commandant left the area. One of his guards, an Italian soldier with a carbine, walked over the C-46 and peered inside the cabin. He saw Red Finkel sitting on the stack of crates that had served as their poker table.

The soldier pointed his carbine at Finkel. He demanded that Finkel open the crates.

Finkel stared at the muzzle of the carbine while he scratched his brain for ideas. He was alone on this plane, and some jerk was pointing a gun at him. In convoluted Italian and English, Finkel persuaded the soldier that he wouldn't open anything until the base commander was present.

While the soldier went to fetch the commandant, Finkel rushed to the cockpit to gather up any potentially incriminating documents. He found one: an envelope addressed to the 101 Squadron commander from Dr. Otto Felix, Israel's Czech operative.

Finkel opened the envelope and saw *his* name on a document: "Aaron Finkel. Typical American. Oversexed. To be watched."

When the commandant returned he was accompanied by Kosteff and Sid Antin and the rest of the crew—and another man. He was the regional chief of police. Unlike the commandant, the chief wasn't friendly.

The police chief ordered Finkel to open one of the crates. Kosteff and the other crewmen tried to persuade the policeman that the crates needn't be opened since they contained only surveying equipment.

The chief wasn't persuaded. He repeated his command, more forcefully this time. *Open the crate.*

So Finkel did. The top crate contained tripods for machine guns. "See," he said, "that's for the surveying equipment."

"Open the rest of it," the chief ordered.

Finkel opened the rest of it. The next thing they saw was the barrel of a Beza 7.92-mm machine gun. "You couldn't call that surveying equipment," recalled Finkel. "It was pretty obvious what it was."

It was more than obvious to the police chief. He placed the entire crew and the two passengers, Finkel and Antin, under arrest.

Finkel asked to make a phone call, and the Italians agreed. He put in a call to Danny Agronsky, still the Haganah's chief operative in Rome and tireless fixer of the problems of the volunteer air crews. He could hear Agronsky groan over the phone. Agronsky promised to see what he could do.

The police grabbed each man's elbow and steered them toward the waiting vehicle. The airmen resisted, yelling at the Italians. They were Americans, goddamnit. They couldn't be treated this way.

The chief stopped. *Americans?* In that case, didn't they want to see the US consul?

The airmen stopped yelling. *US consul?* They were in deep trouble with the Italians, but it was nothing compared to the trouble they'd be in with the US State Department. They were violators of the arms embargo to the Middle East as well as members of a foreign military. They could lose their citizenship, pay big fines, go to prison.

Umm, thanks, but not now, they told the surprised police chief. No need to bother the American consul. Later, maybe.

And then they went to jail.

———

It was the evening of June 7 in Tel Aviv. On David Ben-Gurion's desk was the latest proposal from the United Nations special mediator Count Folke Bernadotte of Sweden. The diplomat had been scurrying between Cairo, Beirut, Tel Aviv, and Amman, negotiating with the leaders of the warring countries the terms of a cease-fire.

Bernadotte's earlier proposals had been rejected by the Arabs, who believed that a quick victory was in their grasp. Momentum had been on their side. Now the war that the Arabs thought would be concluded in two weeks was dragging into a contest of exhaustion. The Arab forces, especially the Egyptian brigades that had penetrated most deeply into Israel, were badly overextended.

And so were the Israelis.

Ben-Gurion and his ministers had been carefully concealing the hard facts from the Israeli public. "We were at the end of our rope," Ben-Gurion wrote later. Israel's troops were exhausted. Losses had been higher than expected. They were short of everything—munitions, food, vehicles, even decent shoes and uniforms.

The war on the ground had been a perilous see-saw match. Israeli forces had been defeated three times at Latrun. They'd lost the Old City of Jerusalem. They were stalemated against the Iraqis in the north. The Egyptians were still solidly encamped 25 miles south of Tel Aviv.

Only against the Syrians had the Israelis gained any ground, and that was due more to Syrian incompetence than to Israeli force of arms. The air war was still tilted in favor of the Arabs, mainly because Israel's meager air force lacked the number of aircraft it required to take command of the skies.

What Israel desperately needed was time. Time to rearm. Time to ship new stocks of arms, ammunition, and precious warplanes from Czechoslovakia. Most of all, time for the weary soldiers of the IDF to rest and recover.

As Ben-Gurion paced the dimly lit hallway in his home, he was becoming certain. A thirty-day respite from war, he wrote in his diary, would be "a golden dream."

That night Ben-Gurion cabled the UN mediator, Count Bernadotte. Israel would accept the terms of the cease-fire.

Hours later, the Arab League, having reached a consensus after a stormy debate, followed suit. The UN announced that the truce would go into effect Friday, June 11, 1948.

The truce would be enforced by UN supervisors. One of the conditions of the agreement was an embargo not only on armaments but also on men of military age entering the war zone.

It was a condition both sides would openly violate.

===

Red Finkel read the news about the truce in the English-language newspaper. When he came to the part about the embargo on men of military age, he had to shake his head.

He and Sid Antin weren't violating any embargo. Not yet. They were still in custody in Treviso.

They spent three days in jail, sleeping on concrete floors and eating prison rations and cursing the Italians until Agronsky managed to pay off the right officials and secure their release. But they still weren't free. The airmen were placed under house arrest, shadowed by an Italian guard, and billeted in a Treviso hotel.

Which wasn't all bad. "You have never seen anything like it," Sid Antin recalled. "It was a huge mansion-type thing—marble columns in the front, very ornate." The airmen spent their time visiting the bars, playing cards, dallying with local women.

One night, just for the hell of it, they got their guard drunk and left him passed out on the sofa of a brothel. "We went back to our hotel," said Antin. "We never heard whether he was fired, or they had a firing squad, or what, but he did get in a lot of trouble, we did hear."

After nearly two weeks, the airmen were released. Dan Kosteff and his crew were allowed to depart in the C-46 for Žatec, but the valuable load of machine guns and ammunition stayed with the Italians. Red Finkel and Sid Antin boarded a steamboat to Venice, where Agronsky had arranged a flight aboard a Jewish-owned South African C-47 to Haifa.

On June 14, 1948, Finkel and Antin finally stepped off the airplane in Haifa. The first person they saw in Israel was a man in a US Army uniform. He had a UN armband around his sleeve. US military personnel were there to enforce the truce.

Finkel and Antin were clearly of military age, a violation of the truce. Worse, they were wearing military khakis. They'd long ago run out of clean civilian clothes during their time in Treviso.

"This big, fat major interviewed each of us as we got off the aircraft," remembered Antin. "We all had a story. I had an uncle in Tel Aviv that I was gonna visit—I was a tourist." Finkel had a similar story. He was just, you know, passing through. "It was a laugh," said Antin, "but we had to say something."

The major wasn't buying it. For the second time since leaving Czechoslovakia, Finkel and Antin were arrested. They were hauled away to a fenced-off area supervised by UN officials.

This time their incarceration was brief. "During that very first night, the Israelis smuggled bodies in for each of us and smuggled us out. We were on our way to the 101 Squadron by early morning."

———

Finkel and Antin weren't the only new volunteers showing up at Herzliya. They were joined by Americans Leon Frankel, a former US Navy torpedo bomber pilot who had won the Navy Cross for sinking a Japanese cruiser in 1945, and Bill Pomerantz, who had four German fighter kills to his credit while flying P-47s with the 318th Fighter Squadron in the Mediterranean.

A week later, four South Africans checked in with the noisy bunch at Herzliya. One was Syd Cohen, a tall, mustached twenty-seven-year-old who had twice left medical school in Johannesburg, first at the beginning of WWII, then again in 1948, to fly fighters for an embattled Israel.

With him came fellow South African Les Shagam, another WWII fighter pilot who, like Cohen, had been recruited by Boris Senior.

The volunteers kept coming. At the end of June another class arrived, including two highly decorated WWII pilots. Rudy Augarten was a lanky twenty-six-year-old with dark, Lincolnesque features who had left his studies at Harvard University to volunteer for Israel.

Augarten had been shot down over Normandy on his twelfth mission in the P-47. He evaded the Germans for two weeks until he was captured and made a POW. After a daring break from prison, Augarten spent another two weeks in the French countryside, evading the Nazis and working his way back to allied lines. Despite the USAAF policy of not returning escaped POWs to combat, Augarten talked his way back into his squadron. In the next few months of flying over Europe, he blasted two German Messerschmitts out of the sky.

Arriving with Augarten was Chris Magee, a tall, thirty-one-year-old ex-Marine who had been Pappy Boyington's executive officer in the Black Sheep squadron. Magee was an ace who had downed nine Japanese warplanes during the Pacific war.

Two more Americans came from California. Bob Vickman was a twenty-six-year-old ex-USAAF photo-reconnaissance pilot in the Asia-Pacific theatre in WWII. At six-two, the lanky Vickman was barely able to squeeze into the coffin-like cockpit of the Messerschmitt.

Arriving with Vickman was his best friend, Stan Andrews, who had flown B-25 Mitchell bombers in the southwest Pacific. The twenty-five-year-old Andrews was an athletic young man with matinee idol looks. The two veterans had met while they were art students in Los Angeles and became best buddies. When Israel's war of independence began, they agreed to volunteer.

Vickman and Andrews arrived in Israel hauling cameras and cartons of art supplies. They wanted not only to fly fighters but to contribute their artistic skills.

They'd been in the squadron only a few days when they got their chance.

=======

It happened one night at the Gallei Yam bar. As usual, the proprietor was keeping a wary eye on the bunch at the big table in the corner. He was still learning about the English-speaking foreigners. He'd learned from experience that the volunteer airmen were rowdy, and the fighter pilots were the rowdiest of them all.

They were easy to spot now. The 101 Squadron pilots wore red baseball caps, courtesy of Red Finkel's sister who shipped a crate of them from New York. Wearing the caps had become *de rigueur* for their forays through the Tel Aviv watering holes. The arrival of the volunteers in the red caps sent bar owners into a state of heightened alert. Their unit quickly received a nickname: the Red Squadron.

But it was still early. The booze hadn't flowed in great quantities, and the Red Squadron pilots were relatively well behaved. One of the reasons they were well behaved was because Modi Alon had joined them, and he was acting like a squadron commander.

Alon had decided that now that they were, officially, a squadron of the Israeli Air Force, they ought to have an official insignia, just like a *real* fighter squadron. Did they have any ideas?

They all had ideas, and an argument soon started. Alon already had his own idea: a winged scorpion, which happened to be the image from his old RAF squadron.

No one liked it.

Then Lou Lenart came up with an idea. How about an angel of death insignia? It had symbolic value, he said, because in biblical lore it was the angel of death who forced the Pharaoh to capitulate in the Passover story.

Getting closer. More drinks were poured. There were more ideas, more arguments. And while the pilots argued, the newly arrived artists, Vickman and Andrews, were hunched over their table doodling on cocktail napkins.

Abruptly the debate ended. Stan Andrews flashed his big grin and held up a napkin. On it was the result of the two artists' handiwork. It was a takeoff on Lenart's angel of death—an image of a skull with dark wings . . . wearing a flying helmet.

The pilots passed the napkin around. They took turns studying the image. Each pilot in turn nodded his head. *Yeah, that's it.*

The decision was unanimous. It was just the sort of death-be-damned hardball symbol fighter pilots had always loved.

By the next afternoon the emblem was being painted on the left side of each Messerschmitt's nose. The artwork of Stan Andrews and Bob Vickman would appear on every new fighter the squadron would acquire and would live on into the next century in the Israeli Air Force.

The truce was in place, and UN peacekeepers were swarming over Israel. Most wore British, US, or Scandinavian military uniforms with black UN armbands. Their assignment was to monitor the cease-fire and to enforce the ban on arms shipments and the entry into Israel of men of military age.

During their forays into Tel Aviv, most of the volunteers kept a wary distance from the armband-wearing enforcers. For their part, the UN officers stayed to themselves, clustering at their own tables in places like the Park Hotel bar and the Gat Rimon.

On a sunny afternoon in mid-June, Leon Frankel, a recently arrived pilot in the Red Squadron, was stepping through the front door of the Gat Rimon, which was one of the squadron's chosen watering holes.

He abruptly stopped in his tracks.

Frankel was looking at a half dozen of the enforcers in the Gat Rimon bar. Each was wearing US military khakis with the UN armband.

One of the armband-wearers was staring at Frankel. Frankel stared back. The UN officer looked familiar . . . a tall guy wearing khakis . . . silver oak leaves on his collar. A US Navy commander.

Frankel recognized the guy. He was the commanding officer of Frankel's naval reserve unit back in Minneapolis. The same unit where Frankel was supposed to be showing up as an active reservist on drill weekends.

The same unit Frankel had left to come to Israel.

Frankel's mind raced. Should he say anything? Maybe the commander wouldn't recognize him. Maybe—

"Frankel?" said the commander. "Is that you?"

Frankel gave him a twisted smile. "Oh, hello, Skipper."

"What the hell are you doing here, Frankel?"

It was a good question. Frankel was still groping for an answer when the commander growled, "Never mind. I *know* what you're doing." He waved his hand. "And I don't want to hear about it."

That was fine with Frankel. Before the commander could change his mind and ask more questions, Frankel made the best move he could think of. He did an about-face and disappeared.

$$=== 24 ===$$

Altalena Burning

OFFSHORE KFAR VITKIN, ISRAEL
JUNE 20, 1948

Moving at slow speed, the heavily loaded ship glided closer to the shore. The sun was low over the Mediterranean as Captain Monroe Fein worked the throttles, trying to steer the vessel's flat bow onto the beach.

In the next minute Fein felt an ominous *scrunch*. The ship's hull was grating on the hard bottom. They were still 300 yards from the shore. They would have to begin unloading the weapons from here.

The *Altalena* was a former WWII US Navy LST—tank landing craft—and she had sailed from southern France nine days ago with a cargo of 4,500 tons of armaments and 940 Jewish volunteer fighters. They had chosen the beach at Kfar Vitkin—nearly the same spot where Milt Rubenfeld had come down in his parachute—because it was far enough from Tel Aviv and the UN embargo enforcers.

Fein could see soldiers and villagers watching them from the beach. Were they waiting to unload the cargo? Fein wasn't sure. He wondered again: *Who are these weapons for?*

$$===$$

Twenty-two miles away in Tel Aviv, a worried David Ben-Gurion had just received the news about the *Altalena*. For eight days he had been tracking the progress of the weapons ship. The munitions on the *Altalena* were originally intended for the splinter paramilitary force called the Irgun, led by a fiery guerilla commander named Menachem Begin.

Begin and Ben-Gurion despised each other. Ben-Gurion considered the Irgun as well as a smaller extremist group, the Stern Gang, threats to Israel's statehood. In the pre-independence era, the Irgun had engaged in acts of terrorism, including bombing the King David Hotel in Jerusalem. Ninety-four Britons, Arabs, and Jews had died in the attack. Irgun fighters had massacred the Arab residents of a village called Deir Yassin, which triggered a series of revenge atrocities against Jewish settlers by Palestinian Arabs.

Begin, for his part, considered Ben-Gurion a lackey of the Americans and Europeans. He denounced the June 11 truce as a "shameful surrender."

When he established the IDF, Ben-Gurion demanded that all the paramilitary units—the Haganah, the Irgun, and the smaller Stern Gang—be melded in a unified army. Each fighter was to forswear his allegiance to his former unit and formally enlist in the IDF.

And Begin, it seemed, was willing to comply. On June 1, he signed an agreement to merge Irgun into the IDF. He further agreed that Irgun would cease acquiring munitions independently.

And then the *Altalena* sailed from France with her cargo of weapons.

On June 15, Begin met with Ben-Gurion's representatives. Without apologies, Begin explained that the Irgun's arms deal in France had been made weeks before the agreement to cease acquiring arms. It was signed, in fact, before the IDF had even been established.

The *Altalena* would soon be arriving in Israel. Ben-Gurion wanted all the arms distributed to the IDF. Begin refused and then relented— but only a little. He wanted 20 percent of the shipment sent to the Irgun defenders in Jerusalem. The remainder could be distributed to the rest of the fighting forces.

Ben-Gurion's government agreed. The two sides had a deal. Or so they thought.

Night fell over Kfar Vitkin. Villagers swarmed down to help with the unloading of the *Altalena*. Food and drinks were hauled in. Over the darkened beach was the sound of singing and laughter. For several hours a spirit of shared purpose united them.

And then, imperceptibly, the mood changed. Someone noticed that the exits from the landing site had been closed off. A force of six hundred troops from the IDF Alexandroni Brigade arrived and took up positions around the beach site. Their orders were to confiscate the arms. All of them. By force if necessary.

Exactly who broke the agreement, who fired the first shots, who gave the orders would be disputed for decades to come. From outside Kfar Vitkin, Irgun forces tried to break through the IDF blockade. They were repelled.

Shots were fired. A gun fight broke out.

Begin fled to the ship in a rowboat. He ordered *Altalena's* captain to make a dash for Tel Aviv where Irgun had support forces. Two Israeli Navy corvettes took off in pursuit. They pumped sporadic machine-gun fire into the slow-moving LST. *Altalena's* crew fired back with deck-mounted Bren guns.

The gun fight on the beach sputtered to an end as the Irgun fighters were overwhelmed and forced to surrender. Meanwhile the *Altalena* steamed for Tel Aviv, hugging the coastline and exchanging fire with the Israeli warships.

In his office in Tel Aviv, Ben-Gurion's face hardened as he received news of the action. Begin's actions amounted to a rebellion.

There could be only one response.

Bomb the Altalena? *A Jewish ship?*

It was unthinkable. At his command post at Sde Dov, Boris Senior agonized over the order he had received. He was to prepare three aircraft to make bombing attacks on the *Altalena* while she steamed in darkness toward Tel Aviv.

The South African pilot had already sworn allegiance to the IDF and considered himself an Israeli. He was duty-bound to comply with the order, but he knew that when the moment came he would find a way out. He would either deliberately miss with his bombs or he'd disable his aircraft. "I could never bomb my fellow Jews," Senior wrote later.

That night Senior was sent out in the darkness to circle the ship, flashing the navigation lights, making a show of strength. Instead of bombing the ship, he would intimidate the *Altalena's* crew into surrendering.

It didn't work. The ship ignored the aircraft, just as she ignored the menacing warships hounding her. The *Altalena* continued her desperate run to Tel Aviv.

More orders went out. The 101 Squadron at Herzliya was alerted for a bombing and strafing mission against the *Altalena*. In addition one of the C-46s from Ekron with a team of bomb-chuckers was assigned to make a run on the ship.

At the Herzliya fighter base, Stan Andrews was vehement. He flatly refused the order. "I came here to kill Arabs, not Jews," he declared.

Andrews wasn't alone. A groundswell of protest swept through the air force. To a man, the pilots said, *Hell no!* They wouldn't take up arms in a civil war.

Which left the IDF commanders with two options: Court-martial the rebellious pilots or discharge them from the service.

As it turned out, neither was necessary.

———

Aboard the *Altalena*, Begin was becoming desperate. He gave the order to Captain Fein, an ex–US Navy officer: Beach the *Altalena*. Drive her ashore on Tel Aviv's downtown beachfront.

Begin was betting that IDF forces would be unwilling to attack a Jewish ship in full view of the public and of the UN truce observers.

It was a bad bet.

Begin was standing on the deck watching the lights of Tel Aviv's beachfront swell in size. Captain Fein was driving the LST through the shallow water toward the beach. And then, with a great lurch, the ship ground to a halt.

The *Altalena's* hull had snagged the wreckage of a sunken Aliyah Bet ship from the 1930s, *Tiger Hill. Altalena* was dead in the water. She was a hundred yards from the Tel Aviv beach.

A motionless target.

The sun rose. Crowds swarmed to the beach to watch the spectacle. From his headquarters, Ben-Gurion ordered chief of staff Yigael Yadin to take the ship by force.

Fighting broke out along the shore and in the streets. IDF troops and bands of Irgun and Stern Gang fighters opened fire on each other. Rounds of fire sizzled through the streets. Glass shattered. Bullets pinged into buildings.

Tel Aviv residents ran for cover. They shuttered their windows and closed businesses as a pall of fear gripped the city. The same question was on everyone's lips: *Is Israel in a civil war?*

On the beach, IDF gunners scurried to set up artillery pieces. The on-scene commander was a tough officer named Yigal Allon, a former commander of the Palmach—the elite commando force that had only recently been integrated into the IDF. Allon radioed the *Altalena's* captain to surrender.

Monroe Fein refused.

Irgun men were unloading equipment from the ship when the IDF machine gunners opened fire. Then the heavy mortars opened up.

The first rounds seemed to be a warning, exploding in geysers near the ship. As the rounds drew nearer, Begin ordered the Israeli flag lowered on the ship's masthead and a white surrender flag raised. No one seemed to notice. The shelling continued. The geysers erupted closer and closer to the ship.

And then it happened. A shell exploded into *Altalena's* hull. Flames gushed from the belly of the stricken ship.

Watching the mayhem from his bridge, Captain Fein worried that the fires would reach the holds where the explosives were stored. He gave the order: *Abandon ship.*

Bullets pinged in the ship as volunteer fighters and crewmen jumped into the water, some swimming, some boarding small boats. After the last of the wounded had been evacuated, Menachem Begin left the *Altalena*. From his clandestine radio station Begin ordered his men *not* to resist the IDF.

Later he would say, "My greatest accomplishment was not retaliating and causing civil war."

─────

The first light of dawn spread over the Tel Aviv seafront. Bewildered Israelis came down to the beach to gape at the destroyed ship. Smoke billowed like a funeral pyre from the hulk of the *Altalena*. The charred ship looked like a symbol from a lost war.

People wept. Others cursed the leaders of both Haganah and Irgun. They were furious that Ben-Gurion had ordered the destruction of the ship and caused the deaths of their fellow Jews. They lambasted Begin for rebelling against the government, causing an unnecessary bloodbath.

IDF forces had rounded up most of the Irgun fighters still in the city. The chief of staff sent the order to disband all Irgun units in the IDF. Former Irgun fighters would be dispersed among other IDF units.

In all, sixteen Irgun fighters and three IDF soldiers had been killed in the confrontation. To Israelis still numb from a month of war with the Arabs, it was a senseless tragedy.

─────

The fight for the *Altalena* was over, but the volunteers were still fuming that they had been ordered to attack the ship. Until now most had seen the infighting between the Israeli factions as a political squabble. It was a running joke among the volunteers: put two Jews together, and you have five political parties.

But this was about more than politics. The *Altalena* affair was a blood feud that could have ripped the new country asunder.

The day after the seizure of the ship, two hundred grim-faced volunteer airmen trooped down to the Yarkon Hotel, a five-minute walk
from the Park Hotel. The four-story hotel had been appropriated for the
air force headquarters. The building was surrounded on all sides by rolls
of barbed wire. Armed sentries inspected the papers of each airman at
the front gate.

Dressed in neatly pressed khakis with the twin silver leaf insignia
of a lieutenant colonel, Haman Shamir stood smoking a cigarette while
the airmen filled the room.

The Bagel Lancers remembered the time in Panama when Shamir
came to quell the mutiny after Bill Gerson's and Glen King's crash in the
overloaded C-46. They recalled Shamir's calm, resolute voice.

Now they were hearing it again.

Shamir began by telling them that the government had absolute
knowledge that Irgun intended to cache the weapons on the *Altalena*
for their own use, possibly in a coup against the government. The pilots
should have obeyed the order to bomb the—

He was interrupted by angry voices. The room filled with a buzz of
heated dissent. Irate pilots and crewmen yelled that they would never
accept such an order.

Shamir lit another cigarette and waited for the clamor to subside.
Then he continued in his calm voice. The Irgun was an army within an
army, he said. They had promised to obey government orders, but then
they broke that promise. There had been no choice but to stop them.

Again Shamir stopped speaking. He let the pilots say their piece.

Stan Andrews, the California artist, declared that he would not,
under any circumstances, participate in a civil war. Nor would he take
up arms against other Jews.

A dozen other airmen yelled out their agreement. Nobody could
make them fly! In fact, they would refuse to enter another cockpit until
the fighting between factions in Israel stopped.

And so on.

Shamir let them finish. Okay, he said, they had made their feelings clear. And he understood. "You have my word that if you feel that

strongly about not taking part in operations against the Irgun you will not be required to do so."

And that was it. The airmen exchanged glances and shrugged. In a sentence, Haman Shamir had defused another potential rebellion. Instead of killing Jews, they would go back to fighting the Arabs.

———

Facts on the ground. It was an expression the sweating and disheveled senior IDF officers had heard many times during the thirty-day truce.

Now they were hearing it again.

Ben-Gurion had brought them together in the sweltering conference room at the defense ministry in Tel Aviv. To Ben-Gurion, "facts on the ground" had a specific meaning. It meant the borders of Israel would be determined *not* by the original UN partition plan. The final shape of Israel would be defined by the territory Israeli forces occupied when a final cease-fire took place.

If the war ended now, most of the Negev would go to the Arabs. Scores of Jewish settlements and villages would be stranded in Arab territory. Israel would be left with even less territory than in the original partition plan.

There was only one way to change the facts on the ground, Ben-Gurion told them. When the truce expired on July 9, Israeli forces must be poised to attack. Shove the Arab Liberation Army out of the central Galilee. Break the Egyptian grip on the Negev. Push the Egyptian Army all the way back to the border in the Sinai.

During the previous desperate battles, the Israelis had fought a holding action. They'd tried to defend what territory they could from the advancing Arabs.

This time would be different. They would take the offensive.

But first they had to neutralize the Arabs' overwhelming air power advantage. The air force would launch carefully coordinated surprise attacks on July 8—the evening *before* the truce expired.

A dozen utility planes—Norsemans, Bonanzas, Fairchilds, Austers— all crewed with bomb-chuckers, would attack the Egyptian positions along the main highway into the Negev. A bomber-configured C-47 Dakota would hit the Syrian Army that was massing on the east shore of the Jordan River.

The biggest—and most important—surprise attack would be by the 101 Squadron Messerschmitts. They would strike the Egyptian air base at El Arish. The strike that had been canceled back in May in order to hit the Egyptians at Ishdud.

It would be a flagrant violation of the UN cease-fire, of course. Neither Ben-Gurion nor his commanders were concerned about such a fine point. Israel was fighting a war of survival.

Playing by the rules could be fatal.

―――――――

Despite all the careful planning, none of the surprise attacks succeeded. In the haze and gathering darkness of July 8, the gaggle of slow-moving utility planes sent to bomb the Egyptian positions on the Negev highway couldn't find their targets. One chucked its bombs on an Israeli kibbutz by mistake. Another became lost and had to dump its bombs in the sea.

The crew of the Dakota bomber, all Machal airmen and none familiar with the Israeli countryside, got lost. After blundering in the darkness around the Jordan River, the crew returned with their bombs to Ramat David.

The surprise attack on El Arish didn't get off the ground. The maintenance team at Herzliya hadn't been able to produce four flyable fighters in time for an evening mission.

The Messerschmitts would take off at dawn.

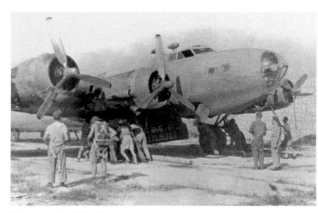

Mitchell Flint with Norseman. *Mitchell Flint Collection.*

Hammers B-17 before a mission. *IDF Archives.*

Chalmers "Slick" Goodlin with the Bell X-1 rocket ship. *Bell Helicopter Textron via Smithsonian National Air and Space Museum (NASM 92-15613).*

Czech-built Messerschmitt (Avia S-199). *Mitchell Flint collection.*

101 Squadron pilots with Messerschmitt: L-R on cowling—Maury Mann, Ezer Weizman, Red Finkel. On wing—Bill Pomerantz, Sandy Jacobs, Sid Antin. Standing: Syd Cohen, Chris Magee (in bandana), Giddy Lichtman, Leon Frankel, Leo Nomis. *Mitchell Flint Collection.*

Lou Lenart, Gideon Lichtman, Modi Alon with the Czech Mule. *Mitchell Flint Collection.*

The Big Bear: Ray Kurtz in a C-54. *Smithsonian National Air and Space Museum (NASM 9A13757).*

P-51D Mustang. *Mitchell Flint Collection.*

C-46 Curtiss Commando. *Mitchell Flint Collection.*

AT-6 Harvards configured as dive bombers. *Mitchell Flint Collection.*

The Red Squadron emblem
designed by Bob Vickman
and Stan Andrews.
Mitchell Flint Collection.

101 Squadron pilots hand-flying: L-R Ezer Weizman, Maurice
Mann, Sid Antin, Intel officer Dave Croll. *Mitchell Flint Collection.*

Modi Alon chases an Egyptian bomber
over Tel Aviv June 3, 1948. *Credit IAF
(https://en.wikipedia.org/wiki/Modi_Alon#/
media/File:IAF_First_Victories_June_3_1948.
jpg) Public Domain.*

Canadian ace John McElroy. *Mitchell Flint Collection.*

101 Squadron commander Modi Alon. *Mitchell Flint Collection.*

Mitchell Flint with P-51. *Mitchell Flint Collection.*

Red Squadron pilots assembled: L-R Back row: John McElroy, George Baker, Rudy Augarten. Standing: Arnie Ruch, Sandy Jacobs, Caesar Dangott, Denny Wilson, Jack Doyle, Ezer Weizman, Syd Cohen, Maury Mann. In helmet Sid Antin. Front row: Wayne Peake, Lee Sinclair, Sye Feldman, Jack Cohen, Bill Pomerantz. *Mitchell Flint Collection.*

Israeli Spitfire fighter. *Mitchell Flint Collection.*

Ezer Weizman in cockpit of a Spitfire. *Mitchell Flint Collection.*

Rudy Augarten in the cockpit. *Budd Davisson, FlightJournal.com.*

"Strange Encounter": Flying a Messerschmitt, Rudy Augarten shoots down an Egyptian Spitfire Oct. 16, 1948. *Courtesy of artist Roy Grinnell.*

Aaron "Red" Finkel with Messerschmitt. *Joshua Finkel collection.*

Chalmers "Slick" Goodlin with a Messerschmitt. *... F Archives.*

Israeli troops capture Beersheba, Oct. 1948.
Credit Mendelson Hugo. https://commons.wikimedia.org/ wiki/File:Beersheba_1948.jpg (Public Domain).

Canada's leading ace George "Buzz" Beurling.
Department of National Defence Canada. (https://commons. wikimedia.org/wiki/File:George_Beurling_Vancouver_1943. jpg) Public Domain.

Altalena burning off Tel Aviv. *Israel GPO. (https://commons. wikimedia.org/wiki/File%3AAltalena_off_Tel-Aviv_beach.jpg) Public Domain.*

Iraq Suwedan fortress under siege (blurry image). *Credit Palmach Archive. (https://commons.wikimedia.org/wiki/File%3AIraq_Suwaydan_1.jpg) Public Domain.*

Ben-Gurion visits the Red Squadron. L-R Giddy Lichtman, Modi Alon, Syd Cohen, Ben-Gurion. *Credit IAF (https://en.wikipedia.org/wiki/Modi_Alon#/media/File:Ben_Gurion_at_First_Fighter_Squadron.jpg) Public Domain*

101 pilots Lee Sinclair and Red Finkel. *IDF Archives*

Maury Mann, Ezer Weizman, Bill Pomerantz with the Mule. *IDF Archives.*

"Wild Man" Chris Magee with a Messerschmitt. *IAF Archives.*

Red Squadron brothers in arms: Syd Cohen, Gideon Lichtman, Modi Alon, Ezer Weizman, Arnie Ruch. *Credit Oritay 200. https://en.wikipedia.org/wiki/Modi_Alon#/media/File:Syd_Cohen.jpg.*

Israeli Piper Cub in Negev. *Credit: Wikimedia Commons. (https://commons.wikimedia.org/wiki/ File%3ANegev_advance.jpg) Used under the Creative Commons Attribution-Share Alike 3.0 Unported license. Public Domain.*

Beechcraft Bonanza configured as a bomber. *Mitchell Flint Collection.*

Downed Egyptian Spitfire May 15, 1948. *Credit Shershel Frank, (https://en.wikipedia.org/wiki/1948_Arab–Israeli_War#/media/File:Egyptian_Plane_TA_1948.jpg) Public Domain.*

25

The Guy with the Cape

Lou Lenart was assigned to lead the four-ship raid on El Arish. The second and third Messerschmitts would be flown by the California duo, Stan Andrews and Bob Vickman. The chubby American, Bill Pomerantz, was in the fourth fighter. Except for Lenart, none had flown a combat mission in Israel.

In the thin morning light the pilots strapped into the Messerschmitts. Each knew the stakes had just gone up. The surprise attack on El Arish the night before had fizzled, and now the truce had expired. Forget the surprise. The Egyptians would be expecting them.

From the cockpit of his fighter, Stan Andrews could see Vickman in the adjoining camouflaged revetment. Vickman was trying to fold his lanky six-foot-two frame into the cramped cockpit.

The two had sometimes discussed what it would be like to bail out of the Messerschmitt. The only volunteer who'd done it was Milt Rubenfeld. But Rubenfeld was a short guy, not like Andrews or Vickman. Their long-legged frames squeezed into the Messerschmitt like compressed springs. Even then Rubenfeld hadn't made a clean exit. He'd hit the tail of the Messerschmitt, receiving serious injuries.

Everyone in the squadron liked Stan Andrews. The twenty-five-year-old volunteer had a happy disposition, and his boyishly handsome face seemed to wear a perpetual smile. In the mix of volunteers at Herzliya,

Andrews and his artist sidekick, Vickman, fit solidly in the camp of the true believers.

Over drinks at the beer garden, the idealistic Andrews would talk about saving his people and defending Israel and righting the wrongs of the past two thousand years. Even the hard-nosed veterans, men like Finkel and Antin, had to grin. Andrews could have been a comic book hero of the forties—a guy with a cape and an upraised fist.

Andrews was not a fighter pilot, at least by experience. He had flown B-25 twin-engine medium bombers in the Pacific during WWII. Andrews had little experience in single-engine fighters like the Messerschmitt.

Andrews didn't seem worried. The guy with the cape was ready for action.

The engines of the four Messerschmitts were running. Lenart had briefed them to be ready to take off without delay. Egyptian fighters could appear at any time to catch them on the ground.

Approaching the end of the runway, the pilots went through their takeoff check lists. The memory cue was TMFRTS—Trim, Mixture, Flaps, Release brakes, Throttle, Set tail wheel locked. Overlooking any of these items could be disastrous on takeoff roll.

Each pilot signaled by hand that he was ready. Lenart nodded and taxied his fighter onto the dirt runway. A cloud of reddish dust swelled behind Lenart's fighter as it hurtled down the runway. Lenart's rudder flapped left and right, countering the Messerschmitt's vicious yawing tendency.

It was Andrews's turn. He lined up on the dirt runway and pushed the throttle forward. Andrews tried to keep the fighter going straight. He was still unable to see over the long nose.

Orange groves whirred past him on either side. Andrews worked the rudder pedals, raising the tail.

And then the fighter swerved to the left. A millisecond too late Andrews shoved in the right rudder pedal. The nose of the Messerschmitt was already pivoting hard, the right wing dropping.

Stan Andrews was no longer in control.

The right wingtip dug into the runway. The fighter's nose burrowed into the ground. Propeller blades snapped. Andrews saw the earth rising to swallow him.

The Messerschmitt hit the ground upside down. The fighter was sliding down the dirt runway tail first. The earth was grinding away at the canopy a few inches from Stan Andrews's head.

Finally it stopped. No more grinding sounds. No more engine noise. Just the ominous crackling of tortured metal.

Andrews was hanging upside down. His head was jammed against the top of the canopy. He was trapped beneath an overturned fighter loaded with 70-kg bombs and high-octane fuel gushing over the ground.

For fifteen minutes Stan Andrews hung in the Messerschmitt. He didn't know whether he would be blown up or burned alive. He heard voices outside the cockpit, but nothing was happening.

More time passed. More fuel dripped on the ground.

Finally the trapped pilot could feel the airplane rocking, tilting, and then hands were grabbing him, tugging him out of the crushed cockpit. A group of Yemenite farmers who lived near Herzliya used long poles to flip the airplane back onto its wheels. The bombs were still attached to their wing mounts.

Andrews was beat-up and shaky. His head had taken a hit when the fighter landed on its back.

The overturned Messerschmitt was still blocking the runway, and the last two fighters—Vickman and Pomerantz—had been unable to take off. Lou Lenart was making a slow orbit of the field, burning precious fuel while he waited for the others to take off.

The farmers and the crash crew managed to shove the damaged fighter off the runway. Andrews heard the sound of a Messerschmitt thundering down the strip, lifting into the morning sky. Seconds later the last Messerschmitt roared past.

Andrews watched the dark specks of the fighters grow smaller. The pilot of the number two fighter in the formation was Bob Vickman. What Andrews didn't know on this pale summer morning was that it was the last time he would see his friend.

Lou Lenart was calculating his fuel. Even when fully fueled, the Messerschmitt held barely enough fuel to fly to El Arish on the Sinai border, drop bombs and strafe the base, and make it back to Herzliya. The twenty minutes he'd wasted waiting for them to move Andrews's fighter off the runway had reduced his fuel supply to a critical state.

Lenart made a gut-wrenching decision. They couldn't strike El Arish this morning. It seemed like a jinx. This was the second time he'd been assigned to lead a strike on the Egyptian air base. Both times the mission fell through. The first was back in May, when at the last minute, headquarters ordered Lenart's four-plane flight to attack the Egyptian column at Ishdud.

Now what? Each Messerschmitt still had two bombs and full canisters of cannon and machine-gun ammunition. They were flying southwestward. Down below Lenart could see the Egyptian-held port of Gaza. Surrounding the harbor was a complex of Arab army facilities. In the harbor was a freighter that appeared to be in the process of unloading supplies.

Legitimate targets. Not as valuable or as morale-crushing as a surprise raid on the El Arish air base, but better than dumping their bombs in the Mediterranean.

Lenart signaled Vickman and Pomerantz to follow him.

It was another uncoordinated, ineffective attack. None of the three pilots knew what the others were doing or how they would egress from the target. Each pilot was on his own. Even before the first bomb struck the ground, Egyptian antiaircraft guns opened up.

Lenart released both his bombs, then swung back to make a strafing pass. As he pulled off the target and pointed his nose northward, he glimpsed the profile of another Messerschmitt—Vickman, he guessed—making a strafing run.

The needle of Lenart's fuel gauge was touching zero when the wheels of his Messerschmitt plunked back down on the runway at Herzliya.

As he taxied to the camouflaged revetment, he saw that Pomerantz had already landed. Standing by the revetments, the two men smoked cigarettes while they waited for Vickman to return.

Minutes went by. There was no drone of an incoming Messerschmitt. No familiar shark-like silhouette coming from the south. The sky was empty.

More time passed. Vickman's Messerschmitt would have consumed all its fuel. For Lou Lenart, it was a replay of his first mission, the four-plane strike he'd led at Ishdud. One aircraft damaged on the runway, another never to return.

For the rest of the day they waited for news about Vickman. Search planes went looking for him. It was dangerous duty because Egyptian warplanes were on the prowl.

They found nothing. Intel listeners picked up no Arab radio communications about an Israeli aircraft shot down or a pilot captured. None of the Israeli ground units in the southern sector reported seeing a downed fighter.

Bob Vickman had disappeared.

By instinct and conditioning, fighter pilots tended to think of themselves as indestructible. It was a deliberate delusion. It shielded them from the pangs of self-doubt, and made them effective warriors. The pilots at Herzliya were no exception.

But a dark cloud of doubt filled the dining room at the Falk House that night. Missing was the high-spirited banter, the jibes and insults that only brothers in arms could fling at each other. They spoke in low tones, speculating about what happened to Vickman. There was a chance that he was captured or hiding somewhere.

Most knew in their gut that Vickman was surely dead.

Those who arrived after the first phase of fighting hadn't known the quiet and scholarly Eddie Cohen, the squadron's first combat loss back in May. But they all knew Vickman. He was one of the pilots who w carousing in Tel Aviv and played pranks on them and swiped cars in town. Losing Vickman was a reminder that despite the high jinks and frat-boy antics they were playing a deadly game.

Stan Andrews was mostly silent. He'd spent part of the day being checked out by the clinic and treated for his head injury. Not until that afternoon did someone tell him about Vickman.

Now Andrews sat slumped in a chair. Gone was the big grin and choir boy expression. He didn't look like a guy with a cape and clenched fist. Stan Andrews looked like someone who'd lost his best friend.

———

Just as affected was Lou Lenart. Though no one was saying it, everyone knew this was the second four-plane strike that Lenart had led—and in which he had lost a wingman. The circumstances in each action were spookily similar: a last-minute change of targets, a messy, uncoordinated attack, every man for himself, each returning to the base alone. Or not returning.

No one was blaming Lou Lenart except, perhaps, Lenart himself. Back when the new fighter squadron was still forming, command of the unit had been informally shared between Modi Alon and Lou Lenart. Because Lenart was the more experienced combat aviator—he'd flown Corsairs in the Pacific War while Alon had seen little wartime action— Alon took administrative command and deferred to Lenart in tactical matters. Since then Alon had been officially designated as the 101 Squadron commander.

In the days following the loss of Bob Vickman, Lou Lenart changed. He seemed to lose his fighter-jock swagger, his zeal for combat. Quietly, without fanfare, he was transferred to the headquarters of the IAF— Israeli Air Force. Lou Lenart would fly no more combat missions.

———

Nor would Stan Andrews, at least in the Messerschmitt. Though he ˜overed from his head wound, Andrews also had changed. It was as ˜gh losing Vickman—the other half of the California duo—had altered his judgment. "Stan started doing stupid things," recalled Baron Wiseberg, who had taken the name Ben-Zvi and was deputy commander at Ramat David.

Andrews's erratic behavior worried squadron commander Modi Alon enough that he ordered Andrews grounded. In a few weeks Andrews was transferred to the Ramat David base as operations officer with the newly formed 69 Squadron, which would be equipped with bombers.

Andrews remained grounded with orders *not* to fly on operational missions. But in a few weeks Stan Andrews was morphing back into his old crusader role.

Grounded? Not the guy with the cape and clenched fist.

=26=

The Nazi Revenge

With the war raging on all fronts, there was no time to grieve for a lost comrade. Calls were coming from besieged ground forces for air support. One of the calls was from the Israeli commander on the northern front where Syrian warplanes—dive-bomber-configured North American AT-6 Harvards—were pounding Israeli positions.

It was the morning after the loss of Bob Vickman. A pair of Messerschmitts scrambled from Herzliya and headed for the battle zone, a place called Mishmar Hayarden near the Sea of Galilee.

In the lead fighter was Maury Mann, a former Spitfire pilot and Battle of Britain veteran. A short, chubby Brit, Mann had an inexhaustible catalog of raunchy songs with which he kept his squadronmates entertained at their nightly gatherings.

On Mann's wing was a slender young veteran of the South African Air Force, Lionel "Les" Bloch. This was the first combat mission of the war for the two men. From 3 miles out the pilots spotted exactly what they were looking for: a pair of Syrian AT-6 Harvard dive bombers.

Most of the Messerschmitts by now were equipped with radios. Mann slid in behind the first Harvard. "I'll take this one," he called to Bloch, "you take the other."

Mann knew the Harvards were slower than the Messerschmitt, but they could be deadly. He was sure that each carried a rear gunner. He also knew that the gunner's firing angle would be limited to either side, not directly rearward or below.

Rapidly overtaking the slower aircraft, Mann opened fire. In the hail of cannon and machine-gun fire from Mann's Messerschmitt, the Harvard spewed debris. Abruptly it plunged straight down into the mottled landscape near the Sea of Galilee.

Mann pulled up and looked around for Bloch. "We were over what was then the Syrian border, and I couldn't see him," Mann recalled. He had last seen Bloch chasing the second Harvard across the border into Syria. Bloch wasn't answering Mann's radio calls.

Mann was low on fuel. He made a quick sweep of the area. He spotted no wreckage, no column of smoke except from the Harvard he'd just shot down.

Dejectedly, Mann turned back to Herzliya. Without Lionel Bloch.

———

Airmen hated mysteries. They especially hated mysteries concerning the disappearance of buddies and squadronmates.

The gloom at Herzliya that night deepened as the Red Squadron dealt with the latest loss. In the two days they'd been back at war, they'd lost two pilots.

The next day another South African, ex-medical student Syd Cohen, was flying a Messerschmitt on a search mission over the northern front. He looked around for signs of Lionel Bloch's fighter. He peered down at the Sea of Galilee, the surrounding shoreline, the adjoining Hula swamp. Cohen spotted nothing that looked like the remains of a Messerschmitt.

Cohen was puzzled. It seemed that Bloch had chased his quarry deep into Syria. And then *something* happened. Was he shot down by the Harvard's tail gunner? Antiaircraft fire?

Or something else?

Cohen had a hunch. He swung the Messerschmitt out over the coast. He squeezed the machine-gun trigger. He felt the rattle of the two nose-mounted 13.1-mm guns. Almost immediately he felt something else.

A vibration that wasn't there before.

Something was wrong, and Cohen had a strong suspicion what it was. He landed back at Herzliya. Cohen climbed down and walked around to inspect the nose of his Messerschmitt.

What he saw made him grimace. All three propeller blades had pieces blown off them. The blades looked as if they'd been hit with . . . *bullets*. His own bullets.

Cohen had come within millimeters of shooting off his own propeller. It meant the synchronizing system of the machine guns—the gearing that allowed the guns to fire *between* the propeller blades—was flawed.

As the realization dawned on the pilots that the Messerschmitt's guns could be shooting off their propellers, the pilots' feelings about the Czech Mule swelled into a full-scale hatred. And it inspired yet another uncomplimentary label for the airplane: *the Nazi Revenge*. The goddamned Nazi Revenge was killing *them*!

Much later, as more evidence came in, their conclusion seemed founded. A high-ranking Egyptian Air Force officer reported that on the day of Vickman's disappearance, a low-flying Lysander utility plane had come under attack by a pursuing Messerschmitt. Just as the Messerschmitt came within firing range, it abruptly flew into the ground and exploded.

Given the timing and location, it could only have been the fighter flown by Bob Vickman. Vickman had either inadvertently flown into the ground or, as now seemed likely, shot off his propeller with his first burst of fire and then crashed.

A postwar Syrian report revealed that a Messerschmitt—it had to be Bloch's—crashed inside Syria while pursuing an AT-6. The pilot was badly injured and died in captivity. Though the unidentified body was returned to Israel in 1949, not until many years later would it be learned that it was in all likelihood that of the crashed pilot, Lionel Bloch.

Did the Messerschmitt kill Vickman and Bloch? There was little proof, but the pilots needed no further convincing. The unsynchronized machine guns were just one more evil attribute of the Nazi Revenge. It became a standard procedure at the beginning of every combat mission to test fire the guns.

Just in case.

On the hazy evening of July 18, with half an hour to go before the next cease-fire, Rudy Augarten took off on his first combat mission in the Messerschmitt.

It was nearly his last.

Augarten hadn't flown fighters—or scarcely *any* airplane—during the three years after the war while he'd been a student in international relations at Harvard. His flying skills were rusty when he arrived at České Budějovice to check out in the Messerschmitt.

Augarten surprised everyone, including himself. He was a quick study, requiring only six hours of training in the Arado two-seater and the Messerschmitt before his Czech instructors declared him combat ready. He'd joined the 101 Squadron at Herzliya in June during the first truce and then sat on the ground during most of the Ten Day Campaign waiting his turn to fly a combat mission.

In Augarten's rush to embark on his first mission, he overlooked an item on the TMFRTS checklist. It was the last T—the one that stood for Trim. He neglected to reset the elevator trim tab from full nose up to the takeoff setting.

Early in the takeoff roll—*too* early—the Messerschmitt's nose pitched up. "One of the wings stalled, going to the left side," Augarten recalled. "Then I realized what happened. I was fighting the stick. The plane was in a slow turn to the left. There was a tree 200 to 250 yards off the runway, and they tell me my wing brushed through."

Somehow Augarten managed to stay airborne. He joined up with Modi Alon and Sid Antin in the other two Messerschmitts. It was Antin's first combat mission also. In a loose V formation the three fighters headed for the southern front, where the entrenched Egyptian Army was trying to seal off the Negev Desert from the rest of Israel.

In the evening light they had no trouble seeing the target. An Egyptian convoy of trucks and armored vehicles was strung out for a mile in the desert south of Beersheba. One after the other the Messerschmitts peeled off, diving on the enemy column.

The attack was quick and deadly. Before the Egyptian gunners could train their fire on the Israeli fighters, the raid was over. Smoke and flames billowed from destroyed vehicles. Panicked troops were scattering in every direction from the burning vehicles. The mission was successful, and now it was over.

And then it wasn't.

Sid Antin's voice crackled over the radio. "Hey, Rudy, there's something on your left!"

Augarten saw them—two sleek shapes, down low, flying parallel to the shoreline. Even at this distance he could see that they were Spitfires. Augarten swung his Messerschmitt's nose hard to the left, descending, sliding in behind the pair of fighters. As he drew nearer he recognized the Egyptian roundel markings on the Spitfires.

For Augarten, it was like old times. In the last months of WWII he'd flown air-to-ground missions, strafing and bombing the enemy on the ground. On one of his last missions, he'd capped it off with a swirling air-to-air engagement, shooting down two German fighters. German *Messerschmitts.*

Now he was flying, of all things, a Messerschmitt. Chasing Spitfires.

"I put my gun sight on one," Augarten recalled, "pulled the trigger, and . . ."

Nothing. He squeezed the trigger again. The guns didn't fire.

It was a fighter pilot's nightmare—the guns weren't working! Then it came to him. "For Christ's sake," he snapped on the radio, "I'm out of ammunition." Augarten had used up his cannon and machine-gun ammo on the Egyptian column at Beersheba.

Modi Alon still had ammunition. Augarten watched from the side while Alon poured a hail of bullets into the Egyptian fighter. Belching fire, the Spitfire went into a shallow dive, then pancaked onto the desert floor in a plume of dirt and smoke.

The second Spitfire pilot, suddenly aware of his nearness to death, was in a frantic diving turn trying to escape. Luck was with the Egyptian. The Messerschmitts were too low on fuel to pursue him. Alon gave the signal to break it off.

It should have been one of those triumphant RTBs—returns to base—that fighter pilots dream of. After strafing and bombing an entire enemy convoy, they'd capped off the mission with a dramatic air-to-air shoot-down. Modi Alon had added number three to his list of enemy kills.

It didn't get any better than this. As usual the rest of the squadron would be standing by the runway watching, counting the airplanes. *Did all three make it back? Did they score any kills?*

Here was the answer. The Messerschmitts roared in low over the field in tight formation. Pulling up one after the other, each set up for the approach and landing. They'd land to the west, into the setting sun.

It was then the triumphant RTB turned into a demolition derby.

The wheels of Modi Alon's fighter had no sooner bonked down on the dirt runway when the fighter took a hard swerve to the right. In a swirl of reddish dirt the Messerschmitt veered off the strip, dragging its left wingtip, careening sideways in a landing gear–bending stop at the edge of the strip.

Next came Sid Antin. He landed hard on the main gear and bounced back in the air. When the Messerschmitt came back down, it porpoised along the runway, nose up, nose down, sliding to a stop with its tail pointing skyward.

Close behind came Rudy Augarten. Squinting against the setting sun, he didn't see Antin's fighter doing its headstand until the last instant. Augarten roared back into the air, barely clearing the disabled airplanes on the field.

He was nearly out of fuel. In the waning light Augarten had to orbit the field while ground crewmen dragged Antin's fighter off the runway.

When Augarten finally plunked the Messerschmitt down on the dirt strip, he could see the audience lined up by the revetments. They had seen the whole show. The Red Squadron pilots were grinning and pumping their arms.

Augarten knew it was going to be a rough night at the bar.

= 27 =

Swifty

The beam of Al Schwimmer's flashlight swept the bomber's darkened cockpit. The panel, the knobs and switches, even the seat mechanism were all unfamiliar to him. They were just as unfamiliar to Leo Gardner, who was climbing into the B-17 with him.

No matter. They'd figure it out. This was the last B-17 of the four Schwimmer had acquired. It hadn't been ready to join the other three on their epic flight to Žatec.

The ex-USAAF officer who sold the airplane to Schwimmer had collected his money and then reported the deal to federal agents. Now the bomber was parked under guard at Tulsa with a sign posted on it: SEIZED BY THE US GOVERNMENT.

But Schwimmer still had connections. The guard at Tulsa was a young mechanic who happened to be a friend of a friend of Schwimmer's. When Schwimmer and Leo Gardner arrived at Tulsa on the rainy evening of July 10, the B-17 was unguarded. And ready to fly.

Only one problem remained. Neither Gardner nor Schwimmer had ever flown a B-17.

＝＝＝＝

For the past week the net had been closing around Al Schwimmer. The black sedans and men in fedoras were swarming around each of his bases. With the publicity surrounding the escape of the first three B-17s, Schwimmer was now squarely in the Feds' crosshairs.

Before they shut him down, Schwimmer wanted to pull off a final mass fly-out of his remaining warplanes. In one swoop he intended to escape with the two Constellations at Millville, still tied up in State Department red tape, plus four Douglas A-20 Havoc twin-engine attack planes that he'd bought and positioned in Ft. Lauderdale, Florida, and the fourth B-17, the one still in Tulsa, Oklahoma, that hadn't been able to join the first three on their escape to Žatec.

There was only one way the plan could succeed. Each of the airplanes would have to be cranked up at their separate bases and flown away simultaneously. Schwimmer selected an out-of-the-way field in New York State, the Westchester County airport at Rye Lake, for their refueling stop before the transatlantic crossing.

Schwimmer knew the Feds would quickly figure out who was behind the operation. By then it would be a fait accompli. The airplanes would be gone. So would Al Schwimmer.

The fly-out date was set for July 11, 1948. Schwimmer instructed his crews in Millville to fuel the two Connies for a long-range flight. The four Havoc attack bombers in Fort Lauderdale were ready and the hired pilots in position.

Schwimmer's carefully coordinated fly-out came apart before it got off the ground. His suspicions that informants had been planted inside his organization were confirmed. Someone at Millville tipped off federal agents that the two grounded Constellations were being fueled for a short "check flight." When the agents swarmed onto the field, they discovered that the airliners' tanks were filled to the top, ready for a long-range journey.

Both Constellations were seized and placed under guard.

At the Fort Lauderdale airport, Schwimmer's hired pilots showed up as ordered, carrying their flight gear. When they approached the A-20 Havoc bombers on the apron, they stopped in their tracks. Parked near the airplanes were black sedans. Gathered around each sedan was a squad of unsmiling federal agents. The Havoc bombers were going nowhere.

That left the lone B-17 in Tulsa.

A soft rain was falling as Schwimmer and Gardner sat in the darkened cockpit and familiarized themselves with the instruments and switches.

After half an hour they were ready. They managed to start the engines. Then they ignored the urgent radio calls from the control tower as they taxied the big four-engine bomber to the runway.

Showing no lights, the big bomber roared down the runway and climbed into the night sky. They filed no flight plan and made no radio calls.

In the early morning, Schwimmer was standing on the tarmac at the Westchester County, New York, airport. It occurred to Schwimmer that snatching the bomber and flying it to New York was the easy part. Getting it across the ocean required the skills of someone *really* clever and gutsy.

Schwimmer already had his man picked out.

==========

Swifty Schindler felt his anxiety level ratcheting up. At a country airport like Westchester, the Flying Fortress stood out like an elephant in a parking lot. It was Sunday, and curious passersby were driving onto the airport to gawk.

This was the "special mission" for which Al Schwimmer had summoned Schindler back from Žatec. That was over a month ago. Since then Schindler had been waiting for this B-17, the last of the four, to be made airworthy. This one was even more beat-up than the three B-17s that had already flown to Czechoslovakia.

The number four engine leaked oil during the flight from Tulsa. A crew of Schwimmer's mechanics was working on the engine, getting it ready for the long leg across the Atlantic.

As Schindler watched them working on the airplane, he kept a watchful eye on the crowd and the cars. So far, no black sedans, no Feds. But the word was already out. A team from the *New York Herald Tribune* was in the airport asking questions, taking pictures.

Schindler told them nothing. He knew if the press was here, the FBI wouldn't be far behind.

While they waited for the bomber's engine to be repaired, one of the new crewmen, a nonpilot, was staring at the beat-up airplane. He said to Schindler, "Man, you have a lot of guts to fly a plane like this."

Schindler laughed. "No, you have a lot of guts to be flying with me. I've never been in the cockpit of a B-17." He saw the young man's face go pale.

It was true. As experienced as he was, Schindler was a transport flyer, not a bomber pilot. But Schindler had extensive multiengine experience, and he was, by nature, an optimist. He'd spent most of the previous two nights studying the B-17 operating manual. In any case, all the B-17 pilots he knew said the B-17 was a pussy-cat airplane to fly. Schindler hoped they were right.

Schindler insisted on taking a familiarization flight with Gardner, whose single flight in the B-17 made him the resident expert. They flew around the pattern a few times and then landed back at the country airport. Schindler's new nine-man crew loaded a collection of mysterious-looking boxes and a spare aircraft engine.

The airport manager seemed surprised when Schindler ordered 3,500 gallons of gasoline to be pumped into the aircraft, enough to keep it airborne for twenty-four hours. With a straight face Schindler told the manager that they were taking off for California on a scheduled training flight.

It was late afternoon, July 11, when the heavily loaded bomber rumbled down the runway again. The crowd at the airport watched the B-17 make a shallow turn to the northeast and gradually vanish in the distance. Only later would someone point out that the airplane didn't seem to be headed for California.

———

Schindler didn't like what he saw ahead. He was four hours into the flight, and darkness was coming. The weather was turning sour. Heading out over the ocean in these conditions was a bad idea.

Just ahead was an airport with long runways, the Royal Canadian Air Force base at Halifax, Nova Scotia. Schindler called for clearance to land.

When he climbed down from the bomber he was met by the deputy base commander—and three armed Royal Canadian Mounted Policemen. They told Schindler that he had just violated Canadian air space and entered the country illegally.

True to his nickname, Swifty Schindler talked fast. He told them he'd been on a training flight, had made a clumsy navigational error, and for safety reasons had decided to land. If they'd just refuel the aircraft and allow him to depart, the matter would be closed and—

The Canadians weren't buying it. News reports had already reached Canada: FBI agents were trying to trace a surplus bomber that had passed through Westchester County Airport in New York. This scruffy-looking ex-military warplane with its civil registration—NL7712M—clearly painted on the fuselage seemed to fit the description. Even more incriminating was the cargo found aboard the aircraft: crates packed with machine guns, ammunition, bomb shackles.

The Canadians impounded the B-17. The crew would be detained while the US State Department was consulted.

Thus began two days of back-and-forth messaging between the Canadian and US governments. The Canadians proposed a compromise. Schindler and his crew would be released if they paid a $100 fine for having illegally entered the country. If Schindler agreed to make the return flight to New York they would provide him with enough fuel for the trip. The B-17 would be met by waiting US government agents.

Nodding solemnly, Schindler agreed.

It took three attempts. On the evening of July 15, Schindler took off, then promptly returned with engine problems. The next afternoon he took off again, escorted by a US Coast Guard aircraft that had come to ensure the B-17 complied with its orders. On takeoff, an engine cowling fell off the B-17. As Schindler headed back to Halifax, two more cowlings flew off, one disappearing in the sea. The Coast Guard monitor plane continued back to the United States.

The next evening the battered Flying Fortress took off again from the Halifax airfield, this time without an escort. As ordered, Schindler turned to the south, in the direction of New York. He continued in that direction until they were out of sight and radar range of their former hosts at Halifax.

Then the B-17 made an abrupt left turn. Two thousand miles ahead waited the Azores.

—————

Schindler knew it would be a close thing. Though the Canadians had provided him with only about five hours' worth of gasoline, Schindler had neglected to tell them that his auxiliary tanks were still nearly full. For the anticipated ten-hour flight to the Azores, he calculated that they would have about a forty-five-minute reserve.

Luck—and a generous westerly wind—stayed with him. The B-17 arrived at the Portuguese Air Force base at Santa Maria in the Azores soon after dawn. They still had nearly an hour's worth of fuel remaining.

The smiling Portuguese air base commander and his staff made Schindler and his crew feel welcome. *Too* welcome, Schindler would later reflect. Instead of refueling and taking off again, Schindler decided to accept the Portuguese hospitality and rest overnight before flying on to Zebra.

It was a fateful decision. While the airmen rested, the American consulate at Ponta Delgada reported the arrival of the B-17 to the US State Department, who quickly determined that it was the fugitive bomber. At the urging of the Americans, the Portuguese impounded the B-17 and arrested the crew.

The next day Schindler and his crew were bundled aboard a Pan Am Constellation and flown back to the United States. Charged with "illegally exporting a warplane," Schindler was prohibited from leaving the country while he awaited trial. A year later a New York court would find him guilty of violating the US Neutrality Act. Schindler's sentence of a year in prison would be suspended.

On Al Schwimmer's desk in New York's Hotel Fourteen lay two issues of the *New York Times*. A July 11 article was headlined: B-17 CARRYING 10 BELIEVED FLYING TO ISRAEL AFTER MYSTERIOUS TAKE-OFF IN WEST-CHESTER. A few days later the paper carried the next installment: B-17 DEFIES CANADA, FLIES ON TO AZORES.

Schwimmer already knew the rest of the story. The B-17 was lost. Schindler and his crew were under arrest. Israel's bomber force had just been reduced by a fourth. The B-17 was irreplaceable because the Feds were shutting down every source of such warplanes.

It meant the end of Schwimmer's operation. As slow-moving as the State Department and the FBI were, they had caught up. Federal indictments were coming down for Swifty Schindler, Charlie Winters, and any day now for Al Schwimmer. Like Schindler, Schwimmer would be banned from leaving the country.

For the rest of the day Schwimmer sat alone in the office, considering his options. Stay in the United States and face charges? Serve jail time? Let the band of volunteers he'd recruited fight Israel's war of survival without him?

Schwimmer knew what he had to do. For months he had been a man without a home. Now he was about to become a man without a country.

The next day Al Schwimmer and Steve Schwartz, the cigar-smoking vice president of Service Airways, boarded a commercial flight for Rome. After a layover and a meeting with Yehuda Arazi, who was negotiating with the Italians for surplus Sherman tanks, they flew on to the Zebra base.

It was like a homecoming. Everywhere Schwimmer went, he ran into volunteers he had recruited in the United States. The field was a beehive of activity—C-46s being loaded, unloaded, or in various stages of maintenance. Messerschmitt fighters waiting to be disassembled and stuffed aboard the transports. He saw the Constellation Sam Lewis had flown from Panama.

Then Schwimmer and Schwartz climbed aboard one of the C-46s for the last leg of the journey. It felt like the culmination of Schwimmer's last nine months of work. The airlift he had put together was taking him to his new home: Israel.

Aharon Remez wasted no time putting the two veterans to work. Al Schwimmer was appointed director of maintenance and engineering for the entire air force. Steve Schwartz was put in charge of personnel for the airlift squadron, which now had an impressive new name: the Air Transport Command.

28

Target Cairo

ŽATEC, CZECHOSLOVAKIA
JULY 10, 1948

Ray Kurtz was a guy who grinned a lot. The oversized, wisecracking ex-B-17 pilot entertained the air crews every night at the Hotel Stalingrad with his offbeat jokes. Like most Jewish kids growing up in Brooklyn in the 1930s, Kurtz knew about anti-Semitism. He'd been called "kike" and "yid" and been bullied by bigger, tougher kids. Then he went through a teenage spurt of growth, metamorphosing into a powerfully built, bear-sized young man. Kurtz became known for being quick with his fists, a reputation that stayed with him throughout the war years and into his later jobs as a cop at Brooklyn's 74th precinct and then as a fireman at Engine Company 250.

Those jobs hadn't been Kurtz's first career choice. Discrimination was a fact in the postwar 1940s. Even after distinguishing himself as a pilot in heavy bombers and covering his chest with medals, Kurtz found that the good postwar flying jobs—airlines like TWA and Pan Am—were closed to Jews.

Then came Service Airways and the war in Israel. And now that he'd landed at the Zebra base in Czechoslovakia, Ray Kurtz was feeling an old stirring inside him.

Parked across the field were the B-17 bombers.

Gazing at them, Kurtz felt himself transported back in time. His WWII bomber, *Flatbush Floogie*, was one of hundreds of B-17s headed

for Germany. He could see again the flak bursts, the mosquito-like silhouettes of Me-109 fighters swarming around them, the thrill—and
terror—of combat over Europe.

Kurtz still hadn't adjusted to his role as a transport pilot. Neither
had his fellow ex-fireman Norm Moonitz or quiet-spoken Bill Katz or
not-so-quiet Al Raisin. They'd all been B-17 pilots. Damn it, they were
bomb-droppers, not trash-haulers.

It was a distinction that sometimes caused friction among the volunteer airmen. One of the ex–bomber pilots, aided by the cheap booze
at the Hotel Stalingrad bar, would make an injudicious remark about
bomb-droppers versus trash-haulers. The bomb-dropper, being outnumbered, always got hooted down.

In any case, most of the trash-haulers were making real bomb runs,
however ungracefully, with the C-46s. All had been flying into harm's
way. No one needed reminding that three of them—Gerson, Cohen,
and Rosenbaum—had already been lost in this short war.

Ray Kurtz's gaze kept returning to the Flying Fortresses at the far
end of the field. As warplanes went, they were a sorry sight—paint peeling, plywood panels where there should be gun turrets, bomb bay doors
sealed shut with a riveted strip. Vital equipment was missing—oxygen
systems, bomb sights, bomb racks, armor, and, especially, guns.

That was changing. Sam Pomerance, Zebra base's aeronautical
engineering whiz, had a team working on the bombers. The work
was going slowly because the C-46s had priority. The cargo planes
were flying round-the-clock supply missions to Israel and required
the most attention.

At Kurtz's urging, Israeli Air Force Headquarters agreed to form a
separate heavy bombardment unit. Assigned as aircraft commanders in
the new unit were the handful of pilots with B-17 experience—Katz,
Moonitz, Raisin. Other airmen with experience in USAAF and RCAF
and RAF bomber units would fill out the B-17 crews. The operations
officer of the new bombing outfit would be none other than the big bear
himself, Ray Kurtz.

Then from Tel Aviv came new orders. The so-called Ten Day War that had begun on July 9 was about to end. Another UN-mandated truce was coming. Before the cease-fire, the IDF wanted to launch a three-front ground offensive.

They wanted the heavy bombers in Israel *now*.

The crews had to scramble. Ready or not, the untested new bomber unit was leaving for Israel. They'd carry with them crews and mechanics, all the makeshift new equipment, plus full loads of bombs that would be put to use after the bombers were repositioned in Israel.

It was then, while he was gazing at the map of the eastern Mediterranean, that an idea took root in Ray Kurtz's mind. Tracing the proposed line of flight with his finger, Kurtz kept noticing something interesting. The route wasn't really that far from . . . *Cairo*. And since they had all these bombs on board . . .

Later it would be argued exactly *where* such an attention-getting idea originated—IAF Headquarters in Tel Aviv or inside the brain of Ray Kurtz. But everyone who knew Kurtz understood that it was his nature to get attention. The crewmen were accustomed to seeing Kurtz parade around the Zebra base with his pet monkey on his shoulder.

Bombing Cairo. It would be the ultimate attention-getter.

And then they decided to raise the ante. As long as they were dropping bombs on something important, why didn't they drop them on *someone* important? And who in Egypt was more important than their playboy king? Farouk I had been one of the prime organizers of the Arab League, the coalition that invaded Israel two months ago.

The top-secret proposal bounced back and forth between Žatec and Tel Aviv. On July 8, Dov Judah, IAF Director of Operations, arrived on a C-46 with the orders authorizing the mission.

The next day came new orders. Scratch the bombing mission. Just ferry the bombers to Israel.

On July 13, Egyptian bombers raided Tel Aviv. Seventeen civilians were killed, and thirty-nine were wounded.

Such a deadly attack could not go unpunished. More orders came from IAF Headquarters. The Cairo mission was on.

Kurtz sent his crews searching for maps and charts. None were to be found in Žatec, at least proper navigational charts that showed the detail they needed. Two volunteers drove into Prague to visit the United States Information Service library. They helped themselves to fold-out map pages from encyclopedias. While they were at it they pulled out guidebook photographs of Cairo's prominent landmarks.

One of the more interesting landmarks was a sprawling building in the center of the city. It was called the Abdeen Palace, and it was the 550-room residence of King Farouk.

—————

It was a peculiar arrangement. Bill Katz, the soft-spoken native of Jacksonville, Florida, had the most wartime B-17 experience and would be the pilot of the lead bomber. Ray Kurtz, as the mission commander, was in the copilot's seat. Watching them like a nervous mother hen was the air force deputy commander, Haman Shamir, who had arrived the day before to accompany the mission.

Kurtz's bomber would hit Cairo. The second two, flown by Norm Moonitz and Al Raisin, would detach from the flight south of Crete and head for their target at El Arish. The lead bomber was the only one fitted with a real bomb sight, although it was a clunky German retrofit model. Sam Pomerance had equipped the other two B-17s with Czech-made gunnery sights—not particularly suited for bombing but better than nothing.

Only the lead B-17 was equipped with an oxygen system, which meant the formation would have to fly *through* any towering cumulus formations instead of climbing to high altitude to fly over the top.

The Flying Fortresses rolled down the runway at Žatec at 10:00 in the morning, July 15. The departure time had been chosen because their time over Cairo would dovetail with the arrivals of two scheduled airline flights. Kurtz hoped—but didn't really expect—that the Egyptians might mistake the big four-engine warplane for an airliner.

Things started unraveling early. Kurtz's bomber lost its attitude gyro—a vital instrument for flying in weather. Then one of the propeller governors froze at 2400 RPM, while the manifold pressure wouldn't go past 18 inches, delivering only half the engine's available power. With the airplane's performance limited, the heavy bomber struggled to climb over the Austrian Alps.

The formation flew into dense clouds over the mountains and had to split up. A hundred miles farther south, nearing the Adriatic coast, they managed to rejoin. And then over Albania appeared a spectacle none of them had seen since 1945: *flak.*

Kurtz couldn't believe it. The goddamned Albanians were shooting at them!

None of the bombers was hit. Bill Katz veered the flight back over the Adriatic, and they flew on for 500 more miles, paralleling the coast of Greece. Abeam the island of Crete, with darkness falling, Moonitz and Raisin flashed their Aldis lamps, and their two B-17s separated from the formation. They were headed for their targets at El Arish and Gaza.

Ray Kurtz watched the two bombers disappear in the gathering darkness. Moonitz and Raisin were supposed to hit their targets before Kurtz arrived over Cairo. The idea was that it would to create a diversion. Now Kurtz worried that it might have the opposite effect. All of Egypt might be alerted. Antiaircraft gunners would be ready and waiting. If Cairo were blacked out, precision bombing would be impossible.

They were approaching 25,000 feet. Kurtz had chosen that altitude because it was high enough to keep them above most antiaircraft fire and provided the best defense against fighters.

Kurtz became aware of a drowsy, lightheaded sensation. Something was wrong, and even in his own fogginess he knew what it was. *The damned oxygen system.* It was a makeshift rig, using tanks of welder's oxygen, all that was available at Zebra. The welder's oxygen tanks lacked the pressure to supply the system.

They pressed on, woozy but conscious, using the emergency pressure control on the oxygen systems. Katz steered toward Cairo, homing in on the navigational beacon the British had conveniently installed at their Fayid Air Base. The B-17 was approaching Cairo along the same arrival route flown by scheduled airline flights.

On the horizon they saw the twinkling lights. Cairo was on the nose. And—a huge relief to the B-17 crew—the city wasn't blacked out. Over the air traffic frequency Jack Goldstein, the radio operator, heard a controller on the ground calling. Would the large plane approaching the Almaza airport identify itself?

Goldstein didn't answer.

The controller repeated the call. Was this the scheduled TWA flight? Were they requesting landing clearance? Would they please acknowledge?

Still no answer. The B-17 continued to Cairo. Tension mounted in the cockpit. They were 20 miles out. Was the controller alerting anti-aircraft batteries? Were fighters on their way up?

Ten miles. The city of Cairo lay sprawled out before them, brilliantly illuminated by thousands of lights. *Too* brilliantly, Kurtz realized. He and his bombardier had worried that if the city were blacked out, they wouldn't pick out their bombing aim point on the ground. Now the aim point—the Abdeen Palace—was a needle in a vast flickering haystack.

It didn't matter. The bombardier would have to locate the aim point the best he could. They would make only one pass over the target.

The bomb bay doors swung open. Kurtz heard a sound he hadn't experienced since 1945: the *swoosh* of air rushing through the open belly of the bomber.

At his station in the glass nose of the B-17, Johnnie Adir, the bombardier, peered through the bombsight. Adir was giving steering signals to the cockpit over the intercom: *Straight ahead . . . ten degrees right . . . hold that heading . . . Bombs away!*

The B-17 lurched as 2.5 tons of high-explosive bombs released from the racks.

Katz swung the B-17 hard left to a northerly heading, toward the open sea. He shoved the nose down, descending to an altitude where they could breathe without oxygen. Half a minute later, amid the lights below, they saw the chain of orange-white explosions pulsing across the center of Cairo.

The darkened interior of the B-17 erupted in spontaneous cheering.

Then something new: *searchlights*. Long shafts of light, a dozen of them, stabbed the night sky, probing for the lone bomber. Bursts of antiaircraft fire began flashing randomly around them.

It was a good time to leave Egypt. From their altitude it was impossible to determine how much damage they'd done. Had they hit Abdeen Palace? Johnnie Adir said he doubted it, given the quirkiness of the German bombsight he was using.

They didn't care. Nothing could suppress the crew's excitement. They'd bombed Cairo and gotten away with it. Even if their bombs hadn't hit the palace, they knew they'd come close. Close enough to scare the hell out of King Farouk.

The other two B-17s flown by Moonitz and Raisin were having trouble. Their primary target, the Egyptian air base at El Arish, was blacked out. The pair turned back to the coast and made a bomb run over the Egyptian complex at Rafah, between Gaza and the Sinai border.

Rafah was clearly visible. And so were the B-17s. It was 9:40 p.m., almost the same time Kurtz's bombs were falling on downtown Cairo, and just as in Cairo, searchlights were lighting up the sky. Flashes of antiaircraft fire opened up around them.

For Moonitz and Raisin, whose WWII bombing missions had all been in daylight, the searchlights were an unnerving new experience. Grimly they droned straight ahead, rocked by the antiaircraft fire, trying to avoid the probing beams of light.

Both made it. Their bombs released, the B-17s continued out to sea. Looking back, the airmen saw the explosions erupting in the Egyptian complex.

All three B-17s landed at Ekron Air Base within minutes of each other. On the tarmac the ecstatic volunteers clapped one another's shoulders and punched the air with clenched fists. Forgotten for the moment was the tension and numbing fatigue of the eleven-and-a-half-hour mission, the clunkiness of the bombsights, the nonworking oxygen system. They'd just made history. By God, they'd bombed Cairo!

By morning, they had the results of their efforts. Johnny Adir's assessment had been correct. They *didn't* flatten Abdeen Palace. The bombs exploded on the palace grounds and in the surrounding neighborhood. They'd destroyed a railway line and killed thirty Egyptians. King Farouk was unnerved but otherwise still intact.

The psychological effect was far more devastating. Cairo was thrown into a panic. For the rest of the night air raid sirens had wailed, searchlights pierced the darkness, antiaircraft guns blazed at the empty sky. Frightened Egyptians headed en masse for the countryside.

The next day the Egyptian press added to the hysteria by reporting a "mass terror raid." According to the media, hospitals and schools and public places had been specifically targeted, causing hundreds of casualties. The attack, by all reports, had been an atrocity of cataclysmic proportions.

In Tel Aviv, news of the raid on Cairo was received with unbounded joy. Israelis were cheering in the streets. Bartenders poured free drinks at the Park Hotel bar and the Gallei Yam.

In his home in Keren Kayemet Boulevard, David Ben-Gurion had been awaiting the news from the raid. When the report reached him, the white-haired prime minister's face broke into a wide grin. It was exactly what Ben-Gurion needed to hear.

Three days remained before the cease-fire. Israel had just sent a message to the enemy. No Arab city was safe from Israeli bombs.

The Usual Suspects

ŽATEC, CZECHOSLOVAKIA
JULY 14, 1948

Sam Lewis had been smitten by the Constellation since the day in early WWII when he first glimpsed that sleek shape. He'd flown the big four-motored Connie throughout the war, then as a captain for TWA, and then for the bogus airline LAPSA. RX121—the only one of the three Connies bought by Schwimmer to make it out of the United States—was the flagship of Israel's new Air Transport Command.

Now Lewis was peering up at the circling Constellation. He didn't like what he was seeing. He was standing on the ramp at the Zebra base, and he could tell that only one of the Connie's landing gear was extended. The other gear and nose wheel were still retracted.

With Marty Ribakoff in command, RX121 had made her seventh trip to Ekron Air Base in Israel. The Connie was returning to Žatec with twenty passengers, including women and children, families of Israeli consular personnel in Czechoslovakia, and deputy air force commander Haman Shamir.

The flight from Ekron had been uneventful until they neared the Yugoslav coast. A Russian-built YAK fighter intercepted them off the Adriatic coast. After looking the big transport over—it still bore the Panamanian LAPSA markings—the fighter pilot waggled his wings and departed.

A few minutes later, as though the brush with the fighter had been a catalyst, the trouble began. The Constellation's main hydraulic line burst. When Ribakoff lowered the landing gear for landing at Žatec, only the left main gear came down. The right gear and the nose gear hadn't moved.

For two hours Ribakoff circled the Žatec air base. By radio he talked with mechanics on the ground while Jimmy Weddell, the flight engineer, went down into the belly of the aircraft and tried to manually crank the other landing gear down.

Nothing worked. The left gear remained locked down. The right gear stayed up.

Sam Lewis and engineering chief Sam Pomerance watched helplessly from the ground. The Connie looked like a one-legged swan droning in circles over the field. It was the worst possible landing configuration, coming in on a single landing gear. The opposite wingtip would drop to the ground and the airplane could cartwheel.

Sam Lewis was racking his brain. How could they get the left landing gear to unstick and retract?

And then Lewis had an idea. He told Pomerance he was going to take off in one of the squadron's BT-13 single-engine training planes. He'd fly beneath the Connie, jam his wingtip against the stuck landing gear, and force it to retract. Of course the BT-13 would probably lose part of its wing, in which case Lewis would bail out.

Pomerance stared at Lewis as if he were seeing an escapee from an asylum. *You're going to do what with your wingtip?* Surely Lewis wasn't serious.

Lewis was. When Pomerance saw Lewis strapping on his parachute, he intervened. Sam Pomerance was nearly as burly as Lewis. He grabbed Lewis's arm and told him there was no way Lewis was going to fly that BT-13. Let Ribakoff land with the wheel down.

They scuffled some more. Red-faced, eyes blazing, Sam Lewis finally backed off.

Minutes later, Lewis and Pomerance and an audience of dozens stood watching Ribakoff bring the four-engine transport down to the runway.

Ribakoff did everything right. He kept the left wing low, gently alighting on the one main landing gear. The spectators on the ground, including Lewis and Pomerance, held their breath. *Will the one gear hold the weight of the airplane? Or will it fold?*

It didn't fold, at least not right away. The big airliner floated down the runway for a thousand feet, balancing on its one gear. Ribakoff strived valiantly to hold the right wing up.

Finally, as everyone knew it would, the right wingtip descended to the ground. The transport veered off the runway. The single gear collapsed and a torrent of sparks and dirt and torn metal spewed behind the airplane. She ground to a stop on her belly, leaving in her wake four freshly dug trenches across the grass field. Almost immediately the passengers and crew were clambering out the doors.

There was no fire. Given the circumstances, it had been as perfect a landing as anyone could have made. The beautiful Constellation was wrecked. A broken main spar jutted through the top of the right wing like the point of a spear. Her propeller blades were bent back at a grotesque angle. Panels of belly and wing skin were ripped from the airframe and strewn in the grass.

Sam Pomerance's mechanics crawled over the airframe, peering at the damage, shaking their heads. It would be a huge task, perhaps an impossible one, to make RX121 flyable again.

Off to the side stood a lone, slump-shouldered figure. Sam Lewis didn't look like Smilin' Jack any longer. He looked like a man who had just lost his sweetheart.

———

At Ekron Air Base in Israel, Ray Kurtz was wearing his trademark big bear grin. He was still on a high from the Cairo bombing mission. Kurtz and his crews had pulled off the most dramatic raid of the war so far.

Then, a few minutes before midnight on July 15, came new orders. They were leaving. The big, easy-to-recognize Flying Fortresses had become the Egyptian Air Force's most sought-after target. IAF Headquarters sent the order: the bombers would be dispersed to different bases in the north to lessen the chance of all three being caught in a surprise air raid.

But first, they had to fly another mission.

The sun hadn't yet risen as Kurtz hauled himself back into the B-17. Fewer than twelve hours had elapsed since they'd rained bombs on King Farouk's palace. Now they were headed for El Arish, the Egyptian air base Moonitz and Raisin had been unable to find in the darkness last night.

This time they had no difficulty spotting the intersecting runways, the rows of parked Egyptian warplanes. Their 6 tons of high explosives pounded the field.

The bombers were gone before the surprised antiaircraft gunners opened fire. No Egyptian Spitfires came up to challenge the Flying Fortresses.

By the end of the day everyone—crews and IAF command—realized that dispersing the bombers to three different bases was a bad idea. Remez countermanded his original order. All the B-17s would be based at Ramat David, the former RAF base in the north of Israel.

During the three-and-a-half days before the July 19 truce, the B-17s flew twenty-three combat sorties, dropping over 100,000 pounds of explosives. They flew in formation, escorted by Messerschmitts from Herzliya.

The bombers' early tactic was to come in low to avoid detection, shoot up the area with the bombers' multiple gun stations, and then come back to drop bombs from altitude. Seeing the big warplanes with the Star of David emblazoned on the wings roaring over their lines was a dramatic morale-booster for the IDF brigades on the ground.

One day remained before the fighting ended. Before the truce went into effect, it was time to send one last message to the enemy.

─────────

Bomb another Arab capital?

Norm Moonitz nodded agreeably. Hell, why not? Moonitz had recovered from his injuries in the C-46 crash last May. He liked the idea that they had bombed the capitals of Egypt and Transjordan so far. Why not Syria?

But this mission would be different. Instead of a three-ship raid, Moonitz would be flying a one-bomber attack.

On the early morning of July 18, Moonitz's B-17 rumbled down the runway at Ramat David Air Base. He banked to the right and pointed the big bomber toward Damascus.

"We made one pass," Moonitz reported. "I was afraid because we only had one B-17 with not a lot of armament. We had no armor . . . we had those crummy Czech guns with the old ring sights."

It was enough. After plastering the city, Moonitz turned his attention to the nearby military airfield of Al Mezze where the Syrian AT-6 Harvard dive bombers were based. He dumped another load of bombs on the airfield and "then on the way back we dove down and we strafed everything we could see."

The raid accomplished its mission. Just as with the raids on Cairo and Amman, the psychological effect on the Syrians counted for more than the actual damage.

And it was time for another air force ritual. The three-bomber force was about to become an official squadron of the air force. To go with the new status, the outfit needed an official label. It would be the same peculiar democratic process by which the 101 Squadron named itself. The crew members of the bomber outfit were told to come up with a designation for their squadron.

They did it the traditional way. They had a party. They kicked ideas around. Some were mundane, some controversial, some utterly tasteless.

The next day the bomber crewmen announced their new designation: 69 Squadron.

Sixty-nine? At headquarters level there were frowns, coughs, a few knowing winks. The fliers stuck to their guns. Some insisted the label came from a decorated USAAF WWII bomber squadron. Kurtz and Moonitz struggled to keep a straight face, saying it was a sentimental number for them. It came from their old New York Fire Department Engine 69.

No one believed them. They believed them even less when the squadron adopted the slogan, "69 Is More than a Number."

To go with the designation, the 69 Squadron took a macho nickname, one that would continue into the next century: *The Hammers.*

———

Emmanuel Zur looked like an English dandy—three-piece suit, buckskin shoes, a trilby hat. He was a thirty-seven-year-old Israeli agent and pilot who had a stack of passports in various names and a portfolio of bogus companies through which he made acquisitions for the IDF.

Zur's mission in Europe was to find attack airplanes. *Real* attack airplanes that could come in fast and low and put a bomb load precisely on target. The Messerschmitt was a poor air-to-ground platform. At best the fighter could carry only a couple of puny 70-kg bombs. Nor was the B-17 an effective low-level attack aircraft. Its most potent use was in terrifying Arab soldiers on the ground.

The twin-engine Douglas A-20 Havoc bombers that Schwimmer purchased in the United States would have been suitable—if they had not been seized by the Feds. Likewise the two dozen P-47 Thunderbolt fighter-bombers Schwimmer had lined up in Mexico—if the purchase hadn't been nixed by the Haganah when they signed the Messerschmitt deal.

On a cloud-covered early July day in Cambridge, England, Emmanuel Zur stood gazing into an open hangar. A smile came to Zur's face, and he nodded his approval. *Yes.* These were the very objects he had been seeking these past six weeks.

Parked in the hangar were two war-surplus de Havilland Mosquito reconnaissance bombers.

The Mosquito was precisely the warplane Israel needed—a fast, multirole fighter-bomber. Both warplanes were in good shape. Zur quickly closed the deal, paying $18,000 for each through one of his cover companies.

Zur's only remaining task was to get the Mosquitoes to Israel. He knew exactly whom to call.

John Harvey could have been a character out of pulp fiction—war hero, spy, deal-maker, daredevil pilot. He was a dapper ex-RAF flier with a ginger-colored handlebar mustache. In Britain he was going by the alias "Terence Farnfield." Harvey's boss was the Israeli agent named Emmanuel Zur.

On the morning of July 5, 1948, Harvey took off from Cambridge in the first Mosquito. Though he had filed a flight plan to Exeter, Harvey turned south and headed toward France.

It wasn't a smooth flight. Because of a fuel system malfunction, he was forced to land at Nice, on the south coast of France. Harvey was promptly arrested.

Zur came to his rescue, paying off French officials, and the next day Harvey was on his way again. After a refueling stop in Ajaccio, Corsica, he was headed for Israel, 800 miles to the east.

Harvey barely made it. Low on fuel, he dropped into Haifa on the coast instead of continuing to Ekron further inland. Nervous Israeli gunners opened fire, thinking the Mosquito was an Egyptian warplane. Dodging flak, Harvey put the Mosquito down on the Haifa airport—and was promptly arrested. Harvey, a.k.a. Terence Farnfield, went to jail for the second time in two days.

Hours passed and numerous phone calls were exchanged between Israel and Britain before it was finally determined that Terence Farnfield was, in fact, one of them.

A few days later, on July 16 in Ajaccio, Corsica, a hired pilot was taking off in the second Mosquito acquired by Zur. Twenty feet in the air, both engines stopped. The Mosquito slammed back into the ground beyond the end of the runway. In a shuddering crash, the fighter-bomber was destroyed.

But it didn't burn. It was discovered that the fuel tanks were empty.

The hired pilot survived the crash, receiving a fractured wrist and a broken nose. He said he hadn't checked the tanks that morning because he had personally supervised the fueling the night before. When he last saw them, the tanks were full.

To John Harvey and Emmanuel Zur, it was worrisome news. They were certain someone had sabotaged their Israel-bound Mosquito. But who? Arabs? Brits?

Radio operator Harold Livingston was in Ajaccio that day on his way to the Zebra base. He spoke with the portly, gout-ridden Commandant Latour who ran the airfield. The commandant assured him he was investigating. The commandant would find the cause of the accident.

Livingston had to laugh. It reminded him of Claude Rains's famous line in *Casablanca:* ". . . round up the usual suspects."

=== 30 ===

The Beaufighter Caper

Emmanuel Zur was still on the hunt for warplanes. During the early summer the Israeli agent had tracked down six surplus warplanes of immense value to the Israeli Air Force: Bristol Beaufighter attack planes. They were stashed at an airfield near Manchester.

Wearing his trademark trilby hat and buckskin shoes, Zur walked across the apron of the Ringway airport to the darkened hangar where the warplanes were stored. Even in the dim light Zur could see that the Beaufighters were in rough shape. Not at all like the two Mosquito fighter-bombers he had purchased.

It didn't matter, Zur decided. They could be fixed. They had to be.

The Beaufighter was a brute of a warplane. Designed as a long-range heavy fighter, it was used by the RAF and commonwealth air forces first as a night fighter and then as an antiship and ground-attack plane.

Unlike sleek fighters like the Spitfire and Mustang, there was nothing sleek about the Beaufighter. Two big radial Hercules engines protruded from the wings ahead of the Beaufighter's blunt nose and cockpit like the claws of a lobster. Despite its looks, the Beaufighter was a fearsome ground-attack machine. It was big and tough and armed with a lethal combination of guns and bombs.

Zur was facing the same problem in Britain that Al Schwimmer had in the United States. Smuggling war birds out of the UK was a dangerous cat-and-mouse game, made even more difficult by the small size of the country. Any interest in ex-military aircraft drew the immediate attention of the Ministry of Civil Aviation and Scotland Yard.

Zur inspected the six Beaufighters more closely. Each had been stripped of its armament. Zur already had a solution for that. He knew of a source through which he could buy cannons, machine guns, and racks to make the Beaufighters true war birds.

The guns and bomb racks couldn't be installed on the Beaufighters in Britain. They would have to be smuggled to Israel in some kind of transport aircraft. Such a mission would be dangerous and difficult, of course.

Another job for Terence Farnfield.

John Harvey, a.k.a. Terence Farnfield, was on his way to Israel again. It was July 20, and this time he was flying a chartered four-engine Handley Page Halifax bomber conveniently reconfigured as a civilian transport. When he chartered the Halifax, Harvey had declared that its purpose was to fly cargo inside Europe.

Stashed in the back of the Halifax were the spare parts and armament for the Beaufighters: forty-one 20-mm cannons, thirty-seven machine guns, four spare engines. The Halifax also carried the hardware needed to convert the transport back to the heavy bomber it had once been.

Harvey had no intention of returning the Halifax to its owners.

Like many of John Harvey's adventures, this one came to a calamitous end. After the eight-hour overwater flight from Ajaccio, Harvey found most of Israel blacked out, including his destination, Ekron Air Base.

It was a too-familiar story. No one on the ground was answering on the discrete radio frequency.

Nearly out of fuel, Harvey plunked the Halifax down on the undersized Sde Dov airport on the outskirts of Tel Aviv. The heavy bomber rolled off the end of the short runway, sheared its landing gear, and bounced across the sand dunes to the darkened beach.

The Halifax was wrecked. Harvey survived the crash, and so did most of the Beaufighter parts and munitions. Pieces of the trashed bomber, including its four Merlin engines, would find their way into other IAF warplanes.

Two days later the imperturbable Harvey, using one of his multiple passports, was slipping back into the UK.

But the stakes were going up. British agents had already been informed that the vanished Halifax bomber had ended up on a beach in Israel. The bloodhounds at Scotland Yard and the Ministry of Civil Aviation were hot on the trail of John Harvey and Emmanuel Zur.

The Beaufighters were nearly ready to go. One major problem remained. How was Harvey going to get them out of Britain?

As usual, Zur had a solution.

⸻

It was simple, Zur explained. They'd make a movie.

Movie? It was a zany idea. Just the kind of zany idea that John Harvey loved.

Zur had already laid the groundwork. He founded another bogus company called the Airpilot Film Company. Its purpose was to produce a movie about a wartime New Zealand Beaufighter squadron.

Zur had most of the pieces in place—actors, production equipment, even a script. The plot included a love story in which the lead actress had a tearful parting from her sweetheart as he and his squadronmates scrambled in their Beaufighters on a dangerous mission against the Japanese. The writers didn't let themselves be sidetracked by niggling details such as the fact that New Zealand's Beaufighters never actually flew in the Pacific.

Meanwhile, with money funneled to him by Zur, Harvey worked on the last missing piece: the airplanes. At the Ringway airfield, using his Terence Farnfield identity, he concluded the purchase of the six Beaufighters. The price for all the aircraft was $36,000, which included the cost of making them airworthy.

Unlike the two nearly new Mosquitoes, the Beaufighters were war-

surplus basket cases and needed extensive overhauls. The worst of the
six was finally used for spares to bring the others up to flyable shape.

Near the end of July 1948, the overhaul crew released four of the
five Beaufighters. Harvey and three hired pilots flew them to the Haddenham airfield in the southern UK, where the film shoot would begin.

Crowds of spectators gathered to watch the filming. The actors
rehearsed jogging out to the Beaufighters, parachutes flapping against
their backsides. Beaufighters taxied around the field followed by cam-
eramen in open cars.

Then, a setback. On the evening of July 28, one of the pilots Harvey
had hired, an ex-RAF airman named Mike Campbell, was delivering the
last of the refurbished Beaufighters. On approach to landing Campbell's
Beaufighter lost an engine and spun into the ground. Campbell was
killed instantly. The Beaufighter was destroyed.

The crash added urgency to the mission. The next morning Zur's
people went ahead with the film shoot. An even larger audience assembled at the field, including curious inspectors of the Ministry of Civil
Aviation. After the crash of Campbell's Beaufighter, they had a keen
interest in the activities of the remaining Beaufighters.

The cameras zoomed in on the climactic departure scene. The tearful heroine clutched at the arm of the heroic pilot. The pilot gazed wist-
fully at her, then looked across the field at his waiting comrades. A long
passionate kiss, and then the pilot tore himself away.

Love yielded to duty, honor, country. The camera followed the hero
in his rush to the waiting Beaufighter, then closed in on the tears flowing
down the heroine's cheeks.

Similar tears were flowing down the cheeks of the spectators. In the
gloom and hard times of postwar Britain, it was just what they needed:
a schmaltzy romance, heroes they could admire, *real* war birds like the
ones that defeated the Axis only three years ago.

Minutes later came the *noise*—the chuffing, deep-throated grunt of
the Bristol Hercules radial engines rumbling to life. The crowd watched,
mesmerized, as the Beaufighters throttled up, all four of them, and

went hurtling down the runway. The combined roar of the eight engines echoed from the walls of the airport buildings.

The thrum of the engines was still in their ears as the spectators watched the warplanes join in formation. The Beaufighters were supposed to bank and come roaring back at low level for the cameras. An old-fashioned buzz job.

Any minute now.

The shapes of the Beaufighters grew smaller. The spectators kept waiting. The shapes dwindled to specks. Then they vanished altogether.

The spectators were mystified. *Where did they go?*

No one knew. Someone said they'd heard that the rest of the film was going to be shot in Scotland because the terrain looked more like New Zealand. Which made sense, most of them agreed. That's where the Beaufighters must have gone, to Scotland in the north.

Not until later would it occur to any of them, including the watch-dogs of the Ministry of Civil Aviation, that the last time they saw the Beaufighters they were flying *south*.

———

John Harvey knew he'd had his last view of England for a long time. After this caper neither he nor Terence Farnfield nor any of the entities on his various passports would be welcome here. Not outside of a jail cell.

Harvey and his crew of hired pilots dropped into Ajaccio, Corsica, where they were met by the portly Commandant Latour, leaning on his cane and hobbling on his gouty leg.

The script hadn't changed. The Frenchman winked, smiled, asked no awkward questions. The most important detail—the matter of payment—had already been handled by Emmanuel Zur.

After another refueling stop in Yugoslavia, the Beaufighters made the five-hour hop to Israel. En route Harvey couldn't help thinking about the previous two calamitous arrivals he'd made—being nearly shot down by Israeli gunners at Haifa, and then finding his destination airport, Ekron, blacked out and unresponsive to his calls.

This time everything clicked. From a hundred miles out the arriving Beaufighters were in contact with the controllers at Ekron. No one fired on them. The warplanes landed in broad daylight. They were quickly hustled off to hangars to be fitted with the guns and bomb racks Harvey had earlier brought in the Halifax.

———

Twenty-two-hundred miles to the northwest, a dark, bubbling anger was spreading through the British Ministry of Civil Aviation. *Someone* had filed a flight plan from Haddenham, the Beaufighters' movie shooting field in southern England, to Scotland.

But not until several hours *after* the warplanes had taken off.

Since then there was no report of Beaufighters landing anywhere in Scotland. Or anywhere else in the UK.

In belated increments they learned the truth. The four attack planes had been sighted in Corsica. Then Yugoslavia. By now there was no question as to what happened to the Beaufighters. Like the Mosquito and the Halifax, they had been smuggled to Israel.

In violation of the embargo. By the same smuggler.

When questioned by the press, an official at the Ministry of Civil Aviation would only say that they had been "fairly bamboozled." "Scotland Yard and the International Police Commission are on the case," he declared. They would catch the bamboozler. He was a shadowy criminal known as Terence Farnfield.

———

On the opposite side of London, another event was attracting international attention. The first summer Olympic Games since 1936 opened in London's Wembley Park. Army bands played while 4,104 athletes from fifty-nine countries marched into the stadium. Britain's royal family arrived to join the 85,000 cheering spectators.

One of those *not* watching the games was pilot Mike Flint, who had just finished Messerschmitt training in Czechoslovakia. Flint's London cousin Audrey, however, dutifully mailed his postcard to his mother.

London, July 29, 1948

Dear Mom,

Hard to believe I am finally here. It's the perfect place for me to have come to after graduating Berkeley. King George opened the games today. The ceremony was spectacular—2,000 pigeons set free and a 21-gun salute.

I plan on meeting our English cousins in the next few days and see some events with them. I love and miss you and hope you are strong and well.

Your son, Mike

Meeting the Red Squadron

HERZLIYA AIRFIELD, ISRAEL
AUGUST 1, 1948

Duffel bag in hand, Mike Flint climbed down from the dirt-streaked lorry. It was late afternoon. Heat waves still shimmered from the winding tar road that led to the fighter base.

The place wasn't like any military field Flint had ever seen. The single dirt runway looked as if it had been freshly bulldozed between groves of orange and fig trees. What appeared to be a control tower was perched atop a rusting water tank. A collection of tents and stone block buildings comprised the base's headquarters. Along one side of the dirt runway Flint could see the snouts of Messerschmitt fighters protruding from their camouflage netting.

Flint had hitched a ride out here. He knew the 101 Squadron had recently moved to this sleepy village north of Tel Aviv. The second UN truce had gone into effect July 19. No airplanes were moving on the field. Except for a few mechanics working on the fighters, the Herzliya base looked quiet.

Flint walked up the path to the command hut. The door was open, and inside he could see a fair-haired man in a neatly pressed bush shirt writing at a desk. Flint rapped on the door frame. The man flashed a brief smile and waved him in.

Flint already knew about Modi Alon, the twenty-seven-year-old commander of the 101 Squadron. He knew that Alon and Ezer Weizman were the only two Israelis in the otherwise all-foreign volunteer squadron. Flint had also heard that the charismatic young officer was a national icon. Alon had been one of the four pilots on the historic first combat mission that halted the Egyptian Army's advance just short of Tel Aviv. Four days later, Alon startled the residents of downtown Tel Aviv by blasting two Egyptian bombers out of the sky directly over their heads.

Now the young officer commanded Israel's lone fighter squadron. Everyone knew that he'd been appointed not because of his experience—most of the pilots, including Flint, had more combat time than Alon—but for the simple reason that he was Israeli. It made sense to Flint. It *was* their country, their air force, their war.

Still, Flint was surprised on first meeting Alon. He had expected a measure of pridefulness, perhaps arrogance. But listening to Alon talk about the squadron and its mission, Flint sensed a maturity that exceeded Alon's age. Modi Alon didn't seem like most of the hell-raising fighter pilots Flint had known.

Alon rose from his desk. It was time, he said, that Flint met his fellow volunteers. For a moment Alon's voice shed some of its seriousness. A hint of a smile flashed over his face.

"You may find these guys a bit . . . different," he said.

It was a five-minute jeep ride. They drove along a rutted road, up the small hill above the field, and then onto a tarred road leading past a few scattered dwellings. Alon wheeled into a lane that stopped at the entrance to a white plaster building with a red tile roof. In the front garden stood a large acacia tree.

The Falk House was a rambling old guest house that had been taken over by the 101 Squadron. The two wings of the building contained the small rooms that were each shared by two of the pilots.

They found most of the pilots hanging out in the screened dining hall. As Alon introduced the new pilot, Flint could feel the curious eyes sizing him up. He knew from experience what to expect. It was the same in every fighter outfit. The US military had a universal term for newcomers: FNGs. It stood for Fucking New Guys.

By tradition, FNGs went to the end of the line. FNGs could expect a barrage of good-natured insults and pranks, and they remained at the bottom of the pecking order until the next FNGs showed up.

Alon's early remark—"You may find these guys a bit . . . different"—came back to Flint. These guys weren't just different. Some were outrageous.

One of the most outrageous was the tall ex-Marine, Chris Magee, who Flint learned would be his roommate at the Falk House. He knew Magee by reputation. As a Marine Corsair pilot in the Pacific during WWII, Magee had earned the nickname Wild Man. He was an ace with nine confirmed kills and a Navy Cross to his credit.

Magee still looked like a wild man. He was wearing a red bandana around his head. He had a pistol strapped to one hip and a trench knife on the other. Deeply tanned from the desert sun, Magee looked more like a pirate than a pilot.

Not until later would Flint learn that besides being a mercenary fighter pilot, Chris Magee's other professions included bootlegger, journalist, and bank robber.

Another wild man was Leo Nomis. Flint already knew Nomis from České Budějovice. Nomis had finished Messerschmitt training sooner than Flint had and arrived at Herzliya a week ago. He was a burly Californian with blunt, dark features.

Leo Nomis had flown Spitfires in the RAF as a member of the American volunteer Eagle squadron. Nomis was proud of his heritage as a Native American—his father was half Sioux—and in the RAF he had painted an Indian head on the nose of his Spitfire. After the war Nomis had made his living as a fly-for-hire crop duster, barnstormer, and fighter pilot.

Like Magee and most of the other non-Jews, Nomis was a mercenary. How much more the mercenaries were paid than the others would become a sensitive subject in late-night drinking sessions.

In his short time in the squadron, Nomis had demonstrated a couple of notable qualities: He was a hotshot pilot who loved to fly. Nomis also loved to drink. Already his binges were becoming the stuff of legend in the 101 Squadron.

Not all the volunteers were as outrageous as Magee and Nomis. Rudy Augarten had arrived in early July, having trained in the Messerschmitt in the same group as George Lichter and Chris Magee. In the mix of rowdy fighter jocks, the mild-mannered Augarten seemed more mature than the rest. Neither a hard drinker nor boisterous prankster, Augarten wasn't inclined to brag about his wartime exploits or embellish combat stories.

Not until Flint got to know Augarten did he learn about his wartime record, that he'd been shot down soon after D-Day, was captured, and then escaped from the Germans. Augarten returned to combat and flew ninety-two more missions, gunning down two German fighters.

Sprawled in a chair in the dining room was Alon's fellow Israeli, Ezer Weizman. The tall, lanky sabra watched the happenings in the room with a bemused smile on his face. Flint learned that the twenty-five-year-old Weizman was a fun-loving warrior who liked flying, partying, chasing women, and playing outrageous pranks on his squadronmates. Especially on FNGs like Mike Flint.

Ezer Weizman, in fact, came from privileged circumstances. The Weizmans were a distinguished Russian émigré family and the closest thing to royalty that Israel had. Ezer's uncle was the celebrated statesman Chaim Weizman, who would be the first president of Israel.

Within his first day, Flint noticed something else about this bunch. None bothered with military niceties such as saluting or yes-sirring or deferring to seniors. The pilots called the squadron commander "Modi" and accorded him no special treatment. As far as Flint could tell, that was fine with Modi Alon.

No one except Alon wore any semblance of a uniform. There were no indications of rank. A few wore cotton flight suits with the sleeves rolled up. Others were dressed in shorts and sandals. Some, like Gideon Lichtman, wandered around shirtless. Like Wild Man Magee, most were burned dark bronze from the summer sun.

All had pistols strapped to their hips. Flint didn't know if the side-arms were for personal defense or a gesture of bravado. Soon enough, he had his own.

━━━━━━

Flint became a member of the squadron, complete with the fighter-jock swagger, the black humor, the pistol on his hip. In this lull between battles, the fighter pilots hung out at the beachside bars and knocked back beers in the Falk House courtyard and walked the Herzliya airstrip at night, listening to the jackals howl from the nearby sand dunes.

Sometimes when they were filled with booze and bravado, they spouted their usual one-liners:

Hell, it's that kind of war.

You know, a guy could get killed doing this.

How do I get out of this chickenshit outfit?

And so on. They were the same one-liners heard in every American combat outfit in WWII.

But here in Israel there was another one-liner—a question—that came up with regularity, usually after the second or third beer.

Why are you here?

At this the airman would scrunch his eyes and light a cigarette and gaze out at the darkened orange groves. It was an uncomfortable question for young men not disposed to soul-baring statements.

Most fell back on one of the easy clichés. "I wanted to help my people." Or, "It was just the right thing to do." A few went so far as to say, "I wanted to fight for a righteous cause."

Which came closest to the truth. It was the reason they had stood in long lines on wintry streets to enlist on the day after Pearl Harbor. It had been the rationale for going off to fight in the name of God, flag, and the homeland. World War II had been the mother of righteous causes.

When the war was finished, it seemed to be the end of such causes. Their lives filled with practical matters—going back to school, learning a profession, starting a family. Good and necessary causes, but . . . something was missing.

Then came the war in Israel. It was unlike any other conflict they had experienced. It wasn't their war, wasn't their country in peril, and for the non-Jews it wasn't even their own people being threatened. It was a war they could walk away from at any time. Several had, but most stayed.

Few of the pilots were good at expressing exactly why they were there. Why they were willing to fight, willing to die. Most just shrugged and stuck to the standard lines. Hell, it was that kind of war.

═════════

The phantom was right on time. The blurry shape had begun appearing over Herzliya once a week since the day the first truce ended.

It was a few minutes past noon on Saturday, August 7. From the dirt ramp at Herzliya the pilots could see the phantom making its weekly pass from north to south. The thing was so high it was impossible to determine the type of aircraft.

They still didn't know what type aircraft it was. A fighter, a high-altitude bomber, or some special photo-reconnaissance aircraft? More important, *whose* aircraft? The Egyptians? Iraqis? Or was it the British, keeping a watch on Israeli military activity and passing the intelligence to their Egyptian clients?

Someone had come up with a name for the mysterious aircraft: *Shufti Kite. Shufti* was from Arabic, roughly meaning "look." Learning the identity of the Shufti Kites had become an obsession with the Red Squadrons.

The problem was, the Shufti Kites were flying at something well over 20,000 feet, high enough to leave telltale white contrails across the sky. The Messerschmitts were not equipped with oxygen systems. The pilots risked losing consciousness before ever getting close to the Shufti Kites.

One of the most obsessed was Gideon Lichtman, who took off on solo patrols during the long truce, climbing as high as he dared searching for the elusive Shufti Kites. So far he hadn't gotten near one.

Most of the pilots believed the high-flier was probably a British-built twin-engine Mosquito bomber. But *whose*? They were determined to find out. And when they did, they'd shoot the intruder down.

Summer dragged on. The truce continued. With more pilots than air-planes and no combat missions to fly, the pilots did what they were most inclined to do. They raised hell. When dusk settled they put on their red baseball hats and headed for the beachside district of Tel Aviv.

By now they were well known among the barkeepers and café owners. The face of the Park Hotel bar manager whitened when he saw them coming. "You fellows," he groaned, "why don't you come one at a time?"

One at a time wasn't the style of the Red Squadron. "However unde-sirable the bar owner found it," remembered Ezer Weizman, "that togeth-erness was the very essence of the squadron. We thought together, lived together, dreamed together, went into combat together."

The scenario seldom changed. As the hour grew late they sang all the raunchy songs they could remember. The South Africans, led by the two Cohens, Syd and Jack, would initiate one of their noisy, foot-stomping Zulu war dances, and all the Red Squadron pilots would get in trail behind them. Sometimes chairs and tables were demolished. Sometime the MPs would show up, break up the party, and send the perpetrators back to their base.

Transportation was always a problem. It was wartime and vehicles, military or civilian, were scarce. Early in the war, the pilots adopted a pragmatic approach to the lack of cars. If a car wasn't available, they stole one. Even the scrupulous ones like Mike Flint and Rudy Augarten saw the practicality in this. It was that kind of war.

But mostly that summer the pilots spent their nights at Kfar Shmaryahu, the village near Herzliya. They did their partying in the Falk House courtyard or at the bistro down the road they called the Roadhouse.

Nearly all the pilots smoked. In the evenings a blue layer of smoke hovered like a canopy over their table. A few, including Red Finkel and Sid Antin, carried pipes, but most stuck to cigarettes.

They smoked American brands when they could get them—Camels, Lucky Strikes, Pall Malls—which were shipped into Israel along with armaments and fuel. British Player cigarettes were okay, arriving via nonembargoed shipments from the UK. When those weren't available, the pilots resorted to Palestinian brands—Dubec or Ayalon—which, remembered Flint, "tasted like camel dung."

And they did what fighter pilots had always done. They swaggered, talked tough, postured. It was a form of whistling in the dark. In their secret hearts there was fear. Not so much fear of dying—they'd come to terms with that back in the Big War—but the fear of . . . *losing*. The gripping fear that they could be throwing away their lives for a doomed cause.

On a warm, moonlit night in mid-August, someone threw a pine board over the tops of a couple oil drums in the Falk courtyard. They dragged out stashes of beer, cognac, and seltzer and placed bottles on the makeshift bar. By the time the light from the full moon was glinting from the Mediterranean a mile away, a classic Red Squadron party was in progress.

Most of the squadron was there—Lichtman, Augarten, Flint, Frankel, Mann, Cohen, Finkel, Nomis—even the commander, Modi Alon, who usually left such gatherings early to go join Mina at their place in the Herzliya village. Sitting beneath the acacia trees, the pilots dipped into the booze and the party gathered steam.

They argued as they always did about who were the better pilots, Yanks, Brits, Canucks, South Africans. They retold their favorite stories. They speculated about what would happen next in this on-again-off-again war.

They talked about Mickey Marcus, whom most knew only by reputation. Marcus was an American army officer, a West Point graduate and distinguished WWII soldier, who, at Ben-Gurion's behest, had resigned his commission in the US Army to come join Israel's cause.

Using the alias "Michael Stone," Marcus undertook the task of organizing the factions of the Haganah into a real army. When Arab armies invaded Israel on May 15, it was Marcus's hit-and-run tactics that kept the enemy off balance while the IDF fought for its existence.

Marcus was dead. The great expectations for the distinguished soldier were snuffed out six hours before the first cease-fire commenced. A young Israeli sentry, unable to understand Marcus's reply to his challenge in the darkness, fired a single, fatal shot.

By ten o'clock most of the airmen were shitfaced except Alon, who was still sipping his drink and wearing his bemused den mother expression. When they started tossing beer on each other, Alon decided it was time to leave. He finished his drink and waved goodbye. The lights of his jeep reflected on the acacia trees as he motored down the roadway toward town.

———

Seventy-five hundred miles away in Oakland, California, Hilda Sarn Flint received another postcard from London.

August 13, 1948

Dear Mom,

The Olympics are nearly over and the Americans have won more medals than any other country. And the California Bears brought home twelve of those golds and one silver. Cal men's crew won nine, perhaps as much or more than any other university. I am so proud of our team.

There is much to do here and the girls are great. London is fun and I may stay on a little while.

Your Son, Mike

32

Dust

ŽATEC, CZECHOSLOVAKIA
AUGUST 12, 1948

The Zebra base was closing.

The Czech commander of the Žatec air base delivered the official notification to Hal Auerbach in his operations shack. The Air Transport Command had *one day* to get out of the country. Everything had to go with them—planes, parts, personnel. No more Israeli presence at Žatec.

No one, including Al Schwimmer in Tel Aviv, could figure it out. No one, for that matter, had figured out why the Czechs were willing to host the Israelis in the first place. One guess was that Czechoslovakia, a client of the Soviet Union, wanted to draw the new Jewish state into the Communist sphere. A more realistic guess was that the Czechs simply needed the cash.

Not until later would they learn the truth: the long arm of the US State Department as well as the British Foreign Office had finally reached Czechoslovakia. Both countries had exerted severe pressure on Czechoslovakia to end its collusion with the Israelis to violate the embargo on arms to the Middle East. The Czechs caved in.

For three months the Zebra base had been the home of the Bagel Lancers. They had flown ninety-five round trips to Israel, made nightly approaches to darkened airfields, dodged hostile and friendly fire, endured crashes, jail cells, and the deaths of three fellow airmen. They'd delivered 300 tons of desperately needed weapons and ammunition.

They'd hauled twenty-five Messerschmitts along with the fighters' spare parts, armament, mechanics, and most of the pilots.

Now it was finished. So was Operation Balak.

For the rest of the day the airmen scrambled to comply with the order. They packed their gear, readied the airplanes, said goodbyes to Czech officers, mechanics, girlfriends in town. The ATC was down to seven C-46s, and everything transportable was stuffed into the cabins along with ground personnel. One of the transports carried a secret passenger: the Czech girlfriend of an American mechanic.

The only airplane not flying out stood like a lone monument in a grassy area of the field. The once-beautiful Constellation, crippled after her disastrous one-gear landing, had to stay behind. The Czechs allowed Schwimmer's chief mechanic, Ernie Stehlik, to remain with the Connie while he labored to make the great ship flyable again.

In Tel Aviv, the Bagel Lancers set down their duffel bags and looked around their new quarters. It wasn't what they expected. They thought they'd be staying downtown, perhaps in the posh Park Hotel, which was close to the beach and vibrating with activity at all hours.

The Bristol Hotel wasn't downtown. It was a dingy-looking three-floor building in a residential neighborhood. No beachside view, no lively restaurant or bar, no bevy of adoring women passing through.

The crews had liked Žatec. Despite chronic shortages of good food and spirits, the place had an old world charm. The meager salaries of the volunteer airmen had gone far in the crushed Czech economy. And despite the admonitions from the Shoo-Shoo boys—Israeli intelligence agents—about fraternizing with local women, the airmen had happily ignored the warnings.

Tel Aviv had a different kind of charm. Even in wartime the beachfront establishments had a fatalistic, drink-and-be-merry spirit.

But the Bristol Hotel wasn't on the beach. It was stuck in a dismal suburb. Instead of a restaurant they had a common dining area where meals were served family style.

Most of the ATC airmen were single, but several married crewmen brought their families to the Bristol. Norm Moonitz's wife, Lillian, and their five-year-old son moved in. So did Ray Kurtz's wife, Ruth, and their five-year-old. Marty Ribakoff's wife and three children joined the group.

Added to the mix was a cadre of newcomers. "These were mainly fighter pilots," wrote radio operator Harold Livingston, "non-Jews, mercenaries rumored to be receiving handsome salaries."

Inevitably, there was friction. Besides the old fighter pilot-versus-transport-driver friction that dated back to World War One, there was resentment about other things: money and moral purpose. True believers versus opportunists.

Part of the discontent was simply because they had time on their hands. With Operation Balak terminated and the truce still holding, the airmen no longer had a vital mission. Missing, at least for the moment, was the sense of a higher purpose.

And then in the third week of August, ten days after they'd arrived in the Bristol Hotel, the Bagel Lancers were given a mission. It wasn't much of a mission, just a demonstration for the prime minister.

What they didn't know was that it would lead to their most dangerous assignment yet.

―――

The midday heat hadn't settled over the sprawling concrete ramp when Ben-Gurion and his entourage arrived. It was the morning of August 17. The occasion was the formal dedication of Tel Nof Air Base—the ex-RAF base the Israelis were still calling Ekron. It was also an opportunity for the air force to show off for the prime minister and his staff.

First came a formation of Messerschmitts. The fighters swept in low over the audience. The combined growl of the twelve-cylinder Jumo engines delivered a satisfying, door-rattling rumble. Next overhead was the air force's single four-motored C-54 Skymaster, now the ATC's flagship after the crash of Sam Lewis's beloved Constellation.

Last came three C-46 Commandos in a loose formation. It was an unexciting flyby. Like a lazy gaggle of fat geese, the transports droned overhead, then landed one behind the other and taxied up close to the audience.

Then came the eye-opener.

The doors swung open. Out of the transports rushed an entire infantry company. Rolling out behind them were jeeps and field artillery. In front of the crowd, the soldiers staged a mock assault.

The spectators were impressed. Especially impressed was the five-foot-tall, white-haired prime minister. Ben-Gurion's eyes remained fixed on the three scruffy-looking transport aircraft, but his thoughts were on the desert that lay to the south.

To Ben-Gurion, a lifelong Zionist, the Negev Desert had always been the *real* promised land. The long triangle of arid desert comprised nearly three-quarters of the territory allotted to Israel in the UN partition plan. Ben-Gurion believed that the Negev would someday be a fertile home to millions of Jews who would settle in Israel.

Since the end of May 1948, the Negev had been occupied by the Egyptian Army. Isolated behind the Egyptian line was a complex of Israeli settlements and a badly depleted brigade of the IDF. Every attempt to resupply and relieve the cut-off units by truck convoy had failed. When the war resumed—and it could at any time—the battle-fatigued fighters in the Negev would be crushed.

The next day Ben-Gurion summoned air force commander Remez to a meeting at IDF headquarters. In the presence of all the IDF senior commanders, Ben-Gurion asked Remez if the isolated Negev settlements could be resupplied by air.

For several seconds the prime minister's question hung in the air. The sour-faced IDF infantry commanders peered at the twenty-nine-year-old air force officer. Remez had a rocky relationship with the tough former Haganah and Palmach commanders. He knew they resented his closeness with Ben-Gurion. He knew they also resented the fact that he had been a lowly sergeant in the RAF during WWII, even though he'd flown over a hundred missions in fighters.

"We can do it all," Remez answered.

Eyebrows raised. A skeptical commander glowered at Remez. "Can you deliver ten tons? It will take that much to save the Negev units."

It was the moment Remez had been waiting for.

"We'll start with thirty tons each night," Remez said. "Then we'll work up to fifty."

A silence fell over the room. There was an exchange of glances, growls of skepticism.

It was exactly what Ben-Gurion wanted to hear. He turned to Remez. Make it happen, he ordered.

═══════

Dust. It was the single enduring feature of this arid terrain. Leo Gardner could feel it and taste it as he landed the Auster utility plane on the old abandoned RAF airstrip.

It was August 19, the day after Ben-Gurion had given the order to send cargo planes into the Negev. Now Gardner was worried. The little Auster had thrown up a cloud of dust when he landed here. He could only imagine the storm the big radial engines of the C-46s would cause.

Gardner was near a settlement called Ruhama, deep in the Negev behind Egyptian lines. The thirty-year-old Gardner had been one of Al Schwimmer's first recruits to his cadre of transport pilots back at Millville. Remez trusted Gardner and had tapped him for the Negev assignment. Gardner's job was to find a site where they could carve out a runway to accommodate the C-46s.

On first inspection, it seemed an impossible task. The abandoned strip was barely identifiable. Gardner estimated that it would take weeks, months, perhaps forever to make it serviceable. Most daunting of all would be making the surface suitable for heavy transport aircraft.

They went to work. From nearby settlements Gardner's team requisitioned tractors, heavy vehicles, a single bulldozer. Day and night the workers pushed and smoothed and lengthened the old surface.

It took five days. When they were finished, they had a 4,000-foot runway with a seven-degree incline. The idea was for the transports to land uphill and take off downhill. All operations would have to be after dark to avoid Egyptian fighters.

That night Gardner brought in the first C-46. The new strip was marked only by a row of kerosene lanterns. Even though he knew what to expect, Gardner was startled.

A cyclone of dust swirled in the darkness around the Commando's propellers. By the time Gardner reached the end of the runway the visibility was near zero.

Even before the engines had been shut down, crews were swarming to the airplane to unload the cargo. They were kibbutzniks (the Hebrew name for kibbutz dwellers), soldiers, elderly people, farmers, teenagers. Each had a pistol or a rifle. They all wore the same expression of relief.

One of Gardner's crewmen was complaining about the dust storm. The kibbutzniks just laughed. The dust was nothing, one of them said. Wait until the rains came. Instead of dust they'd have an ocean of mud.

A load of battle-fatigued Negev Brigade soldiers climbed into Gardner's C-46. An hour after he took off for Ekron, another C-46 landed. Then another. By dawn, half a dozen C-46s had come and departed. That night they delivered 29 tons of supplies.

The next night they were back. This time they delivered 75 tons.

Night after night the C-46s came and went. It was a grueling operation for the air crewmen, sleeping by day and flying by darkness. Each crew made three or four trips a night to the Negev.

The air force gave the operation an appropriate name: *Avak*, the Hebrew word for dust. The young airmen, who remembered the 1930s in middle America, gave it their own name: Operation Dustbowl. The strip in the desert they called Dust Field.

The operation gathered intensity. A second runway was cleared further from the Egyptian positions around Dust Field. The fields became, respectively, Dustbowl One and Dustbowl Two.

The Dustbowl fields were only 30 miles from Ekron, but each flight took half an hour. Outbound aircraft climbed to 5,000 feet over Ekron before heading out over the Egyptian lines to avoid antiaircraft fire. Returning flights did the same in reverse, climbing to 6,000 feet.

Approaching the Dustbowl fields, crews radioed for runway lights. Out of the darkness would appear a single line of flare pots. They were extinguished as soon as the C-46 plopped down in the cascade of dust.

Dust and darkness and the sloping runway weren't the only hazards. Egyptian-held territory was only a few miles away. Tracers sometimes arced into the sky, probing for the darkened shapes of the Commando transports. Egyptian patrols kept a watch on the activity from the nearby hills.

The overworked C-46s had constant maintenance problems, made worse by the dust and the high frequency of takeoffs and landings. Without an inventory of spare parts, resourceful mechanics came up with workarounds and ersatz components. The flight crews knew they were flying airplanes that wouldn't meet the standards of any airline.

Regardless of the airplane's condition, they always left the Negev before daylight. Egyptian Spitfires were on the prowl.

And then on the night of October 6, one of them didn't get out.

━━━━━━

Even before he saw the fighters, Misha Kenner knew what he was hearing: the growl of Merlin engines. Kenner's C-46 had developed an engine problem. He and the crew were stuck on the ground with the disabled airplane.

Dawn was coming. And so were the Egyptian Spitfires.

Kenner jumped down from the C-46 and sprinted for shelter. He barely made it when the fighters swept down, guns blazing.

It was over in minutes. The Spitfires pulled up and headed back south. Kenner clambered out of his shelter and ran over to the C-46. He was astonished. The Egyptians had managed to score not a single hit on the C-46.

The Egyptians didn't come back. By the end of the day Kenner's airplane was repaired and on its way to Ekron.

━━━━━━

At air force headquarters, Remez was dealing with another problem. The air force was running out of fuel. With the end of the truce approaching,

IDF commanders were worried that there wouldn't be enough high-octane fuel for the coming great battle.

It was a critical decision that would have to go all the way to the defense minister. *Cease Operation Dust and save fuel? Continue to reinforce the Negev and hope for the best?*

A freighter called the *Kefalos* was en route from Mexico. The ship was hauling a load of high-octane aviation fuel, which was not on the list of embargoed materials. The IDF commanders believed the freighter would reach Israel in time for the coming battle.

It would be a calculated risk. Ben-Gurion made the call. The airlift would continue.

With both Dustbowl airfields open, the flights increased to eight a night. On one night of superhuman effort, the ATC crews flew thirteen round trips to the Negev. In two months of nonstop flying, the crews of Operation Dustbowl made 417 round trips to the Negev, carrying 4,991 tons of material and 5,098 passengers, most of them troops being rotated into and out of the desert.

Operation Dustbowl had a greater purpose than supplying and relieving the settlements in the Negev. Both sides—Arab and Israeli—understood that what happened in the Negev Desert would determine the outcome of the war.

Ben-Gurion and his commanders were determined that when the war resumed, the Israeli brigades in the Negev would strike from *inside* the ring of Egyptian forces. They would depend on heavy support from the air force—the ATC transports, heavy bombers, and the fighter squadron.

But the fighter squadron had a problem. They were running out of fighters.

The Messerschmitts were crashing at a sickening rate. By now almost every pilot of the Red Squadron had been bitten by the Czech Mule at least once.

Mike Flint had been bitten twice. The first time was when he neglected to check that the gear was fully extended. The Messerschmitt wound up sliding to a stop on its belly. On another landing Flint bounced, then came down in a skid. The right landing gear strut collapsed. It was another metal-bending, dirt-spewing ride down the Herzliya runway.

One day it was Cyril Horowitz's turn. Horowitz was a British ex-RAF pilot with a drooping handlebar mustache. Everyone liked Horowitz, whose clipped accent and style earned him the nickname Esquire.

Horowitz was supposed to fly a reconnaissance mission over the Judean Hills. The other pilots were in their revetments when they heard the crackling sound of Horowitz's Messerschmitt as it started its takeoff roll. The pitch was changing as the fighter accelerated.

Then a metallic *KaWhang!* Followed by silence. The bellow of the Jumo engine was gone.

Gideon Lichtman and Leo Nomis went running toward the runway. They saw the wreckage halfway down the field, about fifty yards off the side of the runway. An ambulance marked with a red Star of David was rumbling across the dirt.

As Lichtman trotted nearer to the wreck, he saw something else. Some kind of green-painted object was merged with the Messerschmitt. It looked like a . . . *jeep.*

It was one of the squadron maintenance vehicles. Horowitz had veered off the runway and run head-on into the jeep.

Lichtman braced himself for the carnage he knew he'd find. Horowitz was surely dead, and those poor guys in the jeep—

They were alive. The two mechanics motoring along in the jeep had looked up in time to get a front-end view of a Messerschmitt boring like a specter from hell straight at them. They abandoned the jeep seconds before the Messerschmitt rammed the vehicle. Locked together, the two machines slid another fifty yards to the boundary of the field.

And then another amazement. Cyril Horowitz wasn't inside the mangled cockpit. He was standing over by the ambulance, dabbing at a nasty cut over his nose. With blood running over his mustache, the Englishman looked like a damaged walrus.

Other than the cut over his nose, Horowitz seemed okay but dazed. He kept asking, "What the hell happened? How did that jeep get in the way?"

No one felt like telling him. He'd figure it out soon enough. They loaded Horowitz into the back of the ambulance and hauled him off to the infirmary at the far side of the field.

Standing by the wreckage was the squadron maintenance officer, Harry Axelrod. He was staring at the crushed nose of the Messerschmitt, shaking his head. Axelrod despised the Mule as much as the pilots, but for a different reason. Out of the twenty-three Messerschmitts placed into service, sixteen had crashed. The damned things were crashing faster than his crews could rebuild them.

Everyone agreed that the Czech Mule was a treacherous fighter. But it was all they had. And they needed more.

———

In Prague, the portly Dr. Otto Felix put on his three-piece suit and went calling on the Czech government. The once-cozy Czech-Israeli relationship had chilled since Felix's last round of purchases. In mid-August the Czechs had bowed to US and UK pressure and evicted the Israeli airlift operation from Žatec. Felix doubted that the Czechs would be agreeable to selling *anything* to the Israelis, especially more Messerschmitts.

Felix was right. After he'd taken a seat in the Czech government official's office, he listened while the official told him exactly what he expected to hear.

No more Messerschmitt fighters were available for purchase. Forget Messerschmitts, the government official told Felix. The Messerschmitts were finished.

But then the official surprised him. His attitude seemed to change. Perhaps, said the Czech, Israel would be interested in purchasing something else.

Something much better.

== 33 ==

Velvetta

Spitfires? Otto Felix was stunned. It seemed too good to be true. The Supermarine Spitfire had been Britain's top fighter in World War II and was still one of the premier air combat aircraft in the world.

During the war, three Czech fighter squadrons had served in the RAF, all equipped with Spitfire LF9 models. In August 1945, all three squadrons flew home to newly liberated Czechoslovakia. Their Spitfires formed the nucleus of the new Czech Air Force.

The official was telling Felix that Czechoslovakia would sell *fifty* Spitfires to Israel.

It was a mystery to Felix. As far as he or anyone else could determine, it was another example of the Czech government bending to the will of a foreign power, this time the Soviet Union. The Soviets wanted to reequip the Czech Air Force with modern Soviet-supplied jets. The cash-strapped Czechs were looking for a buyer for their WWII British Spitfires. One had just walked in the door.

There was the usual haggling over the terms. It was finally agreed that upon inspection and test flight of each airplane, the Spitfires would be transferred to the Israelis for $23,000 each. It was still a steep price for the time, but far more reasonable than the exorbitant amount Israel had paid for the Messerschmitts.

There was one catch. The Spitfires couldn't be shipped to Israel as the Messerschmitts had been—in the cabins of Israel's C-46s. Operation Balak was permanently shut down. The Czechs wanted no more heat from America or Britain about Israeli transports flying from Czech airfields.

Ferrying the fighters to Israel was also out of the question. The Spitfire had a range of only about 600 miles, scarcely more than the short-ranged Messerschmitts. There were still no Israel-friendly refueling bases for fighters along the 1,500-mile route.

The Czechs proposed packing the fighters in crates and shipping them by rail across Yugoslavia where they would be loaded onto an Israeli cargo ship.

Ben-Gurion heard the idea, then summarily rejected it. The next—and maybe last—battle of the war was about to begin. Israel needed the Spitfires *now*.

And then in Czechoslovakia, Sam Pomerance had an idea.

———

Sam Pomerance was the ingenious American engineer who had contrived most of the mechanical miracles for Operation Balak. He was one of the few volunteers still in Czechoslovakia.

Pomerance came from a different background than nearly all the other volunteer airmen. He was an aeronautical engineer with a degree from New York University. He was also a pilot, but his training was in light civilian planes.

Pomerance had been working as an engineer at Ranger Aircraft company when, in March 1948, he left to join the Haganah. Beginning as a flight engineer on Al Schwimmer's fleet of C-46s in Burbank, Pomerance was sent to Europe to be the chief engineer for Haganah's growing fleet of transports and fighters.

The engineer-pilot had flown one of the four Anson light bombers that were impounded in Rhodes after the Greeks were tipped off about the planes' true destination. Pomerance and the others spent four weeks in a Greek jail before being released.

Now it was early September. Pomerance was at the Czech Air Force base at Kunovice, educating himself on the fuel system of the Spitfire.

He knew there was a way. If he could rig external fuel tanks on the Spitfires, they *might* have the range for the flight to Israel with only one fueling stop.

Pomerance's plan was to use the Spitfire's standard belly tank, a streamlined container called a slipper. He would also use two wing-mounted tanks, which, in another stroke of irony, were made for Messerschmitts. To compensate for the extra weight, Pomerance's mechanics would strip everything that could be removed from the Spitfire: guns, ammunition containers, even communications equipment.

Pomerance put his crew to work. Within a week they had the first Spitfire rigged with Pomerance's system. On a humid August day, Pomerance and South African pilot Jack Cohen each test flew the aircraft.

To Pomerance's great satisfaction, his jury-rigged system *worked*. According to his calculations, the external tanks would give the Spitfires *almost* enough range for the trip to Israel.

But not quite. The Spitfires would still need a refueling stop.

And that, for the moment, seemed an insurmountable problem. Yugoslavia had provided refueling facilities for Operation Balak, but now, for obscure reasons, Yugoslavia was flatly refusing to help.

Ben-Gurion dispatched a team to approach the Bulgarian government. They reported back to Tel Aviv: Bulgaria was willing to provide a refueling stop—at an outrageous price: $10,000 per aircraft.

Ben-Gurion was exasperated. The Spitfires were urgently needed. There seemed to be no alternative. The prime minister sent the order: *Pay the Bulgarians.*

And then at the last minute, a breakthrough. In another shift of Cold War politics, Yugoslavia broke its ties with the Soviet Union. The former East-bloc country still had no trade agreements with the west, and its air force needed aviation-grade fuel. Would Israel provide fuel to Yugoslavia? If so, they would grant landing rights for the Spitfires.

A deal was made. The Israeli Spitfires could refuel at the remote Niksic airfield, a dry lake bed in the interior of Montenegro, which, conveniently, was out of sight of international observers. To further hide the nature of the operation, the Spitfires would have to wear the markings of the Yugoslav air force.

The news reached Sam Pomerance in Czechoslovakia. The balding thirty-eight-year-old engineer went to work with a renewed energy. Pomerance and his team labored nonstop to ready the first flight of six Spitfires.

A group of handpicked airmen, most of them WWII Spitfire pilots, arrived in Kunovice from Israel. The pilots flew familiarization flights in the fighters.

Watching his plans come together, Pomerance was pleased. He even liked the name IAF headquarters had assigned to the ferry flights: *Operation Velvetta.*

Boris Senior wasn't as optimistic as Pomerance. Looking at the collection of fighters on the ramp at Kunovice, Senior knew it was a risky operation. The mustached South African veteran had been assigned to lead the first gaggle of Spitfires on the long journey to Israel.

Even with Pomerance's fuel systems, the Spitfires barely had sufficient range. The flight from the Kunovice base in Czechoslovakia to Niksic, Yugoslavia, was only 300 miles, but from there to Ramat David Air Base in Israel was nearly 1,200 miles—a journey of over seven hours. The last two-thirds of it was over open water. The Spitfires would arrive with only twenty minutes of fuel remaining.

For the long overwater segment, the fighters would be led by a mother ship—a four-engine C-54—which would carry dinghies in case someone went down. On board the C-54 would be an experienced navigator. His job was to monitor each fighter's fuel quantity and determine whether the pilot should continue or turn back. Another air-sea rescue ship, a C-47 Dakota, would stage from Ramat David. Even the Israeli Navy was pressed into service, patrolling the last segment of the route over the Mediterranean.

Senior oversaw the familiarization training of the six ferry pilots. All but one—a young South African cadet named Tuxie Blau—had previous Spitfire time. Headquarters had already sent an experienced Spitfire pilot, another South African named Arnie Ruch, to replace Blau.

Senior nixed the assignment. He thought Blau was a good kid, and Senior wanted him to have the mission. He'd already given Blau eight hours of training time. Senior decided Blau was good to go.

It was a decision he would regret.

Of the other four, only Sam Pomerance, the aeronautical engineer and sometime test pilot, had no military flying experience. But Pomerance had already proved himself. He was a natural airman who could become proficient in any new airplane in only a few hours. Even a hot fighter like the Spitfire.

The six Spitfires took off at dawn on September 24. The first leg to Niksic was supposed to be easy, a warm-up for the real show ahead. For this 300-mile flight, Pomerance's experimental fuel system wouldn't be put to the test. All the pilots had to do was hang together in a glistening blue sky.

An hour into the flight, the sky was no longer glistening. Nor was it blue. An angry gray cloud mass covered the southern Alps and obscured most of the landscape. Almost none of the six pilots was proficient at instrument flying, but it didn't matter. The stripped-down Spitfires had only rudimentary flight instruments. In the diminishing visibility it was becoming difficult to keep each other in sight.

Nearing Niksic, they lost sight of each other. The orderly formation flight turned into an every-man-for-himself melee. Each pilot was flitting between cloud layers, flying dangerously low over the mountain range just north of Niksic.

Boris Senior found the airfield first. Niksic was unmarked, situated on a large dry lake bed and surrounded by rugged hills. There was no defined strip, just a large flat surface.

Senior landed the Spitfire, bumped along the uneven ground, then rolled over to the cluster of tents that served as the airfield's command post.

He climbed out of the cockpit and waited for the other five pilots. He was worried about the new kid, Tuxie Blau. Blau had been on his wing when they became separated in the clouds.

An instant later, he stopped worrying. One by one the distinctive shapes of the Spitfires came skimming into view. The first—Senior was sure it was Tuxie—was already on short final approach, flaring above the unpaved runway.

Something didn't look right. The Spitfire was almost on the ground, but something was missing . . . *Oh, hell!*

A geyser of dirt erupted around the Spitfire. Senior watched helplessly as the fighter slid along shedding propeller blades and the crushed remains of the new external fuel tanks. Even before the cascade of dirt had settled, Senior knew what happened.

Blau, the student he had trained, landed with his wheels up.

Senior watched the other four Spitfires land, offering up a silent prayer that nothing else would happen. All the pilots—Sam Pomerance, the two Cohens, Jack and Syd, and 101 Squadron commander Modi Alon—landed and climbed out of their Spitfires.

That evening they huddled in the tents that the Yugoslav Army had provided. Their bathing facility was the cold, fast-running river that flowed next to the field. They shared a common latrine with the soldiers. No one was allowed to leave the airfield. Just to make sure, a platoon of unsmiling Yugoslav Red Army soldiers armed with automatic weapons guarded the facility.

The weather matched their mood, darkening and descending like a thick blanket over the countryside. Senior could barely contain his frustration. Nothing could happen until the weather lifted and the C-54 mother ship got here.

Three days and nights passed. They ate the canned rations they'd brought and tried to make the best of the situation. Five out of six Spitfires were still in the game. No one felt like giving Tuxie Blau a hard time for his mishap.

On the fourth day Boris Senior heard what he'd been listening for: the drone of a large aircraft. A few minutes later he saw the C-54 taxiing to where the fighters were parked. The mother ship had come to collect her chicks.

The next morning, September 27, the C-54 and the five fly-able Spitfires were climbing into a sparkling blue sky. Two Spitfires flew on the C-54's left wing, three on the right. From his cockpit Senior had a superb view of Albania, the Peloponnesus of Greece, the Mediterranean beyond.

Surrounded by such scenery, it was almost possible to relax. Almost. Pomerance's long-range fuel system hadn't yet been put to the *real* test.

To make it all the way, each pilot had to burn *every drop* of fuel from his external tanks before switching to the main wing tanks. For a few heart-seizing seconds the fighter's engine would stop from fuel exhaustion while the pilot switched to his main tanks. Only then, when the Spitfire was running on its main tank fuel, would he know *exactly* how much fuel he had remaining. At that moment the navigator in the C-54 would tell him whether he had enough fuel to make it to Israel from their present position.

Senior was wondering whose engine would quit first when he saw the answer. Modi Alon, flying off the C-54's left wing, abruptly dropped back and veered away from the formation. His external tanks had run dry.

Several seconds elapsed, then he announced that his engine was running again.

But something was wrong. Alon's Spitfire shouldn't have used up its external fuel yet. The navigator in C-54 confirmed the bad news. From where they were, Alon wouldn't make it to Israel with his remaining fuel. He'd have to turn back toward the island of Rhodes.

A few seconds later it happened to Senior. The Merlin engine made a chuffing noise like an animal being strangled. Then it stopped. Everything after that happened in a blur—hands flicking the transfer switch to the main tanks, turning on the fuel boost pump, the Spitfire gliding downward over the Mediterranean.

Senior's engine roared back to life. But he was in the same fix as Modi Alon. The navigator confirmed the bad news. Senior would have to join Alon and land at Rhodes. The remaining three Spitfires would continue toward Israel.

The flight to Rhodes took thirty minutes. Senior had no airport charts, no aviation data for the Greek island. He could make out two airfields on the island, one in the south and a larger one near the city. He chose the larger.

The two Spitfires landed without clearance and taxied to the control tower. Even before Senior climbed out of his cockpit, he was getting a bad feeling. Greece had impounded Israeli airplanes and jailed the crews.

Senior's bad feeling worsened when he saw a Greek air force officer walking toward him from the control tower. The officer wasn't smiling.

"We are short of fuel," said Senior in his most polite voice. "Please ask the Shell agent to come and refuel our aircraft. I have cash with me."

The officer showed no expression. He walked away. A few minutes later he was back, but not with the Shell agent. The officer brought with him a squad of armed soldiers.

―――――

The worst thing about being in jail, observed Boris Senior, was the isolation. He hadn't seen Modi Alon since they'd been arrested and taken to the Greek military headquarters in Rhodes.

From time to time they came to interrogate Senior. The chief interrogator was the commander of the base, an air force captain.

"Where did you come from?" the captain demanded. "Why were you flying fighter aircraft with Israeli markings and no cannons in the wings? What do you want in Rhodes?"

Senior stuck to his story. They'd been on a long-range sea patrol from Israel and ran low on fuel.

The interrogator didn't believe it. Greece was engaged in a bitter civil war with Communist rebels, who were crossing into Greece from the Communist countries of Albania and Yugoslavia. The paranoid Greek military was convinced that Israel was covertly supporting the Communists.

Senior and Alon looked the part. Senior had a thick beard and was wearing scruffy corduroys with a ripped seat. Alon wore faded jeans and a work shirt. Both had revolvers strapped to their waists when they were arrested.

In the cockpit of Senior's Spitfire they found a chart with a penciled course line running through a succession of Communist countries—Czechoslovakia, Yugoslavia, Albania. The South African passport they took from him had a stamped visa from Communist Czechoslovakia.

After five days they bundled Senior into a Greek air force Dakota and flew him to Athens, where he was placed in solitary confinement. A few days later, it was over. The Greeks released both airmen. In an emotional reunion, Senior and Alon hugged each other outside the police station. One of the conditions of the pilots' release was that they were not allowed to return to Israel because of the UN ban on the entry of men of military age.

Both men solemnly agreed to the condition.

Two days later Senior and Alon were stepping off a Pan African charter aircraft at the airport in Haifa. They slipped past the UN observers and entered the country.

It was October 12. Israel's war of independence would resume in three days.

———

Only three of the six Spitfires had made it to Israel. No one knew when the rest would show up. The original plan had been for the Czech Spitfires to form a new unit, the 105 Squadron, to be commanded by Boris Senior. The plan was scrubbed, and the newly arrived Spitfires—and Boris Senior—were assigned to Modi Alon's 101 Squadron in Herzliya.

In addition to the Spitfires, two more modern fighters—P-51 Mustangs—arrived in crates on August 19 in the hold of a US-registered freighter, SS *Enterprise*. The Mustangs were being secretly assembled at an auxiliary field called Ma'abarot near Herzliya. The first would soon be flyable.

Not only was the mix of fighters at Herzliya changing, but the pilots were also. As if timed with the arrival of the fighters, a new cadre of ex-WWII airmen—many already highly experienced Spitfire pilots—checked in at Herzliya. They brought with them a new depth of experience—and different motivations.

One was a blunt-spoken Canadian named John McElroy. McElroy was an ex-RCAF squadron leader—the equivalent rank to a USAAF major. He was a veteran of George Beurling's old outfit at Malta and credited with shooting down eleven Luftwaffe warplanes and a shared credit for a twelfth.

"What are you doing in Israel?" the immigration officer at Haifa asked McElroy.

"I came to fly your fucking airplanes," answered McElroy.

No further questions were asked.

With McElroy came other Canadians, all non-Jews. Denny Wilson was a Spitfire veteran with two Luftwaffe kills. George "Lee" Sinclair was an RAF Spitfire pilot who left the air force at war's end with the rank of Wing Commander. Jack Doyle was another Spitfire pilot in the RCAF who fought in North Africa and Italy, where he downed four enemy aircraft.

Arriving with the Canadians was an American pilot everyone knew by reputation. Chalmers "Slick" Goodlin was an ex-RCAF, ex-navy fighter pilot and, later, a renowned test pilot. In the years after the war Goodlin had gained fame for his pioneering flights in the Bell X-1 rocket ship, the world's first supersonic aircraft. Gillette razor blade ads featured Goodlin's face with the caption, "the fastest man alive."

Another newcomer was an ebullient American named Wayne Peake, who had been a WWII P-51 pilot over Europe. Peake was a good old country boy from North Carolina.

Peake fit right in at Herzliya. At the nightly beer gatherings in the Falk House courtyard, he entertained the squadron, telling stories in his Appalachian drawl and twanging his guitar. During lulls in the war, Peake liked to go off alone to hunt jackals in the sand dunes.

One thing hadn't changed: even with the arrival of the Spitfires and Mustangs, the squadron had more pilots than available fighters. The new guys, no matter how famous or experienced, had to wait their turn.

In Oakland, California, Hilda Sarn Flint was worried. She hadn't received a postcard from her son. The Olympic Games were over weeks ago. She wondered how much longer Mike was going to stay overseas.

One day she was in a grocery store when she ran into a young man named Oscar Morvai, a college friend who stayed in touch with Mike.

"You must be very proud of your son," said the young man.

Something about the way he said it made her wary. Hilda asked why.

"Because of what he's doing for Israel. You know, flying fighters in the war."

She was stunned. *War? Israel?* Hilda was furious. Her own son had *lied* to her. She was going to *kill* that kid when he came home.

If he came home.

═══ 34 ═══

Sea Fury

Most fighter pilots remained loyal to their first loves. The airmen of the Red Squadron were no exception. For the Canadians, South Africans, and two sabras, it would always be the Supermarine Spitfire they had flown in WWII. USAAF veterans Rudy Augarten and Sid Antin were loyal to the tough Republic P-47 Thunderbolt. Ex-navy and Marine pilots Mike Flint, Lou Lenart, and Chris Magee loved the F4U Corsair.

For Gideon Lichtman, it was the North American P-51 Mustang. The Mustang had been his choice in WWII when he blustered his way out of an instructing billet into a fighter squadron. He'd flown the Mustang in the Pacific, in occupied Japan, in the reserves in New Jersey.

Now he was going to fly it in Israel.

The first of the two crated Mustangs smuggled by ship from the United States to Israel had been assembled and was ready for its first mission. After much argument, the assignment went to the tough-talking kid from Newark, Gideon Lichtman.

As he strapped into the fighter, Lichtman remembered why he loved it. Unlike in the claustrophobic Messerschmitt, he had a clear view through the P-51 Mustang's bubble canopy. Instead of the Messerschmitt's spindly landing gear, the Mustang had a wide-track, wing-mounted gear that tracked straight down the runway.

Even starting the engine was more civilized. In place of a mechanic cranking the flywheel of an inertia starter, he had only to toggle the Mustang's starter switch. The big four-bladed propeller snapped around, two, three revolutions—*pocka-pocka-pocka*—and the twelve-cylinder Rolls Royce chuffed to life.

It was supposed to be a reconnaissance mission. The truce was still in effect, which meant Lichtman wouldn't be using the Mustang's .50-caliber machine guns. Not unless the Arabs were obliging enough to fire at *him*. Then it was open season.

His first reconnaissance pass was over the Lebanese air force field in Beirut. Lichtman spotted a cluster of fighters lined up in a neat row like targets in a shooting gallery. For a moment Lichtman was tempted. One high-speed strafing pass and he could blow half a dozen Arab fighters to smithereens.

He moved on. Shooting up Lebanese planes on the ground would be a blatant violation of the truce. Someone's butt would be hung out to dry, and Lichtman knew whose it would be.

He flew over Damascus. He observed nothing of consequence, so he headed south. Lichtman was approaching the coast of Egypt, peering down at the Suez Canal, when the sky around him erupted. *Bloom. Bloom.* The Mustang lurched in the turbulent air. "The heaviest damn flak I'd ever seen," he recalled.

Dodging flak bursts, Lichtman quickly finished his reconnaissance run and headed back north.

He was almost to the coastal border of Israel when he spotted it. Something glimmering like a mirage on the floor of the desert. Lichtman rolled the Mustang up on its wing and peered down at the object.

It was a fighter. An *Arab* fighter, since there were no other Israeli fighters in the air. But this one was different. It had a blunt nose and semi-elliptical wings. He guessed it was a Sea Fury, a fighter no one had reported seeing in this war.

It was worth a closer look.

Lichtman armed the Mustang's guns. He peeled off toward the Arab fighter. "I got right on the guy's ass," Lichtman recalled. "He turned into me, and the fight was on."

Lichtman was surprised. Unlike the bumbling Egyptian fighter pilots he had seen, this one was aggressive. Lichtman wondered if the guy was really an Egyptian. Or was he one of the mercenaries the Egyptians were rumored to be recruiting?

It became a classic *mano a mano* dogfight between the premier propeller-driven fighters of the world. The Sea Fury and the Mustang were flying a tight circle, each trying to get inside the other's turn. In tiny increments, the Mustang gained the advantage.

Lichtman had the Sea Fury in his sights. He saw the pilot turn in his cockpit and look back at him. Lichtman squeezed the trigger.

Nothing happened. No hard rattle of the .50-calibers.

Lichtman squeezed again. And again. He felt himself filled with a seething rage. The goddamned guns wouldn't fire!

The pilot in the Sea Fury was still looking back at him. Wondering if he was about to die.

For several more turns Lichtman stayed on the Sea Fury's tail. He couldn't leave the fight or the Sea Fury pilot would be on *his* tail.

Finally Lichtman saw his moment. He broke away and roared back at high speed for Herzliya. As he flew northward, the anger swelled in him like a mounting storm. He could have been killed because the guns didn't work.

He landed, rolled the Mustang up on the dirt apron from which he'd left an hour before. He stormed across the ramp cursing the Mustang, the unworkable guns, the idiots who installed them, the air force, the whole goddamn war.

By the time he reached the operations building, the message was waiting for him: Report to IAF Headquarters. Immediately.

Lichtman had a reputation for his temper. When he was a kid in New Jersey his temper got him in fights with street kids. "I'd get the shit beat out of me every day," he remembered.

The temper and the quick mouth stayed with him. Lichtman's use of profanity was well known among the volunteers at Herzliya. But not to the senior officers of the IAF. Not until today.

As ordered, Lichtman presented himself at headquarters in the Yarkon Hotel in downtown Tel Aviv. He sat on a hard wooden chair while an air force staff officer questioned him. In the back of the room stood Ahoran Remez, the air force commander. Remez let the staff officer do the talking.

Lichtman didn't like the officer. Although the officer had been an RAF pilot during WWII, he was flying a desk in this war. What most annoyed Lichtman about the man was his *Britishness*—the Alec Guinness mustache, double-creased uniform shirt with epaulettes, web belt. And a *riding crop*.

The officer tapped the riding crop against his leg while he questioned Lichtman. "What type of Arab airplane was it you encountered?"

"I told you. It was a Sea Fury."

"You're mistaken." The officer leaned in until he was face-to-face with Lichtman. "It had to be something else."

"I'm telling you what I saw. And get out of my face while you're talking."

The officer blinked, then backed off. "How do you know what a Sea Fury looks like?"

"I saw a picture in a magazine." Lichtman was nearing his limit. "It was a fucking Sea Fury."

"We know for a fact the Arabs don't have Sea Furies."

Lichtman's limit had been reached. The anger that had gathered in him during the day—the flak over the Suez, the dogfight with the Egyptian fighter, the nonworking guns—all came spilling out. He cursed the staff officer and stormed out of the office.

In any other air force in 1948 it would have been the end of Lichtman's service. He'd be dismissed, maybe court-martialed, perhaps detained, probably kicked out of the country. What he wouldn't be doing was returning to his squadron to fly fighters, which is what happened.

This was the Israeli Air Force, and during this brief window in time the rules were different. Between the volunteers and their Israeli commanders was an unspoken contract. The volunteers could get rowdy, smash furniture, steal vehicles, even be as insubordinate as Gideon Lichtman, as long as they fulfilled their part of the contract. They must be willing to fly, kill, and perhaps be killed.

———

Lichtman heard nothing further about his spat with the air force staff officer. What he did hear a few days later, via Dave Croll, the 101 Squadron intelligence officer, was a tantalizing snippet of information. Intel sources confirmed that the Egyptian Air Force had added to its inventory a potent new fighter.

A Hawker Sea Fury.

The Sea Fury was the last and most sophisticated propeller-driven fighter produced by Great Britain. Powered by a big radial Centaurus engine, the Sea Fury was faster and more heavily armed than any other fighter flown by either side in the 1948 war.

Sea Fury number 701 had been ferried to Egypt in April 1948 by a Hawker factory pilot to demonstrate to the Egyptian Air Force. So enamored were the Egyptians with the new warplane that they seized it, sending the demonstration pilot home and ignoring the flurry of protests from the British embassy.

The requisitioned Sea Fury wound up at the fighter base at El Arish. There it became the personal mount of a handsome, thirty-year-old veteran fighter pilot, Squadron Leader Abu Zaid.

Zaid was Egypt's most celebrated fighter pilot. He was already credited with shooting down one Israeli aircraft and destroying another on the ground. It had been Zaid who shot down the Fairchild Argus off Tel Aviv on June 4, 1948, killing David Shprinzak and his bomb-chucker Mattie Sukenik.

Gideon Lichtman kept remembering the dogfight over the Sinai. The Egyptian pilot had been good. But not good enough. Lichtman would always remember the way the Egyptian pilot looked back at him, waiting for the hail of bullets that never came.

Squadron Leader Abu Zaid. In a war of mostly nameless and faceless adversaries, it was good information. This one had a name and a face.

And he wasn't an amateur like most of his squadronmates. Sooner or later someone would get another shot at Abu Zaid. And this time they'd get that sonofabitch.

━━━━━━━━

The dust-up between Lichtman and the air force staff officer was symptomatic of the friction between the Machal airmen and the IDF commanders. Increasingly, senior commanders made it clear that this was an *Israeli* defense force. Hebrew was its official language. Every senior commander in the IDF was an Israeli.

Even the ATC, despite the grumblings of the Bagel Lancers, was now commanded by a veteran Haganah operative named Munya Mardor. Other than possessing a pilot's license, Mardor had no qualifications for commanding a squadron—except that he was a bona fide Israeli. For his part, Mardor presided over his unruly pilots like a befuddled schoolmaster. He seldom presumed to actually give them orders.

The volunteer airmen were still the angels in the sky who had come to save Israel. But now—well, the volunteers should understand that they were *temporary* angels. Yes, they had a vital place in the IDF—as long as they were needed. If and when the war was concluded, the IDF would revert to what it was supposed to be: a Hebrew-speaking, all-Israeli fighting force.

Then the angels could go home.

Part Three

FORTUNES OF WAR

*Can a country be born in a day or
a nation be brought forth in a moment?*
—ISAIAH 66:8

*In Israel, in order to be a realist
you must believe in miracles.*
—DAVID BEN-GURION

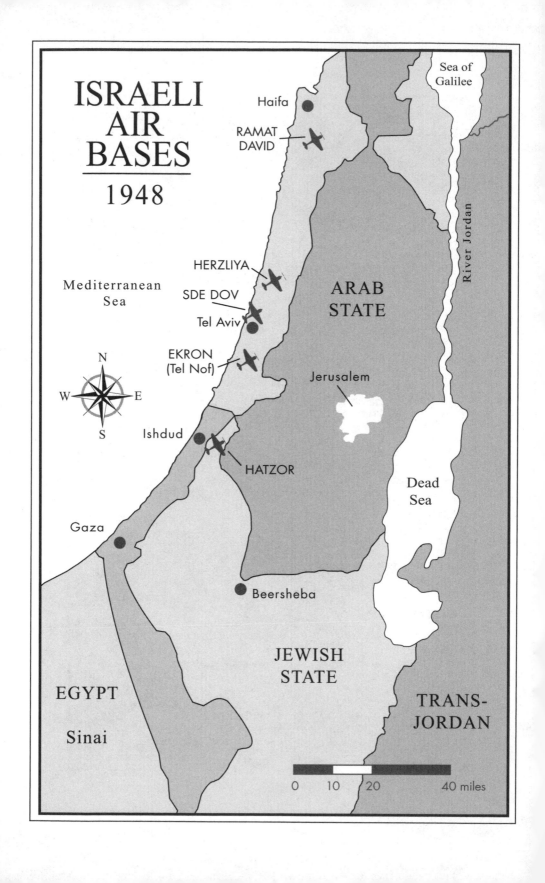

35

Ten Plagues

TEL AVIV
SEPTEMBER 17, 1948

Sitting in the back seat of the Chrysler, Count Folke Bernadotte had begun to relax after an arduous day. The warm September sun shone on the streets of Jerusalem as Bernadotte's three-car convoy wound its way to his next meeting.

Bernadotte was the UN-appointed mediator of the Israeli-Arab conflict. It was Bernadotte who orchestrated the first thirty-day truce between the warring nations and, after ten days of war, it was Bernadotte who negotiated the current cease-fire.

The Swedish nobleman had arrived in Jerusalem that morning. His day had been spent in meetings and inspection tours of the UN-administered territory. Just yesterday Bernadotte had presented to the Security Council his latest proposal for the repartitioning of Palestine. In Bernadotte's plan, the entire Negev as well as control of Jerusalem would be handed to the Arabs. The shape of Israel would be even smaller than under the original UN plan.

Bernadotte's convoy rounded a corner and began the ascent up a narrow road through the Jewish-occupied district of Katamon. Bernadotte was not concerned when he saw a jeep in Israeli military markings wheel in front of the convoy. Military checkpoint stops were common in Jerusalem.

Bernadotte saw three men in military khaki shorts approaching the vehicles. Abruptly one of the men ran directly to Bernadotte's Chrysler. He was carrying a submachine pistol.

Bernadotte, a decorated soldier from two world wars, was trapped. The assassin opened fire.

―――――――

It was nearly midnight, but David Ben-Gurion was wide awake. In the Red House conference room David Ben-Gurion was putting the finishing touches on the response to the plan Bernadotte had presented before he was assassinated.

The killing of Bernadotte was a diplomatic blow to Israel. The assassination was condemned by all sides—the UN, the Arabs, the Israelis—but Ben-Gurion worried that the killing would give the deceased UN mediator's plan heightened significance. In the words of Israeli statesman Chaim Weizman, "what were recommendations . . . now became a political testament."

Bernadotte's assassination had been carried out by member of the *Lehi*—a renegade Jewish underground group called the Stern Gang. The assassins had pumped six bullets into Bernadotte's upper body and then fired eighteen more rounds into the French colonel next to him.

Lehi had regarded Bernadotte as a puppet of the British and their Arab allies. Their motive for killing the Swedish diplomat was the fear that Ben-Gurion's government would agree to his proposals.

It was a groundless fear. What the killers didn't know was that Ben-Gurion and his commanders had already reached a decision about Bernadotte's plan. Israel would never accept a settlement that resulted in the loss of the Negev. They were taking the military option.

It already had a name: *Ten Plagues*.

―――――――

Drive the Egyptians out of Israel. That was the simple—but hugely ambitious—goal of the Ten Plagues offensive.

During the months of the cease-fire, the Egyptians had solidified their hold on the Negev. Both main roads to the desert, one down the

Mediterranean coast and the other a few miles inland, were in Egyptian control. A 6-mile-wide band of bunkers, armed villages, and fortified positions stretched across the desert, sealing off the Negev from the rest of Israel and isolating Israeli settlements behind the Egyptian line.

Controlling both main roads in the desert near Gaza was a massive structure called Iraq Suwedan. It was a former British police fort that the Israelis were calling the Monster on the Hill. For an Israeli offensive to succeed, it would have to drive a wedge through the Egyptian line. And it would have to somehow capture the nearly impregnable Monster on the Hill.

Ten Plagues was a biblical reference to the punishment God visited on the Egyptians after holding the Israelis captive, but soon the offensive was going by another name: Operation Yoav. It was named in honor of a Palmach commander named Yitzhak Dubno, codenamed Yoav, who had been killed in the Negev.

Before Israel could violate the truce, it needed a provocation. The IDF commanders knew exactly where to find a provocation.

One of the provisions of the cease-fire was that Egypt would allow Israeli supply convoys to reach isolated settlements in the Negev. It was a provision Egypt ignored, firing on Israeli truck convoys and making resupply by surface impossible.

A plume of dust rose in the sky on the afternoon of October 15 as a sixteen-truck Israeli convoy rumbled down the main road to the Negev. On board was a team of UN observers. The dust cloud served as an unmistakable signal to the Egyptians.

The Israelis were attempting another supply run to the Negev.

The Egyptians did what they were expected to do. When the Israeli convoy passed the Egyptian stronghold near Kartiya, the Egyptians opened fire. One Israeli truck was set ablaze. The others retreated from the desert.

It was exactly the provocation Israel needed.

The great column of dust from the Israeli convoy was still settling on the desert when three infantry brigades—the Iftah, Givati, and Negev— stormed into the Negev. Supporting them was a newly formed armored regiment, which included two Cromwell tanks stolen from the British Army and a mobile artillery corps. Even the embryonic Israeli Navy joined the battle, shelling Egyptian shore positions in Gaza.

The IDF had learned from the mistakes of previous battles. In Operation Yoav the air force would no longer be a close air support instrument of the infantry. Their first mission would be to seize control of the sky.

And that meant fighters.

Wearing his creased khaki uniform shirt and sunglasses, Modi Alon stood in front of his assembled pilots. In his matter-of-fact voice he read the order of the day from air force commander Ahoran Remez.

"Let every soldier, every pilot and air crew member, every mechanic know that the fate of the corps, the people and state depend on him. Our soldiers at the front will be looking skyward. We will not disappoint them."

A new seriousness had fallen over the squadron. For once the pilots weren't wisecracking or pulling pranks. After the weeks of unsatisfying recon missions and patrols of empty skies and fruitless chasing after the Shufti Kites, they were going into combat.

Today they would fight the Arabs.

Only a few of the pilots in the squadron had seen action. Most had arrived during the long summer break between offensives. Operation Yoav was beginning this evening and the Red Squadron would be the first into action.

But not all of them. As usual, there were not enough fighters for everyone to fly.

Alon read the lineup. The three flyable Spitfires would escort two of the newly arrived Beaufighters from Ramat David in a surprise low-level attack on the Egyptian Air Force bastion in the Sinai, El Arish.

There were nods and mutters. *About damn time.* El Arish had been the intended target for surprise air attacks before. Something always went wrong. Each time they'd lost a pilot. Eddie Cohen and then Bob Vickman.

The pilots assigned to fly the Spitfires on the El Arish strike would be . . . Alon gave them his trademark half smile, letting them hang for a few seconds. Then he named them: Syd Cohen, Rudy Augarten, Jack Cohen.

At this came groans from those not selected. *Everyone* preferred the Spitfire over the Czech Mule.

That left the Messerschmitts. To no one's surprise, Alon announced *he* was leading the three Messerschmitts. They would escort a force of makeshift bombers—two C-46 Commandos and three C-47 Dakotas—on a raid over Gaza.

At the same time a trio of *real* bombers—B-17 Flying Fortresses—would bombard the Egyptian expeditionary forces headquarters at Majdal, just north of Gaza. All three waves of warplanes would hit their targets simultaneously.

In the waning afternoon light the pilots not assigned to the mission stood beside the orange groves as the fighters rumbled down the dirt strip. Little more than an hour had elapsed since the Egyptian gunners in the Negev had obligingly fired on the Israeli truck convoy.

The war was on again.

═══════

Rudy Augarten and Jack Cohen were flying off either wing of the leader, the deep-voiced South African, Syd Cohen. Augarten was pleased that Alon had picked him for the El Arish strike. None of the untested new guys had been assigned to this opening mission. Augarten and Modi Alon had hit it off early. Their styles—Augarten laid back and calm, Alon cool and reserved—complemented each other.

The join-up with the Beaufighters from Ramat David had gone precisely as planned. Now the big twin-engine attack planes were in formation below and behind their Spitfire escorts. The five-plane formation was headed southward, staying just far enough off the coast to remain out of sight. Somewhere behind them the Messerschmitts were escorting the C-46 and C-47 ersatz bombers. Behind them, out of sight, were the B-17s.

In the sprawling brown expanse ahead, Augarten saw it: *El Arish*.

Home base of the Egyptian fighter force. The target the Red Squadron had been unable to hit all these months.

It was 17:40, twenty-nine minutes before sunset. The formation of warplanes swept down on the target.

———

Twenty miles away at Gaza, the plodding C-46 and Dakota bombers were having problems. One of the Dakotas hadn't been ready in time and was scrubbed from the mission. Now the pilots were looking for their targets.

In any other war it would have been a joke, calling the plodding C-46 freight-haulers *bombers*. The big Commandos lacked every essential piece of equipment: bombsights, external guns, bomb bays, and racks. Instead they had bomb-chuckers. Most were young soldiers, though some were air cadets on their way to becoming pilots.

The bombs were secured to the cabin floor in metal trays that fed one bomb at a time onto a metal track. A bomb-chucker would roll the bomb to the open cabin door where another yanked the bomb's pin and another kicked it out the door.

Flying one of the Dakota bombers was an ex-RAF pilot named Gordon Levett. Levett was a non-Jew, and now he was wondering what he was doing there. He had signed up to be a transport pilot—a gentile among the Bagel Lancers—not a bomber pilot.

Prior to the bombing mission Levett had a crisis of conscience. "So far in this war I had not directly killed or maimed," he wrote. "I now had to decide whether I could or should."

Levett reached a decision. Okay, he *would* drop bombs if it were a legitimate military target. He would *not* participate in indiscriminate bombing, possibly killing innocent civilians.

Now Levett was trying to bomb Gaza, and he couldn't *find* a military target. Every building and installation in Gaza was hidden in the gathering darkness.

After several passes without identifying a target, exposed to search-lights and heavy antiaircraft fire, Levett flew out to sea. Then he came boring back in at low altitude. He had both throttles of the C-47 Dakota pushed up to maximum power. The big transport's airframe was rattling and humming like a tuning fork.

This time he spotted a legitimate military target. A railway line.

Levett was roaring toward what he hoped was the target when he felt antiaircraft bursts exploding around him, buffeting the aircraft. Each burst seemed to come closer than the one before.

Levett spotted the rail line. "Bombs away!" he yelled. He heard the bomb-chuckers rolling the weapons out the door. When the last bomb was gone, Levett banked toward the safety of the darkened Mediterranean.

He never learned how many he killed that evening.

Flying high cover for the Beaufighters, Augarten saw the massive explosions as the eight 250-lb bombs erupted on the El Arish base. The two-engine attack planes pulled up, one behind the other, then swept back to rake the neatly parked rows of Spitfires with their machine guns.

The raid was a complete surprise. No antiaircraft fire had yet opened up. No Egyptian fighters were in the air.

Augarten and the two Cohens dove down to join the attack. The Spitfires' speed rose to over 300 miles per hour in the dive.

Augarten streaked low over the boundary of the field. He bored straight toward the smoke column over the main hangar. Waiting . . . waiting . . . Augarten stabbed the release button. *Whump*. He felt the two 70-kg bombs leave the belly of the Spitfire.

With their bombs expended, the Spitfires and Beaufighters swarmed back over the airfield, machine-gunning the parked enemy airplanes. Too late the Egyptian gunners opened up with scattered puffs of antiaircraft fire. No Egyptian fighters had managed—or dared—to get into the air.

Augarten looked back as they exited El Arish. He saw a towering column of smoke and at least four ruined enemy fighters on the tarmac. All the strike planes had gotten away undamaged.

Almost. From one of the Beaufighter pilots came a radio call. He'd taken a hit in his left engine. Augarten and his fellow Spitfire pilots stayed with the damaged Beaufighter as it limped past the Arab lines to a safe landing at Ekron.

The fighters streaked northward over the hills. In the dwindling light, they could barely make out the little strip in the orange groves where the pilots of the Red Squadron were waiting.

36

A Hell of a Ride

First they heard the sound. Even before the silhouettes came into view, there was no mistaking the source of the noise: the staccato rattling sound of the Jumo engines.

Dusk was settling over Herzliya, and the pilots waiting by the runway had heard no news good or bad. *Did we lose pilots again?*

The Messerschmitts were coming in low. Not until they were within a couple of miles of the field could the men on the ground spot them. In the next few seconds the fighters were roaring over the field in a loose echelon.

Three Messerschmitts. The same number that left.

The Czech Mules were still landing, each pilot doing his delicate, rudder-waggling Messerschmitt dance, when the next wave came back. The sound was similar—but distinctly different to those who knew both species of warplane. The throaty, high-pitched growl of the Spitfires' Merlin engines resonated through the orange groves. The men on the ground counted the taper-winged silhouettes.

Three Spitfires. There was cheering, hand shaking, big grins all around. Six fighters departed, six returned. None crashed on landing.

In the history of the 101 Squadron, it amounted to a milestone.

Modi Alon climbed down from the Messerschmitt. Most of his squadron was there—mechanics, armorers, pilots—and they were all happy. For the young squadron commander, it was a moment of supreme satisfaction.

Israel's small fighter force had finally been deployed the way Alon always wanted: to establish air superiority. And they had done it convincingly. The Egyptian fighter base at El Arish, while not destroyed, was in a shambles. Egypt's Spitfire fighters had been kept out of the fight. Not a single Egyptian warplane had threatened Israeli bombers or the infantry brigades advancing into the Negev.

For the bombers, the opening air strikes were a mixed success. Most of them missed their targets. The only real effect of the 5.5 tons of bombs dropped by the B-17s, Dakotas, and Commandos was to spread panic in the Egyptian garrisons at Gaza and Majdal. Scaring the crap out of your enemy sometimes counted for as much as blowing him up.

Among the crowd at Herzliya that night was Mina, Modi Alon's bride. Mina was wearing her usual shy smile. Modi and Mina had planned to go home, but they decided to hang around. Bill Pomerantz, the resident Red Squadron chef, was firing up one of his special dinners at the Falk House. A squadron party was in progress.

Tomorrow, Saturday, was the Sabbath. It would also be the first whole day of the Yoav offensive, and the 101 Squadron would be in the thick of it. Alon was a commander who believed in leading by example. Instead of taking one of the new Spitfires—every pilot's choice over the Czech Mule—Alon again assigned himself to fly the Messerschmitt.

But Alon was also a new husband. He made a promise to Mina. After he'd flown tomorrow morning, he would drive Mina up to her family's place on the Sea of Galilee for the coming Jewish *Sukkot* holiday.

Hearing this, Mina gave him a smile. The former kibbutz nurse was no longer concealing the fact that she was expecting. Their first child was due in six months.

To the other pilots, most of them bachelors, it seemed odd, perhaps overly hopeful, to be starting a family at such a time. Not to Mina and Modi. They had decided to live one day at a time. They wouldn't worry about tomorrow.

═══════

During the night of October 15, three infantry brigades of the IDF—the Yiftach, Givati, and Negev Brigades—had managed to drive a wedge across the Egyptian east–west axis in the north Negev. At the same time a commando battalion of the Yiftach Brigade planted mines along the railway line connecting El Arish with the Egyptian stronghold at Rafah. From their newly captured hilltop positions, units of the Yiftach and Negev Brigades now dominated the critical north–south main road from Gaza to Majdal.

To the east of Faluja, a new IDF unit was clanking into action. A tank battalion—consisting of the two stolen British Cromwell tanks and several Hotchkiss light tanks—was attacking the heavily fortified Egyptian position at Iraq al-Manshiya.

For the inexperienced Israeli tank crews, it was turning into a learning experience. And a bad one. By the end of the day all the tanks would be out of action, destroyed or damaged by Egyptian guns. The accompanying infantry platoon of the Negev Brigade would be driven back by Egyptian artillery.

Eleven thousand feet above the battlefield, Bill Katz had a splendid view from the cockpit of his Flying Fortress. Katz and his two accompanying B-17s were withdrawing from their early morning bombing mission.

Katz and the Hammers of the B-17 squadron had been in action since the evening before, when Operation Yoav kicked off. This morning their target was El Arish. Again no Egyptian fighters came to challenge them or their two Spitfire escorts from 101 Squadron.

Katz had just turned his bombers northward for the trip home when the bombardier called out a bogey—an unidentified aircraft—ahead of them at twelve o'clock low.

Instantly alert, they all peered down at the fast-moving warplane. As it passed beneath they recognized the slender-winged shape.

It was a lone Messerschmitt, headed south.

========

Rudy Augarten's first choice of combat assignments wouldn't have been a photo mission. Flying over places that had just been bombed was, by definition, a high-risk job. By now the antiaircraft gunners at El Arish were in a foul mood and looking for targets.

Augarten was flying one of the two Messerschmitts configured with reconnaissance cameras. It was Augarten's job to photograph the results of this morning's B-17 bombing raid.

The other thing that made photo missions dangerous was that the pilot was on his own. No escorts. Prey for enemy fighters. That was fine with Augarten. Besides the camera mounted in the Messerschmitt's belly, the fighter carried full canisters of cannon and machine-gun ammo. Just in case.

El Arish was easy to spot today. A column of black smoke—the results of the recent B-17 visit—rose on the horizon like a marker beacon. Over the nose of the Messerschmitt Augarten could see the curved roof lines of the hangars.

He leveled at a thousand feet. It was the optimum photo-shooting altitude. It was also a convenient altitude for getting nailed with an antiaircraft round.

The perimeter of the airfield slid beneath the nose of the Messerschmitt. The belly-mounted camera clicked off images of the Egyptian base and forty-five seconds later Augarten was past the boundary and back over empty desert.

He'd been lucky. Not a shot had been fired at the low-flying Messerschmitt. As Augarten climbed to the east to come back for the high-altitude sequence, he gazed around him. El Arish had been hit several times now. *Why hadn't the Egyptians sent fighters up?*

Three seconds later, Augarten knew the answer. They had.

There were two of them, elliptical wings glinting in the early morning sun. They were in a high orbit above El Arish. The Egyptian Spitfire pilots either hadn't spotted the low-flying Messerschmitt yet or they were unwilling to challenge it. Or they were expecting B-17s, not a lone fighter.

Augarten made one more quick scan of the sky, then pulled the Messerschmitt up in a sweeping turn behind the tail of the second Spitfire. He waited, letting the silhouette of the Spitfire swell in his gun sight.

Augarten opened fire. Not until the Messerschmitt's cannon and machine-gun fire was pouring into the Spitfire did the Egyptian pilots realize the danger. The pair of Egyptian fighters broke away like flushed quail, splitting in opposite directions.

Augarten's quarry was racing to the north, diving, frantically trying to get away. Augarten craned his neck around. *Where did the other one go?*

The second Spitfire was nowhere in sight. Augarten returned his attention to the Spitfire in front of him. He fired several short bursts. Pieces were coming off the Egyptian Spitfire. The Egyptian pilot was jinking—racking his fighter in short, ineffective turns—trying to escape the cannon and machine-gun fire.

He couldn't escape. Smoke streamed from the stricken fighter. Augarten stayed on the Spitfire's tail until it crashed in a geyser of debris and smoke in the dunes north of Gaza.

Ten minutes later Augarten was doing a victory roll over Herzliya. In his debriefing he would say that he'd accomplished the recon mission. The film in the fighter's camera contained good damage assessment images of El Arish. And, oh, yeah, while he was at it he'd shot down an Egyptian Spitfire.

As far as Augarten knew, there had been no witnesses to the shoot-down.

————

He was wrong. From another Messerschmitt over the battle zone, Leon Frankel had caught sight of a Spitfire with a Messerschmitt on its tail. Frankel knew exactly what he was seeing. "It was Rudy Augarten," Frankel recalled, "and he was shooting big chunks out of that Spitfire."

And then Frankel received a surprise. "All of a sudden I saw another Spitfire. He was coming at me from below." It was the second Spitfire in the pair that Augarten had encountered over El Arish.

Leon Frankel had not been trained as a fighter pilot. A decorated WWII torpedo bomber pilot, he'd won a Navy Cross and had sixty-seven carrier landings to his credit. But he'd never been in a dogfight.

Until today.

Neither, apparently, had the Egyptian Spitfire pilot. When Frankel dove to get on the Spitfire's tail, the Egyptian abruptly reversed course and headed south.

"By the time I got around, he was halfway to Cairo," Frankel recalled. He chased the Spitfire south until he realized he'd flown *too* far south.

He didn't have enough fuel to make it back to Herzliya. The nearest field en route was Ekron. Frankel decided to land for fuel.

That's when the trouble started. On the ground, Frankel noticed oil dripping from the engine. He called a mechanic to check it out. "He gave it a couple turns with his screwdriver and turned to me with a big smile and said 'Fixed,' and gave me the okay sign."

Frankel took off again. The Messerschmitt wasn't okay. The engine began running rough, stuttering, and it was then that Frankel noticed that the oil pressure gauge was reading zero. He tapped the gauge, hoping the needle would move. It didn't.

Seconds later black smoke was gushing into Frankel's cockpit. He was too far away to make it back to Ekron or even the nearby Lydda airfield.

Frankel was out of options. "I wanted to do a crash landing by the book," he remembered, "and the book says you're supposed to get rid of the canopy."

That meant opening the side-hinged canopy so it would separate from the airplane. But Frankel's canopy wouldn't separate. The canopy was beating against the side of the cockpit like a window shutter in a hurricane.

As the fighter dropped to the earth, Frankel didn't see any clear place to land. There was only a wadi, gullies, a field filled with boulders.

The Messerschmitt hit hard on its belly. It skipped across the wadis and boulders, pieces of aluminum ripping from airplane. A tornado of dirt and sagebrush swirled around the cockpit. Frankel felt one of the rudder pedals smash back against his leg with incredible force.

It was a hell of a ride. Somehow the Messerschmitt stayed upright. When the shattered fighter finally slid to a stop against an embankment, Frankel was amazed that he was still alive.

He crawled out of the cockpit and hobbled away from the wreck. He didn't know where he was. *Israel or Jordan?* He started walking in what he thought was a westward direction.

"There was nobody around," he recalled. "Just me and a dirt road."

But not for long. A truck was motoring down the road. As it came nearer, Frankel saw that it was filled with soldiers. Frankel drew his .38 Smith & Wesson revolver. Like all the volunteers, he knew what the Arabs did to captured pilots.

"I had six shots," he said. "I figured I'd take five of them out and then use the last bullet for me."

As the truck drew near, Frankel lowered his revolver. He could hear the soldiers yelling in Hebrew. They were *Palmachniks*—Israeli commandos—sent to look for him.

Not until late afternoon did Frankel finally get a ride back to Herzliya. When the lorry was still a mile from the base, Frankel saw something ominous rising over the field.

A column of black smoke.

=== 37 ===

Smoke Over Herzliya

HERZLIYA AIRFIELD
OCTOBER 16, 1948

The report reached Modi Alon in the early afternoon. *The Egyptians are pulling out of Ishdud.*

It seemed too good to be true. Ishdud was where Alon, Lou Lenart, Ezer Weizman, and Eddie Cohen had flown the squadron's first combat mission. Ishdud was where they'd stopped the Egyptian march on Tel Aviv. Ishdud had huge symbolic value to both sides.

The Egyptians were pulling their brigade out of Ishdud to consolidate with the main Egyptian force 15 miles south at their stronghold in Majdal. Now IAF Headquarters had a new mission for Alon's squadron: *Hit them as hard as possible. Keep the Egyptians on the run.*

Alon had already flown that morning. Mina was waiting for him in the squadron operations office. More than ever she was looking forward to their afternoon together in the Galilee.

Alon made a decision. It would be a quick mission. And a historic one. One he *had* to fly.

———

Ezer Weizman had just landed after a patrol over the front. Alon grabbed him and said, "What do you say we go fly in Hebrew for a change?"

The ever-eager Weizman just grinned. "Let's go."

On the way out to the airplanes, the two argued over who would fly number 114, a "doll of a plane" in Weizman's opinion, meaning it had shown the fewest nasty tendencies of the Messerschmitts. The other fighter, number 121, was the one in which Leo Nomis made a calamitous belly landing a couple of weeks before.

Alon, being the commander, pulled rank. He took the doll—number 114.

Minutes later the pair was airborne. Each Messerschmitt carried two 70-kg bombs plus their standard load of cannon and machine-gun ammunition.

They had no trouble spotting the Egyptian convoy. The long column was strung out along the road from Ishdud just as they had been when Alon and Weizman first saw them the evening of May 29. The only difference was that this time the Egyptians were *retreating*.

And they could see the bridge at Ishdud. The bridge was still down, just as the Israeli commandos had left it when they stopped the Egyptian advance on Tel Aviv. Now the bridge had a name: *Ad Halom*. In Hebrew it meant "Up to Here."

The Messerschmitts pounced. Diving down through the small arms fire, Weizman planted his bombs in the center of the Egyptian bivouac. Alon dropped his bombs in a neat pattern atop the long row of trucks. Weizman followed the road south to Majdal, strafing the convoys until his ammunition was gone.

In the haze and smoke over the battle front, the pilots lost contact with each other. By radio they agreed to head back to Herzliya separately.

On his own now, Weizman yielded to temptation. He was elated from the historic mission. He felt like buzzing something.

He spotted a suitable target beneath his nose. The enclave of Rehovot, near Ekron Air Base, was the home of his famous uncle, Chaim Weizman, who would soon be elected the first president of Israel.

Weizman brought it in low over the rooftops. He shoved up the propeller pitch—*Whrrrrooooom*—adding volume to the howling twelve-cylinder engine.

It was a classic buzz job. A little reminder to the folks in Rehovot that Chaim Weizman's nephew was alive and fighting.

And then he headed north. He knew that by now Modi Alon should be on the ground.

———

Alon had just requested clearance. Sid Antin, the muscular ex-P-47 pilot, was on duty in the makeshift Herzliya control atop the water tank. Antin cleared Alon to land.

Antin could see Alon's Messerschmitt approaching from the south. It was slowing to land. Two more fighters —Spitfires flown by Syd Cohen and Maury Mann—were at the end of the runway awaiting takeoff clearance.

Antin kept his eyes on Alon's Messerschmitt. The landing gear was coming down. But it didn't look right.

———

Alon was glowering at the main gear indicators on his instrument panel. The indicator showed that the left gear was extended, but the right was not.

It was another of the maddening habits of the Czech Mule, one of the two main gear hanging up. It was an irony that Alon had chosen *this* airplane—number 114—because it was the *least* troublesome of the bunch. He'd stuck Weizman in number 121, which had a history of landing gear troubles.

Like most of the pilots, Alon had encountered the problem before. Usually the stuck gear could be freed by yanking the airplane up and down. Putting G-forces on the airplane would pop the gear out of its cavity in the wing.

And that's what he was doing, yanking hard on the control stick to force the wheel down, when he heard another radio call from Sid Antin in the tower.

Antin had spotted a bogey—an unidentified aircraft coming in from the coast. He wanted Alon to check it out.

Alon didn't hesitate. *An intruder heading for Herzliya.* It could be an incoming bomber. Alon shoved the Messerschmitt's throttle to full power. The landing gear problem could wait. A single enemy airplane could wipe out most of the squadron's airplanes before antiaircraft gunners or fighters could stop it. Roaring westward toward the coast, Alon caught up with the bogey.

It wasn't hostile. The low-flying aircraft—it looked like one of the Auster light planes from Haifa—had the highly visible Star of David emblem on its fuselage. Alon returned to Herzliya and resumed trying to get the Messerschmitt's gear down.

From the control tower Antin watched Alon's yanks and banks. But then he saw something else. Something peculiar.

Smoke. It was a thin wisp, streaming from the nose of the Messerschmitt. Coolant? Engine oil?

Antin called for Alon to check his engine temperatures.

Alon checked. Seconds later he replied that they were fine. He didn't sound worried.

It looked to Antin that Alon's hard yanking of the Messerschmitt worked. The balky landing gear appeared to be down. The Messerschmitt was on a downwind leg for landing.

But something was wrong. The wisp of smoke was still streaming from the engine. The Messerschmitt was flying too slow. Its nose was tilted downward.

The fighter began descending like a stone.

"Get it up!" Antin shouted on the radio. *"Get it up!"*

Alon didn't answer. The Messerschmitt seemed to be out of control. Sid Antin had never felt so powerless in his life. With a sickening feeling he knew what was going to happen.

It took three more seconds. The Messerschmitt plunged into the ground nose first. The impact was felt across the field and all the way up to the control tower. A geyser of flame mushroomed from the spot where the fighter struck the ground.

The rescue and fire crews raced across the field toward the burning wreck. And then abruptly stopped. They heard another sound: a crackling *pop-pop-pop* noise.

The ammunition in the Messerschmitt's canisters was exploding.

Dozens of people watched, all powerless to intervene, while the Messerschmitt burned. No one dared approach it while the ammunition was lighting off. A dense black column of smoke was rising nearly straight up in the still air.

Weizman saw it from 10 miles out. After the buzz job over his uncle's compound at Rehovot, he was returning to Herzliya.

Weizman was stunned. Someone had crashed.

He was still climbing out of the Messerschmitt's cockpit when the squadron maintenance officer, Harry Axelrod, came to him. Axelrod's face was grief-stricken. "Modi's been killed."

Weizman just nodded. He trudged up the path to the squadron operations building where Modi Alon kept his office. He knew that Mina would be inside. She would have seen the crash and the pillar of smoke. Mina knew that only two pilots, Modi and Ezer, were flying this afternoon.

Weizman took a deep breath and walked into the office.

Gideon Lichtman and Boris Senior spotted the smoke from the cockpit of their Piper Cub. What was happening? Was Herzliya under attack? They could see three fighters orbiting over the field. *Are they Arabs? Bombing the airfield?*

Lichtman and Senior were returning from the nearby auxiliary field at Ma'abarot. They'd gone to inspect one of the P-51 Mustang fighters that had arrived in a crate and was still being assembled.

They dove the little utility plane down to the tree line to avoid being seen by the fighters. Not until one of the warplanes zoomed close overhead could they determine its identity. It was a Spitfire. Clearly visible on the fuselage was the Star of David.

Herzliya wasn't under attack. Someone had crashed.

As they flew nearer the airfield they saw the airplane burning in the open space near the southeastern approach to the runway. Lichtman plunked the Cub down, bounced, plunked again—"the worst landing I ever made," he said later—and as he rolled along the runway he had a clear view of the wreck.

He saw that it was a Messerschmitt. Standing in front of the operations hut was a lone figure. She was staring helplessly at the burning pyre of the Messerschmitt, her hands pressed to the sides of her face.

———

The word spread through the frontlines and the kibbutzim and the streets of Tel Aviv. People spoke in mournful voices, wearing expressions of grief.

Modi Alon had become a near-mythical hero. His exploits conjured images of a young David in single-warrior combat against an overwhelmingly powerful enemy. In the first dark days of their war for independence, Modi Alon had given them hope.

At Herzliya, darkness settled over the orange groves and the camouflaged revetments. Most of the pilots had left the airfield. They wandered in twos and threes up the road to the Falk House in the Kfar Shmaryahu village. They stopped a few times to gaze back at the field. Smoke was still rising from the crash site.

Missing tonight were the kibitzing and wiseass banter. No one felt like setting up the makeshift bar—the plank laid over a couple of barrels. Ezer Weizman had left. He'd driven Mina up to her parents' home where Modi had planned to take her that day.

Giddy Lichtman went to the room in the Falk Pension that he shared with Ezer Weizman. He was lying on his cot, all the events of the day whirling through his mind, when the door flew open. Standing in his room was a middle-aged couple. They were Ezer Weizman's parents.

"Who was killed?" the mother blurted. She knew there had been a crash. She also knew that their son Ezer and Modi Alon had been flying together. The Alons and Weizmans were close.

It was Modi, Lichtman told them. Ezer was okay. He'd taken Mina home to her family.

The couple stared at him. The father said nothing. He shook his head and wore a mournful expression. Abruptly the mother burst into sobbing and threw her arms around Lichtman, holding him tightly as she wept.

———

Outside in the courtyard Augarten, Antin, Cohen, and Mann talked about what had happened. The crash was another of the troubling Messerschmitt mysteries. What caused Alon's fighter to abruptly nose down and plunge into the ground? Had the Messerschmitt been damaged by enemy fire over Ishdud?

Sid Antin had been the last to speak with Alon. When Antin spotted the wisp of smoke and told Alon to check his temperatures, Alon had replied in a clear voice that they were fine. But when the Messerschmitt began its steep descent, Alon didn't respond to Antin's frantic calls.

Was Alon incapacitated from the smoke? Had the fighter taken combat damage that made it suddenly uncontrollable? The way the Messerschmitt plunged out of control, it looked like a classic stall-spin accident, perhaps following an engine failure.

The burned-out wreckage provided few clues. The official IAF investigation was maddeningly vague, concluding that "Aircraft crashed out of control, burst into flames and was completely destroyed."

———

Losing a squadronmate was nothing new. Each of the volunteers had seen best friends, wingmen, squadronmates die in battle. It was the nature of war, and the veteran pilots of the Red Squadron had been through the worst of wars in Europe and the Pacific. In Israel they'd already lost buddies: Cohen, Vickman, Bloch, as well as several guys from the other squadrons.

This was different. Modi Alon was not only a buddy but a leader they had come to revere. He was a pilot like them, a WWII vet with similar training to theirs. But he was something else: an Israeli. Alon was a member of the threatened little nation the volunteers had come to help. Alon had made them feel that they were part of a greater purpose.

And now he was gone. Sitting in the gloom of the courtyard at the Falk House, each pilot wrestled with his emotions. "Everybody in the squadron was crying," recalled Rudy Augarten. "In all the wars I've been in, I had never seen anything like that."

=== 38 ===

Maneuver Kill

Who should take over the 101 Squadron?

In their Yarkon Hotel headquarters, air force commander Remez and his staff wrestled with the question until well after dark. The success of Operation Yoav depended on strong support from the air force. The 101 Squadron needed a strong leader.

The Englishman, Maury Mann, had been Alon's number two in command, and in a normal military unit he would succeed the deceased commander. But Mann had been badly rattled by Alon's crash, which he had witnessed from the cockpit of his Spitfire at the end of the runway. So rattled, he'd crashed his Spitfire when he returned half an hour later from his mission in the Negev. According to the reports from Herzliya, Mann was an emotional wreck.

Later that night Remez announced their decision. The new commander of the 101 Squadron would be the tall South African, Syd Cohen. Augarten and Weizman would be promoted to flight leaders.

Alon and Cohen represented two styles of leadership. With Modi Alon the Red Squadron airmen had the sense they were led by a fussy den mother who chided them for their misbehavior. Alon had never disguised the fact that he was ambitious. He was conscious of his public persona, David challenging the Arab Goliath. He embraced the role and added his own flourishes—the sunglasses, the web belt, creased military shirt.

Syd Cohen was different. He was one of them—a big brother, a deep-voiced guy who was as adept at stealing cars as any of the pilots. Cohen had left medical school when WWII began and by 1942 was flying Curtiss Kittyhawks and then Spitfires in North Africa. He was back in med school in 1948 when he dropped out to come to Israel.

To everyone's surprise, the Red Squadron didn't miss a beat. In different ways both commanders—Alon and Cohen—brought out their combative spirit.

The appointment of Cohen created a change in demeanor for the squadron. Gone was the insistence that squadron orders be delivered in Hebrew. Gone were the ass-chewings after a night of bar-trashing or car-stealing. More than ever the Red Squadron was a band of outsiders, a foreign legion within another nation's military. With the sole exception of Ezer Weizman, they were exclusively Machalniks. Volunteers commanded by a volunteer.

━━━━

It was the afternoon of October 17, the day after Modi Alon's death. Leon Frankel was sitting in the back of a jeep when he made a discovery. His limbs had gone numb. "I couldn't move," he recalled. "I was paralyzed." He spent the next several days in the hospital.

Gradually Frankel regained the use of his arms and legs, but the doctors couldn't determine whether his problem resulted from the impact of the crash or was psychological. It didn't matter to Frankel. "I put in my paperwork to go home."

To Frankel's thinking, he had fulfilled his commitment. He'd put his life on the line to help save Israel and his fellow Jews, and new pilots were coming in to replace him. "By a strange coincidence, I had twenty-five missions, the same number I flew in the Navy."

Frankel wasn't the only one to leave. The Wild Man, Chris Magee, had already grown frustrated with the inactivity during the long truce and the lack of combat opportunities. He left Israel only a week before the next outbreak of hostilities.

Another was Leo Nomis, whose drunken binges had made him a

menace to his squadronmates. "We all loved him," recalled Sid Antin. "But when he got drunk, he was a terror. He would fight anybody, break up the goddamned place."

Antin was the only pilot tough enough to handle Nomis. "I'd climb up his back and beat the shit out of him."

In a fit of pique after he was grounded for a buzz job over the beach, Nomis had gone on a rampage in Tel Aviv. He concluded a night of hard drinking by getting into a brawl on the waterfront. After beating up several Israeli MPs, Nomis was tossed into a Jaffa jail.

The volunteers knew there was a line they couldn't cross. They could get shitfaced, smash a few mirrors, steal cars—and know they would be forgiven. It was the kind of war where they could blow off steam—up to a point—and get away with it.

The hard-drinking Nomis had crossed the line. He'd blown off more steam than was allowed. Soon after his release from jail, Leo Nomis was put on a plane out of the country.

Another pilot exiting the squadron was Mike Flint, but for a different reason. Flint had no intention of leaving Israel or the war. After his two landing mishaps with the Messerschmitt, Flint's distaste for the Czech Mule had risen to a full-blown loathing.

The death of Modi Alon only confirmed what he'd suspected since training in Czechoslovakia. The goddamned Messerschmitt was trying to kill *all* of them.

Flint's friend Abie Nathan, an Indian ex-WWII pilot who flew Norsemans in 35 Flight, a tactical transport squadron at Ekron, made Flint an offer he couldn't refuse. Flint could join Nathan's unit. Nathan warned him that the mission—night bombing, resupply and reinforcement at outlying fields—was at least as dangerous as flying fighters. It was about to become even more dangerous because they were going to commence dive bombing with the newly arrived AT-6 Harvards.

"Sign me up," said Flint. Dive bombing was something he'd learned in WWII, and he was damned good at it. Best of all, it meant that he was finished with the Czech Mule.

But the Mule wasn't finished with the volunteers.

It was the late morning of October 17. Giddy Lichtman and Sid Antin were in a pair of Messerschmitts 16 miles northeast of Gaza. Below them was Iraq Suwedan, the hulking fortress the Israeli soldiers called the Monster on the Hill.

From the air the fortress looked like something left from the Crusades—high stone walls with towering parapets that had been built by the British during the Mandate years, before the fortress was occupied by the Arabs.

Iraq Suwedan commanded the road to the Negev. Since the opening of Operation Yoav, Israeli brigades had been in a pitched battle with the Egyptian defenders of the fortress. So far the Monster on the Hill had resisted every attempt to overrun it.

Today they were trying a new weapon. Suspended beneath the wings of the two Messerschmitts were napalm bombs. It would be the first use in the war of the incendiary antipersonnel bomb. Developed and used in the last stages of WWII, napalm was an incendiary mixture of gasoline and a gelling agent. It was a hellish weapon, enveloping its victims in a cascade of flames. The use of napalm produced nearly as much psychological damage as physical carnage.

The fighters dropped down to low altitude over the water and headed toward the Monster on the Hill. Already antiaircraft fire was peppering the sky around the fortress.

Lichtman went in first. He roared in low over the fortress and released his bombs. Pulling up, he swiveled in his seat and looked back. He could see the napalm igniting on the roof of the fortress.

Lichtman was pleased with himself. *Too* pleased. It was then that he made a near-fatal mistake. He stayed in the area around the fortress to use up his cannon and machine-gun ammunition. After his last firing pass over a column of enemy tanks, he found himself back over the fortress—and the guns of Iraq Suwedan.

Then he noticed a different smell in the cockpit. *Burning oil.* The Messerschmitt's engine was streaming oil and coolant.

An Egyptian gunner had scored a hit.

The engine was losing power. Lichtman pointed the nose northward, trying to gain altitude. "I got up to about 300 feet," he recalled, "but couldn't get any higher."

He thought about bailing out. Immediately he dismissed the idea. He was over Arab-held territory. He'd stay with the airplane. Lichtman radioed his wingman, Sid Antin, that he was in trouble.

Smoke was pouring into the cockpit and tendrils of flame were licking around the engine cowling. With no forward visibility, Lichtman snatched the canopy open. A blast of steaming oil hit him in the face, smearing his goggles and burning his face.

Antin joined up on his wing. By radio he tried to steer Lichtman toward Ekron Air Base, about 5 miles ahead. Lichtman extended his landing gear, but then Antin barked on the radio, "Get your gear up, Giddy. Land it on the belly."

It was the right advice. With lousy visibility and a dead engine, a hard landing would collapse the Messerschmitt's flimsy landing gear. There wouldn't be any second chance.

At 150 feet above the desert, the situation went critical. "The engine was farting, cutting out," Lichtman recalled. "The Messerschmitt wouldn't stay airborne much longer."

At 20 feet above the runway he cut the throttle. The fighter settled on its belly, then slid in a shower of sparks to a stop in front of the astonished controllers in the Ekron tower.

It was a near-miraculous ending. The squadron mechanics determined that the fighter had taken flak damage to its cylinder exhaust stack, right wing, and right radiator. The loss of coolant had caused internal damage to the engine.

Two days later, the fighter was flying again.

It was the fourth crash of a 101 Squadron fighter in two days, a horrendous statistic for any fighter unit, especially since three of the crashes were Messerschmitts. It only deepened the distrust the pilots already felt for the Czech Mule.

One of the Mule's early victims, artist and crusader Stan Andrews, was still grounded. He'd been off flight status since his first—and only—combat mission on July 10. It was the day Andrews flipped the Mule on takeoff and his best friend, Bob Vickman, went missing in action.

Andrews had been transferred to Ramat David Air Base, where he was promoted to major and assigned as the liaison officer to the UN peace-keeping force in Israel. The idea was to keep Andrews out of the cockpit.

It didn't work. Against orders, Andrews was flying again. At Ramat David he had found a new comrade-in-arms, a Beaufighter pilot named Len Fitchett.

The twenty-five-year-old Fitchett had been a decorated RCAF Mosquito pilot in WWII, with three confirmed kills and a shared credit for another. Fitchett had been shot down twice himself, once having to evade Nazi troops while he made his way back to allied lines.

Fitchett was not Jewish, but he had been deeply affected when he visited a Nazi concentration camp at the end of the war. In 1948 he was approached by fellow Canadian John McElroy about volunteering to fly in Israel. Fitchett didn't have to think twice. He dropped out of his university studies and joined the Machal airmen in Israel.

In Len Fitchett Andrews found a crusader like himself. As the 103 Squadron "B" Flight commander, Fitchett was able to circumvent the air force order to keep Andrews grounded. He'd take Andrews along in his Beaufighter.

The Beaufighters of 103 Squadron were the same beat-up war birds that Emmanuel Zur had purchased in Britain for his phony film production company. Technically, the attack planes carried only two crewmen, pilot and navigator, but a third observer could be squeezed into the cockpit.

On the morning of October 19, Fitchett and Andrews, with navigator Dov Sugerman, took off to join a naval battle in progress off Majdal. An Egyptian tanker had moved in off the coast to deliver fuel to the

Egyptian garrison at Majdal. The tanker was escorted by the flagship of the Egyptian Navy, the *Emir Farouk*.

When Fitchett's Beaufighter arrived overhead, the battle had been joined by three light warships of the Israeli Navy.

And, unknown to Fitchett, a flight of Egyptian fighters.

Fitchett was in a bomb run on the *Emir Farouk* when he spotted the danger. It was an unfamiliar blunt-nosed fighter—it *had* to be Egyptian—and it was slicing across the sky toward him. As the fighter drew nearer, Fitchett realized he was in trouble. It was a British-built Hawker Sea Fury.

The Beaufighter attack plane was no match for the agile Sea Fury. Fitchett had only one choice. *Dive! Go for the water.*

He jettisoned the Beaufighter's bomb load. He shoved the nose toward the Mediterranean. The Beaufighter and its crew were finished unless they could shake the Sea Fury off their tail.

Over his shoulder Fitchett saw the Egyptian fighter diving with him. The Sea Fury was pulling in behind his tail, almost in firing range. Fitchett banked the Beaufighter hard to the right, then back to the left. He kept the nose pointed at the water. Fitchett could see the wave tops rushing up at him.

He waited until the surface of the sea was filling up his windscreen. At the last instant Fitchett yanked hard on the yoke. It was a brutal, high-G pull-out. The Beaufighter bottomed out of the dive a few feet above the waves. Grunting against G-forces, Fitchett glanced over his shoulder. *Where was the Sea Fury?*

It was gone. In its place was a geyser of blue and green water. It looked like an undersea volcanic eruption. The Egyptian fighter had plunged straight into the Mediterranean.

It was the end of the mission for Fitchett. His bombs were gone. In the official record, Len Fitchett would be credited with a "maneuver kill." He had downed an enemy aircraft not with guns but airmanship.

And it was the end of Egypt's greatest air hero. Squadron Leader Abu Zaid was the commanding officer of 2 Squadron of the Egyptian

Royal Air Force. It was Zaid who surprised Gideon Lichtman with his aggressive fighter tactics several days earlier in the Sea Fury. And it was Zaid who shot down the Fairchild over the Egyptian flotilla.

Today's sortie had been Abu Zaid's seventy-second combat mission of the war. And his last.

On the ground at Ramat David, Stan Andrews climbed down from the Beaufighter. He had defied the standing order keeping him grounded—and it had nearly cost him his life. Now he didn't have to fly into harm's way again.

Instead of being unnerved by the mission, Andrews wanted more. His new friend and fellow crusader, Len Fitchett, who had just splashed the Egyptian Sea Fury, was happy to oblige him.

They didn't have to wait long. There was still time before the next cease-fire. The Monster on the Hill—the intractable Iraq Suwedan fortress overlooking the road to the Negev—had resisted capture. Iraq Suwedan had defied eight attempts by the Israeli Army's Givati Brigade to take it.

With only days, possibly hours before the cease-fire, the Israeli ground commanders were poised to make a final infantry assault. But first they wanted another low-level bomb attack to soften up the Egyptian defenses.

Air force commander Aharon Remez thought it would be a suicide mission, given the intensity of the antiaircraft fire over Iraq Suwedan. He didn't want to assign any of the volunteer airmen.

When Len Fitchett heard about it, he stormed into Remez's office in the Yarkon to demand that *he* be assigned. Remez was surprised. Why would Fitchett, a non-Jew, volunteer for such a mission?

Fitchett didn't bother with modesty. He told Remez he was the most experienced low-level attack pilot in the IAF. "I am the only man here who can do it."

Remez was impressed with the young man's fervor. Reluctantly he agreed. Fitchett could have the mission.

Bombing Iraq Suwedan was dangerous business. Already Gideon Lichtman's Messerschmitt had been hit over the fortress. On his first run over Iraq Suwedan, Fitchett took a hit. He landed his Beaufighter at Ekron with one engine shut down.

The next day Fitchett and South African volunteer Dan Rosin flew practice runs on a dummy target near Ramat David. Finally Fitchett was satisfied. He was sure they could put their bombs on the target.

The next morning the Beaufighters took off for Iraq Suwedan. Fitchett was in the lead. And in Fitchett's Beaufighter—grounding order be damned—was the caped crusader, Stan Andrews.

=== 39 ===

The Monster on the Hill

IRAQ SUWEDAN FORTRESS
OCTOBER 20, 1948

One pass. That was the order from IAF headquarters.

Fitchett acknowledged the order during the mission briefing at Ramat David. As a veteran combat airman, he knew the axiom about low-level bomb runs: "One pass and go to the grass." It meant that after you'd made your first surprise low-level attack, you stayed low and got out of the neighborhood fast.

The Egyptian firepower concentrated at the Iraq Suwedan fortress was sure to be intense. The two Beaufighters would come one right behind the other, drop their weapons, and depart. One pass. Those were the orders.

But some orders begged to be ignored. Fitchett made his first pass over the fortress at Iraq Suwedan, closely trailed by Dan Rosin. They achieved the hoped-for surprise. They met only light ground fire from the fortress's defenders.

But something didn't work. It happened on almost every mission in the beat-up, war-surplus Beaufighters. This time it was Fitchett's bomb racks. Only *half* his bombs released from their racks. Even worse, *none* of Rosin's bomb load had dropped.

It was then that Fitchett made the same critical decision that Gideon Lichtman had made three days earlier. Fitchett ignored the one-pass order. *Damn it*. He still had bombs. He knew he could put them on target. He just needed one more pass.

Rosin's bomb system had an electrical glitch, and he headed back to Ramat David. Fitchett lined up for another run at the Monster on the Hill.

This time the Egyptians in the fort were not surprised.

Tracers arced up from behind the stone walls. Oily bursts of shrapnel exploded to either side and in front of the fast-moving Beaufighter. The air crackled with the bullets from hundreds of small arms.

Fitchett's remaining bombs released. *Ka-boom. Ka-boom*. The explosions reverberated within the walls of the fortress. Fitchett's daring attack succeeded.

But not without penalty. While the Beaufighter was over the target, its bombs still in the air, there was a loud *thunk* that could be heard by Israeli troops on the ground. An ominous trail of smoke and fire spewed from the Beaufighter's left engine.

An Egyptian gunner had scored a hit.

The stricken engine was producing zero power. The Beaufighter was yawing hard to the left. From the ground near the fort, observers could see Fitchett struggling to keep the plane's wings level.

Lou Lenart was the southern front air coordinator. Lenart yelled on the radio at Fitchett. "Turn to the east!" That was where the Israeli troops were.

Fitchett didn't hear. Or else he was unable to turn the damaged aircraft. He continued to the west, toward the shoreline and open beach.

He made it 10 miles. The Beaufighter was shuddering, trailing smoke, hovering on the edge of a stall. Ahead lay the coastal plain, near the village of Ishdud. Fitchett held the nose of the Beaufighter up as long as he could until—*Whomp*—the Beaufighter went in hard. It skidded on its belly over the soft ground.

The airmen—Fitchett, Andrews, navigator Dov Sugerman—were alive. The bottom of the Beaufighter was ripped open, gushing fuel, ready to ignite. Worse, the smoke and dirt column raised by the big downed warplane was a beacon for any enemy patrols in the area.

The crew scrambled out of the cockpit. They had no time to determine whether they'd come down on Israeli- or Egyptian-occupied ground. Over a shallow rise appeared the dark shapes of running men. They were shouting and carrying weapons.

=====

Soon after Fitchett's Beaufighter went down, an Israeli Dragon Rapide twin-engine biplane was dispatched to search the area. In the Rapide were Maury Mann of the 101 Squadron and Smoky Simon from IAF Headquarters. Both were friends of Fitchett and Andrews. They carried with them weapons and ammunition to toss down to the stranded airmen.

It was nearly dark when they spotted the smoke. The wreck of the Beaufighter was still burning. It lay near the beach at Ishdud, about 10 miles from the Monster on the Hill.

The Rapide flew directly over the fire. Gazing down, they determined that, yes, it definitely was the missing Beaufighter. There was no sign of the crew. Near the wreck was a pair of Egyptian army trucks and a cluster of soldiers who promptly opened fire on them.

The slow-moving Rapide was forced to withdraw.

=====

Several days later, Lou Lenart was standing on the beach at the village of Ishdud. Before him lay the wreckage of Len Fitchett's Beaufighter. It was burned to a twisted hulk. By its appearance, it looked as though the aircraft had landed intact, then was intentionally destroyed by fire.

Lenart had rolled into Ishdud along with a well-armed Israeli force in several jeeps and half a dozen trucks. With Lenart was the twenty-six-year-old operations officer for the southern front. He was a sandy-haired, blue-eyed Palmach officer named Yitzhak Rabin.

They had met no resistance. The Egyptian brigade that had occupied the area was gone, in retreat to the south.

At Rabin's order the Israeli troops rounded up the local villagers, including the *mukhtar*, the mayor. An IDF intelligence officer was interrogating the mukhtar in Arabic.

The plane had been on fire when it crashed, the mukhtar said. The villagers tried to save the crew but the fire was too intense.

The intelligence officer asked what happened to the bodies.

The jackals got them, the mukhtar said. He and the other villagers tried to stop them but it was impossible. The fliers' bodies must have been completely devoured by the wild animals.

Lenart didn't believe it. He was a close friend of Len Fitchett's. Lenart had spotted something familiar. "While the mukhtar was reciting this bullshit," recalled Lenart, "my eyes were fixed on his left wrist." The mukhtar was wearing a gold watch. Len Fitchett's watch.

Lenart pulled Rabin aside. He pointed out the wristwatch. Put a bullet in the mukhtar's head, Lenart said. Burn down the village and drive all the villagers out. The Egyptian lines were only a few hundred meters away.

"I can't do that," said Rabin.

"Why not?"

Rabin said that collective punishment was against the Geneva Convention.

Lenart was beside himself. "You think these Arabs are following the Geneva Convention?" he said. "They burned our guys to death, then cut 'em up and fed 'em to their dogs—if they didn't carve 'em up first while they were still alive." Lenart said it again. Shoot the mukhtar and burn the village.

Yitzhak Rabin was a battle-toughened commando and future prime minister. He shook his head. "We cannot do it. If we take such actions, we abandon every principle we are fighting for."

Lenart was overruled. Israel was Rabin's country, not his. He was a foreigner.

The mukhtar stood watching as Lenart and Rabin climbed into their jeep. They drove away without looking back.

———

In his career Rudy Augarten had flown several fighters—the P-47 in which he gunned down two German Me-109s over Europe, the P-51

Mustang recently arrived from the United States, the British-built Spitfire just delivered from Czechoslovakia. And the Czech Mule.

Now Augarten had a new favorite. He'd just taken off from the dirt strip at Herzliya. The nimble Spitfire he was flying had used exactly *half* the length of runway that the Messerschmitt required.

He liked everything about the British-built fighter. It was lighter and more agile than the Mustang. Its cockpit was infinitely more comfortable than the claustrophobic Czech Mule. What Augarten *really* liked was the Spitfire's 20-mm cannons and .50-caliber machine guns. Unlike the quirky Mule's and even the Mustang's guns, the Spitfire's guns were reliable and deadly.

It was a few minutes past 09:00 on October 21. On Augarten's right wing was one of the new guys, Canadian Jack Doyle. Doyle was part of the contingent that included his fellow Canucks John McElroy and Denny Wilson, and American Slick Goodlin. All had WWII experience in the Spitfire. Several, like Jack Doyle, had shot down Nazi airplanes.

Doyle was Canadian by nationality but Irish in temperament. He was born to Irish Catholic parents from whom he inherited a dislike of British rule, whether in Ireland or Palestine. When offered the opportunity to fly for Israel, Doyle had jumped at the chance.

The morning sun cast a golden glow over the desert as the Spitfires headed south. Beneath his left wing Augarten could see Beersheba, the Egyptian-held strongpoint in the central Negev. Off to the west he spotted the dark clusters of the Israeli brigades moving toward the Egyptian concentration at Faluja.

Augarten and Doyle's mission this morning was to intercept enemy warplanes trying to attack the Israeli ground force. Augarten's eyes were scanning the southern sky. If Egyptian fighters had managed to take off from El Arish, they'd be showing up—

In the next instant Augarten spotted them. Four dark shapes, climbing northward from El Arish. Even at this distance he could make out the elliptical wings, the distinctive tapered fuselages.

Spitfires. It was easy to figure out whose air force they belonged to. Augarten and Doyle were flying the only available Israeli Spitfires.

With a 2,000-foot altitude advantage, Augarten and Doyle dove on the Egyptian warplanes. The lead Egyptian pilot spotted them. He hauled his fighter's nose up into an Immelmann—the top half of a loop—toward the Israeli Spitfires.

Augarten was surprised. It was a rare example of aggressiveness by an Egyptian pilot—actually *trying* to get on an attacker's tail.

But not aggressive enough. Augarten cut inside the arc of Egyptian's loop. A few seconds later he was on the Egyptian's tail. He chased the Spitfire through another complete turn. The Egyptian fighter was centered in Augarten's gun sight.

It was over in seconds. The Spitfire's cannons and machine guns spat fire. Smoke poured from the stricken Egyptian Spitfire. The fighter rolled over on a wing and plummeted into the desert, crashing near the Egyptian-held city of Rafah on the border of the Sinai.

Jack Doyle was busy shooting up another of the Egyptian warplanes. Pieces were coming off the enemy Spitfire, but the fighter wasn't going down. Like the other two surviving Egyptian fighters, this one was roaring at full throttle back toward El Arish.

Doyle's quarry got away. The dogfight was over. Back at Herzliya the two fighters pulled up in the now-traditional victory roll over their home field.

Rudy Augarten had earned another distinction in Red Squadron history. He was the first to shoot down a Spitfire—with a Spitfire.

———

General Yigal Allon was the thirty-year-old Israeli commander of the southern front. Under his command Operation Yoav had achieved some—but not all—of its goals. Allon's brigades had driven a wedge into the Egyptian line that stretched from Gaza eastward to Beersheba and to the hills below Jerusalem. The critical road to the Negev had been opened, and the besieged kibbutzim and villages could finally be relieved and supplied by land.

But on prize still lay unclaimed. The city of Beersheba was the capital of the Negev. And an Egyptian stronghold.

Ben-Gurion and the IDF commanders had gambled that the Trans-jordanian Army would not join the battle in the Negev. It was no secret that King Abdullah of Jordan wanted to annex the UN-allotted part of Palestine called the West Bank to his own kingdom when the war was concluded. Abdullah had little to gain by helping the Egyptians in the Negev and much to lose if the Israelis turned their army against *him*.

The gamble was paying off. The Jordanians were showing no inclination to join the fight. The Israeli Army was carefully avoiding confrontations with the Transjordanian-led Arab Legion forces around Jerusalem. Instead, they concentrated their forces on the Egyptian Army's four well-armed brigades in the Negev.

Now Yigal Allon could see his next objective. Shimmering in the distance was the ancient city of Beersheba. To Israelis, Beersheba had immense strategic and symbolic importance. Vital roads radiated like spokes from Beersheba to Tel Aviv in the north, Gaza in the northwest, Hebron and Jerusalem to the northeast.

Allon sent his forces into action at dawn on October 21. A commando battalion of the Israeli Negev Brigade led an attack on Beersheba while other units blocked the roads to prevent reinforcement of the Egyptian force in the city.

The battle was fierce and brief. By 09:00 the battalion-strength Egyptian garrison ran up a white flag.

To the victorious Israelis, the capture of Beersheba, the crown jewel of the desert, felt like the fulfillment of a biblical promise. The land of Israel had just been extended to nearly the same proportions as in the time of King Solomon.

At 15:00 the next day, October 22, the UN-ordered truce took effect. It was the end of Operation Yoav. The Egyptian Army had been pushed back 70 miles and was now divided into isolated forces across the desert.

In Faluja, to the southeast of Gaza, the four thousand troops of the Egyptian 9th Brigade, commanded by Brigadier Sayid Taha, were now cut off from the adjoining Egyptian brigade to the west.

The Monster on the Hill—the fortress of Iraq Suwedan—was still occupied by the Egyptian Army. Despite multiple artillery shellings, bombings, napalm attacks and the loss of Len Fitchett and his Beaufighter crew, the hulking fortress still blocked the key route to the southern Negev.

But not for much longer.

═40═

Faluja Pocket

WESTERN GALILEE
OCTOBER 22, 1948

By UN order, the cease-fire would begin at noon. But at dawn, a fresh battle had already begun in the north. A three-thousand-man guerrilla band called the Arab Liberation Army, in defiance of the UN order, swarmed over a complex of Israeli outposts and settlements in the hills of the western Galilee.

The ALA was an army of volunteers from more than a dozen countries and operated outside the control of the regular Arab forces. Commanded by a self-styled Arab nationalist named Fawzi el-Kaukji, the ALA over the years had been a menace not only to the Jewish settlers of Palestine but to the British occupiers.

Kaukji looked more like a Prussian officer than an Arab—blue eyes, thick neck, close-cropped reddish hair, a body bearing over eighty separate combat wounds. Among his many decorations was the one he prized the most: the German Iron Cross, earned thirty years before in WWI.

Kaukji's early morning assault in the hills above the Galilee came as a surprise to Ben-Gurion and the IDF commanders.

And an opportunity.

The time had come to do something about Fawzi el-Kaukji. Even before the May 15 invasion of Israel by Arab armies, Kaukji's Arab Liberation Army had invaded upper Palestine, attacking Jewish outposts and kibbutzim.

Already in the works was an Israeli military plan that bore yet another symbolic name: Operation Hiram, a reference to the biblical king of Tyre. The operation had been on hold, awaiting a suitable provocation.

Fawzi el-Kaukji had just handed them the provocation.

It was a now-familiar script. Ben-Gurion's representative dutifully protested to the UN. Kaukji's rampage into the Galilee was a flagrant violation of the truce. Just as they had done after each such violation, the UN ignored the protest.

It was all Israel needed. Ben-Gurion himself gave the order: *Launch Operation Hiram.*

The sun hung low over the Mediterranean as the three Hammer Squadron B-17s roared down the runway at Ramat David. It was the evening of October 28, and the bombers were delivering the opening shots of Operation Hiram.

In the lead B-17 was veteran Al Raisin. With him were the bombers flown by Bill Katz and Sam Feldman. Their target was Fawzi el-Kaukji's headquarters in the upper Galilee, a village called Tarshicha.

Sweeping in from the west, each bomber dumped its load of fourteen 100-kg bombs on the guerrilla headquarters. The hills in the Galilee were still shuddering from the impact of the bombs when four IDF units—the Seventh, Carmeli, Givati, and Oded Brigades—stormed into the guerrilla-held territory.

At the head of the force was a tough thirty-seven-year-old major general named Moshe Carmel. During the night Carmel's brigades formed a pincers on Kaukji's main force. In a series of quick and deadly firefights, the Israeli brigades cleared village after village in the northern Galilee. The Carmeli Brigade crossed briefly into Lebanon to block any attempted reinforcements from the Lebanese or Syrians.

On the second night of the campaign, the Hammers flew thirteen more missions, escorted on every mission by Spitfires from Herzliya. No Arab fighters—Iraqi, Transjordanian, or Egyptian—came up to challenge them.

Operation Hiram lasted sixty hours. The B-17s flew thirty-four total missions, dropping 27 tons of bombs on ALA targets. By the time yet another cease-fire took effect at 11:00 on October 31, more than a dozen Arab villages lay in ruins, destroyed by the bombings or demolished by Israeli forces.

As the offensive wound to a close, another grim event was playing out on the roads and paths to Lebanon. Thousands of Arab villagers were fleeing the Galilee. Some went voluntarily. Others were forcibly expelled. They would join the swelling population of Arab refugees in Lebanon and Jordan who would never to return to Palestine. As in the aftermath of previous battles, there would be accusations—and denials—of atrocities committed by Israeli troops.

It was the end of Fawzi el-Kaukji's Arab Liberation Army. The wily guerrilla commander and nearly two thousand of his surviving fighters scattered along secret routes in the hills to Lebanon. They were out of the fight.

Also out of the fight was the Lebanese Army, which showed no inclination to rejoin the war. Likewise, the Syrian and Iraqi forces remained penned up in their preinvasion positions.

Israeli forces now occupied the upper Galilee all the way to the Lebanese border, including the territory allotted to a future Arab state in the UN's 1947 partition plan.

The roles of the warring sides had been reversed. Instead of the Arabs claiming borders to reflect Israeli territory they occupied, Israel was extending its northern boundary into Arab-designated land. The future shape of Israel—assuming there *was* an Israel—would be determined by the territory occupied when a final cease-fire went down.

But not if the United Nations had its way.

———

The demand landed on the prime minister's desk on November 4, 1948: *Israel must withdraw to its previous positions.*

To Ben-Gurion the demand was preposterous—but it couldn't be ignored. It was coming from the UN Security Council. The UN had resolved that all sides must withdraw to the positions they held on October 14.

In the UN-ordered scenario, Israel would relinquish *all* the territory regained in Operations Yoav and Hiram. Israel would hand back the Galilee and withdraw from Beersheba. The Egyptian Army would be allowed to return to Ishdud, where it would again be poised to attack Tel Aviv. Israel would surrender the supply route to the Negev for which it had paid a steep price.

Ben-Gurion knew the source of the demand. The idea, even the language, originated with British Foreign Secretary Ernest Bevin. Since the era of the Mandate and the tragedy of the *Exodus*, the portly Bevin and the British Labour government had supported their Egyptian and Transjordanian allies. Cease-fires and withdrawals were never proposed when the Arab armies were rampaging through Israeli villages and kibbutzim. Now that the Arabs were losing territory they had seized from Israel, Bevin wanted *Israel* to withdraw.

Ben-Gurion snatched up his pen and scrawled his instructions to Israel's envoy to the UN. Israel would seek to have the resolution rescinded— or, at least superseded. In any case, Israel was *not* disposed to withdraw from territory it had regained from the invading Egyptians. Nor would Israel consider allowing Egypt to extricate its isolated forces in the Negev.

Not unless they surrendered.

Ben-Gurion knew where this was going. The war in the Negev Desert was about to resume. It *had* to resume.

———

Israeli Eighth Brigade commander Yitzhak Sadeh's nickname was *HaZaken*—the old man—and he looked the part. The bearded fifty-eight-year-old former commander of the Palmach was a veteran of WWI and the many guerrilla skirmishes in Palestine during the Mandate years.

It was November 8, and Sadeh had just received the order he'd been waiting for. *Kill the Monster.*

The hulking fortress at Iraq Suwedan was more than a nuisance to

Sadeh. Scores of his soldiers had fallen during the assaults across the open ground to the fortress. As long as it remained uncaptured, the Monster was a symbol of the Egyptian invasion of Israel.

In previous assaults, the shells of Sadeh's undersized artillery guns glanced off the Monster's exterior like tennis balls off a brick wall. Now Sadeh's brigade was equipped with something new: lethal 75-mm German antitank guns.

But the truce was in effect. The Israelis, as usual, would need a provocation.

Sadeh already had a plan. He dispatched an army jeep as bait for the gunners in the fort. In clear view of the UN truce enforcers, the Egyptians obligingly opened fire on the vehicle.

It was all Sadeh needed. At dawn, November 9, Sadeh's mortar and artillery fire rained down on the fortress. The new antitank guns opened up from net-camouflaged positions. For half an hour the earth around the fortress shook. Plaster and debris spewed from the pocked walls and smoke billowed from inside.

A hole opened in the Monster's outer perimeter. Sadeh's infantrymen stormed through the breached wall.

The battle ended minutes later. The stunned Egyptians offered only token resistance. After seven bloody failures, the Israelis had captured the Monster without losing a single man.

The noose around the four thousand Egyptians trapped in the Faluja Pocket had just tightened. With the Monster on the Hill no longer covering their flank, the Egyptian 9th Brigade was isolated more than ever from the main force at Gaza and from all land resupply routes.

———

By the end of October, the Egyptians had resorted to a daring new resupply technique. Swooping in at weed-top level, Egyptian pilots released drop tanks from Spitfires over their own garrison in Faluja. The tanks contained supplies for the trapped Egyptian brigade—medicine, ammunition, food, cigarettes. Despite the lack of parachutes, most of the packages survived without bursting.

It was a desperate—and dangerous—tactic. The Egyptian commander at Faluja, Brigadier Sayid Taha, reported that some of the Spitfires were hit by heavy antiaircraft and machine-gun fire, but somehow they all made it.

Truce or not, warplanes of both Israel and Egypt were swarming over the Faluja Pocket. The Egyptians dropped supplies. The Israelis dropped bombs. The stubborn Egyptian force showed no sign of caving in.

The Israelis tried another tactic. One morning the battered Egyptians looked up to see descending on them a cloud of something different. Instead of bombs, they were being pelted with . . . *leaflets*.

In Arabic the leaflets told the Egyptian troops that they had a choice.

If you prefer life, you must yield and surrender. . . . Everyone that comes with this leaflet in hand will get security and we promise him a safe return home. Keep in mind that this is an ultimatum.

The Egyptians weren't persuaded. Winter was settling on the Negev. The Egyptians put the propaganda material to good use. They burned the leaflets for heating fuel.

Second in command of the Egyptian brigade at Faluja was a thirty-one-year-old lieutenant colonel named Gamal Abdel Nasser. The young officer had already been wounded in the chest during earlier fighting in July.

For weeks now Nasser had endured the daily bombings and the shortage of supplies along with his troops. Nasser was embittered with the war and with the army's commanders in Cairo where, he wrote, "No one had any idea what the fighting men in the trenches felt or how much they suffered from orders sent out at random."

Kill this guy or not?

In his cockpit at 10,000 feet, Boris Senior wrestled with the decision. It was the morning of November 4, and Senior was looking at the delta-winged shape of a C-47 Dakota. The transport was heading for the Egyptian air base at El Arish.

Senior was leading a two-fighter reconnaissance mission over the

Egyptian bases in the Sinai. That such flights were flagrant violations of the truce didn't matter, at least to the pilots flying them.

It was supposed to be a routine patrol. What was *not* routine was the assignment of airplanes: two North American P-51 Mustangs. The *only* two in the tiny air force's inventory. In the second Mustang was the ex-P-47 pilot Rudy Augarten.

Senior knew the terms of the truce. Neither side was supposed to take offensive action. Only if an Arab warplane *appeared* to be a threat was he allowed to engage. But there were no UN referees up here in the sky. Senior was prepared to make his own interpretation of the rules.

Senior kept his eyes on the Dakota below. He made a snap appraisal of the situation. *It's an enemy warplane. It may be engaged in offensive activity.*

A stretch of reasoning, but not impossible. The Egyptians used their Dakotas as bombers, just as the Israelis did. Egyptian Dakota bombers had already killed dozens of civilians in Tel Aviv.

Senior rolled the Mustang up on its wing. In a tight downward spiral he dove toward the enemy transport. Augarten followed suit, staying close behind.

The pair of fighters dove until they were directly behind the Dakota. Still at high speed, Senior opened fire. As he skimmed past the Dakota, he could see that it was damaged, heading for the ground. A few seconds behind Senior came Augarten, guns blazing, putting more holes into the Dakota.

Senior pulled up in a tight climbing turn and looked down on his target. A cloud of dust and smoke was boiling up from the desert. The Dakota had pancaked into the ground outside El Arish.

"When I saw that he had crashed," recalled Senior, "I pulled up immediately after firing my guns and turned steeply to get out of range of the antiaircraft guns at the airfield. I didn't see a single antiaircraft shell and realized that our attack was a complete surprise."

As they headed back north, Senior had mixed feelings. This was war. Egypt now had one less bomber they could send against Israel. He knew he should feel exhilarated, but he didn't. "I didn't feel very proud," Senior wrote, "for it was a defenseless transport on its final approach."

Back at Herzliya the pilots walked along the familiar dirt path to the operations shack. As they always did, they gazed at the orange groves and banana trees and rusty water tower. Herzliya had been the Red Squadron's home for nearly six months.

What they didn't yet know was that they were leaving.

= 41 =

Hatzor

The order came directly from Remez at IAF Headquarters. Now that the Egyptians had been pushed 70 miles to the south, the general staff wanted all the fighters—Messerschmitts, Spitfires, the two new Mustangs—moved to Hatzor Air Base, closer to the battle zone.

Hatzor used to be an RAF field called Qastina. It was constructed in 1942 during WWII and still had most of its facilities: hangars, control tower, concrete runways. Hatzor lay just a few miles east of Ishdud, and until the Egyptians were forced out of the area, the field had been in easy range of Arab artillery. Now, flying out of Hatzor, the Red Squadron fighters would be just a few minutes' flying time from the action in the Negev.

There was another reason the squadron had to leave Herzliya. Winter was coming. The seasonal rains would turn Herzliya's red dirt runway into a muddy bog. Landing the spindly-legged Messerschmitt or narrow-geared Spitfire on dirt was hazardous enough. Plopping down in the mud was a guaranteed disaster.

To some of the early arrivals in the squadron—Lichtman, Cohen, Weizman, Finkel—it seemed ironic. One of the reasons for moving to Herzliya was that the Czech Mule was difficult to handle on concrete runways. What they didn't know then was that the Messerschmitt was difficult to handle on *any* runway. The Mule was just as inclined to crash on dirt as on concrete.

The pilots picked up their parachutes and trooped out to the revetments for the last time. Most stopped and took one last look around. They had good and bad memories of the place. They would remember the Messerschmitts that flipped and crashed. They would remember the concrete-walled operations shack where they'd assembled for scoldings by Modi Alon. The same building where Mina watched Modi's Messerschmitt crash and burn.

They gazed up at the shack atop the rusty water tank that served as their control tower. Hidden in the orange groves were the camouflage-netted revetments that had somehow never been discovered by Arab warplanes.

They would always have fond memories of the Kfar Shmaryahu village. They remembered the Falk House and the courtyard where they sat in the lantern light and listened to the jackals howl in the darkness.

Herzliya was where they flew, fought, raised hell, stole cars, mourned lost friends, confronted their secret fears. It was where they became the Red Squadron.

—————

Since May the mysterious reconnaissance aircraft hadn't changed its routine. Once a week, usually Saturday at noontime, the Shufti Kite would fly into Israeli air space from the eastern Galilee, pass directly over Ramat David, and continue south through the Negev. It was always at high altitude, leaving a distinctive white contrail, flying north to south. By the time the report reached the Red Squadron at Herzliya, it was always too late for fighters to scramble and get to high altitude.

Even if they *had* a fighter that could reach the Shufti Kite's high altitude.

Today, November 20, was different. They were no longer at Herzliya. They were 30 miles farther south at Hatzor, giving them more time to scramble a fighter. And now they had a *real* high-altitude fighter.

It was going to be an ambush.

Everyone, of course, wanted the mission. Squadron commander Syd Cohen gave the job to the guitar-plunking, wisecracking North

Carolinian Wayne Peake, who happened to have the most wartime P-51 experience of them all. Cohen would direct the intercept from the Hatzor control tower, where he could watch the action with his binoculars. Gathered at the base of the tower were the other squadron pilots, all listening to the radio dialogue over a loudspeaker.

For Peake, it was a fighter pilot's fantasy come true. He'd flown nearly a hundred combat missions in WWII, but he'd never shot down an enemy plane.

The P-51's Merlin engine was already warmed up. Peake roared down the runway and into the sky, climbing at over 3,000 feet per minute. He figured he'd be at the Shufti Kite's altitude—somewhere around 28,000 feet—in eight or nine minutes. Unlike the Messerschmitt, the Mustang was equipped with an oxygen system, though no one had yet tried it at high altitude.

Peake was scanning the sky above him. *Where the hell was the Shufti Kite?* He didn't see the telltale white contrails.

Cohen could see both airplanes *and* the contrails with his binoculars. He barked over the radio for Peake to keep climbing.

Peake went through 28,000 feet. He *still* didn't see the Shufti Kite. Peake was having trouble concentrating. *Is the damned oxygen system working?*

In the tower at Hatzor, Syd Cohen was spluttering in frustration. He could see the shape of the target—he guessed it was a twin-engine de Havilland Mosquito. The white contrail was coming almost directly over Hatzor. And he could see Peake's Mustang. The two tiny silhouettes were almost merged.

On the tarmac beneath the tower, the squadron pilots were all peering skyward, watching the tiny specks, listening to the radio exchange between Cohen and Peake.

Peake *still* didn't see the Shufti Kite. It was then that Cohen understood. Peake hadn't spotted the Shufti Kite because he was *above it.* The spy plane was almost directly ahead, hidden beneath the long snout of Peake's Mustang. "He's right below you," Cohen called on the radio.

Peake nudged the fighter's nose down and . . . *there it was.* He saw the dark shape of . . . *something*. Peake wasn't sure what he was seeing. His vision was blurring. His oxygen system wasn't working, and he was suffering hypoxia.

Peake blinked his eyes, peering at the target. It was swimming in and out of focus. For seconds at a time Peake saw two of everything. He had the reticles of his gun sight on the blurry shape of the enemy plane.

At the last instant the Shufti Kite pilot realized the danger. He yanked the aircraft hard to the right, toward the Mediterranean. Peake followed—and squeezed the trigger. A stream of tracers poured toward the enemy plane.

And stopped. Peake squeezed the trigger again. Nothing happened.

Peake couldn't believe it. "My fucking guns are jammed!" he yelled on the radio. *One burst of fire!* The guns had jammed in the sub-freezing temperature at high altitude.

Despite his hypoxia, Peake could barely contain his fury, babbling a stream of obscenities over the radio. Meanwhile, the Shufti Kite was motoring westward. It seemed to be unfazed by the encounter.

A single collective groan came from the spectators on the ground. After four frustrating months, one of them had finally ambushed the Shufti Kite. And the bastard was getting away!

In the control tower Cohen kept his binoculars on the fleeing Shufti Kite. It was still heading west, escaping over the coast. But something was streaming from the aircraft. Not a white, vapory contrail. Something dark. Something like . . . *smoke*.

The smoke thickened to a black cloud. As the crowd at Hatzor watched, the speck of the enemy plane morphed into a ball of fire. The Shufti Kite descended like a comet, trailing a plume of fire downward to the Mediterranean.

A cheer went up from the crowd at Hatzor.

Back on the ground, Wayne Peake groggily climbed out of the Mustang. He was met with applause and cheers from his squadronmates. The armorers reported that Peake's machine guns had fired only forty-five rounds before they jammed. It had been enough.

They all wanted to know: *What kind of aircraft was it? Whose was it?* Peake wasn't sure. From his blurred view of the Shufti Kite he hadn't seen any identifying emblems. But he was sure of one thing: It was a four-motored warplane. He couldn't say exactly what kind until they showed him some representative photos. He put his finger on one, declaring, yeah, it was one of *those*—a Halifax four-engine bomber.

Ezer Weizman climbed into the squadron's little Seabee amphibian plane and took off to locate the crash site. He found it, just off the coast at Ishdud. A few pieces of the Shufti Kite were floating on the surface, but there was no sign of the aircraft's crew. It was difficult to judge from the small amount of debris, but Weizman believed that the Shufti Kite had been a two-engine Mosquito, confirming what Cohen had seen in his binoculars.

Peake still didn't believe it. *Damn it, it was a four-engine bomber.* Not until later did they conclude that the oxygen-deprived pilot was probably seeing double. Peake had counted *four* engines on the two-motor Mosquito.

The more important questions were still unanswered: *Whose* air force did the Mosquito belong to? *Which* of the hostile nations had been sending weekly spy flights over Israel?

No more Shufti Kites overflew Israel. No reports of missing reconnaissance aircraft or crews were picked up by Israeli intelligence monitors. It was as if the ghostly warplane had come from an alien planet.

For six more weeks the mystery remained unsolved. Only after the Red Squadron had fought another wave of unidentified intruders would the secret of the Shufti Kite finally be revealed.

⸻

The volunteers didn't like the Hatzor base. Instead of a family-run pension with a friendly village and beer garden like they had at Herzliya, the pilots lived in shabby barracks left over from the British. Instead of orange groves and banana plantations, they had a brown, treeless desert as far as they could see. Winter was bearing down on the Negev. The unheated barracks was freezing at night.

The terrain to the south had been previously occupied by the Egyptians, who left minefields behind them. Not even jackal-hunting

Wayne Peake felt like venturing into the countryside with his pistol, even in daytime.

The mean-tempered Czech Mule didn't adapt to the Hatzor base either. The Messerschmitt had been designed for the grassy sod fields of Europe, not unyielding concrete runways. The Mule wasted no time taking pilots on wild sashays off the concrete and through the sand and sagebrush between Hatzor's intersecting runways.

On a chilly mid-December morning, it was Wayne Peake's turn. The North Carolina country boy was still wallowing in the glory of his shoot-down of the Shufti Kite. Peake was in that dangerous state peculiar to successful fighter pilots: He was invincible. He could handle *any* fighter.

Even the Messerschmitt.

Peake pushed up the throttle. The Jumo engine bellowed and the fighter accelerated down the concrete strip. With no visibility over by the Messerschmitt's long nose, Peake was using peripheral vision, glimpsing references on either side to keep the fighter rolling straight.

The trouble was, there *were* no references. Unlike Herzliya's banana groves and orange trees on either side of the runway, Hatzor had *nothing*. A desert-brown blur was zipping past on either side.

His first indication that something was wrong was when he felt the wheels rolling off the concrete. The tail came up, and the wheels bit into the earth. The paddle-bladed propeller was chewing into the soft ground. The fighter took a sharp swerve to the left and stuck its right wingtip into the ground.

In a tiny flea-speck of his brain Wayne Peake knew what was about to happen. The Messerschmitt skittered along on its nose and right wing-tip, poised for a heart-stopping instant with its tail pointed skyward, then slammed over onto its back.

It was the last thing Peake remembered. The upside-down fighter slid tail-first through the sagebrush. Gasoline was streaming from the ruptured fuel tanks. The destroyed Messerschmitt was a bomb waiting to ignite.

Hatzor didn't have an enclave of friendly Yemeni farmers like those at Herzliya with their long poles to pry up overturned fighters. Not until enough pilots and mechanics had arrived could they lift a wing up high enough to drag the pilot out.

Peake was unconscious. No one, including the medic who had arrived with the ambulance, seemed to know what to do. At that moment the squadron commander—and former medical student—Syd Cohen rolled up. He pushed the medic aside and went to work giving Peake CPR. Minutes later Peake was conscious and breathing.

Peake survived his close call, but he had suffered a concussion. He would be out of action for a while.

As Syd Cohen watched them haul Peake away on a gurney, he realized he had something else to worry about. Another major offensive was kicking off in a week. The Red Squadron was not only short of fighters, but it was also short of pilots. Nearly a dozen had been sent to Czechoslovakia to ferry the new Spitfires.

And they hadn't come back. Time was running out. *What was happening in Czechoslovakia?*

———

Sam Pomerance shivered in the early winter chill. He and his team had been laboring in the big open Czech field getting the Spitfires ready for the long ferry flight.

Pomerance had become a man possessed. Getting the precious Spitfires—*his* Spitfires—fitted with long-range tanks and ferried to Israel in time for the last great battle was his overriding passion.

But the fighters were still mired down in Czech bureaucracy. For weeks the Czechs insisted that all the fighters be crated and trucked to a seaport for shipment to Israel. It meant the Spitfires would arrive far too late to participate in the coming offensive.

And then after much negotiation and payment of more funds, the Czechs relented—but just a little. In early December Pomerance was informed that fifteen Spitfires would be released for a ferry flight to Israel.

Then, another glitch. Yugoslavia, the country that had allowed the previous flight of Spitfires to refuel, was no longer agreeable.

There were more urgent negotiations. In mid-December the impasse was resolved the usual way. Money changed hands. In this case, the cash-hungry Yugoslavian government demanded $300 per ton of aircraft passing through their territory. A deal was finally made at $200 per ton—on a one-flight basis.

There was one more condition, one that reminded Sam Pomerance of the first Velvetta flight. Each fighter had to bear the red star of the Yugoslavian Air Force. The order came directly from Yugoslavian Prime Minister Tito, who was having his own dispute with Russia and didn't want warplanes with foreign markings spotted transiting his country.

As he worked on the Spitfires, Sam Pomerance kept peering up at the heavy gray clouds hanging over the mountains. He could feel the first snowfall in the air.

A hard truth was becoming evident to Pomerance: flying these things to Israel was going to be damned dangerous.

———

On a cool mid-December afternoon, the white-haired prime minister took his customary place in front of his assembled cabinet. "In a few days," he announced in his growly voice, "we will try to end our conflict with Egypt by expelling them from the Negev."

The new offensive already had a name: Operation Horev. Horev was the name given in scripture for Mount Sinai. It would be the largest military thrust Israel had yet mounted. Israel would commit all of its crack infantry brigades to an offensive against the Egyptians in the Negev.

In Operation Yoav, the Israelis had managed to free part of the Negev. But they still faced five well-armed Egyptian brigades—one in the Sinai, two in Gaza, one in the Judean foothills, and the still-formidable 9th Brigade surrounded in the Faluja Pocket.

When Ben-Gurion huddled with his generals in the IDF headquarters, they gave him the hard facts. The success of Operation Horev depended on the air force providing close air support and maintaining control of the sky.

Which was a problem. The air force was running out of fighters. The 101 Squadron was down to three Spitfires, two P-51s, and no more than a couple of Messerschmitts flyable at any given time. The Czech Mules were still crashing at an appalling rate.

Meanwhile, the Egyptian Air Force was restocking its inventory of British-supplied Spitfires, and they had just added a number of Italian-built G-55 Fiat and Macchi MC205V fighters.

Ben-Gurion knew all this. And he was exasperated. *Where*, he wanted to know, were the Spitfire fighters they had bought from Czecho-slovakia at such an outrageous price?

=42=

Velvetta Redux

KUNOVICE AIR BASE, CZECHOSLOVAKIA
DECEMBER 15, 1948

The first snow of winter was falling. The two men worked their way down the row of parked Spitfire fighters, stopping at each airplane, checking for leaks, thumping the tires. Every few minutes one would stop and gaze at the forbidding sky. Each was feeling the same sense of urgency. The outcome of this mission—and maybe the war—depended on *them*.

George Lichter was a trimly built man with a short black beard and a studious expression. The twenty-seven-year-old volunteer had been a distinguished P-47 and then P-51 pilot in Europe during WWII. Before and after his stints as a combat pilot, Lichter had been an air force and then a civilian flight instructor.

Lichter had been in one of the first Messerschmitt classes at České Budějovice. He had impressed his Czech instructors with his ability to tame the nasty-tempered Mule. They were impressed enough that they persuaded the Israelis to make Lichter the new chief instructor in Czechoslovakia.

Grudgingly, Lichter accepted the job. Lichter would rather—*much* rather—have been in Israel flying fighters in combat. Since then he had trained each new class of volunteers, making as many as twelve flights a day in the Messerschmitt.

One of his students had been the American, Red Finkel. "Those planes were so dangerous," recalled Finkel, "I remember seeing Lichter at the end of a day of instruction, and he'd be so shook up he'd head straight for the bar, and couldn't even talk until he had a drink."

Lichter was finished with Messerschmitts. He'd stayed in Czechoslovakia to train the first class of young Israeli cadets in the new Spitfires. Now he was the chief test pilot for each of the Spitfires being fitted with long-range tanks for the flight to Israel.

With Lichter on the field at Kunovice was the engineer-pilot-inventor, Sam Pomerance. The clean-shaven Pomerance was eleven years older than Lichter. Pomerance's improvisations with the Spitfire's fuel system had stretched the fighter's range from 600 miles to a record-breaking 1,500 miles. It was Pomerance's magic back in September that made the Velvetta I operation successful, delivering the first small batch of badly needed Spitfires to Israel.

Pomerance had never flown fighters before, but he had felt comfortable enough to fly one of the six Spitfires on Velvetta I. He was one of the three who made it all the way to Israel. Now he had the job of chief of operations for Velvetta II. He considered it the most important mission of his life. Pomerance would lead the next flight of Spitfires to Israel.

But not until it stopped snowing.

———

Delay the offensive?

Ben-Gurion shook his head. So did IDF chief of staff Yigael Yadin. Every senior commander in the conference room was glowering at Aharon Remez.

The young air force commander was asking them to delay Operation Horev, which was scheduled to begin December 19. With only two days left, the Spitfires from Czechoslovakia were still not here. The fighters were held up by weather and mechanical problems. Remez was worried that the few fighters and pilots the air force had available would be no match for the sixty-five modern fighters and dozen bombers Egypt had moved into the Sinai.

Ben-Gurion gazed around the table. His senior commanders were all scowling and shaking their heads. None wanted to delay the offensive. The pieces of Operation Horev were all in place. Five Israeli brigades were poised to strike into the Negev. Pressure was swelling from the UN, the United States, and especially Great Britain for Israel to return to the October 14 positions. Operation Horev might be Israel's last chance to claim the territory allotted to it in the UN partition plan.

Ben-Gurion made the decision. The offensive would begin on schedule. With or without the Spitfires.

———

"We take off in an hour," announced Sam Pomerance.

The other five pilots nodded glumly. It was the morning of December 18. The sky was still dark and foreboding. For four days the early winter snow storm had been pelting Europe.

Pomerance had just seen the forecast, and it was calling for an improvement. He didn't want to wait any longer. The 300-mile first leg to Niksic, their refueling field in Yugoslavia, should be clear enough.

Pomerance would lead the first flight of six Spitfires. When they had safely arrived, the next six would follow. Already waiting for them in Niksic was the C-46 mother ship and its pilot, Sam Lewis.

Pomerance said goodbye to his wife that morning in their hotel. He'd be back in a few days, he promised. Pomerance was one of the few married airmen among the volunteers. Since mid-October the petite and attractive Elsie Pomerance had been with him in Czechoslovakia.

The Spitfires took off in two clusters, rolling and bumping across the open snow-covered field at Kunovice. Pomerance led the first flight of three fighters, with Bill Pomerantz (no relation to Sam) and ex-navy pilot Caesar Dangott on either wing. The second three, close behind, were George Lichter, newly arrived Canadian ace John McElroy, and a young Israeli cadet named Moti Fein.

Just a few days before, a C-54 flown by Larry Raab had arrived in Prague carrying the ferry pilots for the Velvetta II operation. Ten qualified Spitfire pilots were all the air force had come up with. Even with Lichter and Pomerance, that still made only twelve, and they had fifteen Spitfires.

Desperate for pilots, Lichter drafted the two brightest students in the Israeli cadet class he was teaching. One was Moti Fein, a shy twenty-four-year-old kid who had grown up on a kibbutz, and the other a Haifa dandy named Dani Shapira, age twenty-three.

It was an act of faith for Lichter. His cadets had only about seven hours each in the Spitfire. Neither had more than 140 hours total flying time.

He still had only fourteen pilots, but there was no more time to wait. With the new offensive starting any day, the Spitfires *had* to reach Israel. One of the fighters would have to be left behind. Ten more were already crated and on their way to a seaport for shipment to Israel.

———

The Spitfires rose into the gray murk that covered central Europe. Upward they climbed, higher and higher, looking for clear skies above the cloud deck. At 10,000 feet they were still in the murk.

Only Pomerance's and Lichter's Spitfires had radios and navigational equipment. Each pilot clung tenaciously to the dark silhouette of the airplane directly ahead. To fall back and lose sight of the others in the clouds would be disastrous. The mountain peaks beneath them rose to 8,000 feet.

What neither Pomerance nor Lichter yet realized was that one of their wingmen *had* fallen back. Bill Pomerantz, the creative outdoor chef at the Red Squadron's nightly cookouts, had drifted too far behind. Now he'd lost sight of the formation. Pomerantz was floundering in the clouds, alone and without a radio or map to guide him.

In the lead Spitfire, Sam Pomerance was looking for the break in the weather he'd been promised in the forecast. At 14,000 feet he still saw only grayness. None of the Spitfires had oxygen systems. If they climbed any higher they risked hypoxia and loss of consciousness in the thin air.

Pomerance was still peering at the thickening clouds ahead when he heard Lichter call on the radio. Lichter told him they ought to turn back.

Pomerance didn't answer right away. Damn it, he *knew* he could make it to Niksic one way or the other. But Lichter, who had the most experience, was right. It was too dangerous for an entire formation.

"You take the group back," Pomerance called. "I'll go on alone."

Lichter waggled his wings to gather the other Spitfires. As the little flock began its turn in the clouds, they glimpsed Pomerance's Spitfire fading into the gloom.

* * *

Where the hell is Kunovice?

The weather was no better than when they took off. Lichter couldn't find the snow-covered field they'd left over an hour ago except by dead reckoning—navigating by time and heading.

When he was sure he was clear of the mountains, Lichter brought his flight down through the overcast, flying low over the wintry landscape. To his own amazement, directly ahead lay the nearly indistinguishable little airfield.

It seemed like a miracle. "The pilots thought I was an incredible navigator," recalled Lichter. "It was really just good luck."

Six Spitfires had left Kunovice, but only four returned. No one knew what happened to Bill Pomerantz or Sam Pomerance. Not until the next morning as they prepared for another attempt did they hear the news.

A Spitfire had crashed into a mountain in Yugoslavia.

Who? Either Bill Pomerantz or Sam Pomerance was dead. The other was still missing.

The weather had improved—but not much. No one was feeling cheerful after what happened the day before. John McElroy was the most experienced Spitfire pilot in the bunch. "Nobody's going to lead me this time," he declared. He'd lead his own flight or he wasn't going.

Fine, said Lichter. McElroy could lead a three-ship formation behind Lichter with the American, Caesar Dangott, and the South African,

Arnie Ruch, on his wing. Lichter would lead a three-ship with his two
Israeli cadets, Moti Fein and Dani Shapira.

Off they went again, back into the clouds toward Yugoslavia.

Neither of Lichter's Israeli cadets had much formation flying experience. "If you lose contact with one another," Lichter had briefed them,
"save your life and abandon the airplane."

And then in dense clouds, it happened. Dani Shapira lost contact.
One second he was struggling to keep Lichter's Spitfire in sight, the next
second he saw *nothing.* Fearing a mid-air collision, Shapira banked to the
right, away from the formation. The student pilot was alone, lost in the
clouds. Worse, he hadn't been trained in flying instruments.

It was time to obey Lichter's advice: *abandon the airplane.*

Shapira unfastened his seat belt and slid the canopy open. He was
about to jump over the side when he glimpsed an apparition coming
through the clouds. It was George Lichter's Spitfire. He was trailed by
the other five, all swooping down toward Shapira. "George was waving
his hand," recalled Shapira. "He saved my life."

For three more hours they flew in nearly solid clouds. When Lichter
estimated they were far enough along the coast of Yugoslavia, he took
the formation down through the cloud bank. Flying a few hundred feet
over the Adriatic he led the flight inland and—*there it was*—the big dry
lake bed at the Niksic airfield.

The Spitfires landed in a spread out group and taxied to where Sam
Lewis and the crew of the C-46 mother ship was waiting for them.

Also waiting for them was the bad news. It was Sam Pomerance who
smashed into the mountain. The other missing pilot—Bill Pomerantz—
had been found and he was okay, more or less.

Pomerantz was lucky. After becoming separated from the formation, he had descended blind in the clouds *without* hitting a mountain.
Lost and with minimum visibility, he elected to land the Spitfire on its
belly in a clearing near the northern Yugoslavian coast. Pomerantz was
banged up in the rough landing, but managed to get out of the Spitfire
before it burned up.

Losing Sam Pomerance was a blow. Lichter had spent the past six months working with the brilliant engineer. That night the pilots sat in their chilly quarters and pondered the question: *What caused Sam to crash?*

There would never be a conclusive answer. The consensus among the Velvetta pilots was that Pomerance tried to climb above the weather. He climbed so high he lost consciousness in the oxygen-depleted atmosphere.

The former Luftwaffe airfield at Niksic was just as dreary and inhospitable as it had been back in September. Same cold-water bathing in the nearby river, same unsmiling Yugoslav Red Army guards to make sure no one strayed off the base. The only difference was that this time the airmen slept in former German underground bunkers.

The weather improved. The next day six more Spitfires arrived from Kunovice. The pilots rinsed the water-colored Yugoslav red star emblems off the fighters and replaced them with the Star of David.

As usual, there were problems. One of the fighters had developed a violent knocking sound, and another, a serious fuel leak. They would stay behind and be hauled to Israel the way the Messerschmitts had during Operation Balak: disassembled and loaded in the cabins of C-46s.

Huddled in their underground quarters at Niksic, the pilots wondered: What was happening in Israel? When would Operation Horev begin?

———

It was raining when Ben-Gurion's car pulled up to the Tel Aviv opera house. The performance tonight was Massenet's *Manon*. As Ben-Gurion slipped into his seat, he was joined by the American emissary to Israel, James McDonald, with his daughter. Seated on Ben-Gurion's right were two diplomats from the Soviet Union.

In their polite chatter between acts, neither Ben-Gurion nor the diplomats discussed what was uppermost on all their minds. *Was Israel about to launch another offensive in the desert?*

Ben-Gurion knew the answer. Operation Horev would have begun today, December 19. Sudden winter rains had come to the Negev. The murky weather made effective air support all but impossible. The offensive had to be postponed.

But the Israeli defense minister was also privy to a valuable item of information. In the past few days Israeli agents had intercepted communication indicating that both nations—the United States and the Soviet Union—would block UN sanctions against Israel for its actions in Negev.

To Ben-Gurion it was good news. Neither nation was an ally, but at least they wouldn't be Israel's adversaries. Not yet.

———

For two more days it rained. Israeli monitors picked up Egyptian communications predicting an Israeli offensive in the southern Negev. The Egyptians were certain that the Israelis planned to attack the complex around Gaza. For the past two weeks they'd been reinforcing their garrisons in the Gaza Strip. They were even predicting the time of the Israeli offensive—between December 20 and 25.

The predictions were correct.

On the afternoon of December 22, Operation Horev began with a massive Israeli artillery barrage on Egyptian positions in the Gaza Strip. Elements of five Israeli brigades and other large auxiliary infantry formations surged across the desert, aimed at the entrenched Egyptian Army.

For two days the battle seesawed back and forth. Israeli troops seized their objectives, only to be forced to retreat. Casualties mounted. Little ground was gained. The Israeli offensive seemed to be grinding to a stalemate.

But the assault on Gaza was a deception.

Sixteen miles to the south, two armored brigades of the Israeli Army were slipping into position near Beersheba. They were poised to race southward over the desert to the Egyptian border outpost of Auja. From there they would cut straight across the Sinai to the Mediterranean coast—*behind* the enemy stronghold at Gaza. The Egyptian Army would be encircled.

But the main road was defended by a well-entrenched Egyptian brigade. Israeli archeologists had recently uncovered a Roman trade route from Beersheba to the Sinai. Along this ancient route the Israeli force intended to bypass the enemy fortifications, cutting off all Egyptian forces between El Arish and Gaza.

It was an ambitious plan. Perhaps *too* ambitious, worried some of the IDF general staff. The promised Spitfire fighters from Czechoslovakia still hadn't arrived. How would the air force maintain command of the sky?

═ 43 ═

Appointment in Gaza

EL ARISH, SINAI DESERT
DECEMBER 22, 1948

Guns on a bomber were good, Al Raisin believed. The more the better. It was a lesson Raisin had learned in the skies over Europe during WWII.

Now Raisin was leading a flight of three B-17s to El Arish. Even though the bombers were escorted by a pair of Spitfires from Hatzor, Raisin and his crew were pleased to have the newly installed machine guns on their bomber. When enemy fighters came after you, your own guns were your last defense.

Al Raisin was the new commander of the 69 Squadron—the Hammers—having taken over from Bill Katz, who had replaced the first commander, Ray Kurtz. It was the first day of the Horev offensive, and the Egyptians were putting up a heavy layer of antiaircraft fire. So far none of the bombers had been seriously hit.

Nor had they yet been attacked by Egyptian fighters. No one was sure why. It was either luck or the Egyptian fighter pilots were intimidated by the fighters escorting the bombers.

Or, as seemed likely, the Egyptians knew the Israeli bombers had guns. Lots of them. The gunner's stations on each Fortress bristled with Czech-supplied Beza machine guns.

Every B-17 mission was escorted by fighters, usually a mismatched gaggle of a Messerschmitt, Spitfire, or Mustang. The Red Squadron had begun Operation Horev with only eleven flyable fighters—four Spitfires, two Mustang P-51s, five Messerschmitts. The fighters were doing double and triple duty. When they finished bomber escort missions, they flew bomb-assessment photo missions, patrolled for enemy fighters, then used their ammo to strafe Egyptian ground forces.

Also flying bombing missions again were the Bagel Lancers, now based at Ekron. Though they still called themselves the Air Transport Command, the unit had an official air force designation: the 106 Squadron. The six surviving transports of the C-46s acquired by Al Schwimmer in the Millville-Burbank-Panama days were back in action. The big transports were making daily bomb runs over the Gaza Strip.

Based at Ekron along with the transport squadron was another unlikely bombing unit—35 Flight. Their big, plodding Norseman bush planes had been hauling troops and munitions over enemy territory to outposts like Sdom directly across the Dead Sea from Jordan. Now 35 Flight had been handed a new mission: dive bombing.

Ten North American AT-6 Harvards had arrived from the United States, smuggled in crates labeled "agricultural machinery and equipment." The first five showed up in late November and were hurriedly configured as dive bombers.

Which seemed peculiar at first. The big Pratt & Whitney–powered Harvard had been designed as an advanced military trainer, not a bomber. But this was the Israeli Air Force. Airplanes, like pilots, had to adapt to the mission.

Dive bombing was a more precise—and dangerous—technique than high-altitude bombing. In WWII US Navy Dauntless and Helldiver dive bombers sank 175 Japanese ships, more than any other aerial or surface weapon. Dauntless dive bombers defeated the Japanese fleet at Midway, sinking four aircraft carriers and changing the course of the Pacific war.

By the end of the war, dive bombers were on their way out. They were replaced by sophisticated fighter-bombers like the P-47 and F4U Corsair. The age of the dive bomber was almost over.

But not in Israel. Three years after WWII, dive bombing was about to be resurrected. But precision dive bombing was a specialized skill. A quick scan of 35 Flight's pilots' records turned up only a few who had flown dive bombers in combat.

One was a twenty-five-year-old, red-headed pilot from California.

To Mike Flint, it was like old times. Through the windshield of the Harvard, he was looking straight down at his target, the Egyptian compound at Khan Yunis, south of Gaza.

Flint had learned in the Pacific war that the closer you got to the vertical, the more accurately you could bomb. It was also a matter of survival. The steeper the dive, the harder it was for gunners to kill you.

The problem was, *real* dive bombers had dive brakes to keep the aircraft from accelerating past its design speed limit. This was an AT-6 Harvard, not a real bomber. It lacked refinements such as dive brakes, split flaps, even a bombsight. Flint's airspeed needle was creeping well past the Harvard's red line of 228 miles per hour.

At some point beyond an airplane's red line—its maximum design speed—bad things happened. A vibration, a high frequency buzzing, a sudden flutter and—*Whoof!*—the airplane disintegrated like a smashed piñata.

How far beyond? Flint didn't know. He decided on a maximum of 250 mph. At that speed, he guessed, the airplane would *probably* stay together.

Flint had left the Red Squadron to fly Norseman utility planes with 35 Flight. And though flying supply runs and bomb-chucking missions in the Norseman was interesting, something was missing. In WWII he'd flown the SB2C dive bomber and the Corsair fighter-bomber. He'd shot a Japanese fighter out of the sky. He'd been a warrior. In 35 Flight he was a utility plane pilot.

And then everything changed. Flint was put in charge of the new dive-bombing unit. He picked a team, pilots who had experience in the AT-6 Harvard. One was the 35 Flight commander, Ted Gibson, who had been a WWII noncommissioned pilot in the US Navy. The others were a mixed bag of international volunteers: Abie Nathan, an Indian Jew who had flown with the RAF in WWII, American Dick Dougherty, Canadian Eddie Kaplansky, South African Joe Katzew, a Russian pilot named Grisha Brown, another American, John Soltau.

They worked out dive angles and speeds for the Harvard. Some of the "practice" missions were for real, bombing the Egyptian brigade in the Faluja Pocket. When Operation Horev kicked off, Flint's team was ready.

Now the Egyptian compound at Khan Yunis was swelling like an apparition in Mike Flint's windscreen. His eyes flicked from the windscreen to the airspeed indicator to the altimeter. The altimeter needle was unwinding in a counterclockwise blur—5,000 . . . 4,000 . . . 3,500 . . . 3,000.

Flint had calculated the numbers. If he held the dive to a thousand feet, he'd be four seconds from impacting the earth. Flint jammed the release button. There was a *thump* as the four 110-lb bombs left the airplane. He kept the Harvard in its dive and opened up with the two 7.62-mm machine guns.

Which seemed like a joke. The Harvard was a lousy strafing plane. It didn't have a real gun sight. The machine guns sprayed bullets like a garden hose. Flint could see the bullets spurting into the open ground. At least he was keeping the gunners' heads down.

Grunting against the G-forces, Flint bottomed out at 200 feet above the target. He hunkered lower in his seat, waiting for the *ping* of small arms fire. Over his shoulder he could see the three other Harvards pulling out of their dives. Explosions were mushrooming from the center of Khan Yunis.

They climbed back up to 9,000 feet to do it over again. Two dives, four bombs each. All four dive bombers came off the target without getting hit. They'd land back at Ekron, smoke a cigarette, eat a sandwich, and take off again.

Waiting just off the beach was their fighter escort. Flint recognized the long-snouted shape of a lone Messerschmitt. His old nemesis. But something was missing. They'd begun the mission with *two* fighter escorts.

―――

Flying the second Messerschmitt was the most famous member of the volunteers, American Slick Goodlin. A non-Jew, the twenty-five-year-old Goodlin personified the adventure-seeking, flier-of-fortune esprit of the last wave of recruits to the Red Squadron.

Chalmers "Slick" Goodlin learned to fly in his native Pennsylvania at age fifteen. He joined the RCAF on his eighteenth birthday, flew in combat over Europe as the youngest commissioned officer in the RCAF, then returned to the United States to become a navy test pilot. By war's end Goodlin was a civilian test pilot for Bell Aircraft, where he made twenty-six flights in the X-1 rocket ship.

Goodlin missed his shot at glory when he had a contract dispute with Bell. He was replaced by air force pilot Chuck Yeager, who went on to make history when he flew the X-1 on the first supersonic flight. Soon after Goodlin left Bell in the autumn of 1948, a Hollywood producer named Joseph Berg persuaded him to volunteer to fly in Israel.

Now it was the first day of the Horev offensive. Goodlin and Syd Cohen had been escorting Flint's dive bombers on the Khan Yunis raid. Goodlin was relatively new to the Messerschmitt. He'd heard the stories about the Czech Mule's nasty habits.

Goodlin still had the instincts of a test pilot. While they were over the open water, waiting for the dive bombers to finish, Goodlin decided to fire a short test burst from his nose-mounted machine guns. Just to be sure.

He nudged the trigger—*Brraap*—and immediately released it. Something didn't feel right.

Lucky for Goodlin, it was a *very* short burst. The Czech Mule was living up to its reputation. The guns punched several bullet-sized holes through Goodlin's propeller.

Uttering a string of epithets about Czech engineering and weaponry and the parentage of the idiots who acquired the Mule, Goodlin peeled off from the formation. He nursed the crippled Messerschmitt back to a safe landing at Hatzor.

Just off the Gaza coast at 4,000 feet, Rudy Augarten had a different view of the unfolding battle. He could see the Egyptian encampments at Gaza and the stronghold in Rafah just ahead. A little farther south, just past the international border, he could make out a now-familiar target: the Egyptian air base at El Arish.

When the reconnaissance mission came up, Augarten had jumped at it. Recon flights, especially in fully armed Spitfires, were open-ended missions with a vague set of rules. You were supposed to observe enemy bases, photograph them, avoid trouble.

But sometimes you got lucky. An Egyptian fighter might come sniffing. When that happened, you could forget the other tasks. You had carte blanche to blow him out of the sky.

Flying on Augarten's right wing was Jack Doyle. This was their second mission together, and the two had learned that they made a good team. Both were veteran combat pilots, and each was an eager warrior.

Doyle had credentials as impressive as anyone in the Red Squadron. A Spitfire pilot in the RCAF, Doyle had fought all across North Africa and into Italy. In a single swirling air battle at Anzio he shot down a German Messerschmitt and damaged another before being shot down himself. Badly wounded and unable to bail out, Doyle made a dead-stick, wheels-up landing on the beach.

In a made-for-Hollywood ending, Doyle fell in love with the French-Canadian nurse who tended him in the hospital. He ultimately married her and returned to combat. By the end of the war Jack Doyle was credited with downing four Axis aircraft.

Now Augarten and Doyle were flying southward, staying just over the water and out of range of the antiaircraft batteries around Rafah and Gaza. They spotted nothing remarkable—until they were near El Arish. Through the noonday haze Augarten picked up something— a dark shape down low, flying near the air base.

It was a fighter. But not a Spitfire.

Augarten knew that the Egyptian Air Force had been equipped

with Italian-built Fiat and Macchi fighters. And as he flew nearer the enemy airfield, he saw proof positive. One of the Italian fighters was in the traffic pattern at El Arish.

Nothing about this war lent itself to acts of chivalry or compassion. Like most of the pilots, Augarten had no compunction about shooting an enemy warplane in *any* circumstances—dogfight, on the ground, in the traffic pattern. Augarten reasoned that every enemy warplane, tank, truck, gun emplacement he destroyed saved Israeli lives.

While Doyle flew high cover, Augarten swept down on the slow-moving target. He slid in behind the Egyptian fighter and opened fire with cannons and machine guns.

The engagement lasted only seconds. Augarten's after-action description was cold and factual: "I shot him and he crashed off the runway."

The Egyptian fighter had been caught off guard, but the antiaircraft gunners weren't. A barrage of flak erupted over El Arish. Augarten skimmed past the perimeter of the base. He stayed fast and low over the sand dunes until he was a good 5 miles away. When he climbed up, he saw exactly what he hoped to see. Doyle's Spitfire was sliding in to rejoin him.

The Italian fighter was Augarten's third victory of the war. He had just joined an exclusive club. Counting his two Messerschmitt kills in WWII, Rudy Augarten was now, officially, an ace.

Back on the ground at Hatzor, Augarten gazed around at the handful of fighters parked on the ramp. Operation Horev was in full swing, and the squadron was badly depleted. Where were the new Spitfires they'd been promised?

━━━━━━

Four Spitfires were ready to depart the barren Niksic airfield in Yugoslavia. Two other fighters would have to be left behind with mechanical problems. It was December 23, a day into Operation Horev. The Velvetta II leader, George Lichter, wasn't waiting.

Lichter watched the C-46 mother ship, flown by Sam Lewis, rumble across the unpaved field. When the big transport was off the ground, Lichter and the other three pilots started their takeoff roll.

It would be a test of the strength of the Spitfire's landing gear. Each was hauling a fuel load far greater than the fighter's design limit.

All the fighters made it off the ground without mishap. Quickly they tucked in behind the mother ship and headed out on the dangerous seven-hour overwater journey.

The fighters were limited to a plodding 180 miles per hour, the speed of the C-46 mother ship. The cockpits were miserably uncomfortable. With no heaters and no installations for the pilots to pee, recalled Dani Shapira, "It was very difficult in the last hour and a half."

Near the coast of Israel, the unarmed Spitfires were met by Jack Doyle in a 101 Squadron Mustang to be escorted to Ekron Air Base. The day before, the war had resumed in deadly earnest. Ten minutes before the Spitfires landed, Ekron had been strafed by Egyptian warplanes. Out of fuel and slowed by their external fuel tanks, the Spitfires would have been vulnerable targets.

As quickly as possible each Spitfire was refitted at Ekron with Browning machine guns, Hispano Mk II cannons, radio, and bomb racks.

Three days later the next flight of six Spitfires, led by South African Jack Cohen, arrived from Yugoslavia. The airmen climbed down from the cockpits, just as stiff and weary as the previous bunch.

Ten new Spitfires were parked on the Hatzor ramp. They wouldn't be combat ready for a few days. Looking at them, the pilots wondered: *Will they make a difference?*

———

With the additional fighters in their inventory, the Red Squadron again needed pilots. From nearby Ekron Air Base came an unlikely volunteer. Although he'd been flying C-46s and C-54s with the ATC unit since the war began, the volunteer had also been a Spitfire pilot in the RAF during WWII.

Or so he said.

44

Mano a Mano

TEL AVIV
DECEMBER 23, 1948

Two days earlier, when Gordon Levett made his pitch to Haman Shamir to be transferred to the 101 Squadron, he was telling the truth. He *had* been trained in Spitfire and Hurricane fighters during WWII.

The part that Levett left out was that he had never actually flown a Spitfire in combat. Or any other fighter.

Gordon Levett's war had been spent far from the front lines, first as an instructor in basic training and later as a transport pilot. By the end of the war he had risen to the rank of squadron leader—the equivalent to major. But Levett always felt that he'd been cheated out of the great prize: he'd never been a *real* fighter pilot in a *real* war.

Still, Levett liked the RAF. He liked it enough that after war's end he stayed in—until he was booted out of the service for taking unauthorized leave from his remote Burma base. Down on his luck, the twenty-six-year-old ex-pilot was unable to find a flying job of any kind. He was working in a Jewish-owned diaper laundry in London when he began hearing about the troubles in Palestine.

Levett had no Jewish blood in him. Still, something churned inside him when he learned about the thousands of Jewish refugees being turned back from Palestine—by his own British military. Until then Gordon Levett's postwar life had seemed purposeless. Now he was sensing a mission.

Through his employer, an ardent Zionist named Silver, Levett made contact with a Haganah agent. At their first meeting, the operative asked how much pay Levett expected.

"Board and lodging and pocket money."

"What can you fly?"

"Anything."

The agent wanted proof. Levett presented his logbooks showing the many types of aircraft he'd flown, pilot assessments, and a total of 3,337 hours. There were more questions. Finally the Haganah operative seemed satisfied. He asked, "What do you think about having your genitals cut off and sewn into your mouth?"

Levett didn't have a good answer. He knew the operative was warning him that this wasn't an ordinary war. The Arabs would be taking few prisoners.

Levett shrugged. He said he wasn't worried.

There was a follow-up interview. At the end the agent produced a bottle of vodka and two tiny glasses. They knocked back the vodka and toasted Zion. "I must tell you," said the agent, "I have reported to my superiors that I think you are an agent working for British intelligence. They have decided to play along to see what happens."

Levett had to smile. Even the British, he told the agent, wouldn't send an uncircumcised gentile to be an agent among the Jews.

—————

Levett's timing was perfect. At the moment the ATC squadron had a full complement of airmen. But the 101 Squadron was receiving new Spitfires, and they needed pilots. With a stroke of the deputy commander's pen, Levett was transferred from the ATC to the Red Squadron.

That evening Levett stuffed his possessions into a rucksack and headed for the Gallei Yam bar on the beach. He knew from experience the 101 Squadron pilots would be hanging out there.

A half dozen Red Squadron pilots were clustered in the bar, including squadron commander Syd Cohen. They were drinking beer and wearing their red baseball caps. They invited Levett to join them, and by late evening everyone was pleasantly soused.

With their new squadronmate in tow, the pilots wobbled out to the street to look for transportation. Parked nearby was an American station wagon. One of the pilots quickly hot-wired the ignition. Minutes later they were motoring toward Hatzor in the stolen car.

Watching all this, Levett had to grin. He grinned even more when he settled in at Hatzor and saw the casual nonmilitariness of the squadron. There were no uniforms. Most pilots were going around in battered old leather flight jackets—Army Air Corps or navy issue—with a silk scarf cut from throwaway parachutes.

He watched pilots being driven out to their fighters in jeeps or Chrysler limousines—whatever vehicle had recently been stolen. And he learned the name for the area behind the barracks where they kept the swiped vehicles: Syd Cohen's Used Car Lot.

━━━━━━

Like every new guy, Levett had to prove himself. The squadron pilots watched from the tarmac while Levett made his first flight in the Spitfire—the *only* one of the three fighters he had ever flown before. Except for overcontrolling on takeoff and landing—an inevitable result of going from a 25-ton C-46 to a 5,000-lb fighter—he got the Spitfire up and down without incident.

Then the Messerschmitt. To the surprise of the observers on the ground—and to himself—Levett kept the Czech Mule arrow-straight down Hatzor's thin strip of concrete.

After the Messerschmitt, flying the wide-geared Mustang was almost anticlimactic.

Syd Cohen was satisfied. The new pilot was ready for action. Levett would fly as his wingman for the dawn patrol tomorrow.

That night Levett lay awake thinking about the upcoming patrol. A bothersome truth kept flitting through his mind. He didn't know *any-thing* about flying in combat.

The sun had barely risen on the morning of December 28 when the pair of Spitfires lifted from Hatzor. They climbed toward the Gaza Strip where, just outside Rafah, they spotted an Egyptian train heading southwestward.

And the Egyptians spotted *them*. Almost immediately black-and-white filigree patterns of antiaircraft fire appeared in the dawn sky around them.

Cohen's pair of 250-lb bombs were near-misses on the train. Levett's bombs weren't even close.

Then they came back to strafe the locomotive. It was the first time Levett had ever fired the guns of a fighter. "I was astonished at the clatter and the recoil effect," he wrote later.

This time he didn't miss. He was so enthralled by the sight of his bullets hitting the target he nearly flew into the train. Levett could see passengers jumping from the coach cars. They scrambled for cover from the attacking fighters. "By unspoken agreement neither Syd or I had attacked the passenger coaches," he recalled.

Back on the ramp at Hatzor, Levett climbed out of his Spitfire. In the space of less than an hour he had made the transformation from novitiate to *real* fighter pilot. He had flown in combat.

Of course, it was an air-to-ground mission, not a *mano a mano* dogfight. That wouldn't come until his *next* mission.

It came later that same morning. This time Levett was flying a Messerschmitt. His leader was Jack Doyle, the seasoned ex-RCAF veteran with four kills in WWII. Their mission was to escort a flight of four Harvard AT-6 dive bombers in a raid on the Egyptian force at Faluja.

As the cumbersome formation droned south, Levett peered at the peculiar sight. Big blunt-nosed American-built training airplanes retrofitted as bombers, escorted by a British Spitfire and a German-Czech

Messerschmitt. Even more peculiar was that Levett and Doyle were communicating by hand signals. The radios in the mismatched fighters didn't share a common frequency.

Levett had to shake his head. *Only in the Israeli Air Force.*

The Harvard dive bombers were still diving on the target at Faluja when Levett spotted shadowy dark shapes approaching from the east. They looked like sharks slicing through shallow water.

And then Levett recognized them. Four Spitfires and four Italian-built Macchis, the sleek new fighters acquired by the Egyptian Air Force.

The dive-bomber pilots saw them, too. The Harvards dumped their bomb loads in one pass and exited the area, skimming low over the sand dunes to the north.

Doyle and Levett climbed into the sun until they were 4,000 feet above the incoming fighters. Levett had heard a rumor floating around the squadron. Ex-Luftwaffe aces might be flying with the Egyptian Air Force. It would be a bizarre fate, Levett thought, for an Englishman in a Messerschmitt to be shot down by a German in a Spitfire. A hell of a war.

Doyle and Levett were high with the blinding morning sun behind them. The Egyptian pilots still showed no sign of having seen them.

A perfect ambush.

With no radio communication, Levett was flying close enough to Doyle to see his hand signals. He saw Doyle grin, then point downward. Then he cocked an imaginary gun with his thumb.

Down they swept, each going for a separate target. Doyle pulled in behind an Egyptian Macchi and opened fire. Levett locked on to a Spitfire. Churning in his head were the fighter pilot's maxims: *Wait till he's close . . . fire short bursts . . . keep checking your tail.*

The Egyptian Spitfire was centered in Levett's gun sight. He waited . . . waited . . . then for the first time in his life he opened fire on an enemy airplane.

And to his astonishment, he was *hitting* something. Pieces were flying off the Egyptian fighter. Then, a telltale sign: a white stream of glycol trailing behind the fighter. It meant the Spitfire's Merlin engine was doomed.

Levett was about to give him another burst when something caught his eye. Something behind him.

Another Spitfire. One of the Egyptian fighters was on his right rear quarter. Levett yanked hard into a climbing turn, trying to throw the attacker off his tail.

It wasn't working. The Egyptian was staying inside his turn. Levett looked back over his shoulder. What he saw sent a chill through him.

The twinkling orange muzzles of the Spitfire's machine guns.

The hunter had become the prey. Levett knew the Messerschmitt couldn't win a turning fight with a Spitfire. There was only one way out.

Levett shoved the Messerschmitt into a violent negative-G vertical dive. Dirt and dead bugs flew from the bottom of the cockpit. The Messerschmitt accelerated toward the earth like a descending missile.

Levett glimpsed the airspeed indicator. It was going through 725 kilometers per hour—beyond 450 mph. Only speed and the negative-G maneuver would save him.

Bottoming out of the dive, Levett grunted against the G-load and glanced behind him.

The Spitfire was nowhere to be seen.

Levett zoomed back toward the swarm of warplanes above him. He saw a gaggle of Spitfires, but . . . *which were the Egyptians?* They all looked alike. He couldn't shoot because one of them might be Doyle. Doyle, on the other hand, could blast away at *any* Spitfire he saw, knowing it wasn't his wingman in a Messerschmitt.

And then Levett glimpsed something just off the shoreline—a different silhouette, pointier-nosed than a Spitfire, with tapered, square-tipped wings. It was one of the Macchi fighters. It was low over the water, turning back toward his home base at El Arish.

With his altitude advantage, Levett swept down on the Macchi's tail.

The Egyptian pilot was an inept dogfighter. Levett stayed stay inside his turns, firing short bursts into the evading fighter. The Egyptian was making a clumsy effort to escape being shot down.

Levett wondered if he was wounded. He considered coming alongside and lowering his gear, signaling the Egyptian to surrender.

No, Levett decided. It would slow him down and make *him* a sitting duck for other Egyptian fighters. *Get it over.*

Levett fired more bursts into the Macchi. Black smoke belched from the V-12 engine. The Italian-built warplane went into a steep plunge toward the Mediterranean.

There was no sign of a parachute.

Levett peered around. The sky was clear of fighters. Even Doyle was gone. When Levett landed back at Hatzor, Doyle was on the ramp waiting for him. In their mission report, each pilot claimed one Fiat G55 killed (they were actually Macchi MC.205Vs) and one Spitfire probably destroyed.

Levett couldn't sleep that night. After several hours of staring into the darkness, he rose and switched on the bedside light. He lit a cigarette and reflected on what happened.

He'd shot down one and probably two enemy fighters in air-to-air combat. And nearly been shot down himself. Levett knew that he should be elated, full of himself, filled with a warrior's chest-thumping pride.

He wasn't. Today he had killed a man. Maybe two. Smoking his cigarette alone in the room, Levett wondered about them. Were they young? Old? Married? Fathers? One, he knew for sure, was at the bottom of the Mediterranean still in his fighter.

After all these years of aspiring to be a fighter pilot, this wasn't what Levett expected. None of the high-blown talk about righteous causes and saving a nation and fighting for something greater than himself had been in his mind. Levett had obeyed the warrior's primal command: *Kill or be killed.*

There had been nothing righteous about it.

Levett rose and shuffled through his small collection of books. Finally he located the passage he was looking for. It was in a letter from the French aviator and writer Antoine de Saint-Exupéry to his friend and fellow writer André Gide.

Saint-Exupéry had been in combat for the first time: "I now know why Plato places courage on the lowest rung of the virtues. Never again shall I be able to admire a man who is only brave."

═══ 45 ═══

Storming the Sinai

GAZA STRIP
DECEMBER 25, 1948

Mike Flint's flight of five dive bombers had just pulled off the target in the Faluja Pocket. Staying low to avoid the antiaircraft gunners, they were headed for the coastline. Behind Flint somewhere was his number three dive bomber, Dick Dougherty.

A radio call crackled in Flint's earphones: "I've got a hung bomb!"

One of Dougherty's bombs hadn't released.

And then Flint saw it. Dougherty's AT-6 Harvard was sliding in to rejoin the formation. Flint could see the 50-kg bomb still suspended beneath a wing. It was bad news. A hung bomb was deadly because it could release—and detonate—at any time.

Flint watched Dougherty yank the Harvard up and down, applying G-forces to shake off the hung bomb. Nothing worked. The bomb stayed attached.

"What do you wanna do?" Flint asked on the radio.

"I guess I'll land with it."

Flint just nodded. There were no good choices. Dougherty could land and hope the bomb didn't come off, or he could bail out. Bailing out was a lousy idea, even over friendly territory. Arab militants still roamed the countryside and would make short work of a downed pilot.

Flint and the other three Harvards landed at Ekron and climbed out of their cockpits. They watched Dougherty's Harvard sweeping over the threshold of the runway, flaring to land.

The Harvard was still 20 feet in the air when *something*—a dark object—dropped from the airplane.

Dougherty knew it. He made a violent swerve to the right. The Harvard's landing gear was retracting as the pilot made a desperate attempt to get away from the bomb.

He didn't make it. The bomb exploded into the concrete directly beneath the tail of the Harvard. The sound of the explosion reverberated across the open field. The shattered airplane went down like a shotgunned duck, crashing into the muddy terrain beside the runway.

Flint and the other pilots were already running toward the crash. They saw that the Harvard was a mess. The aft fuselage was riddled by shrapnel. The forward half, including the cockpit, was crumpled from the crash.

The cockpit was empty. Flint peered around. Where was Dougherty?

Then they saw him. Dick Dougherty was standing ankle-deep in the mud several feet from the airplane. He was shaken up but unhurt.

Dougherty was shaking his head in disbelief. The chances of the bomb falling off when it did—the last five seconds of the flight—were infinitesimally remote. A few minutes or even seconds before and the bomb would have detonated far below the airplane, causing no damage. A few seconds later, when the Harvard was on the runway, Dougherty would have been immolated.

The crash made Flint and his team think again about their mission. Dive bombing was inherently dangerous, but it hadn't occurred to them that the bombs they were using to kill Arabs might also kill *them*.

Hung bombs were nothing new. The makeshift bomb racks on the Harvards often malfunctioned, but it had always been possible to get rid of the bomb one way or another. Until today.

The pilots couldn't help wondering: Was Dougherty's accident a fluke, or was it likely to happen again?

In one more day they would find out.

In the ancient desert site of Halutza, a few miles southwest of Beersheba, the commander of the Operation Horev offensive was gazing sourly at the overcast skies.

Yigal Allon was a former commander of the Palmach. Allon was a strong-willed soldier who sometimes had to be restrained by his superiors in the general staff. It had been Allon who, on Ben-Gurion's orders, directed the shelling of the Irgun weapons ship *Altalena*.

Allon was frustrated. It was the third day of Operation Horev, December 25, and the surprise attack against Auja to outflank the Egyptian Army was still delayed because of the rain.

Winter was the wet season in the Negev, and nothing could be done about it. The roads in the desert had turned to swamps. Dry wadis became streams. Tanks and trucks were bogged down. Soldiers were slogging through the muck.

The low-hanging clouds forced the cancellation of most bombing and close air support missions. Allon's only consolation was that the weather was keeping the Egyptian warplanes out of the sky also.

Rain or no rain, the offensive could be delayed no longer. Allon was about to order his two brigades to begin their drive to Auja when he was startled by an oncoming apparition.

A short, stocky figure was tramping through the mud toward him. The figure was accompanied by an entourage of unhappy-looking soldiers. As the group approached, Allon recognized Israel's head of state.

It was classic Ben-Gurion. In his role as defense minister, he had come to send Allon's brigades off on their mission. En route Ben-Gurion's convoy mired down in the mud. For two hours the defense minister, along with chief of staff Yigael Yadin and their entourage, had tramped across the wadis and dunes to reach the brigade.

Allon finished his meeting with Ben-Gurion. Minutes later his two brigades were storming southward across the desert. Despite the mud and rain they quickly rolled over the chain of Egyptian hilltop fortifications.

It was a textbook flanking maneuver. Within hours Auja, the gateway to the Sinai, had fallen. By noon on December 28, Israeli forces were pushing across the border into the Sinai peninsula. The land of their enemy.

It was a historic moment. In a war that began with an invasion of Israel by the Egyptian Army, the soldiers of Israel were now invading Egypt.

"We were suffused with a sense of Jewish power bursting into Egypt," recalled one Israeli soldier. The Israeli troops were singing and hugging each other as their trucks rumbled into the Sinai.

In his armored vehicle near the head of the Eighth Brigade column, General Allon wasn't celebrating. The hard-charging commander was worried that his success might soon be snatched away from him. Allon was receiving a steady stream of cables from IDF head of operations Yigael Yadin in Tel Aviv. Yadin was demanding that he wait for further orders before proceeding deeper into the Egyptian Sinai.

Allon wasn't waiting. Within hours his forces had captured the key Egyptian crossroads at Abu Ageila and then headed for the real prize: the main Egyptian air base at El Arish. With El Arish in Israeli hands, the encirclement of the Egyptian Army would be complete.

═══

Mike Flint was becoming familiar—more familiar than he wanted—with the oval-shaped enclave called the Faluja Pocket. Every day, sometimes several times a day, Flint and his dive-bombing team visited Faluja.

The four-thousand-man Egyptian brigade inside Faluja had become isolated when the main Egyptian Army retreated southward to the Gaza Strip. Despite multiple infantry and armored assaults by the Israeli Alexandroni Brigade and daily barrages from Israeli warplanes, the tenacious Egyptian force held. Eliminating the Faluja Pocket had become a prime objective for the IDF general staff.

It was the fifth day of Operation Horev. Flint's dive bombers were again planting 50-kg bombs on the Egyptian positions inside the Pocket.

The Egyptian gunners weren't improving with practice. The same dispirited 20-mm antiaircraft fire was coming up from somewhere in the enclave, but hitting nothing. So far no dive bombers had been lost to antiaircraft fire.

Flint made his second steep dive on the target. He punched off his last four bombs. Again he opened up with his machine guns to discourage the Egyptian gunners. Then he roared at dune-top height for the safety of the sea.

Over his shoulder he could see the plumes from the explosion inside the Faluja enclave. Once again he'd gotten away with it.

Or so he thought.

Flint's wingman, John Soltau, was sliding up to his left wing. Soltau was waving, pointing to the belly of Flint's Harvard.

"I started to get this sinking feeling in my stomach," Flint recalled. He knew what Soltau was pointing at. It was the same thing that happened to Dougherty. A hung bomb.

Flint put the Harvard through the same yanks, skids, and slews that Dougherty had performed. He pushed the bomber into a dive, then hauled the nose up in an abrupt four-G pull-out. He did it twice.

The bomb didn't budge.

He had the same choices as Dougherty. Bail out or land. Flint had never bailed out before. Doing it over Israel didn't appeal to him any more than it had to Dougherty. There was another option: ditching in the sea. He rejected that one. He'd ditched an SB2C in WWII, and that was enough. In any case, the bomb could still explode when the airplane hit the water.

He would land back at Ekron. Instead of a navy three-point landing—main wheels and tail wheel plunking down at the same time—Flint would fly the main gear onto the runway, then slowly lower the tail.

It was a feather-smooth landing. The main wheels kissed the concrete. Flint let the Harvard slow on the runway, tail wheel coming down, using no brakes.

Flint hunkered down in his seat. If the bomb was going to explode, it would be *now*.

Nothing happened. Flint shut down the engine. The Harvard rolled to a stop, and Flint scrambled out of the cockpit.

Standing beside the airplane, he saw the bomb still suspended beneath the wing. Carefully Flint reached beneath the bomb and cradled it in his arms like a fragile art treasure.

At that moment, 110-lb bomb dropped from its rack.

For a long moment Flint stood there, grunting under the weight of the bomb. It was as if the weapon had a mind—and a heart—of its own. The bomb had waited to drop like a gift into his arms.

Carefully—*very* carefully— Flint lowered his catch to the ground. And resumed breathing.

=====

Yigal Allon was furious. At his command post on the southern front, the young general had just received the most maddening order of his military career: *Stop the advance.*

The order came directly from the IDF chief of staff. Yigael Yadin hadn't minced his words: "What's going on? Halt your advance!"

Furious, Allon climbed into the back of an Auster utility plane from the Sde Dov squadron and flew to Tel Aviv to make his case with Yadin and Ben-Gurion. At IDF headquarters and then at Ben-Gurion's Tiberias home, Allon pleaded for permission to capture El Arish. It was the base from which the Egyptians had been bombing Israel since the first day of the war. Allon's forces were only 6 miles short of it. By seizing El Arish on the coast, his brigades would have the entire Egyptian Army trapped in the Gaza Strip.

Neither Ben-Gurion nor Yadin would budge. The prime minister had a more worrisome consideration. Great Britain was on the verge of entering the war to save Egypt.

In a series of panicky messages, Egyptian ministers were imploring British Foreign Secretary Ernest Bevin to take action under the terms of the 1936 Anglo-Egyptian Defense Treaty. Since Egypt had been invaded by a foreign country, Britain was obligated to defend its ally.

Bevin had put the United States on alert. Ben-Gurion was

informed that President Truman was deeply disturbed by the "invasion of Egyptian territory." According to the US State Department, it
was proof of Israel's "aggressiveness" and "complete disregard" of the
United Nations.

In diplomatic language, Ben-Gurion replied that he had heard no
such demands from either the British or the Americans for the Egyptians
to withdraw from the Israeli territory that they invaded back in May and
which they still occupied. Nonetheless, Ben-Gurion signaled that Israel
would comply with their demands. Israel would pull its forces back to
the international border.

Yigal Allon had his answer. Still seething, he flew back to his command post in the Sinai. With the prize of El Arish snatched from him,
he couldn't close the trap on the eighteen-thousand-man Egyptian Army
as he had planned.

But Allon had an alternate strategy. Instead of attacking the Egyptian Army from their own soil, Allon would return to the border of Israel
and then drive northward for a direct attack on the Egyptian force at
Rafah, just inside Israeli territory. If he succeeded, he might still blockade the Egyptian Army in Gaza and cut off any chance of retreat.

Grudgingly, Allon gave the signal to his second in command. *Begin
the withdrawal.*

─────────

The blond-haired, twenty-six-year-old Yitzhak Rabin was the chief of
operations for the southern front. Like his commander, Yigal Allon,
Rabin was a former Palmach soldier. Both men were frustrated by the
constraints placed on them by the general staff in Tel Aviv. Under vehement protest, they had halted the near-conquest of El Arish.

Now their fast-moving brigades were withdrawing to Abu Ageila.
By tomorrow—New Year's eve—most of the Israeli invasion force would
be back on the Israeli side of the international border. To Rabin, the
withdrawal from El Arish would always be seen as a lost opportunity.

Since their incursion into Egypt, the Israeli brigades had been strafed
and bombed alternately by Egyptian warplanes and on one occasion by

Israeli fighters, whose pilots had not been informed about the presence of Israeli forces deep in Egyptian territory.

Now the Egyptians were back. A pair of fighters—not Spitfires but slick new Italian Macchis—were making strafing passes on the Israeli columns.

And then Rabin and his troops observed something else. Two more fighters were approaching from the north. By their silhouettes they appeared to be Spitfires.

They were swooping down on the Egyptian fighters.

═══ 46 ═══

A Hell of a Way to Run a War

The enemy warplanes were low, one Macchi trailing the other in a circuit around the Israeli encampment at Abu Ageila. Jack Doyle and John McElroy were behind the pair of Egyptians.

Doyle closed in on the leader from the right quarter. At 200 yards he squeezed the trigger, firing short bursts, watching his tracers arc into the Macchi's forward fuselage. Almost immediately black smoke and glycol fluid streamed from the fighter's stricken engine compartment. Trailing smoke, the Egyptian fighter dropped off on its right wing and slanted down toward the desert.

McElroy caught the second Macchi as it was pulling up from a strafing run. Unlike the first Macchi pilot—and unlike most of the Egyptian airmen McElroy had observed—this guy was aggressive.

The Macchi went into a series of evasive maneuvers. He managed to dodge McElroy's bullets. Then he was on the tail of Jack Doyle's Spitfire.

Before the Egyptian could open fire, McElroy put a long three-second burst in him. It was enough to get the Macchi off Doyle's tail. The Macchi turned hard back into McElroy, and the pair went into a violent high-G dogfight.

It took McElroy several circles. Finally he worked his way behind the Macchi's tail. A stream of bullets from the Spitfire's cannons and machine guns sent the Italian-built fighter into an uncontrolled dive into the desert.

Two Egyptian fighters down. No parachute was seen from either of them.

McElroy and Doyle had been surprised by the Macchi pilots, especially the second. In his debrief report McElroy wrote: "Enemy pilots' action during combat denote high combat experience."

Which sounded odd. *High combat experience?* As far as anyone knew, none of the Egyptian pilots had flown in WWII. Being a pilot in the Egyptian Air Force was a glamour job bestowed on the sons of privileged families. Except for Squadron Leader Abu Zaid, who died in his Sea Fury during his encounter with Len Fitchett's Beaufighter, none had shown any particular aptitude for aerial combat.

Until today. It had taken all the skills of John McElroy, one of the world's most accomplished fighter pilots, to shoot down the Egyptian fighter.

The rumor still persisted that the Egyptians had recruited German ex-Luftwaffe volunteers and possibly American fighter pilots. The rumor had never been confirmed.

True or not, the story gave the Red Squadron plenty to speculate about over drinks at the Gallei Yam bar that night. Aerial combat against Americans? A rematch with the Luftwaffe in WWII fighters? It was an intriguing—and worrisome—possibility.

Just as worrisome was another rumor. Egyptian warplanes were being escorted by RAF Spitfires as far as the border. The rumor hadn't been confirmed, but it was troubling.

Many of the Red Squadron pilots had flown in wartime with the RAF. Would they be going into combat against former comrades?

Surely not. Not even in a war as strange as this one.

———

It wasn't the way Denny Wilson had expected to spend New Year's Eve. The twenty-eight-year-old Canadian was in a three-ship flight of Spitfires. Their target was the Egyptian airfield at Bir Hana, deep in the Sinai, where much of the Egyptian Air Force had retreated when El Arish was about to be overrun by Allon's brigades.

Denny Wilson had arrived in Israel in the same group with John McElroy, Jack Doyle, and Wayne Peake. Wilson was a popular guy in the squadron, fun-loving and witty, with a pompadour haircut and Marlon Brando good looks. He was one of fifteen non-Jewish Canadian pilots in the IAF. Wilson had flown Spitfires in the RCAF 411 Squadron in Europe and was credited with shooting down two German warplanes.

Bir Hana had been on the list of objectives during Yigal Allon's lightning thrust into the Sinai, but Allon had been ordered to turn back before his troops could seize the airfield. Instead, the general staff wanted Bir Hana hit from the air. The plan was for fighters to bomb the field and then shoot up whatever they found on the tarmac.

Bombing with the Spitfire was a hit-or-miss exercise. At most the fighter could haul two 100-kg bombs, and the results were wildly inaccurate. But the Spitfire had one great advantage over the B-17s and Harvard dive bombers. It needed no escort. In an instant the Spitfire could shed its bombs and go *mano a mano* with enemy fighters.

Wilson was still in his dive, aiming at the hangar complex on the Egyptian field, when he spotted something coming into his field of vision. It was a couple of thousand feet above the field—an unfamiliar silhouette.

Wilson punched off his two bombs. He bottomed out of his dive and zoomed up to check out the intruder.

It wasn't a Spitfire. As Wilson soared above the incoming aircraft, he identified what he later reported as a Fiat (it was actually a Macchi MC.205V). An Egyptian pilot was returning from a mission, unaware he had blundered into the middle of an Israeli air raid.

Too late, the Egyptian tried to escape. Wilson whipped in behind the fighter. He fired six short bursts. As the Macchi went into a spin toward the desert, Wilson saw the pilot bailing out. The Egyptian pilot was still descending in his parachute when the Macchi crashed into the desert 6 miles west of Bir Hana.

The day wasn't over for Denny Wilson. On his way north, Wilson spotted another item of interest. An Egyptian Spitfire was escorting a Dakota transport plane. The Dakota was dropping supplies to the garrison inside the Faluja Pocket.

Wilson had to make a quick decision. *The Spitfire or the Dakota?*

Wilson slid in behind the Spitfire. The Egyptian fighter went into a tight turn, and Wilson tightened with him. Wilson remembered that they'd been asked not to fire the Spitfire's Hispano cannons unless necessary because ammunition was so short.

He selected the Browning machine guns. Wilson fired a single long burst into the Egyptian Spitfire's engine. He could see pieces and smoke spewing from the stricken fighter.

Wilson's post-action report was succinct: "He spiraled down and blew up."

Roaring back toward Hatzor Air Base, Denny Wilson was exhilarated. One mission, two victories! As many as he had shot down in all of WWII.

It was still New Year's Eve. Now Wilson had something to celebrate.

———

By the time Allon's brigades had received the order *not* to capture the El Arish air base, a commando team had already reached the base's outer periphery.

To their surprise, the base was deserted. The Egyptians had evacuated El Arish and the satellite fields around it. Every serviceable fighter had been flown away to outlying bases in Egypt.

Except one. The commandos had just discovered a completely intact Spitfire fighter left behind.

Allon had received orders to withdraw from the Sinai, but nothing had been said about taking Egyptian hardware with them. Was the Spitfire flyable?

They would soon find out. At the 101 Squadron at Hatzor, Boris Senior and a mechanic were picked up by a utility plane and flown down to the satellite field.

It was a tantalizing prospect, but it didn't work. Sitting in the Spitfire cockpit, Senior tried every way he knew to start the fighter's engine. The Spitfire appeared to be airworthy, but the balky engine refused to start. Senior realized that was the reason the Egyptians had abandoned the aircraft.

They would have to snatch it the hard way. Later, Egyptian and British reconnaissance photos of the long procession of Israeli trucks and armor heading out of the Sinai would reveal a peculiar apparition: a fighter being towed by its tail.

The captured Spitfire made it out of Egypt, but not in one piece. The lightweight airframe hadn't been designed to be dragged like a trailer. After a succession of rude bumps and scrapes a tire burst and then part of the landing gear collapsed.

While the stolen Spitfire was being dismantled and hauled to Israel in pieces, another drama was playing out in the sky over Ekron.

It was 03:00 on the morning of January 4. After a nearly twelve-hour flight from Czechoslovakia, Larry Raab was orbiting Ekron Air Base in a C-54 Skymaster with a load of precious Spitfire equipment.

Now he couldn't land. Ekron was blacked out. No one on the ground was responding to Raab's urgent radio calls. To make matters more urgent, one of the Skymaster's four engines had been shut down while they were still over Greece.

The short, baby-faced Raab was twenty-four, but he still looked too young to drink, let alone fly a four-engine transport. Raab had been one of the early Schwimmer and Schindler recruits back at Millville. Since then he'd lived through all the Bagel Lancers' adventures—Panama, Catania, Žatec and the Balak airlift, the move to Ekron.

To Raab, this was a familiar scenario. The airfield they used to call Ekron had been blacked out back in May when he brought in the first C-46 cargo flight. Not until Raab had nearly run out of fuel did someone finally turn on the runway lights so he could land.

Now they were seven months into the war, and the same thing was happening. No one informed Ekron that the C-54 was inbound.

To hell with Ekron, Raab decided. He'd go to Sde Dov, the little airfield on the north edge of Tel Aviv, with all his lights blinking. Either he'd be shot down by nervous air defense gunners or someone would wake up and turn on the runway lights at Sde Dov.

Neither happened. No one fired a shot. No one turned on the runway lights. Sde Dov stayed hidden in a black gloom along the beach. The radio remained silent. It was as if the four-motored Skymaster was a ghost, invisible to everyone on the ground.

Raab was disgusted. It seemed to be a curse of the Israeli military. For all their élan and innovativeness, the Israelis had a knack for botching operations because one arm of the military wasn't talking to another.

Circling offshore, Raab calculated his remaining fuel. He *might* have enough gas to orbit until dawn when he could see the runway. If nothing else went wrong.

And then as the sky was pinkening in the east, something else went wrong.

A second engine abruptly failed from fuel starvation. With two dead engines, the heavily loaded Skymaster was going down. Raab headed for the shoreline, descending in a shallow glide toward the open sea.

The copilot called out altitudes—Five hundred . . . four hundred . . . *three hundred . . .*

The big transport smacked down on its belly. It skipped once, then plowed to a stop like a flat-bottomed barge. For a long moment Raab and his crew sat motionless, stunned by the abrupt end of their long flight.

As ditchings went, it had been textbook perfect. The C-54 was floating high in the water. Boats were coming toward them from the shore. Too late, someone on the ground was recognizing their existence.

Raab and his crew climbed out through an overwing exit and stood on the wing. None of them had gotten wet. The cargo in the C-54 was undamaged, but the Skymaster was a write-off.

Standing on the Skymaster's wing, Raab and his crew watched the dawn come to Sde Dov. They were disgusted. Through a failure of communication, the air force had lost a precious airplane.

A hell of a way to run a war.

General Yigal Allon hadn't left the land of his enemy quietly. Behind his withdrawing troops lay a trail of scorched earth—wrecked airfields, destroyed bridges, demolished military equipment.

In addition to the Egyptian Spitfire now being hauled northward, a Dragon Rapide two-engine transport had been discovered at the El Arish satellite field. Unlike the Spit, the Rapide was made airworthy by IAF mechanics. Before dark an IAF pilot was flying the prize back to Ekron.

Ben-Gurion had given his okay to Allon's plan to drive northward along the Egypt-Israel border and seize the Egyptian Army's southernmost position in the Gaza Strip, Rafah. Though the road from Auja to Rafah dipped at some points six kilometers back inside Egypt, Ben-Gurion didn't think it would compromise his assertion that Israel's force had completely withdrawn from Egypt.

It wouldn't be the classic encirclement of the enemy that Allon had wanted when El Arish was in his grasp. Still, with a conquest of Rafah, Allon could close the trap on the Egyptian Expeditionary Force.

If the politicians didn't stop him again.

In the crisp dawn of January 4, three of Allon's brigades struck at Rafah. As if it were an omen, the skies opened up and visibility was unlimited. Over the battlefield swarmed fighters, B-17s, dive bombers, light plane spotters.

For the ground-attack aircraft, the danger level was ratcheting up. Since the opening of Operation Horev, the Egyptians had brought in more and larger antiaircraft guns. The sky over Rafah roiled with ack-ack bursts as the Israeli aircraft swept overhead.

A pair of Red Squadron Spitfires flown by the two Cohens—Syd and Jack—showed up to drop bombs and then strafe a train in the enemy complex. Two hours later a pair of Hammer Squadron B-17s rained bombs onto the southern part of Gaza.

A few minutes before noon American Mike Flint, Canadian Eddie

Kaplansky, and the Russian pilot, Grisha Brown, arrived in their Harvard dive bombers. The Harvards each made two steep passes down through the flak, dropping four 50-kg bombs each time on the same Egyptian train and tracks the Spitfires had hit.

Flint's after-action report was matter-of-fact: "Heavy accurate AA fire was encountered from 40mm and 75mm or 88mm guns."

The attacks continued through the afternoon. And so did the intense antiaircraft barrage. Despite the blanket of AA fire, the Israelis had not lost a single airplane.

At least to enemy fire.

= 47 =

"Right with You, Boy"

HATZOR AIR BASE
JANUARY 5, 1949

The scene would replay itself in Red Finkel's mind like a recurring dream. He would never be sure whether it was his fault or if the Spitfire had bitten him like a spiteful pet.

It was a reconnaissance mission, and Finkel was pleased to be back in action. When he was stuck in Czechoslovakia with the other ferry pilots on the much-delayed Velvetta II operation, he had worried that Operation Horev would finish before he could join.

He made it back in time. Today was his third combat mission during the Horev offensive.

Finkel and his flight leader, Boris Senior, made a sweep over the Auja–Rafah road, counting enemy vehicles. They alternated scanning the ground and checking the sky around them. There was always the chance an Egyptian fighter pilot would get his nerve up and jump them.

Like the other pilots, Finkel liked the Spitfire. The arrival of the last ten Spits meant the Red Squadron no longer needed to fly the Messerschmitts, which pleased Finkel. He'd been one of the lucky ones. Finkel had never crashed the Czech Mule.

Mission complete, the pair of Spitfires flew back to Hatzor. Finkel entered the traffic pattern behind Senior, extended his landing gear, and swept over the end of the runway. As he always did, Finkel eased the throttle back and tilted the fighter's nose up, leveling off for the landing.

But something was different about this landing. He'd flared too high. Finkel held the Spitfire's nose up, floating, still 10 feet above the runway—

And then it dropped.

A tire burst. The fighter swerved toward the open ground off the runway. From then on, Red Finkel was along for the ride. The Spitfire's skinny wheels dug into the rain-soaked earth.

The scenario Finkel had witnessed so many times with the Messerschmitt was happening to the Spitfire. The fighter went over on its nose and one wingtip. It slid along, teetering with its tail in the sky, and then slammed down inverted.

Finkel hung upside down for what seemed like hours but in fact was only a few minutes. By now the crash crew at Hatzor had become experts at retrieving pilots from overturned fighters. Within minutes they had dragged Red Finkel from beneath the Spitfire. He was banged up but not seriously hurt.

That evening in the dining room the rambunctious Finkel was uncharacteristically subdued. Whether he liked it or not, he had joined an exclusive club: the Red Squadron pilots whose heads had dangled inches from the ground in an upside-down fighter. What irked Finkel was that he'd done it in a . . . *Spitfire.*

══════

On the morning after Finkel's mishap, two more fighters were taking off from Hatzor. It was another armed reconnaissance mission, and another Red Squadron aircraft mismatch. In the lead was the Spitfire flown by South African Boris Senior. Flying the Mustang on his wing was a twenty-eight-year-old newcomer from Brooklyn named Seymour "Buck" Feldman. Feldman had been a volunteer in the RAF during WWII, receiving a Distinguished Flying Cross from King George for having shot down ten German V-1 rockets with a Tempest fighter.

Feldman and Senior were patrolling the road from Rafah to Auja. The mission had been routine until they were heading back to the coast at 7,500 feet.

Then they spotted them: three Italian-built Macchi fighters. The

Macchis were a thousand feet below, rolling in for a dive-bombing attack on the Israeli forces dug in outside Rafah.

With the morning sun behind them, Feldman and Senior pounced on the Egyptians. The Egyptian pilots awakened to the incoming danger at the last moment and jettisoned their bombs. Two of the Egyptian fighters turned to engage the Israeli fighters.

The Egyptian flight leader chose a different course. He made a hard turn *away* from the danger and was last seen streaking southward toward Egypt.

Senior dove behind one of the remaining Macchis, and Feldman went after the other. Feldman's quarry made a hard turn into him, and the two were immediately engaged in a full-circle dogfight.

Neither was gaining an advantage. Pulling hard into the circle, Feldman managed to squeeze off a ninety-degree deflection shot on the Macchi.

It was a nearly impossible angle. But to Feldman's amazement, some of his .50-caliber bullets scored hits. He saw smoke streaming from the cowling of the Egyptian fighter.

The Macchi was still in the fight. He was still turning hard. After another circle, Feldman found himself in a head-on pass with the stubborn Egyptian fighter.

In the next instant he saw another dark shape swooping on to the Egyptian's tail. It was Senior, who had just finished shooting down the other Macchi.

The South African delivered the coup de grace. The outgunned Macchi rolled over and crashed into the desert. Feldman wrote in his action report: "Observed him prang with black and white smoke pouring out."

Back at Hatzor the excited pilots were doing their usual hand-gesturing replay of the dogfight. The Egyptian pilots had been a mixed bag—one disinclined to fight, one an inept dogfighter, and the third *very* aggressive. As they usually did after the second or third round of drinks, someone speculated about what would happen if they ran up against *real* fighter pilots?

RAF fighter pilots, for example.

The rumors had been confirmed. RAF fighters *had* been escorting Egyptian Air Force warplanes up to the international border. Still, it seemed unthinkable, the notion of going into combat against the RAF. Guys just like *them*.

Could it happen? No one was ruling it out.

═══════

Ben-Gurion was in his office on the afternoon of January 5 when the message came in. The USA Special Representative in Israel, James McDonald, wanted the prime minister to know that Cairo had informed the United Nations, Britain, and the United States that Egypt was ready to begin armistice negotiations—if Israel ceased hostilities.

The irony was not lost on Ben-Gurion. *If Israel ceased hostilities.* After seven months of siege by the Egyptians, an armistice was contingent on whether *Israel* ceased hostilities?

Ben-Gurion had mixed feelings about the Egyptian initiative. It was coming at a time when Israeli forces had their hands on the throat of the Egyptian Army at Rafah. Allon's forces had captured a key crossroads, blocking all reinforcement and resupply to the trapped army. Time was running out for the Egyptians to save their trapped army.

But time was running out for Israel also. Not only was Britain threatening to intervene in the war, but the United States had also become increasingly adversarial. Foreign secretary Bevin was playing the Cold War card, warning that because Israel had received most of its weaponry from a Communist country, Israel would likely join the Soviet bloc. It was a scare tactic, and the United States' senior cold warrior, Secretary of State George Marshall, was a ready believer in such a theory.

The sixty-one-year-old prime minister of Israel was a realist. Israel could continue the war and possibly solidify its gains. And possibly lose everything they'd fought for. Was it worth it? After two thousand years of Jewish longing for a homeland, were they willing to risk throwing it all away?

That evening Ben-Gurion signaled Washington: Israel would be receptive to negotiations with Egypt.

———

The next morning, January 6, a swirling sandstorm swept over the lower Negev and the Sinai. Visibility dropped to near zero. The Hammers managed to get off a single bombing mission and the Red Squadron sent up only a few fighter patrols.

In Washington, London, Tel Aviv, and Cairo, diplomats were exchanging urgent wires. Finally they came up with a new cease-fire deadline in Israel: 14:00 local on January 7, 1949.

One day to go. A new sense of urgency filled the IAF briefing rooms at Hatzor and Ekron and Ramat David. Tomorrow might be the last day of combat. Sandstorms or not, the sound of warplane engines resonated over the desert.

———

An hour past dawn, Mike Flint was peering down through the sand-filled haze at his target. Five Harvard dive bombers had returned to bomb the Egyptian compound in the ancient village just north of Rafah.

The limited visibility wasn't deterring the Egyptian gunners. A heavier-than-usual flak umbrella was blossoming over Khan Yunis this morning. So far none of the Harvards had taken a serious hit from ground fire. Flint decided the gunners didn't need more practice. The Harvards would make just one bombing run.

Flint went first. His target was the police barracks in the village. Flint went into his dive, putting the rectangular shape of the barracks squarely in his windscreen. He jammed the release button and all eight bombs released from beneath the wings.

All the dive bombers made it. As he buzzed at rooftop height toward the coast, Flint swiveled his head from side to side. He could see their fighter cover—a pair of Spitfires circling above them.

Even higher he glimpsed the silhouettes of two Flying Fortresses on their own bomb run over Rafah. Another pair of Spitfires was escorting the bombers.

Not far behind was another flight of dive bombers from Ekron.

January 7 was shaping up to be a hell of a day. Maybe the last day of the shooting war. Flint was certain that the Egyptians would be sending up fighters. Lots of them. *Where were they?*

━━━━

They were there. Six of them, flying in stepped-up formations of two each. They were Egyptian Macchis and they were attacking an Israeli convoy on the road to Rafah.

Jack Doyle spotted them first. He and Boris Senior were in a pair of P-51 Mustangs. They had been escorting the second wave of 35 Flight dive bombers over their target in the Gaza Strip. Finished with the escort assignment, the pair had gone hunting along the Auja–Rafah road.

In the marginal visibility Doyle couldn't determine the type of the fighters or even the nationality. It didn't matter. They couldn't be Israeli. The IAF had never put six fighters in the air at once. These guys were definitely hostile.

The Mustangs pounced from out of the sun. Senior swung in behind the trailing fighter, closing fast. He had time for one long burst before he overtook the enemy warplane. A cloud of brown smoke gushed from the enemy fighter as Senior zoomed back up in the sand cloud over the desert.

Senior promptly lost sight of everyone, including his wingman. "Where are you?" he called to Doyle.

"Right with you, boy," came the answer in a thick Irish brogue.

Doyle, in fact, was busy gunning down one of the fighters that had been strafing the Israeli convoy. "Started firing from 700 yards," his debrief report stated, "strike in wing, wing cowling came off, strikes on engine and fuselage. Aircraft went away pouring brown and black smoke."

Then Doyle went after a second enemy fighter, getting a few rounds into him before he overshot. "I was going so goddamned fast I went whistling straight by them."

The Macchis scattered. Within seconds they were invisible in the low visibility.

The fight was over. Above the sand cloud and clear of the battle zone north of Rafah, Senior and Doyle rejoined and headed back to Hatzor. Each would be credited with one kill apiece of an Egyptian Macchi fighter (which again were mistakenly reported as "Fiats").

The cease-fire was due to go into effect in less than two hours. Back at Hatzor it seemed that Senior and Doyle might have fought the last air-to-air duel of the war.

They hadn't. Fifty miles to the south, the greatest—and most controversial—air battle of the war was just beginning.

=48=

Twisting the Lion's Tail

AUJA–RAFAH ROAD, NEGEV DESERT
JANUARY 7, 1949

The four British Royal Air Force Spitfires arrived over the Israeli column five minutes after the Macchis departed. The leader of the flight, Flying Officer Geoff Cooper, had spotted the towering smoke columns from the convoy the Macchis had set ablaze.

Cooper wanted a closer look. Over the radio he issued a quick command. Two fighters would fly high cover at 1,500 feet. Cooper and his wingman would go in low at 500 feet. As Cooper flew nearer toward the convoy, he saw the source of the smoke. Three trucks in the Israeli armored column were burning.

The first two Spitfires were almost over the top of the armored column when Cooper's fighter was hit by ground fire. At the same moment he heard his wingman yell on the radio that he'd been hit in the engine.

Cooper yanked his Spitfire up in a soaring turn. In his rear quarter he saw his wingman's fighter trailing smoke, climbing, the canopy blowing free. The pilot was bailing out.

In the next instant Cooper glimpsed something else—a pair of dark shapes materializing out of the haze above them. *More fighters. Whose?*

═══

The gunner atop the Israeli Eighth Brigade armored car let out a lusty cheer. He'd gotten one of the fighters! The armored column had been caught by surprise by the first wave of Egyptian warplanes that sneaked in from the east and hit them before anyone could get off a shot. Three trucks destroyed, several soldiers killed.

When this second bunch came in, the gunners were ready. A hail of small arms and 20-mm fire went up from nearly every vehicle in the convoy—and hit at least one of the fighters. A fresh pillar of smoke marked the spot where the enemy fighter crashed. A parachute was descending to the desert close to the convoy. Troops were already on the way to capture the enemy pilot.

And the action wasn't over. From his perch atop the armored car, the gunner could see another pair of fighters swooping down on the enemy warplanes from above.

―――――

John McElroy issued a crisp radio call to his wingman, Slick Goodlin: "Enemy aircraft at twelve o'clock, right in front of us." They looked like Spitfires to McElroy, and they weren't friendly. These Spits were making a run directly on the Israeli Eighth Brigade column moving along the Auja–Rafah road.

McElroy and Goodlin were the poster boys of the Red Squadron. One was Canada's eighth-highest ranking WWII ace and the other a renowned test pilot. Neither was Jewish. Neither was an idealist or a crusader. McElroy and Goodlin had come to Israel for the same reason volunteers had been drawn to battle since the Peloponnesian War. They missed the thrill of combat.

The two fighter formations—both flying Spitfires—had arrived over the Israeli convoy almost simultaneously. Seconds after the low-flying RAF Spitfire was hit by ground fire, McElroy and Goodlin were pouncing on the three remaining intruders.

Before he opened fire, McElroy wanted to be sure of his target. He slid in close enough to the trailing Spitfire to see the pointed wingtips, the round fin and rudder. They were not the clipped-wing Spitfire version flown by the IAF. They were hostile fighters.

McElroy dropped back into firing position and opened up with a four-second burst. He saw explosions erupting from the Spitfire's engine and cockpit. Pieces were flying back from the shattered wings. Too late, McElroy tried to duck the cloud of debris. *Whap whap.* Parts of the plane were thunking into his own fighter. Below him the shattered enemy fighter was in a steep dive to the desert.

McElroy pulled up and swiveled his head, looking for the other fighters. *There!* Two o'clock, slightly low, another Spit. It had the same pointy wings, which meant it couldn't be Goodlin.

"I just dropped my sights on him—it was 400 yards—and let fly," McElroy reported. He saw his tracers chewing up the length of the Spitfire's fuselage, all the way to the engine.

Another kill. In less than a minute McElroy had gunned down two enemy Spitfires. Now he was worried about his own fighter, which had taken damage from the debris of the first kill.

As he exited the combat area, McElroy peered around in the sandy murk. He saw nothing. Where was Goodlin?

———

Goodlin was a mile away, in a near-vertical climb. He was chasing the fighter he'd jumped over the convoy. He wasn't getting any closer. The enemy Spit was a later model than Goodlin's, with better climb performance.

In a full-throttle upward chase, the two fighters broke out of the haze at 10,000 feet, still climbing. Goodlin clung to the enemy's tail, too far behind to use his guns. Sooner or later this guy had to run out of energy and come back down.

At 16,000 feet, he did. The enemy Spitfire abruptly reversed and swung into Goodlin. For an instant Goodlin had a frontal view of the oncoming Spitfire, its guns blazing.

Goodlin dodged the oncoming fighter, then tried to maneuver behind his tail. The two Spitfires went into a classic scissors duel, crossing noses in a head-on pass, reversing to come back in another head-on pass.

There was no graceful exit from a scissors fight. To turn and run gave your opponent an easy shot at your tail. A scissors fight continued until one fighter managed to turn more tightly than the other and get *inside* his turn. Then he gunned him down.

With each nose-to-nose cross and reversal, Goodlin, the WWII veteran and master test pilot, gained a tiny advantage. As he worked his way toward the enemy Spitfire's rear quarter, Goodlin saw the pilot glancing over his shoulder.

And then Goodlin noticed something else. Something he hadn't observed in the swirling sand haze or in the nose-to-nose scissors passes. On the enemy Spitfire's fuselage was a distinctive round emblem. Not the green-bordered circular emblem of the Egyptian Air Force, but a large blue-white-red roundel.

The emblem of the British Royal Air Force.

A storm of conflicting thoughts swirled through Slick Goodlin's mind. Why was he in a dogfight with a British fighter? Why were RAF fighters attacking an Israeli column? Had the Brits entered the war on the side of the Egyptians?

At the moment, it didn't matter. The scissors duel was drawing to its inevitable conclusion. The RAF Spit had already fired on Goodlin. There was only one way for this fight to end.

Goodlin pulled his nose further inside the RAF Spitfire's turn. He waited . . . waited . . . pulling tighter . . . *There!* A decent firing angle. He squeezed the trigger. Goodlin saw his tracers arcing into the enemy Spitfire's cowling.

The dogfight was over. The Spitfire rolled inverted and the canopy blew off. A dark shape dropped from the cockpit. Seconds later the pilot was descending beneath the white canopy of his parachute.

Goodlin found McElroy waiting for him above the still-smoking Israeli convoy. With McElroy in the lead, the two Spitfires roared low across the runway at Hatzor and then each pulled up in a classic victory roll.

John McElroy was grinning when they climbed down from their cockpits. The grin remained in place until Goodlin told him what they'd done. They'd just shot down three British warplanes. Another had been downed by Israeli gunners.

McElroy's faced turned ashen. "Oh, no," he blurted. "You're crazy. The British wouldn't be down there."

But they would. Israeli intelligence reported that the British had been sending armed recon flights over the battle area since yesterday. An earlier flight of two Mosquito reconnaissance aircraft with four Spitfire escorts had overflown the battle zone without being challenged.

Then came a telephone report from the front. Two of the downed RAF pilots had parachuted directly over Israeli positions. Both were captured. One was a noncommissioned officer named Frank Close. He was the pilot of the Spitfire shot down by Israeli ground fire. The other was Flying Officer Tim McElhaw, who had been McElroy's second target.

The flight leader, Flying Officer Geoff Cooper, was the Spitfire pilot Slick Goodlin had shot down after the scissors duel. Cooper parachuted into the desert south of the battle zone where he escaped on foot, eventually being rescued by Bedouins and transported by camel to the Egyptian Army.

The fourth British airman was a noncommissioned pilot named Ron Sayers. He was flying the Spitfire that McElroy shot down on his first firing pass.

Sayers was dead. He'd been killed at the controls of his Spitfire and crashed into the ground near the Israeli lines.

The news stunned the Red Squadron pilots at Hatzor. Not until later would someone point out the irony that in the most dramatic air-to-air encounter of the Arab–Israeli war, *none* of the combatants was Arab or Israeli or even Jewish.

McElroy, the hard-bitten Canadian ace who had fought alongside RAF squadrons throughout WWII, was distraught. The Brits were his allies and comrades in arms. And he'd just killed one of them.

Most of the pilots, including Slick Goodlin, took a pragmatic view. Hell, this was war. Why were the Brits sending armed fighters into Israeli air space in the midst of a battle? It was either a gesture of hostile intent or gross stupidity.

In either case, what happened—the downing of four RAF fighters— was perfectly justified. Didn't the IAF pilots have a *duty* to defend Israel's air space and its troops on the ground?

A fever of excitement swept through the barracks and squadron ops room at Hatzor. The cease-fire was supposed to begin in an hour. No one knew what to expect. Would the RAF retaliate? Was the skirmish with the RAF the beginning of an Israeli–British war? How would Israel react to British intrusions in Israeli air space?

With a sense that the end was near, the fighter pilots were clamoring to fly one last mission. 101 Squadron commander Syd Cohen was at a staff meeting in Tel Aviv. Deputy commander Rudy Augarten and ops officer Ezer Weizman were in charge. Before the cease-fire, they wanted to send up more fighters.

At 13:20, Canadian Denny Wilson and South African Arnie Ruch were given the go-ahead to fly a patrol over Rafah and El Arish. Minutes later, over Abu Ageila, the pair found exactly what they were looking for: a swarm of eight Macchi fighter-bombers, flying in two four-ship formations. All were armed with bombs.

In the melee Wilson and Ruch managed to damage several but failed to shoot any down. The most they could accomplish was to force the Egyptian fighters to jettison the bombs they would have used against Israeli positions at Rafah.

Even though the truce had gone into effect at 14:00, Rudy Augarten wangled a clearance from headquarters for one more reconnaissance mission. Ten minutes beyond the official truce time, Augarten and his fellow American Wayne Peake took off in their Spitfires to fly over Rafah and along the road to Auja. They were looking for enemy activity, especially *air* activity.

They found nothing. The sky was empty.

With the truce in place, the fighting was supposed to stop. No more flying over enemy territory.

But what about the British? No one seriously believed that the RAF was going to ignore the shooting down of four of their fighters and the capture of two pilots.

In the ops office, Ezer Weizman argued on the phone with Dov

Judah, Director of Operations at IAF headquarters. "Listen," said Weizman, "there's a cease-fire? Okay. But those Egyptians—I don't know whether they'll start again or not—but I think it would be good for morale to fly over El Arish with a foursome, to display our presence, and to remind them that they'd better keep to the cease-fire."

Over the phone came the sound of agitated breathing. Both Judah and Weizman knew that morale was not a priority with the truce in place. The Egyptians were not Israel's greatest worry. An entire RAF four-ship patrol had gone missing.

The British were coming. They had to.

From the director at headquarters came the order: "Go!"

═══════

The fighters rolled down the runway at half past three o'clock. As usual, the Hatzor mechanics had struggled to get the Spitfires mission-ready. Today would be one of the rare occasions when the Red Squadron put four fighters in the air together.

Weizman assigned himself to fly the lead. With him was Sandy Jacobs, an RAF-trained pilot like Weizman. Jacobs was born in Palestine to British parents and was the youngest member of the squadron.

Flying number three was Caesar "Danny" Dangott, a former US Navy fighter pilot. On Dangott's wing was Bill Schroeder, also ex–US Navy. Both Dangott and Schroeder had been Velvetta II ferry pilots and missed most of the action in Operation Horev. Schroeder was a new guy, still an unknown quantity. Today was his first operational mission with the squadron.

The winter sky was gray and hostile. Despite their jackets and fur-lined gloves, the pilots shivered in the unheated cockpits at 7,000 feet.

Weizman took a direct course for El Arish. Droning southbound, he could see the other three Spitfires in a wide combat spread. None of the pilots knew what to expect. *Will the Egyptians send up fighters?*

Will the British?

The British already had. At almost the same time Weizman's flight was taking off, four Spitfires of RAF 208 Squadron—the same unit that had sent the morning four-ship patrol—launched from their base at Fayid to search for their missing squadronmates.

This time the Spitfires brought escorts. With them were two flights of modern Hawker Tempest fighters. The Tempest was a sleek, round-motored, high-performance fighter developed late in WWII. Seven Tempests were assigned to fly medium cover for the Spitfires. Another eight Tempests flew top cover at 10,000 feet.

The nineteen-fighter armada joined up over Fayid and headed north. Toward Israel.

Weizman spotted the telltale black specks. There were two formations of at least eight each. They were at twelve o'clock level, coming from the south. From Egypt.

Weizman waggled his wings, signaling his wingmen to close up the formation. He shoved the power up on his Spitfire and started a climb to a higher altitude. Altitude converted to speed. Speed was life in a dogfight.

The enemy formation—Weizman didn't yet know *which* enemy—was approaching the international border. Weizman's flight was at 8,500 feet, almost directly over the oncoming formation. To Weizman they looked like Spitfires. They appeared to be carrying bombs.

They were entering Israeli air space. It was all he needed to know.

"Going in," Weizman called. Down swept the four Spitfires.

The first to draw blood was Bill Schroeder. Schroeder zeroed in on the trailing enemy fighter—an RAF Tempest. Schroeder blasted him with machine-gun and cannon fire.

It was quick and deadly. Schroeder saw the Tempest go into a spin and plunge into the desert near Rafah. There was no parachute.

The twenty-three-ship engagement turned into a melee, every man for himself, each pilot fighting for his life. Fighters slashed through the sky. Cannons and machine guns spewed fire. The frantic Tempest pilots fired at *every* Spitfire—including their own.

There was no further doubt about the identity of the intruders. The distinctive RAF roundels were visible on the British Spitfires and Tempests.

Weizman went after another Tempest. He caught one, sat on his tail and opened fire. Weizman saw hits, but the Tempest kept flying.

And shooting back. For a perilous few seconds Weizman was a target. He felt the *whap whap* of machine-gun bullets punching through the tail of his fighter. He managed to outturn the Tempest behind him.

The chaotic battle ended as abruptly as it began. Weizman rolled his Spitfire up on a wing and peered around. He was alone. He didn't see any of his wingmen. The British fighters had scattered in all directions.

The dogfight had taken Weizman down to a low altitude. Now the Egyptian antiaircraft guns at Rafah were shooting at him. It was time to get away.

Weizman landed back at Hatzor. To his great relief, he found all three of his wingmen waiting for him.

Only then did it fully dawn on them what they'd done. With four cobbled-together fighters their little squadron had taken on nineteen modern warplanes of a world power. They'd blown one out of the sky, seriously shot up another, and scattered the rest like quail. Except for the bullet holes in the tail of Weizman's Spitfire, the Israeli fighters had been untouched by the warplanes of the Royal Air Force.

Bill Schroeder had shot down an adversary on his first and only air-to-air combat mission of the war. He was instantly given a new squadron name: "Sudden Death" Schroeder.

It was a heady moment. And a scary one. Weizman tallied up the day's score. "Five planes, the property of the British Empire, were now buried in the desert sands. Two of the British pilots were killed, we captured two others, and one of them walked back to his base."

Now what? The little ragtag Israeli Air Force had just twisted the tail of the British lion. Anyone who knew anything about the mighty RAF knew that such a humiliation could not go unpunished.

The speculation ran rampant through the squadrons at Hatzor and Ekron and Ramat David. "The most common guess," wrote Weizman, "was that a score of bombers, escorted by dozens of fighters, would swoop down on the Hatzor airfield and wipe it off the face of the earth."

So the pilots did what came naturally. They headed for their favorite watering hole, the bar at the Park Hotel. The story of the Red Squadron's battle with the RAF was already making the rounds in Tel Aviv.

"It was a party to beat all parties," recalled Weizman, "with Israelis, American tourists—in fact, anyone who loved a good story and a drink—coming to join us."

Not until well after midnight did the pilots make their way back to their bases to meet whatever the dawn would bring.

=== 49 ===

"What a Beautiful Day"

TIBERIAS, ISRAEL
JANUARY 8, 1949

The sun rose over the Negev. Pilots sat strapped in their cockpits at Hatzor. They were ready to intercept incoming warplanes.

An hour passed. Then another. No swarms of bombers appeared. No waves of British fighters. There was no reprisal attack.

At their bases in the Canal Zone the furious RAF Spitfire and Tempest squadron commanders were begging for clearance to launch a massive retaliatory strike. RAF headquarters withheld permission.

The British Foreign Office fired off a stormy protest to the Israeli government and demanded compensation for the loss of airmen and aircraft. The Air Ministry issued a blustery warning that RAF aircraft would henceforth regard as hostile any "Jewish aircraft" encountered over Egyptian territory. To further demonstrate their outrage, the British sent reinforcements to their garrison at Aqaba, at the southern tip of Jordan adjoining Israel.

And that was it.

The Air Ministry continued to insist that its warplanes had *not* entered Israeli air space. They had been conducting "unarmed reconnaissance flights." Since the first four Spitfires had been shot down over Israeli lines, it meant either the Israeli forces were in Egyptian territory or the RAF fighters were in the wrong place.

The wreckage of the Tempest fighter shot down by Bill Schroeder had fallen 4 miles inside Israeli territory. The evidence from all the crashed airplanes as well as the statement from one of the captured RAF pilots made it clear that the British warplanes were indeed armed. Slick Goodlin would long remember seeing the blazing machine-gun muzzles of his Spitfire adversary.

Still, no one in the squadron felt cheery about fighting the RAF. Nearly all of them had flown with or alongside RAF airmen in WWII.

The Red Squadron pilots sent a message to the RAF 208 Squadron:

Sorry about yesterday, but you were on the wrong side of the fence. Come over and have a drink sometime. You will see many familiar faces.

January 8 was the Sabbath. That morning the prime minister was gazing through the window at his country retreat in Tiberias at the placid water of Lake Galilee. To the consternation of his staff Ben-Gurion had left Tel Aviv during a crucial moment in the war.

In his diary Ben-Gurion wrote, "What a beautiful day. Has the war really ended today?"

By mid-morning it seemed clear that it had. The British response to yesterday's air action was limited to sword-rattling. Peace talks between Egypt and Israel were scheduled to begin. Even the bellicose British foreign secretary wasn't willing to launch a new Middle East war against Israel.

For the four thousand Egyptian troops still encircled in the Faluja Pocket, the truce meant a blessed end to the steady bombardment they'd been enduring. Throughout the winter offensive, the tenacious Egyptian brigade had managed to repulse every Israeli assault on their position. Saving the trapped brigade was a key motivator for Egypt to reach an armistice with Israel. For Israel, the Faluja Pocket was an important bargaining chip.

Still trapped with his soldiers in Faluja was Lt. Col. Gamal Abdel Nasser. Nasser had been with the brigade since the early triumphant march that ended at the bridge in Ishdud. Nasser's experience in Faluja had left him more bitter than ever. He wrote that he was "in a state of revolt against everything . . . in revolt against the smooth, closely-shaven chins and the smart and comfortable offices at General HQ, where no one had any idea what the fighting men in the trenches felt or how much they suffered from orders sent out at random."

The young officer blamed Egypt's defeat on its inept general staff— and the corrupt King Farouk. One of the ways Nasser had kept himself occupied while encircled behind Israeli lines was by recruiting other young officers into a secret group.

One day soon, Nasser vowed, his little cabal would overthrow Egypt's corrupt government.

———

Twenty-two hundred miles away in London, Britain's Labour government was taking heat from the United States over the air battle of January 7. Why, demanded the Truman administration, were armed British warplanes meddling in a Middle East conflict in which Britain had no role? With a delicate peace process underway, *why* did they send warplanes into the area?

The heat spilled over onto the floor of the House of Commons. During the debate over the downing of the British warplanes, former Prime Minister Winston Churchill stood up and shocked everyone. Churchill demanded an explanation for the unreported downing of *another* British warplane: a Mosquito fighter-bomber shot down over the coast of Israel the month before.

Mosquito fighter-bomber? The British Air Ministry at first tried to dodge the question. In a rambling, evasive answer, the ministry declared that the aircraft had strayed off course during a training mission. It was inadvertently shot down over the Mediterranean.

Churchill wouldn't let it go. Under his stubborn questioning, the Air Ministry finally admitted that, umm, yes, the Mosquito had been on a . . . *reconnaissance* mission over Israel. In fact, the Cyprus-based Mosquito squadron had been regularly flying such missions over Israel since the beginning of hostilities.

And with that revelation, a mystery was solved. The elusive Shufti Kite had at last been identified. The high-flying spy plane shot down by P-51 pilot Wayne Peake, which in his oxygen-deprived condition he thought was a Halifax bomber, was a twin-engine, high-altitude Mosquito.

A *British* Mosquito. The overall tally of British aircraft downed by the IAF had just been raised to six.

———

Two of the Red Squadron pilots didn't feel like celebrating. One was John McElroy. Even in lighter moments McElroy never laughed as much as the others or engaged in squadron high jinks. In temperament McElroy was more like his fellow Canadian Buzz Beurling, a dour type for whom air-to-air combat was a serious, all-consuming obsession. McElroy and Beurling had flown in the same RAF Spitfire squadron during the WWII defense of Malta, where each of them became aces.

Weighing heavily on McElroy's mind was the mission he'd flown with Slick Goodlin. McElroy had shot down *two* RAF Spitfires. He had killed one of the pilots. McElroy knew in his gut that he'd done what was required of him. Still, he couldn't get over the bad feeling.

The next day McElroy made a phone call to Air Headquarters. Then he caught a ride up to Tel Aviv. He made his way to IAF Headquarters in the Yarkon Hotel, where he was taken to the room where the prisoner was being interrogated.

McElroy introduced himself.

The prisoner's name was Tim McElhaw. He was one of the pilots McElroy shot down two days ago. The one who was still alive. McElhaw was wearing his RAF tunic with wings and epaulets displaying his rank: flying officer.

McElroy and the captured pilot had a polite conversation. Each was careful not to say anything of operational significance. Though McElroy didn't describe his precise role in the engagement, the young pilot seemed to know that McElroy was one of the shooters. As McElroy left, he wished the Brit pilot well. Now that the truce was in place, he would surely be repatriated soon.

John McElroy had seen a lot of war, but for him this was a new experience. It was the first time he'd gotten to meet someone he'd just shot down.

━━━━━━

Bill Schroeder was even more troubled than McElroy. Schroeder didn't like his new nickname—"Sudden Death"— and he didn't like the way he earned it. The ex-navy fighter pilot had flown exactly one air-to-air combat mission in Israel and scored one kill. The fact that Schroeder's kill had been not an Arab but a young Englishman named David Tattersfield was haunting him. It haunted Schroeder so much that even though he'd just joined the squadron, he'd had enough.

The next day Schroeder packed his bags and was gone.

Soon after, a letter arrived at the British Air Ministry to be forwarded to the father of Flying Officer Tattersfield.

> *I am writing you hoping to ease the bitterness you must feel toward those people responsible for your son's death. . . . On the afternoon of 7 January, we encountered twelve RAF Spitfires [actually fifteen Tempests] loaded with bombs, heading for our fighter bases. . . . Four of us attacked and I fired on the plane your son was flying.*
>
> *Please understand that the policy put forward by Britain's Foreign Department is alone responsible for recent events.*
>
> *I have nothing but remorse knowing that David Tattersfield died needlessly. I have come to Israel to help defend the country best I can. I am not a Jew but I feel it my duty to aid this struggling state.*
>
> *What can I say? Words are so inadequate. I can only say that I deeply regret the death of David and hope you can or will understand some day.*

The letter was unsigned but presumed to be from Bill Schroeder.

For the second time Yigal Allon, the commander of the southern front, had the Egyptian Expeditionary Force by the throat. His brigades had cut off the Egyptians at Rafah and were in position to retake all the territory known as the Gaza Strip.

And for the second time Allon was being ordered to withdraw.

The order came directly from the defense minister. As a condition of the truce, all Israeli forces were to be gone from Egyptian territory by January 10. "Egyptian territory" included the land held by the Egyptian Army in the Gaza Strip.

The young general could not contain his outrage. Allon fired off a vehement response to IDF headquarters, which drew immediate rebukes first from the chief of staff and then from Ben-Gurion himself. "You are a good commander," Ben-Gurion said to the impulsive officer, "but you have no political experience. Do you know the value of peace talks with Egypt? After all, that is our great dream!"

Grudgingly, Allon complied with his orders. That night he withdrew his brigades from their blocking positions around Rafah, allowing the Egyptians access to the vital supply road from El Arish to Rafah.

Two days later, on January 12, the delegations of Israel and Egypt landed on the Greek island of Rhodes to begin UN-sponsored peace negotiations. The UN mediator was an American, Ralph Bunche, who had succeeded Count Bernadotte. For his efforts, Bunche would ultimately receive the Nobel Peace Prize.

Since Egypt's invasion of an outgunned Israel nine months earlier, the balance of power had tilted. Egyptian delegates were desperate to negotiate a settlement to save the badly mauled Expeditionary Force that was strung out along the Gaza Strip. An Egyptian brigade was cut off and starving inside the Faluja Pocket. Egypt itself was on the brink of revolution. Its military and citizens alike were furious at the vast loss of life and treasure in the sands of Palestine.

Israel, too, had a strong motivation to negotiate a peace. The tiny new country was weary of war. Its exhausted soldiers wanted to rejoin their families and resume their lives.

The peace talks went on for six weeks. During this time a blessed silence fell over Israel. There was no thunder of artillery. No rattling machine guns. No howling warplanes battling over the desert. Red Squadron fighters patrolled the borders, but there were no more skirmishes with Arab—or British—warplanes.

The representatives of Israel and Egypt signed an armistice agreement in Rhodes on February 29, 1949. With Egypt, the major player, out of the war, the other Arab belligerents had little choice except to follow. Lebanon signed an armistice on March 23, 1949, followed by Jordan on April 3, then Syria on July 20. The Iraqis refused to enter negotiations but followed the other coalition members and ceased hostilities.

The miracle of Israel's victory had come at a staggering price. More than six thousand Israelis and volunteers—1 percent of the population—had lost their lives. Hundreds of groves and farms and kibbutzim lay in ruins. Israel's economy was in tatters, with thousands of new refugees pouring into the country.

Over seven thousand Arabs had died in the war, and more than seven hundred thousand were now refugees—a calamity that would spawn bloodshed for decades to come.

———

By March 1949, the guns were silent, but certain facts on the ground were still unresolved. The 120-mile-long triangle of desert extending from Beersheba southward to the port of Eilat on the Red Sea was still up for grabs. At the southernmost tip of the desert, the Eilat seaport was a vital gateway to Africa and the Far East. Since the end of the fighting, Jordan had been quietly establishing its own facts on the ground, infiltrating troops into the southern desert.

Thus began Israel's last offensive. It had an appropriate name: Operation Uvda. Uvda was Hebrew for "fact."

Rather than an armed confrontation with yet another Arab enemy, Operation Uvda's purpose was to establish Israel's claim, once and for all, on the vast wasteland of the Negev, Ben-Gurion's dreamed-of settling place for future immigrants.

Operation Uvda became a race between two IDF units—the Golani and Negev Brigades. The finish line was the Red Sea shore at Eilat. Each brigade advanced at night along separate routes. They had orders to avoid conflict with the Jordanians on the east and the Egyptians along the western border.

The Golani Brigade moved southward from the Dead Sea, through a desolate gap called Scorpion's Pass, directly toward Eilat. The Negev Brigade took a different route, a zigzag path from Beersheba, along the international border with Egypt, circling around Eilat and approaching it from Egyptian territory in the south.

Negev Brigade troops had carved a landing strip called Avraham in the wilderness 30 miles north of Eilat. On March 6, newcomer Slick Goodlin brought in the first C-46 from Ekron. Behind him came another C-46. Then another, all hauling reinforcements, water, ammunition, and food for the fast-moving Israeli brigades.

To the Bagel Lancers, Uvda was a replay of Operation Dust. Just as before, they were flying round-the-clock missions from Ekron to a desert outpost. Their unit was now officially the 106 Squadron of the IAF, under the command of Englishman Gordon Levett, who had just transferred back after his tour with the Red Squadron and shooting down two enemy fighters.

On March 10, five days after Operation Uvda began, vehicles of the Negev Brigade, covered with dust and filled with cheering Israeli soldiers, rolled into the ancient port of Eilat. They met no resistance. The Transjordanian occupying troops had already gone home.

An hour later the Golani Brigade entered Eilat from the north to join the riotous victory celebration. One of the nurses from an ambulance unit came up with a bedsheet on which they painted an Israeli flag. A young captain named "Bren" Adan—later to be a major general—earned a place in history by slithering up a makeshift flagpole to mount what would be called the "Ink Flag."

The two brigades and the 106 Squadron had achieved one of Israel's most significant victories—without firing a shot. In a bloodless five-day campaign, Israel had doubled its land mass. The raising of the Ink Flag over the former police hut at Eilat marked a symbolic end of Israel's war of independence.

───

With the shooting war over, the Red Squadron's mission had become an unexciting routine of reconnaissance flights and patrols over the new nation's borders. Missing the rush of air-to-air combat, several said to hell with it, packed up, and left. Among them were the Canadian pilots—Wilson, McElroy, Doyle, Sinclair. They were off to seek adventure elsewhere.

The exodus continued. Squadron commander Syd Cohen announced he had to return to South Africa before his slot in medical school expired. George Lichter was going home to New York to salvage the fabrics business he had left behind. Gordon Levett decided to return to England and start a new life. Red Finkel hung around long enough to help move the squadron to Ramat David, and then he was on his way home.

A few of the early volunteers were still there, some changing squadrons and jobs. Mike Flint left 35 Flight to return to the Red Squadron, and so did his dive-bomber colleague, Grisha Brown. Happy to fly Spitfires and Mustangs instead of the Czech Mule, Flint reclaimed his old job description: *fighter pilot*.

Americans Rudy Augarten, Sid Antin, and Caesar Dangott stayed long enough to help train the up-and-coming young Israelis who would replace them. Among them were the young Velvetta pilots Dani Shapira and Moti Fein, both destined for greatness in the future Israeli Air Force.

And then Augarten left. He was going back to complete his degree at Harvard. Slick Goodlin finished his tour of duty with the transport squadron and took up the job of air force chief test pilot.

The Red Squadron was still an English-speaking, mostly volunteer outfit. But not for much longer. On a crisp spring morning, April 1, 1949, the 101 Squadron lined up on the ramp at Hatzor. Standing in front of his pilots, Syd Cohen slipped off his flight jacket and passed it to Ezer Weizman. It was a symbolic change of command.

Such an occasion, of course, called for a party. Even by Red Squadron standards, Cohen's farewell bash was one for the record books. The affair started early in the Park Hotel bar. By nine o'clock the clamor of raunchy songs, boisterous toasts, and the foot-stomping cacophony of Zulu war dances reverberated down Ben Yehuda Street, continuing until well past midnight.

The next morning the Universal Airways DC-3 carrying Syd Cohen took off from Lod airport. The Red Squadron was there to give their old commander a proper send-off. As Weizman recalled, "Four Spits from the world's youngest air force attached themselves to his plane, circling in formation and entertaining him with aerobatics until he was twenty miles out to sea."

Several Bagel Lancers found a long-sought opportunity in Israel. The job that had been denied them in America—the captain's seat in a real airline—was becoming a reality. The former Air Transport Command was metamorphosing into Israel's national airline, El Al.

Sam Lewis, the mustached senior pilot of the group, was staying on to be an El Al captain. So were ex-fireman Norm Moonitz, Floridian Bill Katz, and the B-17 smuggler, Swifty Schindler. Tryg Maseng, former Columbia student and aspiring writer, had fallen in love with an Israeli girl, converted to Judaism, and would become a captain for Arkia, a start-up Israeli domestic airline.

The mastermind of the armaments smuggling operation, Al Schwimmer, returned to the United States to face trial for conspiracy to violate the US Neutrality Act. One of the charges against Schwimmer—that he had transferred contraband airplanes to a Communist country—he refuted by having Sam Lewis fly the newly repaired Constellation from Czechoslovakia back to the United States. It was a mostly symbolic act. "I didn't want anybody to say I had given it to the Reds," Schwimmer said.

Schwimmer was not surprised that one of the witnesses for the prosecution was his nemesis from the days at Burbank, the fedora-wearing FBI agent Bernarr Ptacek.

The trial went on for over three months. In February 1950, Al Schwimmer, Leo Gardner, and Ray Selk were found guilty. None was sentenced to prison. Each was fined $10,000 and stripped of many of his rights, including his veteran's benefits.

In separate trials, Swifty Schindler and Charlie Winters were also found guilty of violating the Neutrality Act. A New York judge gave Schindler a suspended prison sentence of one year and a year on probation. A Miami judge sentenced Charlie Winters, the only non-Jew to be charged, to eighteen months in federal prison.

MAY 15, 1949

It was a glistening spring morning in Tel Aviv. Over two hundred thousand deliriously happy Israelis—nearly a quarter of the country's population—were jammed onto sidewalks, alleys, and storefronts all the way down to the beach. Ben Yehuda Street was cordoned off. Brigades of IDF troops, tanks, and armored vehicles rolled past the cheering crowd.

One year had elapsed since the first Egyptian bombs crashed into downtown Tel Aviv. That the tiny upstart nation of Israel had survived the Arab invasion and then *defeated* the armies of five opposing nations was a still nearly unfathomable miracle.

The crowd was already hoarse from yelling. Then a new sound rolled in from the north. It started as a low rumble and then swelled in volume. Not until the sound was nearly over them could they see the source.

The battered, patched-together warplanes of the world's unlikeliest air force were flying in Israel's first victory parade.

First came the slow-movers—Cubs, Austers, a bi-winged Dragon Rapide. They were low—so low that some of the dangling wheels were nearly rolling over the rooftops. Behind them came a formation of AT-6 Harvards, a Bonanza, a Norseman, a Lodestar.

Then came the *real* noisemakers—a massive formation of C-46s, B-17s, Dakotas, and a solitary Beaufighter. Leading the five C-46s—all that remained of the ten Al Schwimmer had acquired in California— was Englishman Gordon Levett. Levett had to grin as he peered around at the gaggle of worn-out warplanes. Like old soldiers, Levett recalled, "they all had stories to tell."

Last came the fighters. The new Red Squadron commander, Ezer Weizman, took the formation of twelve Spitfires, three Mustangs, and the remaining flyable Messerschmitt down low, directly over the upturned faces in the audience. The collective howl of sixteen V-12 engines rattled windows and prickled the skin of every spectator in the street.

Flying a Spitfire in the middle of the formation was Mike Flint. As Flint's eyes flicked from the Spitfire ahead of his right wing to the sprawling crowd 200 feet below, he felt himself filled with a new pride. This was a day, he told himself, he was going to remember for the rest of his life.

Israelis in the streets were weeping openly. The massed thunder of the warplanes' engines was vivid proof that they had truly won their independence. After two thousand years, the promised rebirth of Israel was a fact.

The day was just as emotional for the men in the cockpits. They were as diverse a bunch as the conglomeration of warplanes they were flying. They came from the United States, Britain, Canada, France, Belgium, South Africa, Austria, Holland, Russia, Norway, Poland, Czechoslova-kia, Israel.

They were the angels who had come to save a new nation. They'd done what was expected of them. Today was their farewell performance.

It was time to go home.

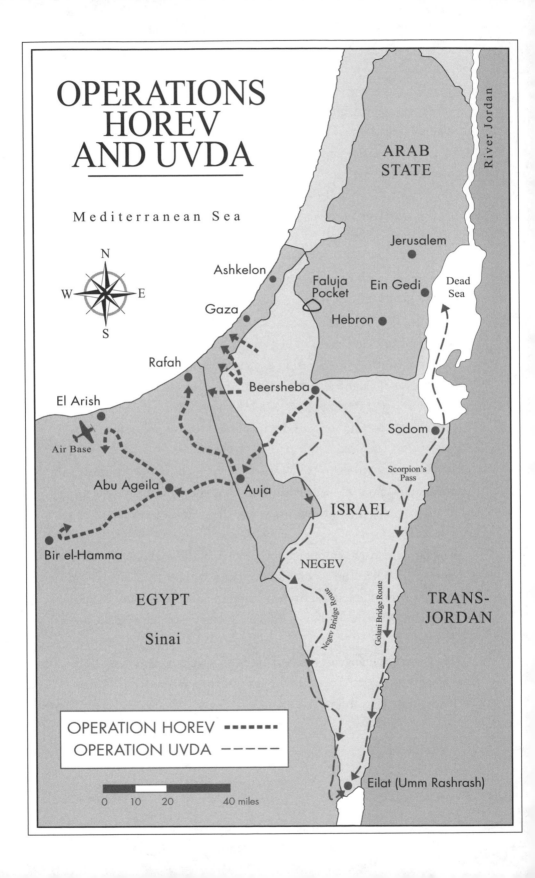

Epilogue

Old men forget: Yet all shall be forgot.

But he'll remember with advantages
What feats he did that day.

—SHAKESPEARE, *KING HENRY V*

The volunteer airmen scattered around the world. They became lawyers, teachers, test pilots, military officers, doctors, screenwriters, airline pilots, business moguls, movie producers. A few stayed to build successful careers in Israel.

For the next half century and more the aging veterans came together to tell stories, toast each other's successes, celebrate weddings, bar mitzvahs, graduations, and, with increasing frequency, bury one of their own.

They held reunions in Israel, including a monumental fiftieth anniversary of the country's independence. They walked the old airfields, gazed at the changed skyline of Tel Aviv, listened to the lapping of the waves at night along the Mediterranean. They paid solemn visits to the gravesites of fallen Machal comrades. Most of all they marveled at the changes in the country they helped save.

Even as their numbers dwindled, the volunteers would remain what they had been since 1948. They were brothers in a righteous cause.

RUDY AUGARTEN earned fame as one of only a handful of US aces to score kills in two wars, achieving his five victories in four different types of fighter. Augarten finished his degree at Harvard, then returned to Israel to serve for two years as commander of the IAF base at Ramat David with the rank of lieutenant colonel. Augarten went back to the

United States, earned another degree in engineering, and then worked as an engineer and real estate businessman in Seal Beach, California. He passed away in 2000 at the age of seventy-eight.

SYD COHEN, the much-respected Red Squadron commander, completed his studies and practiced medicine for several years in South Africa. At the urging of Ezer Weizman, Cohen and his family resettled in Israel in the mid-1960s. Cohen served as an airborne combat medic in the Six-Day War and the Yom Kippur War and held the post of Chief Medical Officer for El Al. Cohen died in Israel in 2011 at the age of ninety.

JOSEPH JOHN "JACK" DOYLE followed his fellow volunteer, John McElroy, back to Canada and the RCAF, serving in the same squadron, flying fighters with NATO forces in Europe.

AARON "RED" FINKEL worked in several professions before settling in commercial real estate in California. He was a ringleader of the American Machal pilots and returned to Israel several times to renew friendships. He died in 2006 at the age of eighty-six in Encino, California.

MITCHELL "MIKE" FLINT returned to California to confess to his mother about the bogus postcards from the 1948 Olympics. He was working as an engineer for Lockheed when he was recalled to active duty in the navy during the Korean War. After Korea, Flint went to law school, earned a JD, and established a successful practice in Los Angeles. He retired from the naval reserve with the rank of commander. In Israel on his ninetieth birthday, Flint was awarded the rank of Rav Seren—major—in the Israeli Air Force, the rank he had turned down sixty-four years earlier.

LEO GARDNER, after his conviction with Al Schwimmer for conspiracy to violate the Neutrality Act, became a pilot for El Al. Later, with Gordon Levett, the adventuresome Gardner ferried warplanes to and from Israel. He passed away in Boca Raton, Florida, in 2003 at the age of eighty-nine.

CHALMERS "SLICK" GOODLIN served as chief test pilot in the IAF. He then flew DC-4s for Near East Transport on humanitarian missions carrying refugees to Israel. Goodlin was involved in various aviation ventures, becoming CEO of the Burnelli company, developer of the "lifting fuselage." He was portrayed—unfairly in his opinion—in the movie about test pilots and astronauts *The Right Stuff*. Goodlin died in Florida in 2005 at age eighty-two.

RAY KURTZ, leader of the Cairo raid, returned to the United States to start a new freight airline. In May 1951, he was reported missing while ferrying a Mosquito bomber to Israel with navigator Seymour Lerner. Wreckage was eventually found on the shore of Greenland, but no trace was ever found of the airmen. Kurtz was thirty-two years old.

LOU LENART airlifted thousands of Jewish refugees from Iraq to Israel, flew for El Al, worked as general manager for the San Diego Clippers basketball team, and served as a producer on several movies, including *Iron Eagle* and *Iron Eagle II*. Lenart died in 2015 at the age of ninety-four at his home in Israel.

GORDON LEVETT, the former orphan and diaper-laundry worker, left Israel with the rank of lieutenant colonel. He was involved in multiple warplane-ferrying operations, wrote the biographical *Flying Under Two Flags* (London: Frank Cass, 1994), married twice, and became a father for the first time at the age of forty-eight. Levett died in England in 2000 at age seventy-nine.

SAM LEWIS, the Smilin' Jack look-alike, became the first chief pilot for El Al, where he remained until his mandatory retirement age, then continued flying for Schwimmer's company in Israel and later for an Israeli tycoon. Lewis passed away in 2004.

GIDEON LICHTMAN, the tough-talking fighter pilot, stayed active in the USAF reserve and flew combat missions in Korea. Later he returned to Israel as a test pilot for Al Schwimmer's company. Returning once again to the United States, Lichtman became a high school teacher and settled in Miami, Florida.

HAROLD LIVINGSTON, the wisecracking Bagel Lancer radio operator, went home to become a novelist and screenwriter. He wrote the screenplay for the first *Star Trek* movie, earning an Academy Award nomination. Among Livingston's seven books is *No Trophy, No Sword* (Chicago: Edition Q, 1994), an account of his service flying as a radio operator with the Air Transport Command in Israel's war of independence.

CHRIS MAGEE, bored with the lack of combat action during the long summer truce, returned to the United States and became a bank robber. The Marine ace and Navy Cross winner eventually served eight and a half years in federal prison. When he was released in 1967, his old squadronmates held a grand party for him. Magee worked as a journalist in Chicago until his death in 1995 at the age of seventy-eight.

JOHN McELROY missed flying fighters. After he was sure he wouldn't be arrested for having shot down two RAF warplanes, he rejoined the Canadian Air Force and flew Sabre jets in Europe. He left the military in 1963 and became a real estate salesman in Ontario, Canada.

NORM MOONITZ, the tough ex–New York fireman, stayed in Israel to fly with El Al, and later worked as a test pilot for Lockheed, a contract pilot for Lufthansa, then for Trans International Airlines, from which he retired in 1981. A hardy man who ran the New York marathon at age 61, sailed, surfed, and skied, Moonitz died in 1998 at the age of seventy-seven.

WAYNE PEAKE returned to the United States and joined Flying Tiger Airlines. The guitar-strumming fighter pilot died in 1979 of cancer at age fifty-five. In compliance with Peake's wishes, he was given a military funeral in Israel. Peake was laid to rest near the grave of another non-Jewish volunteer, Buzz Beurling.

MILTON RUBENFELD, after his dramatic mission over Tulkarm, became a businessman in Oneonta, New York, and then Sarasota, Florida. He and his wife appeared in the 1988 movie, *Big Top Pee-wee*, starring their son, Paul Reubens, better known as Pee-wee Herman. Rubenfeld died in Sarasota in 2004 at the age of eighty-four.

IRWIN "SWIFTY" SCHINDLER became one of the first pilots for Israel's national airline, El Al, moving with his family to Israel for two years. After he left El Al he became a Miami, Florida, developer, mortgage broker, and a talk-show host on a radio station. He died in September 2007 at the age of ninety-one.

ADOLPH "AL" SCHWIMMER was persuaded by David Ben-Gurion to return to Israel in 1951, where he founded Israel Aircraft Industries, the country's largest employer and developer of much of Israel's high tech military hardware. Schwimmer received a pardon from President Clinton in 2001 for his Neutrality Act conviction. Schwimmer died in Israel at the age of ninety-four.

BORIS SENIOR remained in the IAF until 1952, when he left with the rank of colonel. Senior became a manufacturer of photographic materials and an international investor. During his wartime stint at Herzliya he became smitten with the nearby village of Kfar Shmaryahu, where he built a home and lived until his death in 2004 at the age of eighty-two.

EZER WEIZMAN rose to become commander of the Israeli Air Force between 1958 and 1966. As deputy chief of the general staff he directed the surprise air attacks during the Six-Day War in 1967, destroying the Egyptian Air Force in three hours. After serving as defense minister in

1977, Weizman was elected president of Israel in 1993, serving until 2000. He died in 2005 at the age of eighty.

CHARLES "CHARLIE" WINTERS settled in Miami after his eighteen-month prison sentence for violation of the US Neutrality Act and founded an export company. When he started a family, he never told his children about the B-17 caper or his prison time. Winters died in 1984 at the age of seventy-one. He was posthumously pardoned by President George W. Bush in 2008.

Acknowledgments

This story came to life on a glorious spring afternoon in Israel. Michael Flint and I were standing beside the runway of the former fighter base at Herzliya. With us was Michael's father, Mitchell Flint, who had flown Messerschmitts from this field sixty-seven years before. The old fighter pilot showed us the revetments where the Messerschmitts and Spitfires had been concealed. He pointed to the ancient water tank that had served as their control tower. He took us through the crumbling concrete building that had once been the squadron operations office.

It was then, just for a moment, I could hear it: the deep-throated growl of V-12 engines. The staccato rattle of 13.1-mm machine guns. I could sense the urgency of Israel's epic battle for survival.

I knew this was a story that had to be told.

———

My first thanks go to my collaborator, Michael Flint. Capturing the story of the Machal airmen on the screen and in print has been Mike's ongoing passion for many years. He was an invaluable source and research guide throughout the writing of the book and during our forays to Israel and New York.

Michael's father, the iconic Mitchell Flint, deserves special thanks. Despite his unique distinction of having flown four of World War II's most famous fighters in combat—the F4U Corsair, Messerschmitt, Spitfire, P-51 Mustang—Mitchell "Mike" Flint remains what he has always been: a modest and gracious gentleman. During the many months of helping research this book he became a second father to me.

A number of researchers and scholars of Israel's war of independence deserve mention. Canadian historian and journalist Lawrence "Laurie" Nyveen, who oversees the 101squadron.com website, contributed his extensive knowledge about the Red Squadron and its 1948 exploits. Dr. Ralph Lowenstein, Machal veteran and historian, assembled the immensely valuable collection of questionnaires from his fellow veterans that are now archived in the American Jewish Historical Society in Manhattan. During my research at the AJHS I was ably assisted by the Director of Library and Archives, Susan Malbin, and her efficient staff.

In Florida I was helped and entertained by veteran fighter pilot and feisty raconteur Gideon Lichtman. In California Machal veterans Lee Silverman and Benno Katz contributed their valuable reminiscences. I owe thanks to Joshua Finkel, son of the colorful Aaron "Red" Finkel, and to Mark Augarten, son of leading fighter ace Rudy Augarten, for sharing photographs and documents from their fathers' collections. Steve Katzew provided material about his father and Flight 35. Aaron Friedman, former bodyguard to David Ben-Gurion, offered valuable anecdotes about the dynamic first prime minister of Israel.

In Israel we were generously assisted by Lt. Col. Amos Cohen of the Fisher Institute for Air & Space Strategic Studies; IAF colonel and former Knesset member Eliezer "Cheetah" Cohen; Avi Moshi Segal, chief curator of the IAF Museum; Elan Frank, decorated IAF veteran and documentary film maker; David Farer, writer and historian of the 1948 war; Dan Moskowitz, who arranged our terrific Tel Aviv accommodations; Udi Gazit, son of Gen. Shaya Gazit; Dr. Gil Mileikowsky, who connected us with valuable sources in Israel; Elie Inbar, the intrepid aviator who flew us over Israel; Yael Shany, who organized the media blitz for Mitchell; Yehuda "Udi" Zorani, who accompanied us from the United States and served as interpreter, guide, and genial travel companion.

A number of Michael Flint's team members and long-time supporters deserve special mention: the indomitable Cheri O'Laverty; Barbara Press Fix, who smoothed the path in many ways; Lt. Col. Francisco "Paco" Hamm, USAF (ret.), who assembled the many hours of archived film footage; Joyce Flint, Mitchell's wife and mother of Michael; attorney Konrad Trope; super agent David Warden; Michael's brother, Guy Flint.

Others who were part of the *Angels in the Sky* journey include Capt. Woody Berzins, USNR, journalist Tom Tugend, Tony Mulligan, Varda Yoran, Dan Mokady, Iris Mileikowsky, Neville Johnson, Chris Rehr, Audrey Thomson and her son David, Jerry Meadors, Eddie Kugler, Mark Lanksy, Mark Jonathan Harris.

South Africa produced more IAF volunteers per capita than any other country, and the veterans and their families contributed much to this project. They include Alon Zimmerman, Saul and Smoky Simon, Rod Margo, Cynthia Cohen-Kaplan, Joel and Sonny Ospovat, Noreen and Zan Swartzberg, Clifford Solarsh.

The splendidly detailed maps of Israel and the battle zones were produced by friend and graphics whiz Alan Norris. Old pal Ben Omensky deserves thanks for connecting me with the Flints and planting the seed for our collaboration. Author Steven Pressfield has my gratitude for his encouragement and permission to quote from his superb account of the Six-Day War, *The Lion's Gate* (New York: Sentinel, 2014). Artist Roy Grinnell has my thanks for his permission to reproduce the dramatic painting *Strange Encounter.* Roy's aviation art is on display at www .roygrinnell.com.

A salute and sincere thanks to John Glusman, vice president and editor-in-chief at W. W. Norton & Company, who shepherded this book from its inception to publication with precision and skill. Special thanks to John's amazing assistant, Lydia Brents, for her talent, patience, and sense of humor. My thanks to Francine Kass, art director at W. W. Norton, for indulging my several last-minute tinkerings.

Another round of applause for Alice Martell, my long time literary agent and chief cheerleader, who was an early believer in this project. Thanks again to Alice's able assistant, Stephanie Finman, for her ongoing loyalty.

As always, my heartfelt gratitude to my wife and staunchest fan, Anne Busse-Gandt, for her encouragement, love, and willingness to stay the course.

Timeline

===

ISRAELI WAR OF INDEPENDENCE

1947

NOVEMBER 29: UN votes to partition Palestine into Jewish and Arab states.

DECEMBER 3: Civil war erupts between Arab and Jewish factions in Palestine.

1948

JANUARY 15: Schwimmer Aviation Services opens in Burbank, California.

APRIL 11: Service Airways C-46s fly away from the Millville, New Jersey base.

APRIL 20: Bill Gerson and Glen King killed in Mexico City crash.

MAY 14: David Ben-Gurion declares establishment of the State of Israel.

MAY 15: Arab armies invade Israel. First air attack on Tel Aviv.

MAY 20: George "Buzz" Beurling killed in Norseman crash in Rome.

MAY 24: Bill Malpine and fellow airmen captured by Egyptians.

MAY 29: First air strike by IAF fighters against Egyptian Army at Ishdud.

MAY 31: Establishment of the Israeli Defense Force.

JUNE 3: Modi Alon shoots down two Egyptian Dakota bombers over Tel Aviv.

JUNE 11–JULY 8: First truce.

JUNE 21: *Altalena* shelled and seized by IDF off Tel Aviv.

JULY 9–JULY 19: "Ten day campaign" followed by second truce.

JULY 9: Aborted strike on El Arish; Stan Andrews crashes; Bob Vickman disappears.

JULY 10: Lionel Bloch vanishes while pursuing Syrian warplane.

JULY 15: B-17 bombing raid on Cairo. Three B-17s arrive in Israel.

JULY 19–OCTOBER 15: Second truce.

AUGUST 23–OCTOBER 21: Operation Avak (Dust).

SEPTEMBER 24: Operation Velvetta. First Spitfires fly from Czechoslovakia.

OCTOBER 15–22: Operation Yoav; offensive in the Negev.

OCTOBER 16: Death of Modi Alon in Messerschmitt.

OCTOBER 20: Deaths of Len Fitchett and Stan Andrews in Beaufighter.

OCTOBER 28-31: Operation Hiram; Upper Galilee captured by Israel.

NOVEMBER 9: Red Squadron moves to Hatzor Air Base.

NOVEMBER 20: Wayne Peake shoots down Shufti Kite.

DECEMBER 18: Operation Velvetta II; next wave of Spitfires fly from Czechoslovakia.

DECEMBER 22: Operation Horev; offensive to push Egyptian Army from the Negev.

1949

JANUARY 7: Climactic air battles with the RAF. Final cease-fire goes into effect.

FEBRUARY 24: Armistice signed with Egypt; Lebanon and Transjordan soon follow.

MARCH 5–10: Operation Uvda (Fact); Israel gains possession of the entire Negev.

JULY 20: War officially ends with signing of Israel–Syria peace agreement.

AIRCREW OF THE ISRAELI AIR FORCE
KILLED OR MISSING IN THE
1948 WAR OF INDEPENDENCE

Modi Alon	Israel
Stan Andrews	United States
Amon Berman	Israel
George "Buzz" Beurling	Canada
Lionel Bloch	South Africa
Spencer Boyd	United States
Daniel Bukstein	Israel
Wilfred Canter	Canada
Ed Cohen	South Africa
Leonard Cohen	Britain
Shlomo Cohen	Israel
Willy Fisher	Canada
Len Fitchett	Canada
Bill Gerson	United States
Oliver Holton	United States
Glen King	United States
Zohara Levitov	Israel
Leon Lightman	Britain
Ralph Moster	Canada
Sam Pomerance	United States
Moses Rosenbaum	United States
Emmanuel Rothstein	Israel
Shlomo Rothstein	Israel
Itschak Shakelnowitz	Israel
Yariv Sheinbaum	Israel
David Shrpinzak	Israel
Zvi Shusterman	Israel
Fred Stevenson	United States
Dov Sugerman	Britain
Matitiyahu Sukenik	Israel
Israel Tannenbaum	Israel
Bob Vickman	United States
Zviu Zivel	Israel

Notes

Prologue

xv   Lenart was stunned by what he saw: Lenart's impressions during the raid come from Steven Pressfield, *The Lion's Gate* (New York: Sentinel, 2014), p. 47.

xvi   A Hebrew phrase came to his mind: *ein brera*: Ibid., p. 47.

xvi   "The worst piece of crap I have ever flown": Ibid., p. 43.

xvii   "I wanted to kill as many Nazis . . .": Ibid., p. 43.

xviii   Israelis were certain the pilot was dead: Ami Isseroff, "The Debut of the Israeli Air Force," Zionism Israel Information Center, http://zionism-israel.com/his/israel_first _air_battle.htm.

PART ONE: A WAR WAITING TO HAPPEN

Chapter 1: Yakum Purkan

4   "The General Assembly of the United Nations, by a vote of thirty-three": Larry Collins and Dominique Lapierre, *O Jerusalem!* (New York: Simon and Schuster, 1972), p. 39.

4   "I could not dance, . . . I could not sing": Ibid., p. 46.

5   "The Land of Israel is surrounded": Benny Morris, *1948: A History of the First Arab-Israeli War* (New Haven, CT: Yale University Press, 2008), p. 87.

5   the armies of five surrounding Arab countries: Steve Chawkins, "Lou Lenart Dies at 94; War Hero Was 'The Man Who Saved Tel Aviv,'" *Los Angeles Times*, July 22, 2015, http://www.latimes.com/local/obituaries/la-me-lou-lenart-20150722-story.html; Brian Cull, Shlomo Aloni, and David Nicolle, *Spitfires Over Israel* (London: Grub Street, 1990); Ehud Yonay, *No Margin for Error* (New York: Pantheon, 1993); and Benjamin Kagan, *The Secret Battle for Israel* (New York: World Publishing, 1966).

9   "Come in again sometime": Leonard Slater, *The Pledge* (New York: Simon and Schuster, 1970), p. 100.

10   "Expenses": Ibid., p. 143.

Chapter 2: A Righteous Cause

12   Flint had the feeling that he'd served a righteous cause: Interview with Mitchell Flint, May 13, 2016.

14   Lenart grew up feeling . . . anti-Semitism: Steve Chawkins, "Lou Lenart Dies at 94; War Hero Was 'The Man Who Saved Tel Aviv,'" *Los Angeles Times*, July 25, 2015, http://www.latimes.com/local/obituaries/la-me-lou-lenart-20150722-story.html.

14   "Nobody bullied me anymore": Amos Kamil, "The Israel Air Force and the Americans Who Helped Make it," *Newsweek*, January 31, 2015, http://www.newsweek.com/2015/02/13/israel-air-force-and-americans-who-helped-make-it-303346.html.

14   "I understand you're interested in flying": Dialogue from Lenart's recruitment comes from *They Were All We Had: The Birth of the Israeli Air Force*, a 1988 documentary film by Jonathan Paz; and Ehud Yonay, *No Margin for Error* (New York: Pantheon, 1993), p. 6.

16   "No names were exchanged": Dialogue and impressions come from Gideon Lichtman interview with the author, November 10, 2015.

16   Schwartz was the newly appointed vice president: Leonard Slater, *The Pledge* (New York: Simon and Schuster, 1970), p. 232.

Chapter 3: Schwimmer and Company

19   *How* expensive? Bernstein wanted to know: Leonard Slater, *The Pledge* (New York: Simon and Schuster, 1970), p. 144.

20   a check from Bernstein for $45,000: Ibid., p. 144.

21   Felix was to return immediately to Prague on an arms-buying expedition: Ehud Yonay, *No Margin for Error* (New York: Pantheon, 1993), pp. 23–24.

22   the ten C-46s that were coming: Slater, *The Pledge*, p. 145.

22   Schwimmer was paying well—$1.95 an hour: Ibid.

Chapter 4: Dark Suits and Fedoras

24   Lewis and Gardner . . . Schwimmer: David Bercuson, *The Secret Army* (New York: Stein and Day, 1984), p. 39.

25   He flipped open his credential case. His name was Bernarr Ptacek: Leonard Slater, *The Pledge* (New York: Simon and Schuster, 1970), p. 168.

27   he'd be goddamned if he'd have a Jew as a captain: Ibid., p. 221.

28   Martin Bellefond: Ibid., pp. 222–223.

Chapter 5: "How Much Would We Have to Pay You?"

31   Beurling as "untidy, with a shock of tousled hair": Group Captain Percy "Laddie" Lucas, DSO and Bar, DFC, a former *Daily Express* columnist and a commander of Beurling in Malta, as quoted in an article by Peter Worthington, "Death of WWII Flying Ace Buzz Beurling Still a Mystery," *Toronto Sun*, April 16, 2013, http://www.torontosun.com/2013/04/06/death-of-wwii-flying-ace-buzz-beurling-still-a-mystery.

31   blood from the headless pilot: "George 'Buzz' Beurling, Ace of Malta," *Historic Wings*, June 10, 2012, http://fly.historicwings.com/2012/06/george-buzz-beurling-ace-of -malta/.

32   "I would give ten years of my life": "George 'Screwball' Beurling: The Falcon of Malta," *Aces of WW2*, http://acesofww2.com/can/aces/beurling/.

33   "Are you Aaron Finkel?": Quotes and circumstances of recruitment recalled by son Joshua Finkel, September 20, 2016.

34   "How much would we have to pay you?": Ehud Yonay, *No Margin for Error* (New York: Pantheon, 1993), p. 36.

Chapter 6: Service Airways

35   Schwimmer had chosen the Millville: Leonard Slater, *The Pledge* (New York: Simon and Schuster, 1970), p. 224.

36   picking out Jewish-sounding names: Ibid., pp. 229–230.

38   "A latter-day Flying Tigers volunteer group": Harold Livingston, *No Trophy, No Sword: An American Volunteer in the Israeli Air Force during the 1948 War of Independence* (Chicago: Edition Q, 1994), p. 59.

38   Trygve "Tryg" Maseng: Ibid., p. 89.

40   Were some of the mechanics . . . government spies?: Schwimmer's suspicions about spies among his mechanics were founded. At Schwimmer's trial in 1949 for conspiracy to violate the US Neutrality Act, one of the government's witnesses was a mechanic who testified against Schwimmer. Lee Silverman interview with the author, July 9, 2015.

Chapter 7: Black Sedans

43   It was almost departure time: There are several slightly different published versions of the departure from Millville. This one has been compiled from Harold Livingston, *No Trophy, No Sword: An American Volunteer in the Israeli Air Force during the 1948 War of Independence* (Chicago: Edition Q, 1994), pp. 45–46; Leonard Slater, *The Pledge* (New York: Simon and Schuster, 1970), pp. 250–253; and Bill Norton, *Air War on the Edge: A History of the Israel Air Force and Its Aircraft Since 1947* (Hinckley, England: Midland, 2004), p. 93.

44   "I'll be back in a second": Livingston, *No Trophy, No Sword*, p. 43.

45   "If you want to stop them": Ibid., p. 46.

47   *The Bagel Lancers*: Ibid., p. 59.

47   "Where's the weight and balance": Slater, *The Pledge*, p. 254.

Chapter 8: Incident in Mexico

50   Mexico City had a long runway: Accounts of the Gerson crash are drawn from Bill Norton, *Air War on the Edge: A History of the Israel Air Force and Its Aircraft Since 1947* (Hinckley, England: Midland, 2004), p. 93; and Harold Livingston, *No Trophy,*

No Sword: An American Volunteer in the Israeli Air Force during the 1948 War of Independence (Chicago: Edition Q, 1994), pp. 70–71.

51   Marty Ribakoff saw it from the air: Jeffrey Weiss and Craig Weiss, *I Am My Brother's Keeper* (Atglen, PA: Schiffer, 1998), p. 88.

52   Bill Gerson . . . was dead: "William Guy Gerson," *World Machal*, http://machal.org.il/index.php?option=com_content&view=article&id=363&Itemid=625&lang=en.

54   "I'm told you guys are blaming me": Livingston, *No Trophy, No Sword*, p. 79.

54   Greenspun . . . yacht captain: Weiss and Weiss, *I Am My Brother's Keeper*, p. 97; "Hank Greenspun," *World Machal*, http://www.machal.org.il/index.php?option=com_content&view=article&id=616&Itemid=985&lang=en.

Chapter 9: The Great Flyaway

56   Each Messerschmitt would cost $44,600: Bill Norton, *Air War on the Edge: A History of the Israel Air Force and Its Aircraft Since 1947* (Hinckley, England: Midland, 2004), p. 109; Leonard Slater, *The Pledge* (New York: Simon and Schuster, 1970), p. 261.

58   number of Jewish dead in the civil war: Ze'ev Schiff, *A History of the Israeli Army* (New York: Macmillan, 1974), p. 25.

59   the day came for the flyaway: Slater, *The Pledge*, pp. 274–276; Harold Livingston, *No Trophy, No Sword: An American Volunteer in the Israeli Air Force during the 1948 War of Independence* (Chicago: Edition Q, 1994), pp. 81–82.

61   Raab was getting a bad feeling: David Bercuson, *The Secret Army* (New York: Stein and Day, 1984), p. 108; Slater, *The Pledge*, p. 285.

Chapter 10: When in Rome

62   "Everyone spotted me for an American": Lichtman interview with the author, November 10, 2015; Leonard Slater, *The Pledge* (New York: Simon and Schuster, 1970), p. 272.

64   Lichtman spotted the strange woman: Slater, *The Pledge*, p. 272; Lichtman video interview, September 23, 2014, provided by Machal Productions, Los Angeles.

65   La Biblioteca . . . punches were thrown: Jeffrey Weiss and Craig Weiss, *I Am My Brother's Keeper* (Atglen, PA: Schiffer, 1998), p. 118.

66   "We spent the night getting it on": Lichtman interview with the author, November 10, 2016.

67   "King of Lampedusa": Brian Cull, David Nicolle, and Shlomo Aloni, *Spitfires over Israel* (London: Grub Street, 1990), p. 79.

67   a sheet of flame: Peter Worthington, "Death of WWII Flying Ace Buzz Beurling Still a Mystery," *Toronto Sun*, April 16, 2013, http://www.torontosun.com/2013/04/06/death-of-wwii-flying-ace-buzz-beurling-still-a-mystery; "George (Buzz) Beurling," *World Machal*, http://www.machal.org.il/index.php?option=com_content&view=article&id=187&Itemid=486&lang=en.

67   Bill Malpine saw it first: Weiss and Weiss, *I Am My Brother's Keeper*, p. 119.

68   "They wanted to get Beurling": Lichtman interview with the author, November 10, 2015.

69   a former British army sergeant named Levingham: David Bercuson, *The Secret Army* (New York: Stein and Day, 1984), p. 114; "George 'Screwball' Beurling: The Falcon of Malta," *Aces of WW2*, http://acesofWW2.com/can/aces/beurling.

Chapter 11: Meeting the Mule

71   The pilots . . . asked for Dr. Otto Felix: Ehud Yonay, *No Margin for Error* (New York: Pantheon, 1993), pp. 24–25.

72   A senior flight instructor and . . . officers: Ezer Weizman, *On Eagles' Wings: The Personal Story of the Leading Commander of the Israeli Air Force* (New York: Macmillan, 1976), p. 62.

74   They were amazed that Lenart was alive: Yonay, *No Margin for Error*, p. 26.

74   The Czechs had lost their supply of the powerful Daimler-Benz DB 605 engines: A postwar fire destroyed the building where the Avia company stored their supply of Daimler-Benz 605 engines.

74   heavier and less powerful Jumo 211F engine: Described by historian Lawrence Nyveen, "101 Squadron," http://101squadron.com/101/101.html.

Chapter 12: "Will They Bomb Tel Aviv Tonight?"

76   "by virtue of the natural and historic right of the Jewish people": Ben-Gurion's reading Israel's declaration of independence, the celebrations, and the Egyptian bombing: Benny Morris, *1948: A History of the First Arab-Israeli War* (New Haven, CT: Yale University Press, 2008), p. 178; Larry Collins and Dominique Lapierre, *O Jerusalem!* (New York: Simon and Schuster, 1972), p. 422.

77   "Will they bomb Tel Aviv tonight?": Ehud Yonay, *No Margin for Error* (New York: Pantheon, 1993), p. 27.

78   "Not yet, you still have lots to learn": Ezer Weizman, *On Eagles' Wings: The Personal Story of the Leading Commander of the Israeli Air Force* (New York: Macmillan, 1976), p. 63.

79   "Fuck them on the ground": Yonay, *No Margin for Error*, p. 28.

79   a phone call to Ehud Avriel: Weizman, *On Eagles' Wings*, p. 64.

80   "They're tricky airplanes . . . We're glad to be rid of them": Leonard Slater, *The Pledge* (New York: Simon and Schuster, 1970), p. 293.

Chapter 13: The Sound of Spitfires

82   shot down in his P-40: Boris Senior, *New Heavens: My Life as a Fighter Pilot and a Founder of the Israel Air Force* (Washington: Potomac, 2005), pp. 11–25.

82   "Yes, we know": Ibid., p. 168.

83   "I warned them and now look at this": Ibid., p. 177.

86   The Catania base wasn't going to work: Bill Norton, *Air War on the Edge: A History of the Israel Air Force and Its Aircraft Since 1947* (Hinckley, England: Midland, 2004), p. 94.

87   "Talk to them in Hebrew and see what answer you get": Leonard Slater, *The Pledge* (New York: Simon and Schuster, 1970), p. 288.

88   "You are either smugglers or thieves": Ibid., p. 289.

Chapter 14: Zebra Base

91   Schindler . . . could see what appeared to be military facilities: Harold Livingston, *No Trophy, No Sword: An American Volunteer in the Israeli Air Force during the 1948 War of Independence* (Chicago: Edition Q, 1994), pp. 105–107.

91   codenames used for staging bases: Leonard Slater, *The Pledge* (New York: Simon and Schuster, 1970), pp. 298–299.

93   a contract crew: Zdeněk Klíma, "Air Bridge Žatec - Ekron Summer 1948," *The Jews of Saaz/Žatec*, http://www.saaz-juden.de.

94   "What the hell is that?": Dialogue from Lichtman interview April 24, 2014, provided by Machal Productions, Los Angeles.

94   "Where's my Nescafé?": Ibid.

95   "There was no cockpit check": Ibid.

Chapter 15: Or Die Trying

96   the Rome base was finished: Lichtman interview with the author, November 10, 2015.

97   Malpine . . . finally agreed: Jeffrey Weiss and Craig Weiss, *I Am My Brother's Keeper* (Atglen, PA: Schiffer, 1998), p. 122.

100 "They're fucking Arabs!": Ibid., p. 124.

100 they'd landed in enemy territory: Vic Shayne, *Ups and Downs with No Regrets* (San Bernadino, CA: CreateSpace, 2012), p. 497.

100 "This is the Egyptian Army": Weiss and Weiss, *I Am My Brother's Keeper*, p. 124.

100 Malpine wasn't lucky: The description of Malpine's capture and imprisonment has been compiled from Malpine's answers to Ralph Lowenstein's questionnaire, now in the archives of the American Jewish Historical Society, 15 West 16th St, New York, NY; Leonard Slater, *The Pledge* (New York: Simon and Schuster, 1970), pp. 289–290; Brian Cull, David Nicolle, and Shlomo Aloni, *Spitfires Over Israel* (London: Grub Street, 1990), p. 150.

101 They were the fortunate: The five captured airmen would be freed in a prisoner exchange in March 1949.

Chapter 16: Where Is Moonitz?

102 "Find out where Auerbach is": Harold Livingston, *No Trophy, No Sword: An American Volunteer in the Israeli Air Force during the 1948 War of Independence* (Chicago: Edition Q, 1994), p. 100.

103   the monkey . . . could replace his copilot: Ibid., p. 90.

104   "Four hundred . . . three hundred": Ibid., p. 103.

104   fuselage ripped loose: Details of Moonitz's crash have been compiled from Moonitz
       interview in the Jonathan Paz documentary film, *They Were All We Had: The Birth
       of the Israeli Air Force*, 1988; and Aaron Finkel's video interview of Moonitz, 1988,
       provided by Machal Productions, Los Angeles.

105   Moonitz and Eichel had managed: Finkel's 1988 video interview of Moonitz.

Chapter 17: Ad Halom

108   It implied that Israel had *many* fighter squadrons: Bill Norton, *Air War on the Edge:
       A History of the Israel Air Force and Its Aircraft Since 1947* (Hinckley, England: Mid-
       land, 2004), pp. 110–111.

109   "We couldn't sit around doing nothing": Ezer Weizman, *On Eagles' Wings: The Per-
       sonal Story of the Leading Commander of the Israeli Air Force* (New York: Macmillan,
       1976), p. 65.

110   "We need your planes now": Steven Pressfield, *The Lion's Gate* (New York: Sentinel,
       2014), p. 47.

111   Eddie Cohen: "The Debut of the Israeli Air Force," Zionism and Israel Information
       Center, http://zionism-israel.com/his/israel_first_air_battle.htm.

112   "There is no making light of this moment": Pressfield, *The Lion's Gate*, p. 47.

115   *We have come under attack by enemy aircraft, we are dispersing*: Benny Morris, *1948:
       A History of the First Arab-Israeli War* (New Haven, CT: Yale University Press,
       2008), p. 240; Pressfield, *The Lion's Gate*, p. 48.

116   The Egyptian brigade would not cross the bridge at Ishdud: In the Israeli city of
       Ashdod, formerly called Ishdud, the bridge where the Egyptians were stopped still
       stands. Near it is the *Ad Halom* memorial. Ad Halom means "thus far and no fur-
       ther" (literally, "up to here").

PART TWO: BESIEGED

117   *I declare a holy war, my Moslem brothers*: Saul S. Friedman, *A History of the Middle
       East* (Jefferson, North Carolina: McFarland, 2006), p. 249.

Chapter 18: Gefilte Fish

120   "so cocky he seemed to swagger even while sitting down": Zachary Solomon, "Pee-wee
       Herman's Crazy Dad," Jewniverse, May 27, 2013, http://thejewniverse.com/2013/
       pee-wee-hermans-crazy-dad/. Rubenfeld was the father of actor Paul Reubens, bet-
       ter known as Pee-wee Herman.

120   Iraqi forces at Tulkarm: Brian Cull, David Nicolle, and Shlomo Aloni, *Spitfires Over
       Israel* (London: Grub Street, 1990), p. 153.

122   Messerschmitt was gone. So was the parachute: Ezer Weizman, *On Eagles' Wings: The*

Personal Story of the Leading Commander of the Israeli Air Force (New York: Macmillan, 1976), p. 69.

123   "*Gefilte fish!*": Drawn from the several versions of the event, including ones by Lawrence Nyveen, "Milton Rubenfeld," *101 Squadron*, http://101squadron.com/101/101.html; Ehud Yonay, *No Margin for Error* (New York: Pantheon, 1993), p. 34; Harold Livingston, *No Trophy, No Sword: An American Volunteer in the Israeli Air Force during the 1948 War of Independence* (Chicago: Edition Q, 1994), p. 131; and Weizman, *On Eagles' Wings*, p. 69.

123   "I seem to have been hit": Weizman, *On Eagles' Wings*, p. 69.

Chapter 19: The Sparrow and the Condor

126   farmers of Kfar Vitkin . . . salvaged the machine guns: Lawrence Nyveen, "Milton Rubenfeld," *101 Squadron*, http://101squadron.com/101/101.html.

126   how long the party lasted: Weizman describes the squadron party and his accident in Ezer Weizman, *On Eagles' Wings: The Personal Story of the Leading Commander of the Israeli Air Force* (New York: Macmillan, 1976), p. 70.

127   "The Messerschmitt was so full of holes": Ehud Yonay, *No Margin for Error* (New York: Pantheon, 1993), p. 34.

128   Spitfires swoop over Ekron: Weizman, *On Eagles' Wings*, p. 71.

128   squadron had to move: Yonay, *No Margin for Error*, p. 40.

131   Alon swept down: Weizman, *On Eagles' Wings*, p. 70; and Brian Cull, David Nicolle, and Shlomo Aloni, *Spitfires Over Israel* (London: Grub Street, 1990), pp. 156–157.

Chapter 20: Bogeys

133   "It thrilled me": Lichtman interview, April 24, 2014, provided by Machal Productions, Los Angeles.

134   "Giddy, wake up": Ibid.

136   he saw hunks of metal spewing off the Spitfire: Brian Cull, David Nicolle, and Shlomo Aloni, *Spitfires Over Israel* (London: Grub Street, 1990), p. 164.

137   "We just got a confirmation": Ibid.

137   "Better than getting laid": Lichtman interview with the author, November 10, 2015.

Chapter 21: Message to Amman

139   "If you do not fly, you get a bullet in the head": Boris Senior, *New Heavens: My Life as a Fighter Pilot and a Founder of the Israel Air Force* (Washington: Potomac, 2005), p. 187.

141   "We would be bound to defend ourselves and attack Jewish aircraft": Brian Cull, David Nicolle, and Shlomo Aloni, *Spitfires Over Israel* (London: Grub Street, 1990), p. 155.

142   "Get that bloody thing out, you fool!": Ibid., p. 160.

143 Missing was the Fairchild flown by David Shprinzak: Senior, *New Heavens*, p. 194.

145 the Frankenstein fighter: Lawrence Nyveen, "Spitfires," 101 Squadron, http://101 squadron.com/101real/spitfires.html; and "The Israel Air Force—Spitfires Over Israel," *World Machal*, http://www.machal.org.il/index.php?option=com_content&view= article&id=122&Itemid=176&lang=en.

145 Now Senior was having second thoughts: Senior, *New Heavens*, p. 209.

Chapter 22: Bombers

147 Schwimmer tracked down four: David Bercuson, *The Secret Army* (New York: Stein and Day, 1984), pp. 131–133; Zvi Aloni and Shlomo Avidor, *Hammers: Israel's Long-Range Heavy Bomber Arm: The Story of 69 Squadron* (Atglen, PA: Schiffer, 2010), pp. 9–10.

147 "guiding them to somewhere in Europe?": Leonard Slater, *The Pledge* (New York: Simon and Schuster, 1970), p. 229.

148 "Due diligence on the part of customs officials": David Bercuson, *The Secret Army*, p. 132.

148 Eli Cohen had stepped on a plywood panel: Aloni and Avidor, *Hammers*, p. 10.

149 "By a stroke of luck we were able to pick up the airway radio beacon": Ibid., p. 10.

149 "I'm going to crush your skull": Ibid., p. 10.

149 Winters pulled out the sealed envelope: Slater, *The Pledge*, p. 311.

150 For twelve more hours: The journey of the B-17s is drawn from several accounts: Dario Leone, "Here's How Israel Managed to Get Three Second Hand B-17 Flying Fortress Bombers," *The Aviationist*, July 22, 2014, https://theaviationist.com/2014/07/22/ how-israel-got-the-b-17/; Bill Norton, *Air War on the Edge: A History of the Israel Air Force and Its Aircraft Since 1947* (Hinckley, England: Midland, 2004), p. 138; Brian Cull, David Nicolle, and Shlomo Aloni, *Spitfires Over Israel* (London: Grub Street, 1990), p. 172.

150 He was astonished at what he saw: Ibid., pp. 311.

151 Winters . . . knew he was going to need a lawyer: Jerry Klinger, "Charles Winters," http://www.palyam.org/OniyotRekhesh/Charles_Winters.

Chapter 23: A Truce of Sorts

154 "Typical American": Aaron Finkel to historian Lawrence Nyveen, "Aaron 'Red' Finkel," 101 Squadron, http://101squadron.com/101/101.html; "Aaron 'Red' Finkel," World Machal, http://www.machal.org.il/index.php?option=com_content&view=a rticle&id=590%3Aaaron-qredq-finkel&catid=45%3APersonal+Stories+&Itemid=9 60&lang=en.

154 "See, . . . that's for the surveying equipment": Dialogue from this scene: Sid Antin to Lawrence Nyveen, "Syd Antin," 101 Squadron.

155 "We were at the end of our rope": Larry Collins and Dominique Lapierre, O *Jerusalem!* (New York: Simon and Schuster, 1972), p. 552.

156   a condition both sides would openly violate: Benny Morris, *1948: A History of the First Arab-Israeli War* (New Haven: Yale University Press, 2008), pp. 265–267.

156   "You have never seen anything like it": Antin to Nyveen, "Syd Antin," *101 Squadron.*

157   "This big, fat major interviewed each of us as we got off the aircraft": Ibid.

159   Their unit quickly received a nickname: the Red Squadron: Ehud Yonay, *No Margin for Error* (New York: Pantheon, 1993), p. 51.

160   a skull with dark wings: The 101 Squadron death's head emblem had no symbolic connection with the state of Israel, but as one of the pilots recalled, it "seemed singularly apt to represent the undisciplined, war-scarred and unheralded collection of volunteers in Israel's first fighter squadron": Leo Nomis, *Desert Hawks: An American Volunteer Fighter Pilot's Story of Israel's War of Independence, 1948* (London: Grub Street, 1998), p. 73.

161   "Frankel? . . . Is that you?": Dialogue from Leon Frankel interview by Red Finkel, 1988, provided by Machal Productions, Los Angeles.

Chapter 24: *Altalena* Burning

162   cargo of 4,500 ton of armaments: Shlomo Nakdimon, *Altalena* (Jerusalem: Idanim, 1978), pp. 162–163.

163   Deir Yassin: Larry Collins and Dominique Lapierre, *O Jerusalem!* (New York: Simon and Schuster, 1972), pp. 286–296.

163   truce as a "shameful surrender": Ibid., p. 572.

163   The two sides had a deal. Or so they thought: Smoky Simon, "The Altalena Affair," World Machal, http://www.machal.org.il/index.php?option=com_content&view=article&id=235&Itemid=331&lang=en.

165   "I could never bomb my fellow Jews": Boris Senior, *New Heavens: My Life as a Fighter Pilot and a Founder of the Israel Air Force* (Washington: Potomac, 2005), p. 202.

165   "I came here to kill Arabs, not Jews": Harold Livingston, *No Trophy, No Sword: An American Volunteer in the Israeli Air Force during the 1948 War of Independence* (Chicago: Edition Q, 1994), p. 153.

167   "My greatest accomplishment": Avraham Avi-Hai, "Menachem Begin: Moments of Greatness, Moments of Error," *Jerusalem Post*, November 27, 2014, http://www.jpost.com/Opinion/Menachem-Begin-Moments-of-greatness-moments-of-error-383064. Years later Begin and Ben-Gurion laid aside their old enmity. In 1967 Begin led a delegation to persuade Ben-Gurion to accept the premiership again. After the meeting, Ben-Gurion wrote that if he had then known Begin as he did now, the face of history would be different: Yehuda Lapidot, "The Altalena Affair," Jewish Virtual Library, http://www.jewishvirtuallibrary.org/jsource/History/Altalena.html.

167   sixteen Irgun fighters and three IDF soldiers had been killed: Daniel Gordis, *Menachem Begin: The Battle for Israel's Soul* (New York: Schocken, 2014), p. 91.

168 "You have my word that if you feel that strongly": Livingston, *No Trophy, No Sword*, p. 158.

170 none of the surprise attacks succeeded: Ehud Yonay, *No Margin for Error* (New York: Pantheon, 1993), p. 41.

Chapter 25: The Guy with the Cape

171 Everyone in the squadron liked Stan Andrews: Lawrence Nyveen, "Stan Andrews," 101 Squadron, http://101squadron.com/101/101.html; Lichtman interview, September 23, 2014, provided by Machal Productions, Los Angeles.

172 a millisecond too late: The account of Andrews's crash is drawn from Lawrence Nyveen, "Stan Andrews," *101 Squadron*; Ehud Yonay, *No Margin for Error* (New York: Pantheon, 1993), pp. 41–42; and Eliezer "Cheetah" Cohen, *Israel's Best Defense: The First Full Story of the Israeli Air Force* (New York: Orion, 1993), pp. 33–34.

175 Bob Vickman had disappeared: In Brian Cull, David Nicolle, and Shlomo Aloni, *Spitfires Over Israel* (London: Grub Street, 1990), p. 183, Egyptian Air Commodore Mikaati reported being pursued by a Messerschmitt at an altitude of a hundred feet. "The Israeli must have been concentrating on keeping me in his sights because he dropped his nose to follow. He overshot and went right in, almost level with me."

177 "Stan started doing stupid things": Ibid., p. 183.

Chapter 26: The Nazi Revenge

178 "I'll take this one, . . . you take the other": Mavis Wolff, "Lionel (Les) Morris Bloch," World Machal, http://www.machal.org.il/index.php?option=com_content&view=article&id=189&Itemid=487&lang=en.

179 "We were over what was then the Syrian border, and I couldn't see him": Ibid.

180 or, as now seemed likely, shot off his propeller: Brian Cull, David Nicolle, and Shlomo Aloni, *Spitfires Over Israel* (London: Grub Street, 1990), p. 183.

181 "One of the wings stalled": Murray Rubinstein and Richard Goldman, *The Israeli Air Force Story* (London: Arms and Armour, 1979), p. 43.

182 "Hey, Rudy, there's something on your left!": Lon Nordeen, *Fighters Over Israel: The Story of the Israeli Air Force from the War of Independence to the Bekaa Valley* (New York: Orion, 1990), p. 17.

182 "I put my gun sight on one, . . . pulled the trigger": Ibid., p. 17.

182 pancaked onto the desert floor: The Egyptian pilot killed was a senior officer, Wing Commander Said 'Afifi al Janzuri.

183 Augarten . . . barely clearing the disabled airplanes on the field: Ehud Yonay, *No Margin for Error* (New York: Pantheon, 1993), p. 43.

Chapter 27: Swifty

184 The last B-17: Most accounts place the B-17 in Tulsa, but in Zvi Aloni and Shlomo Avidor, *Hammers: Israel's Long-Range Heavy Bomber Arm: The Story of 69 Squadron*

(Atglen, PA: Schiffer, 2010), pp. 11–12, Schwimmer has it in "Ekron, Ohio," which is probably incorrect. This was the second of the two bombers Schwimmer bought from Donald Roberts of Tulsa.

184   parked under guard: Brian Cull, David Nicolle, and Shlomo Aloni, *Spitfires Over Israel* (London: Grub Street, 1990), p. 172.

187   "you have a lot of guts to fly a plane like this": "Irvin 'Swifty' Schindler," World Machal, http://machal.org.il/index.php?option=com_content&view=article&id=55 1&Itemid=902&lang=en.

187   the airplane didn't seem to be headed for California: "B-17 Carrying 10 Believed Flying to Israel after Mysterious Take-Off in Westchester," *New York Times*, July 12, 1948.

189   Then the B-17 made an abrupt left turn: "B-17 Defies Canada, Flies on to Azores," *New York Times*, July 19, 1948.

189   Charged with "illegally exporting a warplane": Aloni and Avidor, *Hammers*, pp. 12–13; Leonard Slater, *The Pledge* (New York: Simon and Schuster, 1970), pp. 312–313.

190   B-17 DEFIES CANADA, FLIES ON TO AZORES: "Pictorial History: Acquir-ing Arms and Personnel," Aliyah Bet & Machal Virtual Museum, http://www.israelvets.com/pictorialhist_acquiring_arms.html.

190   Arazi . . . negotiating . . . for surplus Sherman tanks: Slater, *The Pledge*, p. 313.

Chapter 28: Target Cairo

192   Ray Kurtz was a guy: Ellen Rabinowitz Kurtz, "Ray Kurtz and Squadron 69," World Machal, http://www.machal.org.il/index.php?option=com_content&view=article&id=213&Itemid=301&lang=en.

194   orders came from IAF Headquarters. The Cairo mission was on: Zvi Aloni and Shlomo Avidor, *Hammers: Israel's Long-Range Heavy Bomber Arm: The Story of 69 Squadron* (Atglen, PA: Schiffer, 2010), p. 14.

195   interesting landmarks . . . Abdeen Palace: Leonard Slater, *The Pledge* (New York: Simon and Schuster, 1970), p. 311.

195   Haman Shamir . . . to accompany the mission: Zvi Aloni and Shlomo Avidor, *Hammers*, pp. 14–15.

196   *The damned oxygen system:* Munya Mardor, *Strictly Illegal* (London: Trinity Press, 1964), p. 220; Kurtz, "Ray Kurtz and Squadron 69," World Machal.

196   Katz steered toward Cairo: Details of the Cairo raid differ in various accounts. This scene is drawn from Bill Katz's memoir: "Bill Katz," World Machal, http://www.machal.org.il/index.php?option=com_content&view=article&id=250&Itemid=344&lang=en?; Bill Norton, *Air War on the Edge: A History of the Israel Air Force and Its Aircraft Since 1947* (Hinckley, England: Midland, 2004), p. 139; and Mardor, *Strictly Illegal*, pp. 219–220.

198   Moonitz and Raisin . . . rocked by the antiaircraft fire: Aloni and Avidor, *Hammers*, pp. 14–15.

Chapter 29: The Usual Suspects

201 no way Lewis was going to fly that BT-13: Bill Norton, *Air War on the Edge: A History of the Israel Air Force and Its Aircraft Since 1947* (Hinckley, England: Midland, 2004), p. 99; Harold Livingston, *No Trophy, No Sword: An American Volunteer in the Israeli Air Force during the 1948 War of Independence* (Chicago: Edition Q, 1994), p. 173.

202 a lone, slump-shouldered figure: Norton, *Air War on the Edge*, p. 99.

203 6 tons of high explosives pounded: Zvi Aloni and Shlomo Avidor, *Hammers: Israel's Long-Range Heavy Bomber Arm: The Story of 69 Squadron* (Atglen, PA: Schiffer, 2010), pp. 15–16.

203 B-17s flew twenty-three combat sorties: Brian Cull, David Nicolle, and Shlomo Aloni, *Spitfires Over Israel* (London: Grub Street, 1990), p. 196.

204 "We made one pass . . . I was afraid because we had only one B-17": Ibid., p. 196.

205 "69 Is More than a Number": Aloni and Avidor, *Hammers*, p. 21.

205 $18,000 for each: Norton, *Air War on the Edge*, p. 127.

207 Livingston . . . reminded . . . of . . . "round up the usual suspects": Livingston, *No Trophy, No Sword*, p. 171.

Chapter 30: The Beaufighter Caper

209 Harvey plunked the Halifax down: Harold Livingston, *No Trophy, No Sword: An American Volunteer in the Israeli Air Force during the 1948 War of Independence* (Chicago: Edition Q, 1994), p. 133; a slightly different version is given by Rob Wubbenhorst, "War of Catastrophe and Independence," http://www.flamesofwar.com/portals/0/documents/wargamesillustrated/wi310-webarabisraeliairwar.pdf.

211 the Beaufighters throttled up: Peter Chamberlain, "1945–1963: Arms Smuggling etc," http://www.haddenhamairfieldhistory.co.uk/beaufighters.htm.

213 fitted with the guns and bomb racks: 30 Squadron RAF Beaufighter Association, http://www.30squadron.org.au/index.php/beaufighter/bristol-beaufighters-in-the-worlds-air-forces.

213 Ministry of Civil Aviation . . . "fairly bamboozled": "Scotland Yard Hunting Four Missing Fighter Planes; Believed Bound for Palestine," Jewish Telegraphic Agency, September 10, 1948, http://www.jta.org/1948/09/10/archive/scotland-yard-hunting-four-missing-fighter-planes-believed-bound-for-palestine.

213 Flint's . . . postcard to his mother: courtesy of Mitchell Flint.

Chapter 31: Meeting the Red Squadron

216 "You may find these guys a bit . . . different": Mitchell Flint interview with the author, July 8, 2015.

217 One of the most outrageous: Magee, Nomis, and Augarten profiles from Mitchell Flint interviews with the author, May 12–15, 2016; Lawrence Nyveen, "Chris Magee," *101 Squadron*, http://101squadron.com/101/101.html; Lawrence Nyveen,

"Leo Nomis," *101 Squadron*, http://101squadron.com/101/101.html; Lawrence Nyveen, "Rudy Augarten," *101 Squadron*, http://101squadron.com/101/101.html.

220   *Shufti Kite:* Leo Nomis, *The Desert Hawks: An American Volunteer Fighter Pilot's Story of Israel's War of Independence* (London: Grub Street), p. 65.

221   "You fellows, . . . why don't you come one at a time?": Ezer Weizman, *On Eagles' Wings: The Personal Story of the Leading Commander of the Israeli Air Force* (New York: Macmillan, 1976), pp. 74–75.

222   "tasted like camel dung": Mitchell Flint interview with the author, August 15, 2016.

222   classic Red Squadron party: Flint and Lichtman interview, April 2, 2013, provided by Machal Productions, Los Angeles; Nomis, *Desert Hawks*, pp. 80–81.

223   postcard from London: courtesy of Mitchell Flint.

Chapter 32: Dust

225   They'd hauled twenty-five Messerschmitts: Bill Norton, *Air War on the Edge: A History of the Israel Air Force and Its Aircraft Since 1947* (Hinckley, England: Midland, 2004), p. 95.

225   the Czech girlfriend of an American mechanic: Jeffrey Weiss and Craig Weiss, *I Am My Brother's Keeper* (Atglen, PA: Schiffer, 1998), p. 174.

225   The once-beautiful Constellation: The Constellation would require eighteen months of repairs before Stehlik, Schwimmer, and Sam Lewis flew it back to California.

226   "These were mainly fighter pilots": Harold Livingston, *No Trophy, No Sword: An American Volunteer in the Israeli Air Force during the 1948 War of Independence* (Chicago: Edition Q, 1994), p. 200.

227   Out of the transport rushed an entire infantry company: Ehud Yonay, *No Margin for Error* (New York: Pantheon, 1993), p. 47.

227   "We can do it all": Ibid.

228   Make it happen: Munya Mardor, *Strictly Illegal* (London: Trinity Press, 1964), pp. 222–225.

229   The fields became . . . Dustbowl One and Dustbowl Two: Leonard Slater, *The Pledge* (New York: Simon and Schuster, 1970), pp. 315–316.

230   Egyptian patrols kept a watch on the activity: Eliezer Cohen, *Israel's Best Defense: The First Full Story of the Israeli Air Force* (New York: Orion, 1993), p. 45.

230   Egyptians had managed to score not a single hit on the C-46: Brian Cull, David Nicolle, and Shlomo Aloni, *Spitfires Over Israel* (London: Grub Street, 1990), p. 247; Norton in *Air War on the Edge*, p. 95, asserts that the Egyptian fighters chose not to fire because of the truce.

231   Operation Dustbowl made 417 round trips: Norton, *Air War on the Edge*, p. 95.

233   "What the hell happened?": Lichtman interview with the author, November 10, 2015; Cull, Nicolle, and Aloni, *Spitfires Over Israel*, p. 235.

Chapter 33: Velvetta

234 Spitfires would be transferred to the Israelis for $23,000 each: Brian Cull, David Nicolle, and Shlomo Aloni, *Spitfires Over Israel* (London: Grub Street, 1990), p. 236.

237 Spitfires would have to wear the markings of the Yugoslav air force: Ibid., p. 243.

237 Operation *Velvetta*: Alternate spellings in various accounts are "Velveta" and "Velveeta." One account attributes it to the sunscreen lotion labeled "Velvetta" that IAF pilots carried in their survival kits. Another version comes from volunteer Les Shagam, who was in Air Headquarters when someone asked if the Spitfire ferry operation had a name. Shagam's eyes fell on a newspaper ad for a popular cheese spread: Velveta (as it was spelled in Europe in the 1940s; in America it was "Velveeta").

239 Senior . . . offering up a silent prayer: Boris Senior, *New Heavens: My Life as a Fighter Pilot and a Founder of the Israel Air Force* (Washington: Potomac, 2005), pp. 217–220.

240 His external tanks had run dry: The malfunction of Senior's and Alon's fuel system was explained later by Jack Cohen (Lawrence Nyveen, "Spitfires," *101 Squadron*, http://101squadron.com/101/101.html): "What I think happened is we had little breather pipes fitted to the wing tanks with the cut-away edge facing forward, and I think what really happened there was the pressure of the wind up against this little pipe was sufficient to pressurize the tanks and, acting as a pump, force the fuel into the full main tank, which would then simply pump the extra fuel overboard from the relief valves. When they did go onto main tank there was nothing left in their wing tanks. So we learned our lesson from that and the second time (Velvetta 2) we put the breather pipes in, but facing the wrong way and we had no problem."

241 "Please ask the Shell agent to come and refuel our aircraft": Senior, *New Heavens*, p. 220.

241 "Why were you flying fighter aircraft with Israeli markings": Ibid., p. 221.

242 The Greeks released both airmen: Though Senior and Alon were released, the Greeks kept the two Spitfires. A Greek pilot crashed one in a fatal accident, and the other was returned to Israel in 1950.

243 "I came to fly your fucking airplanes": Murray Rubinstein and Richard Goldman, *The Israeli Air Force Story* (London: Arms and Armour, 1979), p. 53.

243 "the fastest man alive": Lawrence Nyveen, "Chalmers 'Slick' Goodlin," *101 Squadron*, http://101squadron.com/101real/people/goodlin.html.

244 "You must be very proud of your son": dialogue from Mitchell Flint interview with the author, May 15, 2016.

Chapter 34: Sea Fury

246 reconnaissance mission: Lichtman interview with the author, November 10, 2015.

246 "The heaviest damn flak I'd ever seen": Ibid.

246 "I got right on the guy's ass": Ibid.

248 "What type of Arab airplane": Dialogue and details of the Lichtman exchange with the staff officer from Lichtman interview with the author, November 10, 2015: Brian Cull, David Nicolle, and Shlomo Aloni, *Spitfires Over Israel* (London: Grub Street, 1990), p. 251.

249 Zaid was Egypt's most celebrated fighter pilot: Ibid., p. 162.

PART THREE: FORTUNES OF WAR

251 *In Israel, in order to be a realist you must believe in miracles:* Ben-Gurion quoted by Roman Frister, *Israel: Years of Crisis, Years of Hope* (New York: McGraw-Hill, 1973), p. 45.

Chapter 35: Ten Plagues

254 The assassin opened fire: Benny Morris, *1948: A History of the First Arab-Israeli War* (New Haven, CT: Yale University Press, 2008), pp. 311–312.

254 "what were recommendations . . . now became a political testament": Chaim Herzog, *The Arab Israeli Wars* (London: Arms and Armour, 1982), p. 88.

255 One Israeli truck was set ablaze: Some accounts claim the Israelis blew up one of their own trucks just for effect. "We had our pretext," recalled Yitzhak Rabin, *The Rabin Memoirs* (Boston: Little, Brown, 1979), p. 37.

256 "Let every soldier, every pilot and air crew member, every mechanic know": Morris, *1948*, p. 323.

258 "So far in this war I had not directly killed or maimed": Gordon Levett, *Flying Under Two Flags* (London: Frank Cass, 1994), p. 179.

259 He never learned how many he killed that evening: Ibid., p. 181.

260 Augarten . . . stayed with the damaged Beaufighter: Brian Cull, David Nicolle, and Shlomo Aloni, *Spitfires Over Israel* (London: Grub Street, 1990), p. 257.

Chapter 36: A Hell of a Ride

262 drive Mina up to her family's place: Ehud Yonay, *No Margin for Error* (New York: Pantheon, 1993), p. 55.

263 units of the Yiftach and Negev Brigades now dominated the . . . north–south main road: Benny Morris, *1948: A History of the First Arab-Israeli War* (New Haven, CT: Yale University Press, 2008), p. 325.

265 Augarten . . . shot down an Egyptian Spitfire: Brian Cull, David Nicolle, and Shlomo Aloni, *Spitfires Over Israel* (London: Grub Street, 1990), p. 259.

265 "It was Rudy Augarten": Frankel quotes from Leon Zdon, "Leon's Other War," *Minnesota Legionnaire*, October 2012, p. 8.

267 Frankel felt one of the rudder pedals smash back against his leg: "I still have one leg shorter than the other," he said half a century later in an interview with Aaron Finkel, 1988, provided by Machal Productions, Los Angeles.

Chapter 37: Smoke Over Herzliya

268 *Hit them as hard as possible:* Eliezer Cohen, *Israel's Best Defense: The First Full Story of the Israeli Air Force* (New York: Orion, 1993), p. 52.

268 "What do you say we go fly in Hebrew for a change?": Exchange between Alon and Weizman from Ehud Yonay, *No Margin for Error* (New York: Pantheon, 1993), p. 55.

269 Alon, being the commander, pulled rank: Ezer Weizman, *On Eagles' Wings: The Personal Story of the Leading Commander of the Israeli Air Force* (New York: Macmillan, 1976), p. 77.

269 It was a classic buzz job: Ibid., p. 77.

270 Antin cleared Alon to land: Antin interview with Lawrence Nyveen, "Syd Antin," 101 Squadron, http://101squadron.com/101/101.html.

271 "Get it up!": Yonay, *No Margin for Error*, p. 56.

272 Weizman took a deep breath and walked into the office: Weizman, *On Eagles' Wings*, p. 78. Mina Alon was three months pregnant when Modi crashed. Their daughter, Michal, was born April 29, 1949. Years later she would serve in the IAF in the 101 Squadron—the same unit her father commanded when he was killed.

272 "the worst landing I ever made": Lichtman interview with the author, November 10, 2015.

273 "Who was killed?": Ibid.

274 "Aircraft crashed out of control": Brian Cull, David Nicolle, and Shlomo Aloni, *Spitfires Over Israel* (London: Grub Street, 1990), p. 260.

274 "In all the wars I've been in, I had never seen anything like that": Yonay, *No Margin for Error*, p. 57.

Chapter 38: Maneuver Kill

275 Mann was an emotional wreck: Ehud Yonay, *No Margin for Error* (New York: Pantheon, 1993), p. 56; In an interview with Lawrence Nyveen ("Maurice 'Maury' Mann," 101 Squadron, http://101squadron.com/101/101.html), Aaron Finkel asserted that IAF Headquarters thought Mann was "too aggressive."

275 Syd Cohen: Leo Nomis, *Desert Hawks: An American Volunteer Fighter Pilot's Story of Israel's War of Independence, 1948* (London: Grub Street, 1998), p. 62.

276 "I couldn't move . . . I was paralyzed": Frankel interview with Aaron Finkel, 1988, provided by Machal Productions, Los Angeles; Leon Zdon, "Leon's Other War," *Minnesota Legionnaire*, October 2012.

277 "We all loved him": Antin about Nomis, quoted by Lawrence Nyveen, "Syd Antin," *101 Squadron.*

277 Nomis was put on a plane out of the country: Yonay, *No Margin for Error*, p. 52.

277 "Sign me up": Flint interview with the author, July 9, 2015.

279 "I got up to about 300 feet": Quotes and details of crash from Lichtman interview with the author, November 10, 2015; Brian Cull, David Nicolle, and Shlomo Aloni, *Spitfires Over Israel* (London: Grub Street, 1990), p. 263.

281 Fitchett . . . credited with a "maneuver kill": "Flying for Your Life: Leonard Elmer 'Len' Fitchett," The Canadian Fighter Pilot & Air Gunner Museum, http://flyingfor yourlife.com/pilots/ww2/f/fitchett/.

282 "I am the only man here who can do it": Yonay, No Margin for Error, p. 59.

Chapter 39: The Monster on the Hill

285 "Turn to the east!": Steven Pressfield, The Lion's Gate (New York: Sentinel, 2014), p. 57.

286 They were shouting and carrying weapons: The circumstances of Fitchett's down-ing are conjectural, drawn from the account by Lou Lenart in Pressfield, The Lion's Gate, pp. 56–59, and based on the early sightings of the wreckage described by Jef-frey Weiss and Craig Weiss in I Am My Brother's Keeper (Atglen, PA: Schiffer, 1998), pp. 231–232.

287 "While the mukhtar was reciting this bullshit": Lenart and Rabin quotes from Press-field, The Lion's Gate, pp. 58–59.

288 What Augarten really liked: Budd Davisson, "Rudy Augarten: The Passion to Fight," Flight, November–December 1996.

289 the two fighters pulled up in . . . victory roll: Augarten received official credit for downing one of the Egyptian Spitfires. Though Doyle claimed one shot down and one damaged, he received official credit only for one damaged enemy plane.

289 Operation Yoav: Near the end of Operation Yoav, General Allon requested permis-sion from Ben-Gurion to launch an attack on Hebron and into the Jericho valley all the way to the Jordan River. Ben-Gurion withheld permission. He was concerned about engaging the Transjordanian Army and inviting British intervention.

Chapter 40: Faluja Pocket

292 Fawzi el-Kaukji: Larry Collins and Dominique Lapierre, O Jerusalem! (New York: Simon and Schuster, 1972), pp. 159–160.

293 Operation Hiram: "Hiram" had been the biblical king of Tyre who was instrumental in building the First Temple of Jerusalem.

294 Accusations . . . of atrocities by Israeli troops: Benny Morris, 1948: A History of the First Arab-Israeli War (New Haven, CT: Yale University Press, 2008), p. 346, quotes an October 31 order from General Carmel to his brigade and dis-trict commanders: "Do all in your power for a quick and immediate clearing of the conquered areas of all the hostile elements in line with the orders that have been issued. The inhabitants of the areas conquered should be assisted to leave." Whether this order came at the direction of Ben-Gurion was never clear. Fol-lowing the cessation of fighting, Ben-Gurion ordered an investigation into the massacres at four villages. In at least one case, an officer was court-martialed and sentenced to several years imprisonment, according to Yoav Gelber, Palestine 1948: War, Escape, and the Emergence of the Palestinian Refugee Problem (Sussex, UK: Sussex Academic Press, 2006), pp. 227–228.

295 Not unless they surrendered: Ben-Gurion's response to the November 4 UN resolution: David Ben-Gurion, *Israel: A Personal History* (New York: Funk & Wagnalls, 1971), p. 291.

295 Yitzhak Sadeh: "Yitzhak Sadeh," *Jewish Virtual Library*, http://www.jewishvirtual library.org/jsource/biography/sadeh.html.

296 Sadeh . . . dispatched an army jeep as bait: Professor Hillel Daleski, in an interview by Nathan Cole: "Prof. Hillel Daleski: The Early Years," http://www.academy.ac.il/ SystemFiles/20596.pdf.

296 Egyptian 9th Brigade was isolated: David Bercuson, *The Secret Army* (New York: Stein and Day, 1984), p. 217.

297 Egyptian commander . . . reported . . . Spitfires were hit by . . . fire: Brian Cull, David Nicolle, and Shlomo Aloni, *Spitfires Over Israel* (London: Grub Street, 1990), p. 277.

297 *If you prefer life, you must yield and surrender*: Cull, Nicolle, and Aloni, *Spitfires Over Israel*, pp. 277–278.

297 Nasser . . . wrote: "No one had any idea what the fighting men in the trenches felt": Gamal Abdel Nasser, *Memoirs of the First Palestine War* (Amazon Digital Services, 2015), p. 27. Four years later, Nasser would become Egypt's first president.

298 "When I saw that he had crashed": Boris Senior, *New Heavens: My Life as a Fighter Pilot and a Founder of the Israel Air Force* (Washington: Potomac, 2005), p. 237. Flying the Dakota was Egyptian Wing Commander Amr Shakib, who was wounded with a bullet in his chest. He and all fifteen passengers survived.

Chapter 41: Hatzor

302 Peake's intercept of the Shufti Kite: Bill Norton, *Air War on the Edge: A History of the Israel Air Force and Its Aircraft Since 1947* (Hinckley, England: Midland, 2004), p. 122; Ehud Yonay, *No Margin for Error* (New York: Pantheon, 1993), p. 69.

302 "He's right below you": Yonay, *No Margin for Error*, p. 69.

303 "My fucking guns are jammed!": Jeffrey Weiss and Craig Weiss, *I Am My Brother's Keeper* (Atglen, PA: Schiffer, 1998), p. 243.

304 a Halifax: Yonay, *No Margin for Error*, pp. 68–69.

305 Peake pushed up: "Wayne Peake," World Machal, http://www.machal.org.il/index.php? option=com_content&view=article&id=555&Itemid=907&lang=en.

307 "We will try to end our conflict with Egypt by expelling them from the Negev": Benny Morris, *1948: A History of the First Arab-Israeli War* (New Haven, CT: Yale University Press, 2008), p. 353.

Chapter 42: Velvetta Redux

309 "Those planes were so dangerous, . . . I remember seeing Lichter": Ehud Yonay, *No Margin for Error* (New York: Pantheon, 1993), p. 63.

310 *Delay the offensive?*: Brian Cull, David Nicolle, and Shlomo Aloni, *Spitfires Over Israel* (London: Grub Street, 1990), p. 293.

312   the two brightest students: Lichter's cadets, Moti Fein and Dani Shapira, would dis-
       tinguish themselves later. Fein, who changed his name four years later to Modi Hod,
       would rise to be the commander of the IAF during its stunning victory in the 1967
       Six-Day War. Shapira would fly combat in every subsequent war and become Israel's
       most famous test pilot.

313   "You take the group back": Lichter quotes during the ferry flight: Vic Shayne, *Ups
       and Downs with No Regrets* (San Bernadino, CA: CreateSpace, 2012), p. 336.

313   "Nobody's going to lead me this time": Jeffrey Weiss and Craig Weiss, *I Am My
       Brother's Keeper* (Atglen, PA: Schiffer, 1998), p. 250.

314   "George was waving his hand": Cull, Nicolle, and Aloni, *Spitfires Over Israel*, p. 294.

315   Ben-Gurion slipped into his seat: Benny Morris, *1948: A History of the First Arab-
       Israeli War* (New Haven, CT: Yale University Press, 2008), p. 357.

316   Operation Horev began: Operation Horev objectives from IDF archive 922/75//561.

Chapter 43: Appointment in Gaza

320   This was an AT-6 Harvard: Flint interview with the author, July 9, 2015.

322   Slick Goodlin: NASA History, "X-1 Biographies—Chalmers H. (Slick) Goodlin,"
       https://www.history.nasa.gov/x1/goodlin.html.

323   Doyle fell in love with the French-Canadian nurse: Mike Finegood, *American Veter-
       ans of Israel Newsletter*, October 1995.

324   "I shot him and he crashed off the runway": Brian Cull, David Nicolle, and Shlomo
       Aloni, *Spitfires Over Israel* (London: Grub Street, 1990), p. 298. The pilot of the
       Egyptian Macchi fighter was Flt. Lt. Shalabi al Hinnawi, who was badly wounded
       but survived the crash. Following Egypt's disastrous losses in the June war of 1967,
       al Hinnawi became commander of the Egyptian Air Force.

325   no installations for the pilots to pee: Cull, Nicolle, Aloni, *Spitfires Over Israel*, p. 295.

Chapter 44: *Mano a Mano*

327   "What can you fly?": Dialogue and details of Levett recruitment: Gordon Levett,
       Flying Under Two Flags (London: Frank Cass, 1994), pp. 127–128.

328   Syd Cohen's Used Car Lot: Murray Rubinstein and Richard Goldman, *The Israeli Air
       Force Story* (London: Arms and Armour, 1979), p. 52.

329   "I was astonished at the clatter and the recoil": All quotes in this scene: Levett, *Fly-
       ing Under Two Flags*, p. 199.

329   This time Levett was flying a Messerschmitt: Ibid, p. 199. Other accounts, includ-
       ing the one in Shlomo Aloni, *IAF Operations in the 1948 War* (West Midlands, UK:
       Helion, 2015), p. 22, have Levett flying a Spitfire on the mission with Doyle. Levett's
       detailed description of the Messerschmitt's performance during the encounter indi-
       cates that his account is more accurate.

330   It would be a bizarre fate, he thought: Levett, *Flying Under Two Flags*, p. 199.

330   Doyle pulled in behind an Egyptian Macchi: Doyle reported it as a Fiat G55 (similar

in appearance). Not until after the war would they learn that all the Egyptian "Fiats" the IAF engaged were Macchi MC.205V fighters.

332 "I now know why Plato places courage on the lowest rung": Levett, *Flying Under Two Flags*, p. 201.

Chapter 45: Storming the Sinai

333 "I've got a hung bomb!": Radio dialogue recalled by Mitchell Flint, interview with the author, July 9, 2015.

335 classic Ben-Gurion: Benny Morris, *1948: A History of the First Arab-Israeli War* (New Haven, CT: Yale University Press, 2008), p. 361.

336 "We were suffused with a sense of Jewish power": Ibid., p. 363.

337 "I started to get this sinking feeling in my stomach": Flint interview with the author, July 9, 2015.

338 "What's going on? Halt your advance!": Yitzhak Rabin, *The Rabin Memoirs* (Boston: Little, Brown, 1979), p. 40.

339 Truman was deeply disturbed by the "invasion of Egyptian territory": Morris, *1948*, p. 366.

Chapter 46: A Hell of a Way to Run a War

341 Doyle closed in on the leader from the right quarter: Shlomo Aloni, *IAF Operations in the 1948 War* (West Midlands, UK: Helion, 2015), p. 37.

342 "Enemy pilots' action . . . denote high combat experience": Ibid., p. 37.

342 Aerial combat against Americans?: Faulty intelligence reports led 101 Squadron to believe that a pair of Americans, a 40-year-old with the last name of Ellsworth and 29-year-old John Packard, flew as mercenaries for the Egyptians: Lawrence Nyveen, *101 Squadron*, http://101squadron.com/101/101.html.

342 Denny Wilson: "Denny Wilson," World Machal, http://machal.org.il/index.php?option =com_content&view=article&id=644&Itemid=1020&lang=en.

343 Wilson was still in his dive: Aloni, *IAF Operations in the 1948 War*, p. 41.

344 they'd been asked not to fire the Spitfire's Hispano cannons: Brian Cull, David Nicolle, and Shlomo Aloni, *Spitfires Over Israel* (London: Grub Street, 1990), p. 307.

344 "He spiraled down and blew up": Ibid., p. 307.

345 The captured Spitfire made it out of Egypt: Aloni, *IAF Operations in the 1948 War*, p. 42.

346 The C-54 was floating: Ibid., p. 49; Larry Raab questionnaire response in Jewish Historical Society archives, accessed March 15, 2016.

348 "Heavy accurate AA fire was encountered": Aloni, *IAF Operations in the 1948 War*, p. 57.

Chapter 47: "Right with You, Boy"

349 The scene would replay: Shlomo Aloni, *IAF Operations in the 1948 War* (West Midlands, UK: Helion, 2015), pp. 58–59. IAF reports almost never attributed accidents

to pilot error. Takeoff and landing accidents, including those of the Messerschmitts, were usually blamed on blown tires or brake failures. Finkel's swerve off the runway was blamed on a burst tire.

351 "Observed him prang with black and white smoke": Ibid., p. 62. "Prang" was a much-used word of the period, meaning "crash."

354 *Where were they?*: Flint interview with the author, July 8, 2015.

354 "Where are you": Radio dialogue: Boris Senior, *New Heavens: My Life as a Fighter Pilot and a Founder of the Israel Air Force* (Washington: Potomac, 2005), pp. 241–242.

354 "Started firing from 700 yards": Aloni, *IAF Operations in the 1948 War*, p. 68.

354 "I was going so goddamned fast I went whistling straight by them": Murray Rubinstein and Richard Goldman, *The Israeli Air Force Story* (London: Arms and Armour, 1979), p. 54.

Chapter 48: Twisting the Lion's Tail

356 Cooper wanted a closer look: Brian Cull, David Nicolle, and Shlomo Aloni, *Spitfires Over Israel* (London: Grub Street, 1990), pp. 314–315.

357 "Enemy aircraft at twelve o'clock": Murray Rubinstein and Richard Goldman, *The Israeli Air Force Story* (London: Arms and Armour, 1979), p. 56.

358 "I just dropped my sights on him": McElroy account, Cull, Nicolle, and Aloni, *Spitfires Over Israel*, p. 316.

360 "Oh, no. . . . You're crazy": Rubinstein and Goldman, *The Israeli Air Force Story*, p. 56.

360 RAF pilots had parachuted: Yitzhak Rabin, *The Rabin Memoirs* (Boston: Little, Brown, 1979), p. 41.

362 "Listen, . . . there's a cease-fire?": Ezer Weizman, *On Eagles' Wings: The Personal Story of the Leading Commander of the Israeli Air Force* (New York: Macmillan, 1976), p. 80.

363 "Going in": Ibid., p. 81.

363 Schroeder saw the Tempest go into a spin: Ibid., pp. 80–81.

364 "Sudden Death" Schroeder: Recalled by Aaron Finkel in 1988 group reunion video.

364 "Five planes, the property of the British Empire": Weizman, *On Eagles' Wings*, p. 81.

365 "It was a party to beat all parties": Ibid., p. 82.

Chapter 49: "What a Beautiful Day"

367 *Sorry about yesterday:* Variations of the 101 Squadron's message to the RAF appear in different sources. This version is from "Israel v the RAF—Caught in the Middle—Air Combat between Israel and the RAF," http://web.stanford.edu/group/tomzgroup/pmwiki/uploads/3229-Spyflight-a-JHS.pdf.

367 "What a beautiful day": Ehud Yonay, *No Margin for Error* (New York: Pantheon, 1993), p. 70.

368 Nasser . . . "in a state of revolt against everything": Gamal Abdul Nasser, *Nasser's Memoirs of the First Palestinian War, Journal of Palestine Studies* 2 (Winter 1973): 27.

368   Churchill stood up and shocked everyone: Yonay, *No Margin for Error*, p. 69.

369   McElroy introduced himself: Brian Cull, David Nicolle, and Shlomo Aloni, *Spitfires Over Israel* (London: Grub Street, 1990), p. 326.

370   letter arrived at the British Air Ministry: "Tattersfield Family Website: Tatters-fields in the Military," http://www.tattersfield.net/tattersfield-family-history/tattersfields-in-the-military/.

371   "You are a good commander, . . . but you have no political experience": Benny Mor-ris, *1948: A History of the First Arab-Israeli War* (New Haven, CT: Yale University Press, 2008), p. 369.

373   slithering up a makeshift flagpole: "Former IDF General Avraham Adan Dies at 86," *Haaretz*, September 29, 2012.

375   "Four Spits from the world's youngest air force attached themselves to his plane": Ezer Weizman, *On Eagles' Wings: The Personal Story of the Leading Commander of the Israeli Air Force* (New York: Macmillan, 1976), p. 83.

375   "I didn't want anybody to say I had given it to the Reds": Leonard Slater, *The Pledge* (New York: Simon and Schuster, 1970), p. 320.

377   Like old soldiers, . . . "they all had stories to tell": Gordon Levett, *Flying Under Two Flags* (London: Frank Cass, 1994), p. 215.

377   Flint . . . felt himself filled with a new pride: Flint interview with the author, May 15, 2016.

References

The following is a partial list of the sources consulted in the writing of this book. The list covers the technical and historical range of the story and is offered as a guide to readers interested in further information.

BOOKS

Allon, Yigal. *Shield of David: The Story of Israel's Armed Forces*. New York: Random House, 1970.

Aloni, Shlomo. *Arab–Israeli Air Wars, 1947–82*. Oxford: Osprey, 2001.

———— *Israeli Air Force Operations in the 1948 War*. West Midlands, UK: Helion, 2015.

———— and Zvi Avidor. *Hammers: Israel's Long-range Heavy Bomber Arm*. Atglen, PA: Schiffer Military History, 2010.

Bercuson, David J. *The Secret Army*. New York: Stein and Day, 1984.

Bracken, Robert. *Spitfire: The Canadians*. Erin Ontario: Boston Mills, 1995.

Cohen, Eliezer "Cheetah." *Israel's Best Defense: The Full Story of the Israeli Air Force*. New York: Orion, 1993.

Collins, Larry, and Dominique Lapierre. *O Jerusalem!* New York: Simon and Schuster, 1972.

Cull, Brian, David Nicolle, and Shlomo Aloni. *Spitfires Over Israel*. London: Grub Street, 1990.

Gelber, Yoav. *Palestine 1948: War, Escape, and the Emergence of the Palestinian Refugee Problem*. Sussex, UK: Sussex Academic Press, 2006.

Gordis, Daniel. *Menachem Begin: the Battle for Israel's Soul*. New York: Schocken, 2014.

Heckelman, Joseph. *American Volunteers and Israel's War of Independence*. New York: KTAV Publishing, 1974.

Herzog, Chaim. *The Arab–Israeli Wars: War and Peace in the Middle East*. London: Arms and Armour, 1982.

Ilan, Amitzur. *The Origin of the Arab-Israeli Arms Race: Arms, Embargo, Military Power and Decision in the 1948 Palestine War*. New York: Macmillian, 1996.

———. *Bernadotte in Palestine*. New York: Macmillian, 1989.

Kagan, Benjamin. *The Secret Battle for Israel*. New York: World Publishing, 1966.

Kaplansky, Eddie. *The First Fliers: Aircrew Personnel in the War of Independence*. Jerusalem: IDF, The Air Force History Branch, 1993.

Levett, Gordon. *Flying Under Two Flags*. London: Frank Cass, 1994.

Livingston, Harold. *No Trophy, No Sword: An American Volunteer in the Israeli Air Force during the 1948 War of Independence*. Chicago: Edition Q, 1994.

Mardor, Munya. *Strictly Illegal*. London: Trinity, 1964.

Markovitzky, Yaacov. *Machal: Overseas Volunteers in Israel's War of Independence*. Ministry of Education, Israel Information Center. Internet edition 2007. http://www .mahal-idf-volunteers.org/about/Machal.pdf.

Morris, Benny. *1948: The First Arab-Israeli War*. New Haven, CT: Yale University Press, 2008.

Nomis, Leo, and Brian Cull. *The Desert Hawks: An American Volunteer Fighter Pilot's Story of Israel's War of Independence, 1948*. London: Grub Street, 1998.

Nordeen, Lon. *Fighters Over Israel: The Story of the Israeli Air Force from the War of Independence to the Bekaa Valley*. New York: Orion, 1990.

Norton, Bill. *The Israeli Air Force and Its Aircraft Since 1947*. Hinckley, England: Midland, 2004.

Pressfield, Steven. *The Lion's Gate: On the Front Lines of the Six Day War*. New York: Sentinel, 2014.

Rabin, Yitzhak. *The Rabin Memoirs*. Boston: Little, Brown, 1979.

Rubinstein, Murray, and Richard Goldman. *The Israeli Air Force Story*. Englewood Cliffs, NJ: Prentice-Hall, 1979.

Schiff, Ze'ev. *A History of the Israeli Army: 1874 to the Present*. New York: Macmillan, 1985.

Senior, Boris. *New Heavens: My Life as a Fighter Pilot and a Founder of the Israel Air Force*. Washington: Potomac, 2005.

Shayne, Vic. *Ups and Downs with No Regrets: The Story of George Lichter*. San Bernadino, CA: CreateSpace, 2012.

Slater, Leonard. *The Pledge*. New York: Simon and Schuster, 1970.

Weiss, Jeffrey, and Craig Weiss. *I Am My Brother's Keeper: American Volunteers in Israel's War for Independence 1947–1949*. Atglen, PA: Schiffer, 1998.

Weizman, Ezer. *On Eagles' Wings: The Personal Story of the Leading Commander of the Israeli Air Force*. New York: Macmillan, 1976.

Yonay, Ehud. *No Margin for Error: The Making of the Israeli Air Force*. New York: Pantheon Books, 1993.

RESPONSES TO QUESTIONNAIRES DISTRIBUTED BY
DR. RALPH LOWENSTEIN AND ACCESSED THROUGH COURTESY
OF THE AMERICAN JEWISH HISTORICAL SOCIETY,
15 WEST 16TH ST, NEW YORK, NY 10011.

Auerbach, Hal
Augarten, Rudy
Finkel, Aaron
Flint, Mitchell
Frankel, Leon
Friedman, Aaron
Gardner, Leo
Katz, Benno
Lichtman, Gideon
Malpine, Bill
Moonitz, Norm
Nomis, Leo
Raab, Larry
Ribakoff, Martin
Silverman, Lee
Wilson, Denny

ONLINE RESOURCES

101 Squadron: Nyveen, Lawrence. 101 Squadron. Accessed October 25, 2015.
    http://101squadron.com/101/101.html.
Ad Halom: Brody, Lazer. 2016. "The Miracle of Ad Halom." http://www.breslev
    .co.il/articles/holidays_and_fast_days/yom_hazikaron/the_miracle_of_ad_halom
    .aspx?id=11806&language=english.
Altalena: World Heritage Encyclopedia. "The Altalena Affair." http://www.gutenberg
    .us/articles/the_altalena_affair.
    Lapidot, Yehuda. "The Altalena Affair." Accessed September 15, 2016. http://www
    .jewishvirtuallibrary.org/jsource/History/Altalena.html.
B-17 to the Azores: Aliyah Bet & Machal Virtual Museum. "Pictorial History: Acquiring
    Arms and Personnel." Accessed June 10, 2016. http://www.israelvets.com/
    pictorialhist_acquiring_arms.html.
B-17 Cairo raid: World Machal. "Bill Katz." Accessed June 16, 2016. http://www
    .machal.org.il/index.php?option=com_content&view=article&id=250&Itemid=344
    &lang=en?
Beaufighters general information: 30 Squadron RAAF Beaufighter Association. "Bristol

Beaufighter Squadrons of WWII." Accessed July 5, 2016. http://www.30squadron
.org.au/index.php?option=com_content&view=article&id=27&Itemid=356.

Beaufighters missing: Jewish Telegraphic Agency. "Scotland Yard Hunting Four Missing
Fighter Planes; Believed Bound for Palestine." September 10, 1948. http://www
.jta.org/1948/09/10/archive/scotland-yard-hunting-four-missing-fighter-planes-
believed-bound-for-palestine.

Beurling, George "Buzz": Historic Wings. "George 'Buzz' Beurling, Ace of Malta." June
10, 2012. http://fly.historicwings.com/2012/06/george-buzz-beurling-ace-of-malta/.
Aces of WW2. "George 'Screwball' Beurling." Accessed February 17, 2016. http://
acesofww2.com/can/aces/beurling/.

Cohen, Eddie: Isseroff, Ami, and Zionism and Israel Information Center. "The Debut of
the Israeli Air Force." http://zionism-israel.com/his/israel_first_air_battle.htm.
World Machal. "George (Buzz) Beurling." Accessed November 30, 2015. http://www
.machal.org.il/index.php?option=com_content&view=article&id=187&Itemid=486&
lang=en.

Finkel, Aaron "Red": World Machal. "Aaron 'Red' Finkel." Accessed September 10,
2016. http://www.machal.org.il/index.php?option=com_content&view=article&id=5
90&Itemid=960&lang=en.

Fitchett, Len: Flying for Your Life. "Leonard Elmer 'Len' Fitchett." Accessed August 21,
2016. http://flyingforyourlife.com/pilots/ww2/f/fitchett/.

Gerson, Bill: World Machal. "William Guy Gerson." Accessed March 12, 2016. http://
machal.org.il/index.php?option=com_content&view=article&id=363&Itemid=625&
lang=en.

Goodlin, Slick: NASA History. "Chalmers H. (Slick) Goodlin." Accessed May 30, 2016.
https://www.history.nasa.gov/x1/goodlin.html.

Harvey, John: Wubbenhorst, Rob. "War of Catastrophe and Independence."
Accessed August 21, 2016. http://www.flamesofwar.com/portals/0/documents/
wargamesillustrated/wi310-webarabisraeliairwar.pdf.

Katz, Bill: World Machal. "Bill Katz." Accessed July 15, 2016. www.machal.org.il/index
.php?option=com_content&view=article&id=250&Itemid=344&lang=en?

Kurtz, Ray: World Machal. "Ray Kurtz and Squadron 69." Accessed July 16, 2016.
http://www.machal.org.il/index.php?option=com_content&view=article&id=213&It
emid=301&lang=en.

Peake, Wayne: World Machal. "Wayne Peake." Accessed October 10, 2016. http://www
.machal.org.il/index.php?option=com_content&view=article&id=555&Itemid=907&
lang=en.

Pomerance, Sam: World Machal. "Jack Cohen." Accessed July 28, 2016. http://www
.machal.org.il/index.php?option=com_content&view=article&id=331%3Ajack-cohen
&catid=45%3APersonal+Stories+&Itemid=569&lang=en.

Rubenfeld, Milt: Odessit, Eric. "Rudy Augarten—Avenging the Holocaust."

Accessed March 21, 2016. https://conservativlib.wordpress.com/history/rudy-augarten-avenging-the-holocaust/.

Schindler, Swifty: World Machal. "Irvin 'Swifty' Schindler." Accessed July 15, 2016. http://machal.org.il/index.php?option=com_content&view=article&id=551&Itemid=902&lang=en.

Wilson, Denny: World Machal. "Denny Wilson." Accessed April 21, 2016. http://machal.org.il/index.php?option=com_content&view=article&id=644&Itemid=1020&lang=en.

Winters, Charlie: Klinger, Jerry. "Charles Winters." Accessed September 16, 2016. http://www.palyam.org/OniyotRekhesh/Charles_Winters.

Žatec Air Bridge: Klíma, Zdeněk. "Air Bridge Žatec–Ekron Summer 1948." Accessed February 11, 2016. http://www.saaz-juden.de/html/body_operation_balak_air_bridge_zatec_-_ektron_izrael_.html.

INDEX